Law and Politics in Modern China

Law and Politics in Modern China

Under the Law, the Law, and Above the Law

Sharron Gu

CAMBRIA
PRESS

AMHERST, NEW YORK

Requests for permission should be directed to:
permissions@cambriapress.com, or mailed to:
Cambria Press
20 Northpointe Parkway, Suite 188
Amherst, NY 14228

Library of Congress Cataloging-in-Publication Data

Gu, Sharron.
    Law and politics in modern China : under the law, the law, and above the law/
    Sharron Gu.
      p. cm.
    Includes bibliographical references and index.
    ISBN 978-1-60497-604-5 (alk. paper)
    1. Law—China—History. 2. Rule of law—China—History. 3. Law—Political
aspects—China. 4. Law reform—China. I. Title.

    KNQ120.G8 2008
    349.51–dc22

2009000875

TABLE OF CONTENTS

ACKNOWLEDGMENTS

I would like to thank my editor, Norman Christie, who has unconditionally supported my writing and research for the past ten years. His great gift of empathy and sensibility for the sound and rhythm of language has made him the first non-Chinese person that I have ever known who truly understands China and its history, culture, and people. He became a favourite friend of my family during the time of our field research in 2004 and 2005. Norman's English perspective has contributed a great deal in making this book a good read for a wide global audience.

I also would like to express my gratitude to Cambria Press, whose high degree of efficiency and professionalism has made my publishing experience a pleasant surprise. I want to especially thank editor Paul Richardson and copy editor Sharon Berger for their hard work, patience, and dedication. Sharon, along with her team of editorial experts, provided excellent advice on style and technical issues. The clarity of my argument has been greatly enhanced through their efforts.

Law and Politics in Modern China

INTRODUCTION

This is a book about Chinese law and politics. It follows my first book, *The Boundary of Meaning and the Formation of Law* (McGill-Queen's University Press, 2006), which compares the cultural and linguistic foundation of Chinese imperial law and English common law. This is an interdisciplinary study of Chinese law, its language, and political institution in a modern environment.

It is a history book with strong contemporary implications. It attempts to portray modern and contemporary China in terms of historical consistency and to interpret modern Chinese politics within the historic context of its native language rather than within the limitations of "universal" (often Western-oriented) sociological or developmental theories. It demonstrates that modern China is an experience beyond the horizon of any established theory of social sciences and humanities. Chinese politics possess a cultural refinement and sophistication that Western languages have only begun to encounter during the second half of the twentieth century. The logical consistency of modern and contemporary China can be found only in its own cultural heritage and political establishment.

This book illustrates that China is not a pre-law developing country, as many scholars believe. The career of Chinese law has a much longer and more complex history. The fact that the Chinese words of law and political rhetoric have influenced and penetrated each other has made it impossible for Chinese law to function with the same efficiency as does the Western legal system. The political interference of legislation and legal administration derives less from the ideological choices of the Chinese leaders than from their cultural and linguistic environment.

With a legal tradition more than two thousand years old, China has been dealing with legal bureaucracy and corruption during the entire pre-modern, modern, and contemporary periods. Since China inherited a longstanding tradition of interweaving and fusion between law and state, law and politics, law and ideology, and law and business, Chinese law has failed to function as a detached mechanism through which social negotiation, mediation, and distribution are carried and regulated. A highly rhetorical language, law, with its words alone, cannot specify, define, and hold principles, regulations, and rulings without intervention of political interpretation and personal authority.

The impossibility of separating law from politics and officialdom is deeply rooted in China's nonabstract and personal language. As Chinese legal concepts and reasoning evolved within a complex literary and narrative framework, the Chinese concept of law has never attained the status of the English concept of common law as an abstract and externally imposed institution that enjoys the respect of its politicians and citizens. Chinese always see their law as human in origin, political in interpretation, and fluid in meaning. As an inherited attitude, the Chinese state and its individual citizens see legal regulation as a moving and shapeless encumbrance that must be pushed, bent, and even altered as circumstances allow. In the West, torts are determined by precedents, and new precedents are severely tested as they occur. This has acted as the primary motivator in the English based system and has reinforced its respectful status, which the general population as well as its legislators hold as customary for law. Chinese words of law, however, did not enjoy the same force as that of the modern statutes.[1] Although Chinese laws have developed concrete and detailed codes, they are unable to classify and distinguish levels of legislation. Chinese rulers, regardless of their political ideologies, often have the power to define (or redefine) and control the words of law. Thus, their personal preferences have always dominated rulings, which have in turn fostered a highly unregulated and even authoritarian power.

This traditional political monopoly of law has existed for thousands of years, and the Chinese people have learned that the law changes as often as their rulers and administrators change. The general populace is disinterested in matters of law and only becomes interested if individuals are personally affected by a particular judgement. China has evolved into a society that operates less within levels of law, as Western societies do, than around law, the boundary of which is slippery, fluid, and elastic according to pragmatic need.

Two extra levels of society in China float around law: the above law and under (out) law. The former is above law because its members have sufficient political influence to redefine the meaning of law and to distribute individual shares of rights as they please, without referring to any constitutional and legal principles. Without an English abstract concept of law and justice, Chinese politics is not regulated by its words of law, but rather by the words of those who have political power. Chinese legal administration has a historic tendency to override legislation. In China, politics is law, and politicians are the legislator, the jury, and the judge. Therefore, the degree of Chinese justice, regardless of its scale (municipal, regional, or national), is determined less by constitution and regulation than by the personal characteristics and preferences of the incumbent rulers and administrators.

With this lack of clarity in legal boundaries, institutional discipline, and interlocked regulations, political power has a natural tendency to subvert. Legal and political corruption is widely accepted as a normal part of life in contemporary China. There are two currencies in China: money and political connection. Unlike the West, where these currencies follow separate channels (markets) and flow according to separate rules, interacting only occasionally, in China, money, power, and law circulate within a singular channel that is managed by the same group of people. As a result, the rapid pace of economic development has widened the gap between the people who have everything and those who have nothing. The gap is also widened between powerful and influential people with their pre-laminated entourage of economic and political hangers-on, and those whose basic rights are constantly violated and even nullified. Through a careful manipulation of an always-revocable financial or political license, each layer of Chinese influence is effectively managed by the layer immediately above it. This creates a limited vision in which the individual only comprehends those portions of society that are at the same level as he is and the levels immediately adjacent to this position. Hence, the Chinese concept of "place" emerges, offering support to the general administrative structure from the bottom.

Political corruption inevitably creates a level of under law. Chinese under law does not carry the same meaning as the English term *outlaw*, which means 'people who break the law'. Chinese under laws are people who are neglected or left out of the rule of law. In most cases, they are repressed and stripped of their entitled rights because someone who is more powerful wants to acquire a larger share of rights to increase his or her influence. The majority of Chinese citizens do not believe that they are born with rights, as most Westerners do. Human rights as universal entitlement is a concept that remains alien to the Chinese mind. After several thousand years of such repression, the common Chinese have cultivated a tolerance or even numbness towards inequitable treatment and corruption. They have come to accept a highly fluid scheme that simultaneously degrades (or harvests) individual entitlement to rights (in the Western sense) and redistributes them as privileges within a politically expedient superstructure. Unequal rights have become the norm, and they are heard and seen inconspicuously, and are acknowledged only subconsciously by the collective.

Based on this level of social consciousness (or rather unconsciousness), Chinese social change has been unconstitutional (in the English sense) throughout its history. As words failed, swords had to take over. Lacking a legal protocol to amend the system, military intervention is a constant element of Chinese social change. Since there is no negotiable channel for social change (the voice of the under laws has never been heard), modification must be initiated through an armed action of under laws against those above law. [2] Under laws occasionally resort to an outlaw revolution when the government becomes extremely corrupted or insensitive to public grieving so that social reorientation can proceed.

For thousands of years, almost every new dynasty in China has emerged, more or less, through this sort of revolution of outlaw peasants. The revolutions did not change the law itself, as it was quickly re-announced after the coronation of the new emperor, but they changed the people who administrated the law. The system remained intact while the people occupying the positions above law and under law simply changed places. As the revolutionary outlaws crowned themselves as the new masters (above law), the cycle was completed and once again prepared to repeat itself.

These unconstitutional characteristics of social change are rooted in Chinese culture and language rather than merely the personalities of China's leaders. Mao's Chinese Revolution, also referred to as the Communist Revolution, in the first half of the twentieth century, which overthrew the Nationalist government and established the People's Republic of China in 1949, was a revolution of outlaws. Mao was the only Chinese leader who had the vision to acknowledge that his once revolutionary but now ruling syndicate was, much to his dismay, becoming a privileged class (above law). Although he chose different political theory, rewrote the law, and risked everything to launch another revolution, his vision and the actions that he undertook failed to pull China away from its intrinsic system of stratification and the inherent corruption that it bred. He had followed the same road as scores of emperors before him. He was a peasant hero (of the under-law group) who had elevated himself to the status of above law. He became the mouth of law, and his words became doctrine. Even with his exceptional personal charisma, Mao failed in his attempt to dismantle the level of society above law. When he lost control, his beloved China was left in a state of lawless chaos.

Contemporary Chinese leaders are acutely aware of the possibility that the under-law portion of society could become outlaw. Social instability is the biggest threat to their plan for economic prosperity and modernisation. During the past three decades, they have been trying very hard to establish an impersonal authority of law despite strong internal resistance from within the party.[3] They have successfully reduced the political influence of the military,[4] which has been and still is the most flagrant source of above-law corruption. They have demonstrated their intolerance of illegal trade and embezzlement through the implementation of harsh, even capital, punishment. They have compelled regional administrations to deal with public outcries for justice in matters concerning labour disputes and social benefits. To reduce the cruelty of Chinese capitalism, with its inhumane disregard of any living creature, the central government has consistently championed the weak and the repressed. However, so far, they have only just reached the foothills of the long high mountain range that is the organised corruption of China.

To establish the authority of constitution and apply law equally to every citizen is a struggle against China's heritage. The very foundation of China's social and political fabric is based on personal connections and influence. The thought of dealing with people who do not possess personal distinction is almost non-Chinese. A language of law disregarding personal connotation is not imaginable, as deeply rooted cultural custom has nurtured a codependency that binds the various layers of society together into a seemingly impenetrable and inflexible mass. To accept the authority of constitution requires a general change of attitude, habit, and way of thinking, not just a political directive to do so.

A change of this nature needs many generations to reach completion. Hence, Chinese modernisation will follow a different path from that of Western countries during the early modern period and that of other developing countries during the twentieth century. Unlike the West, where business and labour interests are regulated by the authority of legislation determined by a representative democratic system, and economic growth and social distribution are balanced within a wide spectrum of political presentation, Chinese law is contemplated, written, administered, monitored, and adjusted by a singular authority.

The Chinese single-party system has a mechanism distinct from the Western multiparty systems in which concerned groups are consulted during the decision-making process. Western policies are routinely modified by a wide variety of public opinions, producing a two-way transparency and a continuous dialogue between the electorate and the government. Chinese policies are modified through internal government discussion and are rarely brought into the public forum for debate. With this freedom from the scrutiny of the public eye, those in positions of influence tend to pursue their own interests. Chinese leaders must ultimately be correct in the first instance, as any error in policy direction could spark either an insurrection of the under-law portion of local society or the withdrawal of the sanction of global partners who offer China opportunity to modernise. Either consequence would undermine the very legitimacy of the current state and the accomplishments that it has made since 1949.

Chinese leaders have a challenging task, as they must attempt to balance policy that cannot appear offensive to several apparently conflicting factions. Hundreds of millions of Chinese live at a level of poverty that the modern world does not comprehend. These are the under laws, farmers and peasants who eke out a living in their little villages on the mountains and along the streams and rivers of the interior. It is important to the Chinese leaders that this critical mass must believe that corruption is being addressed diligently and that the personal standard of living is improving at a satisfactory rate. The central government is well aware of the risks if this huge group loses faith in the integrity of the system. The military must be disarmed of its influence in government affairs and stripped of its corrupt procedures in its day-to-day operations. Officials at all levels of public service must operate in a transparent environment.

This is why there must be a balance between "socialist" image and "capitalist" pursuits, as well as between a mass of humanity living around the poverty level and the privileged few who benefit from modernisation. There is a need for a general belief that progress is being made, or once again risk the chaos of the Cultural Revolution. Therefore, China, in the eyes of the rest of the world, has to appear to be double-faced and simultaneously heading in opposite directions until it builds a new legal system based on the impersonal language of law and creates a real channel for public participation.

China developed a civilian stability after cultivating a state institution of long history. In theory, this stability worked the same way that the Western legal system does today. There was a separation between law and its administration, and between ideology and its implications. However, since the language of law has developed a wide spectrum of rhetoric alternatives, Chinese law could change more radically than did the English laws. Chinese law often fails to produce any compromising solutions in political disagreements and could only work before and after a change of political power and state.

Social and political change in China often operates within a spectrum that is much wider than its "legal" systems and beyond the terms that are specified in its law. Political change has had to involve the above law, under laws, and outlaws. In the time of anarchy, Chinese personal authority beyond the established legal boundary becomes the mouth of law and the hands behind legislation. The words of authority can change the meaning, connotation, and implication of the established rules or even overturn the entire legal system and moral establishment.

Until the middle of the 1960s, the political struggle within the Communist Party took the form of moral rectification and title shuffling, justified by constant ideological campaigns. After official ideology exhausted all its options and failed to motivate designated political action, Mao launched the Cultural Revolution, a deliberate attempt to involve under laws and to create a majority to control the legislative authority and change the destinies of many of his administrators.

This has created a highly complex relationship between the authority of Mao and his bureaucracy, and between the interests of the military and civilian societies. It took Mao Zedong twenty years to realise that his personal authority, even with a highly advertised divine code (of his own definition), could not control the minds and deeds of billions of souls who were left to make their own ("by-me") laws. The anarchy, which he created to destroy his ideological and political opponents, eventually came to defeat him, as well as the system that he had spent his entire life to build. This is because no one, even Mao with all his power and charisma, could control the connotations, intended meanings, and implications of Mao's own words in a language that has been used and abused for more than five thousand years.

* * * * *

The book demonstrates this line of argument through a historic narrative divided into six chapters, each of which represents a political era in Chinese modern history. The linear chronology is a deliberate attempt to establish Chinese legal background so that comparison can be made to the legal and political ideas of the West. This comparative footing makes it easier to show how and why foreign ideas of law and democracy often fail to take root in China. The idea of law without (or above) political interruption is simply inconceivable in the Chinese mind. After two thousand years of accumulation and cultivation, the codified language of law has become too vast and fluid to hold its original principles. It has become a slippery rhetoric used by legal practitioners, rather than a guideline defended by the judiciary.

CHAPTER 1: IMPERIAL LAW, REVOLUTION, AND REFORM

This section begins with a brief history of Chinese imperial law, which describes how the political administrations of various dynasties have struggled to maintain political power by manipulating the inherited laws. It is not a conventional legal history that studies how rulings are created, accumulated, reclassified, and become an increasingly complex "legal" structure. It focuses instead on how law is made, remade, applied, and administrated, constantly motivated by state politics.

By the end of the nineteenth century, the words of Chinese law had lost their binding power and had become a tool of imperial politics. Both the content and implication of the imperial law would change each time a new emperor was crowned, and a local legal administration arrived as the provincial judges rotated in their assignments.

It was a challenge for Chinese reformers to find an alternative for the imperial law, which has had a historic tendency to submit to political power. It proved to be almost as difficult as changing the Chinese language itself. During China's thousand years of history, reform movements had emerged many times from both the bottom and the top segments of society, but none of them were able to shake the foundation of the traditional power structure. Large-scale peoples' movements, such as the White Lotus Rebellion (1796–1804), inspired by Buddhism, and the Taiping Rebellion (1850–1864), motivated by Christian social ideas, were repressed by the imperial court, but not before seriously weakening and almost toppling the Qing dynasty. The ineffectiveness of imperial authority was proven when Emperor Guanxu's Hundred Days' Reform (1898) failed.

CHAPTER 2: WORDS AND SWORDS OF THE REPUBLICAN REVOLUTION

Unlike the republican revolution in Western Europe and North America, where peace was proclaimed in the words of constitution, the Provisional Constitution of the Republic of China (1912) marked the beginning of war among several influential warlords who, in the name of the republic, had designs of the throne.

While the Western constitutions could negotiate and redistribute interests and power, as well as override opposition, Chinese words of law, including those of the Constitution, became worthless as they awaited the outcome of these military actions. The Republican Revolution of 1911 led by doctors, scholars, and other men of letters could not succeed without a war because no politician was willing to give up power without a fight.

The Constitution could prevail only with thousands of soldiers standing behind it, as they did in the Northern Expedition (1926–1928). It died with the dissolution of the military coalition between nationalist and communist troops. As Chiang Kai-shek turned his guns on his former allies, who had threatened his authority by provoking unrest in the cities and the countryside, the rule of law was replaced by the white terror in 1927.[5] In Chinese politics, words were only as strong as the army that stood behind them; political debate and negotiation meant a physical confrontation that could only end with the annihilation of the opposition.

CHAPTER 3: NATIONALIST LAW AND THE COMMUNIST REVOLUTION

Western democracy is based on the premise that the louder voice will carry the day. But the debates and negotiations always continue. Chinese political dialogue is not conducted as an exchange between equals but rather as shouting match that continues until one voice has completely silenced that of the other(s). In order to gain and stabilise this total control, the Nationalists assembled a huge mass of soldiers and embarked on a mission to eradicate the forsaken Communists who had retreated to the countryside (1928–1934). At the same time, the corruption of the Nationalist government created a large section of society whose basic rights were neglected, nullified, and abused. The Japanese occupation of Shanghai (1932) and subsequent invasion (1937–1945) sharpened popular resentment against the government led by Chiang Kai-shek.[6]

The Communists organised this section of society and turned them from under laws to revolutionaries of outlaw, and they eventually (between 1946 and 1949) drove the Nationalists off of the mainland.[7]

CHAPTER 4: COMMUNIST PARTY AS LEGISLATOR AND ADMINISTRATOR

The Communist Party assumed power in the name of the under law and rapidly became the new above law. To establish a new order, it turned society upside down and reorganised it based upon the citizens' degree of loyalty to their new regime. A purge was undertaken at every level of governmental institution to remove all who were openly disloyal or suspected of being so. This distrust was further expanded to include family, friends, and business associates of those who were considered to be opposed to the leadership. Instead of extending the same rights to each citizen, a spectrum of degraded rights was distributed to ranked social groups according to assumed political attitude.

The Communists were not satisfied with a new Constitution of 1954 or with their status as the ruling party, as is customary in Western majority governments. Like the Nationalists before them, the Communists' victory had to be complete and their supporters had to be pure. Therefore, they launched endless political movements (between 1951 and 1965) and segregated anyone who had differing opinions, even those with the best of intentions.[8] Nothing could stop them in their quest for absolute control, not even the law. Once their opposition was totally silenced, they set about the task of establishing a new political hierarchy to ensure their above-law position.

The Communist Party had become the sole legislator, legal administrator, and judge of the Chinese people. A mountain of specified, degraded, and unequal rights and entitlements that stipulated a unique place for each citizen was enacted, thus guaranteeing the absolute control of the party.

CHAPTER 5: WORDS OF MAO AND LAW IN THE CULTURAL REVOLUTION

The Cultural Revolution (1966–1976) created a lawless state in China. Unlike the West, where political movement often emerges from grassroots activity, the Cultural Revolution was conceived and orchestrated every step of the way by the divine voice and words of Chairman Mao. For ten years, all rules of Chinese law—be they constitutional, patrician, moral, ancient, or modern—were completely overridden by the words of a single man.

The Cultural Revolution was planned in one mind and distributed by the words from one mouth. The words of Chairman Mao became an institution the moment that they were spoken, a new divine law. Like any Chinese law, it lost its power as quickly as it was used and eventually became only symbolic. As the ultimate rhetoric, it was widely quoted, argued, and abused for different purposes and ideas. It recognised no ideological boundary and crossed all legal and moral standards; it became a weapon to establish, to motivate, to move, and to kill. It mutated from the words of law, which distinguish the lawful from the unlawful, into a force that could transform anyone's words for political gain.

CHAPTER 6: LAW, UNDER LAW, AND ABOVE LAW IN CONTEMPORARY CHINA

It took China more than ten years of internal disaster and, perhaps more importantly, the 1976 death of its god and emperor, Mao, to shake free from his divine instruction. Deng Xiaoping, the last Chinese leader who possessed the personal charisma that was characteristic of the first generation of the Chinese Communist Party, launched economic and political reforms. Once order was restored, Deng retired, leaving China still in need of effective law that could abolish the corrupt practices of administrators and officers at all levels of business, government, and the armed forces. Historically, Chinese words of law have rarely been honoured on their own merit, and they require the endorsement of respected political personalities. The adjective *respectable* is not often associated with the noun *politician* by the Chinese. Since the influence of the military provides a fortified haven for the granting of favours, political leadership has chosen to resurrect the divine image of Mao as a useful symbol in its struggle to reduce corruption and graft.

In the post-Mao period, a group of under laws, consisting mainly of powerless peasants, the city poor, and young people influenced by Western ideas of democracy, has emerged to champion reform policies. Previously, although material conditions were generally pathetic, everyone was relatively poor, including those with political power.

During the most difficult times of modern China, the older generations of Communist leaders (even those at the highest level) lived as their people did. With Mao and his closest associates maintaining a modest lifestyle, very few in the party dared to step out of line. Later, as influential persons abandoned modesty and began to flaunt their power, the common people once again observed the traditional corruption and mismanagement of party officers. A widely based resentment of these behaviours has swept the country, and as the gap widens between the rich and the poor, an intolerance, disgust, and distrust have developed that will test the very legitimacy of the one-party system.[9]

In contemporary China, political influence has become the most fluid currency in the market, and above law corruption is now rampant.[10] Administrators, holding onto a longstanding promise by the central government that it will never allow another political purge, have misconstrued this directive as a guarantee of immunity from the legal consequence of their unlawful activities. Since 1990, when China decided to embrace some of the concepts of Western-style business and encourage foreign investment, there has been a virtual stampede of influence peddling as many try to cash in their power for personal benefit. Embezzling public funds, buying and selling political favours, and purchasing influential positions have become a normal part of officials' lives.[11] This blatant disregard of law and public interest has gone far beyond the point that drove Mao to embark on his second revolution.

Chapter 7: Conclusions

China needs a voice that can speak words as binding and powerful as Mao's, but it cannot risk another dictatorial revolution. The answer lies in the silent words of law, free from Chinese political rhetoric, impersonal and unshakeable lines that cannot be altered and abused by anyone regardless of political title. China must learn to respect its words of law and defend them vigorously.

CHAPTER 1

IMPERIAL LAW, REVOLUTION, AND REFORM

The fundamental difference between Chinese legal tradition and that of the West lies not so much in if law works, but rather in what kind of law regulates social and political institutions and how that law is written, announced, implied, and administered. To understand Chinese law, one has to acquire a considerable knowledge of the history of the language in which law evolved and legal thinking was cultivated. One has to consider a much wider spectrum of the Chinese legal tradition when comparing it to Western laws, which are primarily made of positive rules separated from moral and political judgement.[1]

Long and uninterrupted literary tradition sets the Chinese language apart from other languages. Chinese is not the only language that has a five-thousand-year history, but it is the longest continuing literary tradition in the world. Writing was used in Greece and Crete during the Bronze Age, but the written material that survives from these cultures consists mainly of inventories and other administrative records, rather than literature. Greek was an oral language, or more precisely a collection of regional dialects, until the eighth century BC, when the Phoenician alphabet was successfully adopted. At that time, written Chinese (in literary texts) was at least several centuries old and contained a considerable written vocabulary.[2] All other ancient languages that had produced original scripts and utilised phonetic systems either have died or have been replaced, completely or partially, by subsequent languages. As universal languages, Sumerian, ancient Egyptian, Babylonian, and Latin are no longer spoken and are rarely written. Ancient Semitic languages have reoriented many times, have adopted various scripts, and have been replaced by several ancient and modern languages.[3] Like Latin, Sanskrit and Biblical Hebrew became so abstract and inaccessable that they cloistered themselves from the daily lives of the common people who used different oral and/or written languages.[4]

Because of its unique and continuous written language, Chinese law evolved differently from those of both Western and Middle Eastern legal traditions because it did not experience any linguistic change. Without a single linguistic rupture, Chinese literary tradition has managed to maintain its basic characteristics throughout its long history. Chinese law was made and remade, and continues to be made, in the same written language that has corresponded to hundreds of regional vernaculars.

Western legal tradition, which replaced Latin with its modern European languages, made a relatively clean break from the Christian canon law that had produced a sophisticated universal order and moral code during the medieval era. This linguistic reorientation made it possible to create a boundary between legal and political discourse and between secular and religious codes. A majority of the legal traditions of ancient Semites was buried with their languages after repeated linguistic changes from the original Sumerian, Babylonian, Assyrian, and Aramaic. When law was initially written in Biblical Hebrew, it inherited a relatively vague and open concept of divine authority and moral rules. It took religious leaders and biblical scholars many centuries to gradually specify and refine its language.

Due to the continuity of Chinese literary language, Chinese law did not have to choose between natural and moral laws, between precise and vague rules, or between man and God. It harvested and assimilated all of the religious (ritual), legal, and moral connotations and reprocessed them into one diverse and flexible system through centuries of conceptual classification and juxtaposition. By the same token, Chinese law was and still is unable to make clear distinction between legal and moral rules and between law and politics. Until recently, Western scholars have been reading legal (*fa*) and moral (*li*) sides of Chinese law as if they were the same as the Western opposites of religious/secular and legal/moral laws. They overlooked the cultural significance of an ancient and continuous language that combines both legal and moral discourse and allows this discussion to continue as it intermingles. These deep linguistic roots are absent or shallow in the history of most modern European languages.[5]

Most European languages experienced linguistic change during the late medieval period. The ongoing linguistic accumulation of written Chinese made conceptual distinctions between legal, moral, and political rules fluid and elastic. In Christian Europe, these crucial distinctions that shaped the emergence of Western legal tradition were made possible by linguistic change from Latin to European vernaculars. After thousands of years of reclassifying and juxtaposing legal and extra-legal languages, and redefining its legal and moral order, the Chinese language was able to combine nature and human society into a seamless universal order. A similar universal order appeared in medieval Europe and was reconstructed in modern languages during the Enlightenment.[6] The universal order in the Chinese language is a world of perpetual flux that is constantly flowing in and out of social order and disorder, within and outside of established legal rules.[7] The foundation of conceptual barrier that underlies the distinction between law, on one hand, and moral and political rules, on the other hand, has been submerged by the natural growth and maturity of the Chinese language.

This fluid concept of order created by the Chinese language, with elastic meanings and multidimensional reasoning, is the main challenge that has been facing the Western (or Western-trained Chinese) scholars of Chinese law.[8] It is a daunting and painful task to pin Chinese words and their multiple connotations down to the specific domain of English or German concepts, and it is difficult to force Chinese legal history to fit into a Western framework. Imagine binding a foot, distorting its natural shape, pushing it into a shoe that is two sizes too small, and then going for a walk—not impossible, just painful.

Many fundamental concepts underlying contemporary Western legal theories no longer make any sense in describing and analysing Chinese legal history. For example, the distinction between "rule of law" and "rule by law" exists only in academia. It does not hold ground even in the contemporary legal practice in the West, where words of law have long been used as means to justify political needs and commercial interests, rather than as pure legal and nonmoral or nonpolitical measurement.[9] If contemporary English law is conceived as the pure legal and nonpolitical language in the past, it can and will flow out of codes and courtrooms; its distinction from political and moral languages has begun to disappear.

The continuous language of China inherited not only a highly specific, complex, and sophisticated system of law, but also a much richer collection of nonlegal rules to sanction the social conduct of its citizens. This moral background behind the law was a repertoire of moral codes cultivated by a literary tradition that is thousands of years old. These codes have elevated social and civil order from an externally imposed system that sanctions behaviour into a realm of shared convictions about proper and improper conduct. The maturity of literary language also flattened out the gap between words and deeds, rules and implication, and the language of law, as well as that of morality and politics.

As legal language lost its absolute boundary, Chinese law created its last frontier to maintain social order: legal and political administration. Politicisation of law, a new phenomenon in the contemporary West, has been a fact of life for many centuries in China. Law has been a mistress of Chinese rulers because it had never stood alone without the guidance of the administrators, the hands of the state, or the protection of an army.

Unlike in Western democracy, where the loudest (collective) voice often carries the day, no major Chinese political shift has occurred that employs the use of words alone. The power to define the meaning of law and to administrate legal applications has become a prize to win through the uses of military action, conspiracy, and manipulation. In fact, most founding emperors had military backgrounds and were able to control an army, which was the only way to usurp an established dynasty. It required a strong leader with a highly organised army to win the war and to take and maintain the right to rule regardless of his social or ethnic background.

This tendency continued well into the modern era, although the contemporary Chinese leaders have changed political ideologies. Words and ideas alone never stood a chance in the political arena of modern China. Chinese politicians and social reformers had to learn to lead an army and fight their way to the top.[10] Just like the founding emperors of the past, the emergence of both Chiang Kai-shek and Mao Zedong were backed up by their military troops.[11] Mao defeated Chiang not because his Marxist ideology was more popular (as the Communist propaganda claimed) but because he was a superior military commander and political strategist. Although they embraced different ideologies, Mao and Chiang shared the same attitude towards law and employed the same methods to deal with lawmaking and legal administration. For both, law was simply an additional tool to aid them in achieving and justifying their political agendas. Each of them created a multileveled administrative hierarchy based on personal loyalty that they had cultivated in their early military careers. The various degrees of personal loyalty became the prime deter-mining factor in the formation of the structure of their organisations and general power distribution within each of the Communist and Nationalist Parties during the middle of the twentieth century.

THE IMPERIAL LAW

The Chinese imperial law was a well-developed and complex legal system with very detailed codes and procedures that engaged a hierarchy of different types of lawmaking. Codes were drafted in general terms and kept up-to-date then applied to particular circumstances by substitutions or imperial edict. These specific decisions were made on legal points and prevailed over conflicting, generally applicable code provisions.[12] In cases of conflicting rulings, legal issues would be decided by higher courts in which ministers made their suggestions and then sought ratification by the emperor himself. There was also a multileveled court system, which had specific procedural regulations covering all aspects of litigation. It had distinct and well-classified rulings to deal with legal actions, from the filing of a complaint to pretrial investigation, to the trial, judgement, and appeal. This system remained constant with minor variations as redefined and enacted by each imperial dynasty.[13]

This mature and complex system was the result of over two millennia, during which rules were repeatedly made and boundaries were defined. As boundaries became less relevant, they had to be reclassified and refocused in order to reestablish their authority and limitations.[14] As the impact of words gradually diminished after repeated use and abuse, an army of legal administrators and surveillance personnel came to be organised and institutionalised. Their functions were to stand behind words of law and protect the integrity of the increasingly softer and more elastic boundaries that were emerging.[15]

Two thousand years ago, when the Chinese language was still formative, its law was young and vigorous, as were the early Roman law of the same period and the laws of various European vernaculars of the early modern period. Chinese law was publicly announced, recorded, confirmed by the appropriate authority figure, and then administrated by a civil body.[16] China took many centuries to establish a comprehensive legal system and a complex legal administration to serve it.

The distribution of power was clearly defined in the law of the Han dynasty (206 BC–AD 220).[17] The emperor and the chancellor each had what we might today call a secretariat. In the Secretariat of the Emperor, the emperor had six masters (*liushang*). They were the master of clothing (*shangyi*), master of food (*shangshi*), master of head gear (*shangguan*), master of feasts (*shangxi*), master of baths (*shangyu*), and master of writing (*shangshu*). The first five of these offices were designed to oversee the daily personal life of the emperor. The last was actually the secretary of the imperial palace.

The Secretariat of the Chancellor was composed of thirteen bureaus (*cao*), which are similar to divisions of contemporary cabinet ministry (*si*). The most important divisions were the following: West and East Bureau (*xicao, dongcao*) were the personnel ministry, responsible for the appointment and employment of all military and civilian officers; the Bureau of Households or Revenue (*hucao*) managed the sources of revenue for the imperial household; the Bureau of Memorials (*zoucao*) constructed and maintained all governmental memorials; the Bureau of Complaints or of Litigation (*cicao*) was an office of adjudication of civil law; the Bureau of Regulations or of Standards (*facao*) controlled all standards of weights and measures, as well as the timetable for postal service; the Bureau of Commandant or of Military Transportation (*weicao*) arranged the transfer of military troops; and the Bureau of Bandit Suppression or Control (*zeicao*) and Bureau of Decisions or of Criminal Executions (*juecao*) had duty of suppressing insurgents and had the jurisdiction over criminal violations and punishment.

As in modern Japan and England, Chinese legal administration in Han dynasty was mainly in the hands of chancellors (prime ministers, in modern terms) rather than the hands of the imperial house or monarchy. The emperor had only one office for administrative affairs. To serve the office, he had only one library and a staff of four. The chancellor had thirteen bureaus, which supervised a much broader jurisdiction. These bureau chiefs became ministers of the state in later dynasties.

The classification and distribution of responsibility (power) between the royal family and the state institution of the chancellor and the constant shifting of the boundary between them had become an important characteristic of the entire tradition of legal and political form.[18] This type of power struggle between the government and the crown did not merely involve the use of legal words (drafting the Constitution, as well as passing legal regulations and amendments) as was the case in the West. Instead, those holding administrative titles embarked upon a constant negotiation concerning a redefinition of entitlement of their positions, their judicial boundaries, and their rankings.

In early Chinese legal history, administrative positions were repeatedly created, eliminated, reestablished, classified, and reclassified. As rising stars in the legal administrative structure, newly appointed administrators could override the judgements of the established ones. They could disappear just as quickly based on the political whims of the emperor or his bureaucracy. For example, the position of commander in chief (*da sima*) was created in the late years of the former Han dynasty (206 BC–AD 9). The commander in chief's appointees were either real or nominal regents. When Wang Meng (an illegitimate heir of the crown) occupied the throne (AD 9–23), he designed a strong central government to curb subordinate resentment. He refused to give power to any regent. The position of commander in chief (until AD 51) was stripped of most its power and reduced to the rank of a regular cabinet member. Liu Xiu, the founder of the later Han dynasty (AD 25–220), continued Wang Meng's practice. Although he retained the position of commander in chief, he reduced and limited its responsibilities to general supervision of the officialdom, which did not include responsibility of the military.[19]

The legal system of the later imperial period China rarely focused on how to write code, statutes, and regulations, which followed an inherited form. Rather, it was concerned about how to interpret the ancient law, how to apply the law, who would be trusted to administrate the law, and how much power an administrator should be granted in order to not interfere with the ranks of his peers. Emperors often used edicts to alter the jurisdictional boundaries of a particular post or shuffled administrators among the more favourable jurisdictions based upon their personal preferences.[20] During the former Han dynasty, the emperor appointed the higher ranking officials from among a list of candidates that the chancellor had proposed. In the later Han dynasty, the emperor may have sought advice from a wider circle; however, he was not bound by these recommendations.[21]

After a period of time, this imperial title shuffling became redundant as it accomplished little that favoured the throne. No matter how the emperor redefined administrative titles and rankings or reassigned his chief administrators, the imperial intentions almost always clashed with the goals of ambitious officers who were willing to challenge him.

Generations of Chinese rulers adopted a strategy of separation to allow the ruler to maintain authority and strategic control during this power struggle with his officialdom. High-ranking officers were isolated, and each and every one of their legal boundaries were severally limited and interlocked. Judicial barriers between officials were set very high so that the emperor could deal with his challengers individually instead of facing a collection of ministers who could collaborate in order to challenge his authority. During the later Han dynasty, the formal power of the chancellor was replaced by the informal power of the grand commandant. These high-ranking but nominal ministers could be tripped up on some of the many laws, and some were dismissed for the most trivial of offences. From AD 107 onward, the throne intermittently blamed the subversive criticism of administrators on the three excellencies and dismissed several of them.[22] In the most serious cases, the ministers who criticised the emperor would be executed or forced to commit suicide.

During the former Han dynasty, relations between the throne and the high officials were relatively smooth. Tensions arose in the middle period, particularly the reign of Emperor Wu (141–87 BC). By the later Han dynasty, the conflicts between the cabinets and the throne intensified as it became obvious that the former appeared to be less willing to be subservient to the latter.[23] After the first fifty years of this dynasty, the high officials were replaced more often and more rapidly.

Despite the wishes of the emperors, the power of the bureaucracy continued to expand, and it became more complex. The evolution of legal and administrative titles of imperial government reflected the history of repeated classification and redefinition of legal jurisdictions and functions, as well as perpetual power redistribution. The title of chancellor (*cheng xiang*) was in use from the very beginning of the former

Han dynasty. Until 8 BC, the chancellor was the highest ranking civil official, and could act ex officio as spokesman for the bureaucracy.[24] In 8 BC, the cabinet was profoundly changed. The position of grand secretary was abolished and replaced by that of the grand minister of works and the commander in chief (regent). They were elevated to the same rank as the chancellor.[25] Now, there were three excellencies who jointly inspected all aspects of local administration; the dual-headed system of the former Han dynasty, which had been dominated by the chancellor, was now replaced by a tripartite cabinet consisting of three excellencies, whose members were codependent and equal. The Office of Chancellor, which used to be a strong competitor of the crown, has never recovered from the loss of status suffered in 8 BC. It was the grand commandant that gradually became the most influential part of the cabinet.[26]

The attempt to separate power between the imperial household and government continued in the Tang dynasty (AD 618–907). Tang emperors divided the responsibility of the former chancellorship among several departments. They were much more hands-on and met with high-ranking officers more often to discuss government policies than did Han emperors. During the Tang dynasty, the organisation of legal administration changed from a linear structure to a pyramid. In the previous dynasty, the emperor dealt with a chancellor, who was in charge of the administrative apparatus; the chancellor employed a vice-chancellor to control administrative supervision. Tang emperors had to deal with three departments of administration (*sansheng*) that shared the functions and the powers that originally belonged to a single man, which were the Imperial Secretariat (*Zhongshusheng*), the Imperial Chancellery (*Menxiasheng*), and the Executive Department (*Shengshusheng*). The supervision of censorial power, however, lay outside any of their jurisdictions.[27]

As the administration expanded horizontally, Tang emperors further classified the legal functions of various official postings to avoid excessive overlap. This created a more complex hierarchy of increasingly specific legislative and judicial functions. Two officers headed the Imperial Secretariat. These were the secretary general (*zhongshuling*) and imperial chancellor. A single presiding minister (*shangshuling*) headed the Executive Department. The Tang bureaucracy as a whole was vertically divided into nine grades, the first two of which were reserved for elder statesmen. The actual responsibility for administration lay with officials of the third grade and lower. The secretary general, the chancellor, and the presiding minister were all third-grade officials. They exercised the same functions as those of the chancellor of the Han dynasty.

During the Tang dynasty, the most important government legislation took the form of imperial decrees (*zhi*), which were issued by the Imperial Secretariat in the name of the emperor. His Imperial Majesty did not draft the law himself; it was written by lower officials of the Imperial Secretariat known as drafting officials (*zhongshu sheren*). There were seven or eight such officials under two assistant secretary generals (*zhongshu shilang*). This procedure was called "deciding the intent and issuing the decree" (*ting zhi ch'u ming*).

Although the emperor was the mouth of the imperial law, the legislative power, which put the words into the imperial mouth, rested in the hands of the government that drafted and issued the imperial decrees. In this system, the drafting officials drew up a number of draft memorials, from which the secretary general or assistant secretary general would chose one and revise it into a formal decree. This decree would be submitted to the emperor for his signature (*hua zhi*) and then sent to the Imperial Chancellery for review.

This procedure guaranteed a clear separation of power between legislation and administration of the law. The head of the Imperial Chancellery would immediately review each decree and ask for additional opinions from its reviewing officers (*jishizhong*), who were lower ranking officials under the Imperial Chancellery. Whenever the imperial chancellor was opposed to the decree, the document would be returned to the Imperial Secretariat with comments for revision. This power of review, which lay with the Imperial Chancellery, is what could be called, in modern terms, the *countersignature*.

The refusal to give this countersignature (which was necessary to validate the decree) would kill the legislation, even an imperial proclamation. Once the necessary procedures had been completed, the decree would be sent to the Executive Department for enforcement. A decree signed by the emperor but refused by the Imperial Secretariat became nullified and could be reviewed once again in a Hall of State Conference (*Zhengshitang*), the highest legislative organ of central government. All imperial decrees had to be stamped with the seals of the Imperial Secretariat and the Imperial Chancellery character *zhi* (meaning "imperial decree"). The Imperial Secrateriat and the Imperial Chancellery were required to provide their seals if the Hall of Conference approved the legislation.[28]

Under this system, the emperor did not have absolute control of legislation. An imperial decree that did not include the seals of the Imperial Secretariat and Imperial Chancellery was considered to be illegal. However, some strong and ambitious emperors were not afraid to ignore the established legal procedure. Empress Wu Zetian (AD 690–705) broke the inherited procedure, exercised her prerogatives, and directly proclaimed her decrees without having them endorsed by the Imperial Secretariat and the Imperial Chancellory. She also ruthlessly silenced opposition of the secretariat and the chancellery by killing dissenting officials, thus setting a precedent for absolute imperial control of legislative and legal matters.

This practice was followed by Emperor Zhongzong (AD 705–710), who succeeded Wu. The direct, or unapproved, decrees were often signed by the emperor in black ink, rather than the customary red. These documents were called slant-sealed black-ink decrees (*xiefeng mozhi*), indicating that they had not gone through the normal channels of the Imperial Secretariat and the Imperial Chancellery. The emperor himself could not be certain that the lower levels of administrators would always recognise the authority of these decrees. The officials who were appointed by this extraordinary imperial procedure were often called slant-sealed officials (*xiefengguan*). The word *xie* translated literally means "leaning on one side and not straight (or upright)", and therefore, either inappropriate or illegal. At the time, the improper appointment of higher officials did cause grave bureaucratic problems.[29] Gradually, the exceptional precedent became rule after repeated usage.

During the Song dynasty (AD 960–1279) the power of the emperor continued to expand. This preserved the centralised structure initiated by the Tang dynasty as a whole and discouraged the undertaking of major institutional innovations.[30] This change initially took place less due to any dark plot or personal ambition than due to the circumstance in which the founder of the Song dynasty became an emperor. The founding emperor of the Song dynasty (*Sung Taizu*), Zhao Kuangyin (AD 960–976), had never sought the throne. He was merely a commander of the Imperial Guard when he was suddenly elevated to a high-ranking position by the former emperor. His military campaigns were so successful that he was compelled to proclaim himself as the emperor of a new dynasty almost overnight. During the proceeding troubled years of the Five Dynasties (AD 907–960), several new emperors had ascended to the throne and had failed to earn the respect of their administrators because their authority was created by the action of their soldiers. As rulers in terms of learning, experience, and administrative capacity, they were inferior to their chief ministers, a large collection of career officials who had served in the previous imperial government.

The chief ministers believed that the authority of the emperor needed to be reestablished and respected, as Chinese law had never worked without a strong leader. The ministers decided to humble themselves and show their loyalty to the new regime and the law for which they had worked very hard to establish and maintain. They changed the traditional procedure by which imperial decrees were formulated. Instead of drafting a decree themselves, as they did in the Tang dynasty, they produced an instruction (*zhazi*) in which they summarised opinions and presented the emperor with a number of views on how he might proceed with a given matter. This procedure was termed "taking up audience whether to pursue or abandon a matter" (*mianqu jinzhi*). Afterwards, the chief ministers would formally draw up a decree that reflected the emperor's view.

This new procedure completed an important transformation in imperial legislation. It transformed from the Tang process, in which the highest ministers of state routinely made new laws for the emperor, to a system that presented the emperor's personal decision. With this change, the throne now held control of the legislative structure. As imperial decisions became a higher level of legislation, the chief ministers' role was reduced to that of administrators who merely put the decrees into effect. The influence of the emperor increased at the expense of that of his chief ministers.

This action, which was originally an emergency measure, changed legislative procedure for many centuries. In the Tang dynasty, the Hall of State (an assembly of ministers) could issue orders on its own, called "directives" (*tangtie*). This practice continued in the early Song dynasty, and these directives were considered more important than imperial decrees. However, this situation changed when the Imperial Secretariat was no longer permitted to issue Hall of State directives on its own; they were superseded by the aforementioned imperial instruction. After Emperor Taizong (976–997), all official business had to be settled with imperial decrees, which paved the way for total control by the throne in legislative procedure.[31] The source of imperial legislation had begun to transfer from outside of the palace to the inner court.

During subsequent dynasties, imperial power was further consolidated by strong and authoritarian emperors. One of the most efficient ways to curb the influence of the state bureaucracy was to abolish overly influential office, and to separate those who exhibited the potential to challenge the power of the throne.

At the beginning of the Ming dynasty (1368–1644), the central government agencies followed the Yuan dynasty (1271–1368) structure.[32] The Imperial Secretariat (*Zhongshu Sheng*) was the administrative office and presided over the Six Ministries: Personnel, Revenue, Rites, War, Justice, and Public Works. The Censorate (*Yushi Tai*) maintained disciplinary surveillance over officialdom, and the Chief Military Commission

(*Dudu Fu*) commanded the armies. In 1380 Hu Weiyong, the prime minister (d. 1380), was charged with plotting rebellion and was executed along with thousands of others. The Emperor Zhu Yuanzhang (1328–1398), the founding emperor of Ming, then abolished the Imperial Secretariat and took direct control of the Six Ministries.[33] Meanwhile, he splintered the Chief Military Commission into five equal agencies known as the Five Commissions (*wufu*), each of which reported directly to the throne. In addition, the Censorate was abolished in 1380 and replaced by the inspector (*Du Chayuan*), which in turn fragmented and was placed in the hands of low-ranking investigating censors who also reported directly to the emperor. The reorganisation of the central government during the middle of Zhu's rule marked the zenith of the growth of imperial autocratic authority in China.[34]

An even more efficient way for an emperor to excise legislative power was to be personally involved in the codification of law and to put his own words into the imperial code. Zhu Yuanzhang compiled the Great Ming Code (*lu*) and the Commandment (*ling*). At this time, the *lu* and *ling* developed into two parallel forms of legislation, each of which stated the regulations from different angles to serve various purposes. Zhu not only laid out the principles for drafting the Ming Code but also took an active part in some of the specific codification language. He ordered members of the Code-Drafting Commission to consider each article to the best of their abilities and present them to him daily so that he could discuss the articles with them.[35]

Both the Great Ming Code (*lu*) and the Commandment (*ling*) were promulgated at the same time under the personal supervision of the emperor. Zhu Yuanzhang also clarified the relationship between these two laws in his imperial edict. He declared that the Commandment was enacted to educate people before wrongful acts were committed, whereas the Ming Code was intended to punish people after they have committed crimes. He hoped that people would observe the Commandment so that they would not fall into the realm of the Ming Code and be punished.[36]

The Commandment was the first precedent of legislation juxtaposing the emperor's own words with the words of law. It was a code of case law written personally by an emperor employing colloquial (nonlegal) language.[37] It consisted of four parts: three compilations (*bian*) aimed at the emperor's subjects in general and one volume addressed to the military. It took the emperor only two years to compile and enact the 236-article document. When one considers this relatively short time span and the extraordinarily harsh penalties specified in the document, it becomes easy to see the founding emperor's scepticism towards the existing legal procedures that he inherited and his commitment to eliminating undesirable social elements.

Zhu Yuanzhang ordered that every household in the country had to possess a copy of his law, the Commandment. He also announced that the penalties for a criminal (beating with a stick, penal servitude, or life exile) could be reduced by one degree if the convicted possessed a copy of the law. Punishment would be increased by one degree for those who did not have their copy. As the second and third compilations were completed, Zhu announced that those who did not respect, or did not possess copies of, the law were not his transformed subjects and thus should be banished from the Chinese Empire. This law took effect with legally binding force on the very day that it was issued.[38]

To prevent the officialdom from breaking the law through corruption and forging court cliques, Zhu Yuanzhang also announced three jurisdictional codes against offences by officials, especially offences such as abusing powerful positions, including embezzlement of tax grain. His administrative law took a form imitating a chapter of the Book of Documents (*Shangshu*), the Grand Pronouncement (*Dagao*).[39] From 1385 to 1386, Zhu proclaimed three volumes of Grand Pronouncement: the Grand Pronouncement (*Dagao*) in 74 articles, the Supplement to the Grand Pronouncement (*Dagao xubian*) in 87 articles, and the Third Part of the Grand Pronouncement (*Dagao sanbian*) in 43 articles.[40]

Compared to the Ming Code, the Grand Pronouncement specified much more severe punishment for crimes than was stipulated in the Ming Code and the Commandment. Zhu regularly admitted that many of the sanctions he employed in the Grand Pronouncement were "extralegal" (*fawai*) punishment. The Grand Pronouncement employed a number of brutal punishments, such as exterminating criminals' clans, execution by slow slicing, pulling out sinews, severing fingers, removing the kneecap, sentencing to military exile, amputating legs, and castration.[41] He explained to the officials why he had stipulated such extralegal measures to deal with crimes:

> It has been more than forty years since I first took up arms; I have since personally ordered the affairs of the realm. I have experienced all of the good and bad, true and false of human nature. Those who were wicked and crafty by nature and committed serious crimes obviously beyond doubt had been specifically ordered to be punished by extralegal penalties. This was intended to make people take heed and thus not lightly dare to break the law. However, this is just an expedient measure to punish the wicked; it is not the regular law [changfa] of the ruler who preserves the accomplishments. From now on, when my descendants become emperors they shall only enforce the Code and the Grand Pronouncement. They certainly shall not employ any punishments like tattooing, cutting off the feet, cutting off the nose, and castration. Because the succeeding rulers will be born and raised in the palace, they would not have enough knowledge and cannot possibly distinguish good from the evil. I fear that their poor judgement might harm the innocent by mistake. If any officials, civil or military alike, dare to use these punishments, he should be immediately executed.[42]

According to Zhu, different rulers with different experience and judgement should be trusted with power to administrate different kinds of laws: regular law or special (or expedient) measure. An extraordinary ruler, with extraordinary experience and ability to judge human character, could use extralegal measures while ordinary rulers should follow the regular laws, which would prevent them from making mistakes and harm the innocent.

The Ming Code and Zhu's Grand Pronouncement were buried with the death of Ming Empire; however, Zhu Yuanzhang's attempt to make his mouth the fountain of law did not die with him. It was repeated and superseded in a much grander scale in the twentieth century, when

Mao Zedong spoke and wrote words that not only paralleled the law but also created laws. During the Cultural Revolution, Mao's words replaced all Chinese laws, legal as well as moral, that had been inherited since ancient times.

Not every emperor had the ambition and energy to personally excise this power, as did the founding emperor. Emperor Chengzu, also known as the Yongle Emperor (1402–1424), initiated the practice of asking a few Hanlin (Confucian academy) grand secretaries to join him in confidential discussions of state affairs. The responsibility of the grand secretaries increased during the succeeding reigns so that by the 1430s all matters of state, important or not, were referred to Yang Shiji and the other grand secretaries for decision. They eventually became "de facto prime ministers" (chen zaixiang).[43]

This shift of power from the imperial house to the bureaucracy was not a repetition of the legal debate between the crown and its ministers of the past dynasties. It reflected a personal preference of the emperors themselves. When the Zhengtong Emperor (1435–1449, 1457–1464) was young, his grandmother, the Empress Dowager, made decisions about state affairs. She met with her ministers regularly. The child emperor was forbidden to meet with his grand secretaries in private. It became obvious that someone who enjoyed a close relationship with the crown could run the country through the authority of a weaker emperor. When the Jiajing Emperor (1521–1567) came to the throne, Xia Yen, then a supervising secretary, submitted a long memorandum in which he urged the emperor to be sure to consult his ministers and not to issue decrees on the advice of the people near him.[44]

As imperial power increased, concerns arose from administrators. How much power would the emperor use? How much would the throne be influenced or even abused by those close by? Could an emperor be as unpredictable in his rulings as his personality indicated? The people who had the ears and eyes of the emperor had more opportunity to manipulate the crown, and therefore the nation's business.

Throughout Chinese dynasties, imperial law had always forbidden eunuchs (the castrated imperial servants) from interfering with government affairs.[45] Zhu Yuanzhang, who foresaw the increasing power of eunuchs, even erected an iron tablet inside the palace gate that read "Eunuchs are forbidden to interfere with affairs of the state" (*Neichen bude ganyu zhengshi*).[46] However, no words, even the words of the founding emperor, had succeeded in curbing the illegal influence wielded by this important group. By the end of the Ming dynasty, the number of eunuchs had grown to more than seventy thousand. They were employed as special investigators, tax collectors, and supervisors of military commanders. They had become a dominating factor in Ming politics.[47]

The eunuchs abused the judicial system at an alarming rate.[48] The void between the emperor and his grand secretaries created other opportunities for the eunuchs in the palace to assume the role of go-betweens. Communication had to pass through the hands of the eunuchs within the palace. Lazy emperors would ask their closest eunuchs to sign documents for them, thus allowing the eunuchs to usurp the imperial power of endorsing in royal red ink (*pihong*), and becoming, at least for a moment, the de facto emperor. Some eunuchs became so corrupt and lazy that they left important documents lying around and eventually allowed them to be used to wrap food. Eunuch corruption and complacency reached its nadir during the late Ming dynasty.[49]

Like any other Chinese dynasty, the Qing took the throne by military force. In 1644 North China was the scene of two crippling blows to the decaying Ming State. Chongzhen, the last Ming emperor, was overthrown by rebellious troops, and he hung himself in his back garden when the peasant forces of Li Zicheng (1606–1644) sacked Beijing. In April 1644 Li proclaimed himself as the Emperor of Shun Dynasty, *Shunwang* (meaning "Thunder/Great King"). In May the short-lived new regime was ousted by the combined armies of the Manchu regent Dorgon and the Ming general Wu Sangui, who had defected to the Qing. With the considerable collaboration of both military and civilian Ming officials, the Qing proceeded and consolidated its position in North China.[50]

The Qing regime was a Manchu State that had adopted enough Chinese tradition to attract the favour of large numbers of native Chinese statesmen and intellectuals. It retained the Ming legal and administrative structure as the basis of government and represented itself as a group of righteous avengers, upholding the institutional order, who worked to punish the unruly hordes of peasants that had destroyed Ming.

Early in the Qing dynasty, the regime's success in administration presented a good example of how a foreign culture could rejuvenate an ageing, ailing, and corrupted system. It also demonstrated how a young language and vigorous culture could gain political control of an old civilisation like China. By adopting Chinese language and culture, Manchu rulers succeeded in administrating the empire longer than any native Chinese dynasties. But the Manchu paid a heavy price for this success. They eventually lost their ethnical and cultural distinction. Manchu, as an ethnic group, was absorbed by Chinese in culture, language, as well as in mind and body (through generations of intermarriage). After a few generations, the Manchu lost their efficiency and, just like many of the Chinese dynasties before them, lost their empire to sloth and corruption.

The best way to understand how the early Manchu emperors transformed Chinese administration is to study the organisation of the Qing's inner court, called the Grand Council (*junji chu*). The Grand Council provided a Qing solution for the agelong and costly power struggle between the inner court (*nei ting*), and outer court (*wai chao*), which it had inherited from previous dynasties.[51] The inner court was composed of the emperor, his palace household, and his private council. The officials who presided over the departments that administered the empire formed the outer court. The Grand Council of the Qing emperors transformed many of the central government agencies by personal and direct dealings with the multiplicity of subordinate agencies in the capital. In most instances, these supervisory responsibilities were held by a small group headed by the monarch, a few ministerial assistants, and small staffs. This transformation coordinated the activities of the imperial staff, the administration, and the military. It created an organisational efficiency that allowed China to defeat her ancient Mongol enemy on the northwestern frontier and set the stage for the military successes of the Quianlong Emperor's Ten Great Campaigns (1755–1792), which pushed the boundaries of the Chinese Empire to their greatest extent in history. The governing style of these Qing emperors was ruling as a joint monarchical-conciliatory administration rather than ruling by direct and personal imperial decree. This allowed the dynasty to rise to greatness during its middle years and eventually prolonged its life.[52]

As seen in previous dynasties, in Qing the distribution of power and juridical boundaries of the two courts varied according to the personalities of the emperors and their chief administrators. Strong emperors might direct the administrators; strong bureaucrats might isolate the emperors, empty the imperial power, and administer the realm independently. In some periods, battles were fought entirely within the inner court, sometimes with the palace eunuchs playing a leading role. With the notable exception of Huang Pei, who astutely grasped the significance of the Grand Council's early history as, essentially, a replacement of the inner court. The evolution of the two courts remained at the heart of the Qing government and is intimately related to the development of the Grand Council.[53]

The two communication systems utilised by each of the Qing courts supplies a good example of this bifurcation. The routine communication system inherited from the Ming was reinstalled and flourished in the outer court. This was an open, public, and regulated bureaucratic channel. Many of its documents were eventually published in the *Peking Gazette*. To support and make further use of the routine communications system, the outer court had its own archival installations and drew on its archival holdings for official compilations, such as the court chronicles (*shi lu*) and official histories (*guo shi*).

By contrast, the palace memorial system began in the period of the Kangxi Emperor (1661–1722) as the emperor's private channel, with its documents kept secret and limited to circulation between the inner court and provincial correspondents. Official records indicate that incoming palace memorials more than doubled from their ahistorical average, and their corresponding written responses almost tripled. Archives were established. During the next reign, the inner court's Grand Council acquired authority over its own publication projects, supplying both secrecy and access to important information for the monarchs and their inner-court ministers.

The outer-court bureaucracy consisted of the major administrative organs mostly inherited from the earlier dynasties up to Ming. The chief mission of these agencies was to process the documents of the routine system reports from all over the empire concerning nearly all of the major spheres of government enterprise. To fully comprehend eighteenth-century developments, it is important to understand that the outer court operated according to statutory prescription: The administrative code governed the outer-court staffs that ran the empire.[54]

This structure provided a natural division between daily administration and imperial supervision. The imperial power, which was independent and well-informed, had the rights to override and interfere with the state administration. However, this imperial power hung on the personality of the crown and tended to change from reign to reign and from emperor to emperor. Although the Yongzheng Emperor (1722–1735), allowed his father's deliberative princes and ministers (*I-zheng wang da chen*) and the southern (imperial) study (*Nan shu fang*) to continue, they were used less often and gradually declined. In their place, he conceived a new design for his inner court and appointed top echelons of his favourites (one to four high-assisting ministers) and two new middle-level staffs—the Board of Revenue's Military Finance Section and the High Officials in Charge of Military Finance. The Qianlong Emperor (1736–1795) made another major change. He combined Yongzheng's three new inner-court entities into one. He called the new organisation the Grand Council, revived from an old name for the Office in Charge of Military Strategy (*Pan li jun ji chu*). This Grand Council became the major central government administrative body for the duration of the dynasty.

Qianlong's reign was the longest in China's dynastic history and was the heyday of the Grand Council. During this period, the Grand Council expanded its capacity in great spurts and acquired the shape that it would carry until imperial rule ended in the early twentieth century. The council was able to expand chiefly because of its vantage point from the inner court, the prestige of its closeness to the throne, its secrecy, and its inherited unofficial status. This freed it from the traditions, administrative rules, and transparency that were simultaneously constraining the older outer-court agencies.[55]

The unity between military and civil administration, as well as between the crown and its bureaucracy, illustrated the success of the Grand Council. Grand Council in Chinese is *jun ji chu*, which consists of three characters. The first two descriptive characters have a double meaning: *jun ji* could mean both "military affairs" and "affairs of the state". At the early eighteenth century, the character *jun* was often combined with xu and meant "military supplies" or "military finance". Gradually, *jun* began to combine with *ji* (strategy) and conveyed the concept of military planning or strategy. At the end of the Interim Council, the revived term was employed in its second sense of affairs of state. It captured the amalgamated mission of the council, which included more than military campaign alone.[56]

The council's early edict-drafting responsibilities involved mainly two types of documents: the publicly promulgated edicts and the court letters. During Qianlong's reign, a streamlined form developed for handling certain types of edicts. This type of drafting consisted of writing down all particulars except for the part that required an imperial decision. A blank space would be left for the emperor to personally inscribe his decision with vermilion ink: a man's name for an appointment, for instance, or a sum of money for the distribution of imperial largesse. A common example of these forms were "edicts with blanks for (the emperor to write) names" (*kong ming yü zhi*). The blank-name edicts would be fully written out with all appropriate information (the date, the type of edict, and the position rank and place) except for the name of the imperial designee. Frequently, the draft would be accompanied by a list of candidates and a Grand Council memorandum of explanation. Once the draft edict had been placed before him, the emperor would fill in the blank with vermilion calligraphy.[57]

The Qing dynasty continued the moralisation of Chinese law, initiated by Zhu Yuanzhang's publication of moral personal instruction and the penal rules. Emperor Shunzhi (1644–1661) stressed the importance of the Six Instructions (*Liu Lu*). The Kangxi Emperor expanded upon the original texts and issued his *Sheng Yu* (Sacred edict) in 1670.[58] His son, the Yongzheng Emperor, added still more to the early Ming text in his *Sheng Yu Guangxun* (Sacred edict with amplified instructions) in 1724. The Qing orchestrated its efforts to promote the injunctions of the *Sheng Yu* by making them the focus of the *xiangyue* (village covenant) system, which had served as a local control system for centuries.[59] The village covenant system imposed state-sponsored and supervised lectures that were administered by the village elite and rural commoners in a network of edification designed to both emphasise Confucian values and discourage deviance from the norm.[60]

Qing rulers freely borrowed Zhu Yuanzhang's moral exhortations to village commoners first outlined in the *Liu Yu*. It was contained in his *Jiaomin bangwen* (Placard of people's instructions) of 1398: Perform filial duties to your parents, honour and respect your elders and superiors, maintain harmonious relationships with your neighbours, instruct yours sons and grandsons, let each work peacefully for his or her livelihood, and do not commit wrongful deeds.[61]

Kangxi and his son, Yongzheng, were two of the most successful Manchu rulers of the Qing dynasty.[62] They favoured the adoption of moral institution as a priority for creating a good government and peaceful society. They made good use of Zhu's model of didactic injunctions as they attempted to control the behaviour of their subjects at the grassroots level.

Qing was the last dynasty to place on the throne a series of foreign rulers who occupied and ruled China. By the later period of the Chinese imperial state, law and legal institution had become so corrupted and inefficient that the government could not nullify the military efficiency of Mongolia and North China. Several non-Chinese dynasties ruled during the two hundred years that immediately followed the Song dynasty. It did not take long for the non-Chinese rulers to realise that it was much easier to obtain power by force than to actually run an empire as complex as China. Many foreign dynasties failed to maintain power as the well-entrenched civil administration protected the traditional Chinese system. The injection of foreign political culture prolonged Chinese imperialism by selecting and utilising the best of its new and inherited characteristics. Qing was the longest and most successful period of foreign rule because Manchu rulers chose to remake themselves completely into Han (the ethnic majority of Chinese), culturally, mentally, and eventually physically. However, this choice that ensured their dominance was also a curse that led Qing to its eventual decline. The institutionalised corruption inherent from the Chinese system did not allow its Manchu rulers to escape the historic fate of every single Chinese regime before them.

Qing adopted an administrative system that relied mainly on the rule of man rather than on the rule of law. After thousands of years of use and abuse, words had lost their binding power. Law alone was no longer able to function in Chinese society except with an army of state bureaucracy behind it. The state bureaucracy itself, which was also not to be trusted without imperial surveillance, was sanctioned and controlled by both external (legal and administrative) and internal (moral) means.

External control of the administration was accomplished through the institution of an imperial surveillance and disciplinary system: an administration of the administration. The Chinese emperors created the world's first legal administration that was exclusively designed to take charge of monitoring, impeachment (*tanhe*), and disciplinary investigation (*jiucha*) of the action of their own governments.[63]

The Imperial Censorate was an ancient institution. It was built on the ancient principle that everyone should be subject to, monitored by, and scrutinised by the law of the land, including the rulers and state administrators.[64] From the Qin dynasty (221–206BC) on, with the expansion of state bureaucracy, the structure of central government fell into a stable general pattern that emphasised the censorial functions. The top echelon of the government, those directly under the emperor, was always tripartite and included a supreme military establishment, a supreme general administration, and the Censorate, usually bearing the literal designation Tribunal of Censors (*yushi tai*). The Han dynasty's governmental hierarchy was headed by a triumvirate called the "three dukes": a grand marshal, a grand councillor (chancellor), and a censor in chief (*yushi tafu*).[65]

During the Han dynasty, the imperial secretary exercised the power of censorship or surveillance in the broad sense of supervision or oversight of all governmental agencies. His jurisdiction included both central and local officials and even extended to the imperial household and palace staff. The palace assistant to the imperial secretary (*yushi zhongcheng*) was a deputy imperial secretary whose duty was to inspect the imperial family and the court, and he personally oversaw the surveillance of the emperor.

This organisation came from the general belief that everyone, including the emperor, was subject to legal scrutiny. During times when the law was clear and words were binding (regardless of social status), the institution of the Censorate was powerful, and it carried a strong mandate (or sanction) to ensure that everyone in the realm was following the rules. The assistant imperial secretary (*yushi cheng*) was the "eyes and ears" for the chancellor, who oversaw government administration at all levels. The assistant imperial secretary supervised the implementation of the orders issued by the chancellor to the throne so that, initially, this power of surveillance reached right into the palace.[66] At this time, imperial power was bound by state laws and regulations.

Towards the end of the former Han dynasty, when imperial power had increased, the imperial secretary had to withdraw from the palace. A new Office of the Imperial Secretary (*Yushitai*) was formed with responsibility limited to inspecting the government. It did not have any authority over the emperor or the court. Yet, there were still remonstrators (*jianguan*) who inspected the emperor, officials who dated back to the chief remonstrator (*jianyi dafu*) of the early Han period who were attached to the superintendent of the imperial court (*guangluxun*). According to the meaning of their official title in Chinese, it was their duty to remain close to the emperor and to offer criticism of his words and deeds. The superintendent of the imperial court, as one of the nine chief ministers, was under the control of the chancellor.

By the beginning of the Tang dynasty, the remonstrators became more powerful. By their attachment to the Imperial Chancellory, their office expanded to include policy reviewing officers who were in charge of document control, literally sealing and rejecting (*fengbo*) decrees. This office also included such censorial officials as chief remonstrators (*jian guan*), completioners (*shiyi*), and reparationers (*pujue*). Although these officers were often of low rank and lacked authority, they were highly respected in the government because they had the ear of the emperor. The completioner's job was to remind the emperor of the matters that he might have forgotten, while the reparationer's responsibility was to make amends for any mistakes that the emperor might have made.

Since it was the sole function of the remonstrators to criticise the mistakes and shortcomings of the emperor, another Tang official called the censor in chief (*yushi dafu*) was established to sanction the behaviour of officialdom. There were different types of censorial officials: those for surveillance (*taiguan*) and those for remonstrators (*jien guan*). The surveillance censors were the eyes and ears of the emperor, whereas the remonstrators were the lips and tongue of the chief ministers.[67]

It was not until the Song dynasty that censorial officers gained institutional autonomy. In Song, the remonstrators were organised independently in a Bureau of Remonstrance (*jian yuan*), and supervising secretaries staffed six separate, independent bureaus (*fang*) that were forerunners of the autonomous Offices of Scrutiny of Ming times. Their new organisational status gave the speaking officials even greater prestige and a more influential political role than they had previously enjoyed.[68]

In the meantime, the social origins of the speaking officials began to change. As the majority of speaking officials came from the Han and the dynasties after Han, great families, their official titles, and family connections symbolised the dignity of eminent personages and independent status from imperial patronage. They could almost claim equality with the emperor, who treated them as a council of peers whose advice and admonitions rested upon a sharing of interests and viewpoints with the throne.

This relationship changed, however, after the speaking officials became regular officials of the Imperial Chancellery and Imperial Secretariat as the officialdom as a whole came to be dominated by civil service bureaucrats. As the government became more autocratic, it created a gulf between the emperor and his remonstrators, who were now more employees than colleagues. This transition had affected both the remonstrators, who had to remonstrate with a more self-conscious aggressiveness, and the emperors, who had to prepare to see hostility in remonstrance more often than sympathy.

This system changed again in Song.[69] A Bureau of Remonstrance (*jian yuan*), an autonomous agency, was established and removed from the power of the chief ministers. It soon became an instrument of the emperor to monitor the chief ministers. In Song, the remonstrators and government administration were set against each other, and the censorial system became an institutionalised opposition to the government rather than to the crown. It placed chief ministers as a barrier between the emperor and his critics. An irresponsible and undisciplined group of critics emerged, consisting mainly of remonstrators who presented their individual opinions.

Song chief ministers could not simply disregard this kind of "pure criticism" (*qingyi*), since the function of remonstrators was not to oppose the government but to uphold public justice. The remonstrators had great moral power, and if a chief minister did not listen to one of them, the remonstrator would resign, resulting in an enhancement of his integrity and reputation. In such a case, the succeeding remonstrator would take the same position as his predecessor and continue the opposition.

The censorial tradition had the following functions. First, the Censorate was not subordinate to any other branch of government. It had direct access to the throne, which guaranteed that it could present its opinions directly to the emperor, bypassing any line of administrative officials of either the civil service or the military service. This was a valuable asset when the censorial officials undertook to impeach or to censure powerful officers or to denounce policies supported by court favourites. However, the power of these censorial officials was limited and interlocked. They were vulnerable to retaliation. Other officials could impeach them for abuse of privileges. Moreover, since censorial personnel failed to form a separate personnel corps, they were subject to normal promotion and demotion procedures of the general civil service. Their enemies in other agencies eventually had some opportunities to harm the career of individual censorial officials. This individual retaliation was not always effective, but it could entirely silence or intimidate the censorial agencies.

With its prestige and imperial connections, censorial officers enjoyed a degree of autonomy. This freedom of action was derived from the traditional right of an individual to submit memorials directly to the throne without consulting with his administrative superiors, an inherited notion from the early Tang period. This privilege was dramatically withdrawn from personnel of the Censorate in the year AD 726, from which time forward they had to submit impeachment through established channels. They were required to consult with both the vice censor in chief and the censor in chief. Moreover, their impeachment had to pass through a routine document control process in both the Imperial Chancellery and the Imperial Secretariat. This restriction was not removed until the eleventh century.[70]

The Yuan dynasty transformed the censorial system and made it highly centralised. The Mongol rulers created a highly centralised and intricately articulated government with a three-way division of responsibilities.[71] They did away with the old Imperial Chancellery and Department of State Affairs, but retained the Imperial Secretariat as a general organ of civil administration. Its officials served as an advisory council for the emperor and directed detailed administrative operations through six subordinate ministries.[72] The Censorate was established in 1268 to investigate the morality of all officials, as well as the policies and functions of the government. The Censorate had its own widespread network of subsidiary units, through which it maintained surveillance over all local governments. It monitored court routines, general administrative activities, the military establishment, and legal procedures. Its officers periodically inspected the records of all government agencies, and they accepted and investigated complaints about injustices. At all three levels of jurisdiction, they went out either annually or semiannually to make systematic and thorough tours of inspection. The Yuan censorial system was, consequently, far more invasive and complete than any preceding one, and its degree of tightly knit centralisation was never exceeded by the later dynasties.[73] As the Emperor Kublai Khan put it, "The Secretariat is my left hand, the Bureau of Military Affairs is my right hand, and the Censorate is the means for my keeping both hands healthy".[74]

The Yuan surveillance officials were also explicitly endowed with magisterial powers. Oftentimes, even an individual censorate was expected to punish, and also discover, offenders. An official of a Surveillance Office was empowered to punish functionaries who were not of the nine civil services ranks, as well as those officials of the lowest ranks (6–9) whom he found guilty of lesser crimes. Only in this era, censorial officers of Yuan ceased to be critics of the government and were instead utilised as a tool for imperial legal and administrative control.[75]

Early Ming's censorial system was mainly based on that of Yuan. By this time, the censorial system, like Chinese law and civil bureaucracy, had become a mutual institution, which could adjust to the requirement and persuasions of the emperor. The existence of the censorial institutions was not in itself a guarantee that vigilant surveillance would be maintained, either over the officialdom or over the ruler. It was definitely not a guarantee that censorial impeachment and remonstrance would effectively check government irregularities at any given time. The effectiveness of any important censorial action always depended upon the ruler's reaction to it, and this was in turn shaped by the total political environment of the time. The value of criticism depended upon the personalities of the censorial officials, and particularly upon their conscious or unconscious appraisal of the total political environment. They could have a variety of motives: personal, corruptive, political, or vindictively partisan. As an institution, however, the historical significance of the Censorate lies in its mandate to serve as a deterrent to unjust and illegal activities in government.[76] Although its functions varied according to personalities and the needs of the emperors, the Censorate's existence and capacity to intervene was a valuable instrument for maintaining the balance of power between the throne and the administration.

Sometimes, when the power of the civil servants appeared to threaten the imperial authority, the censorial system became a tool of high-ranking political purge. From 1620 to 1627, the imperial censorial officials concentrated their impeachment proceedings on the highest ranking officials of three groups. The first group was composed of the grand secretaries and the ministers of the Six Ministries, who dominated the operation of the central government. The second group comprised the supreme commanders, or viceroys, who directed the defence of Liaotung Peninsula and were in charge of substantial multi-province regions elsewhere. The third group was composed of the grand coordinators, who served as governors of the provinces. Denunciation and accusations forced many Donglin civil servants to resign as their peers were arrested, tortured, and murdered. [77]

This ancient right to oppose was gradually diluted by imperial power. The Office of Remonstrators became merely another bureaucracy that abused its function of speaking out and opposing government for the sake of advancing individuals' status. It became increasingly acrimonious, truculent, violent, and absurd, and the office lost its integrity within society and government. Its opinions came to be slighted and ignored. As its influence disappeared, opportunistic ministers and corrupt officials came to the fore.[78]

The last attempt to bring justice and legality to the imperial court was made by Yang Lien, the vice censor in chief of the left wing in Ming. Yang's denunciation of Wei Zhongxian became the most famous censorial memorial of Ming. In his document, Yang reminded the throne that the imperial law prohibited eunuchs from interfering with state affairs. It denounced the fact that Wei disrupted the court's orderliness and intimidated the entire court.

Yang had investigated and accused Wei Zhongxian of twenty-four major offences against the imperial law that involved illegal activities used to create personal influence and power that overrode the power of the emperor. For example, Wei usurped the Imperial Secretariat from its privilege to prepare prescripts for imperial consideration attempting to remove the supervising secretary, Sun Jie, and the grand secretary, Liu Iqing, by inciting the former to denounce the latter. He attacked loyal and righteous ministers and ousted them from office: the minister of rites, the minister of justice, and the minister of works. Wei punished anyone who uttered a remark that offended him. He murdered the emperor's favourite concubine while the emperor was away. He forged an imperial order that caused a pregnant imperial concubine to commit suicide. He arranged the death of the emperor's first son to prevent the emperor from having an heir. He built a tomb for himself that should only have been designed for an emperor. He showered honours and titles upon himself and his relatives. He ordered the execution of a man on the frivolous charge of illegally opening a mine, when all the man had done was complain that a coal pit was interfering with his ancestral graves. Wei imprisoned and tortured men for the minor offence of trespassing on grazing lands, after they had already been dealt with by proper local judicial authorities.

However, by this time, the censorial system had long lost its judicial power. The denunciation of Wei had no legal standing except for the imperial ear, which at the time was monopolised by palatial eunuchs. Eunuch secret police and palace guards were allowed to accumulate such power that if an imperial official spoke out and offended a eunuch, even unintentionally, he was subjected to exaggerated accusations and thrown into the eunuch-run prisons. By 1641, some 140 top-ranking officials were in jail. The traditional Board of Punishments was unwilling to step up and enforce justice, and so the eunuchs were allowed to accuse, torture, and punish anyone who got in their way. During the Qing dynasty, the right to write directly to the emperor became more and more restricted. Generally, the regular right to present a document (*t'i-pen*) regarding administrative issues was possessed only by the head officials (*t'ang-kuan*) of capital offices, governors-general, governors, and three ranks of military officers.[79]

Moral cultivation of the civil servants became increasingly important as the external disciplinary tradition proved to be less and less effective. Moralisation of law was an inherited characteristic of Chinese legal tradition; it became more dominant when law as impersonal regulations had worn out. As legal administration alone was no longer enough to sanction behaviour, especially the behaviour of the state officials, moral rules became crucially important in order to maintain social order. In an effort to reestablish a moral force within the state administration, Confucianism was constantly reinterpreted. The throne invested considerable resources to recruit Chinese intellectuals who would invigorate the civil service.

Unlike the monastery learning of medieval Europe, which attempted to retreat and detach from contemporary politics and focus on religious and spiritual pursuit, Chinese academies (*Shuyuan*) often had a long and complex relationship with the state and its politics. The private characteristic of Chinese academies was relative in the sense that the academies had increasing ties with the state bureaucracy. Some of the most prominent early academies were founded by nonofficial scholars who had independent incomes. However, they often were or had been state officials, sought imperial permission for what they did, received official endowments of land, and acquired teachers through agreement with the government.[80]

The relationship between private education and state politics varied from time to time. For example, the political turmoil of the Five Dynasties stimulated a desire for scholarly retreats. By the time of Southern Song (1127–1279), though life was more settled, some scholars, especially in the Zhuxi school, had reservations about the conduct of official education and the effects of the examination system on scholarship.[81]

During the Yuan dynasty, many more schools were established, and the Chinese State began to supervise academies more closely. It began to encourage the building of academies by granting lands for their construction and supplying books for their libraries. At the same time, the state began to assign teachers, who were given a place at the board tables of provincial education officials.[82] In Ming, some academies, nearly always dedicated to great scholar-philosophers of the past, contained libraries, which soon became meeting places for literati as well as centres of higher learning. During times of their greatest vigour, prominent scholars supervised the students at these locations.

Student life involved training and self-cultivation aimed at the achievement of personal virtue, success in the state examinations, and personal intellectual pursuit. The students followed a schedule of systematic study: regular lectures, discussions, and sometimes interviews with prominent intellectuals.[83] Academies like this became an issue as they presented a threat to the authority of the state during the Ming period.

The structure of education changed during Ming. From the Han dynasty through Tang and Song, every Chinese intellectual started his career as a minor official, but all could hope to qualify for a high office.[84] From Ming and afterwards, the examination system created two levels. On the lower level were the cultivated talents and the recommended men, who had to wait their turns to be qualified for high office. On the upper level were the doctors of letters and the Hanlin academicians, who had never started at the bottom.

During the Ming and Qing dynasties, many of the best and brightest men studied at the Hanlin Academy. The academic structure had changed. In the Han dynasty, the training ground for administrative functions was placed within the ranks of minor officialdom. In Tang, it was in the households of the great families, and in Song, it was in service as compilers of historic documents and literary works for the central government's archival and research institutions. The Ming doctor of letters within the Hanlin system provided the government with a pool of talented and job-ready intellectuals for the present and future needs of the civil service.[85]

On both levels of the educational system, Confucianism cultivated an army of intellectuals who were loyal to the state establishment. These Confucian intellectuals personally identified themselves with their country (*guoja*) (lit., home-nation—one word with two characters). In their minds, China as a nation identified with her ruler. These intellectuals were inclined to depict themselves as maligned and misunderstood loyal servants of the emperor who were frustrated by vicious intrigue. Confucian scholars were saturated with historical lore; they provided vivid representations of a continuing validity and immediate relevance to their own moral choices.

The morality of the intellectuals was based on centuries of Confucian learning. Confucians often had the career goal of occupying the *Zaixiang* (prime office), through which they could decisively influence the reform of the entire society. It has been pointed out that the most idealistic Song schools viewed the prime office, rather than the emperor, as the crucial governmental position and as the political fulcrum of change. Since they considered the empire to be their own responsibility, they attempted to transcend rulership through their learning.[86]

The idea that officials should take the affairs of the empire as their own responsibility became a cliché during the Qing dynasty. However, intellectuals still believed that the state of order in the empire was directly related to the condition of scholarship (*xueshu*). The health of the political system had to do with—more than anything else—honourable officers presiding over affairs instead of the wicked and corrupt. The Confucian attitude virtually always called for the discipline of bad officials through punishments such as dismissal but wavered on whether or not humiliating punishments should be used.

During Qing, the pendulum swung back towards harshness, as the rulers gradually tightened the conditions for the reduction of criminal sentences. In 1655 a basic principle was introduced that did not permit leniency if the crime involved corruption, such as the illegal taking of wealth. In 1801 the Jiaqing Emperor eliminated any routine appeal for officials and other gentry of sentences consisting of penal servitude or higher (military labour, exile, execution, etc.) However, officials could still petition to have the Board of Punishments advise the emperor on appropriate sentencing.

Confucian intellectuals considered military action as the pursuit of the uneducated, therefore, that of the low life. They would not lower themselves to commit outlaw activities and considered it a personal disgrace to face criminal proceedings. They refused to take arms even when they were betrayed by the emperor, to whom they had devoted their service. The scholar's battlefield should be his paper and his weapon his pen.

Qu Yuan (340–278 BC) was the most famous intellectual martyr of this period. He committed suicide to protest his ruler who refused to listen to his honest advice for a righteous state. Qu Yuan left behind a poetic legacy of his concerns and sorrow that have been read, sung, and performed by the Chinese for many centuries. His passionate and agonising words inspired many generations of intellectuals who refused to serve evil or foreign rulers. Some of these scholars included Liu Kun, a loyal servant of the Jin who was unjustly slandered, imprisoned, and killed in AD 317. Ji Shao died in battle in AD 304 defending the emperor against rebels. His blood actually spattered the emperor's clothes. Wen Tianxiang (1236–1283) died for refusing to serve the Mongol dynasty (Yuan), a foreign rule that replaced the Han dynasty (Song).[87]

For most Confucian intellectuals, learning, politics, and righteousness were separate issues. Unlike the politicians and academics of the early modern West, whose political views were associated with their ideologies, the political loyalty and righteousness of Chinese intellectuals were associated with personal integrity and pride. Their attitude towards and relationships with the throne were a matter of personal choice, which they could maintain, while at the same time they could remain cynical about policy and ideological changes. Instead of organising themselves as, for example, liberals and conservatives, Chinese intellectuals and bureaucrats were divided among loyal ministers (*zhongchen*) and disloyal ministers (*jianchen*). Chinese bureaucrats might choose a different leader to serve; universally, they believed that personal loyalty was morally correct, betrayal was a moral offence, and to rebel by a means other than spoken or written words was a disgrace. With this sense of righteousness, the only alternative to serve an unrighteous ruler was to retire and pursue nonpolitical (literary) writing.

Chinese intellectuals, saturated and tamed by their Confucian teachings, had never been able to provide an alternative to the political system until the end of the Qing dynasty. Their political activities had been maintained within the established structure because their very existence depended upon the support of the crown. There was no substantial or growing organisation of scholars that could be comparable in cohesiveness to the Mongol or Manchu tribes. Nor had the Chinese literati ever entertained thoughts of plotting to seize control of the government themselves.[88]

Without an external source of law, divine or otherwise, the Confucian notion of separate laws for different sections of citizens made it possible to stabilise the Chinese state formation in the sense that the educated and official career hopefuls often refused to resort to outlaw solutions to pursue social change. According to Confucius, "The *li* do not reach down to the common people; penal law does not reach up to the great officials".[89] The intellectual oppositions in Chinese history, very much like the modern Western political oppositions, rarely break the law or allow themselves to be seen as rebellious criminals. However, unlike the West, their dissenting voices could hardly be heard and their opinions did not matter, and their concerns could easily be silenced by the authoritarian system.

Only those under law, the peasants and farmers who were completely shut out of the imperial system, were left to rebel. During the later days of Ming, there were endless armed disturbances that erupted in the majority of provinces.[90] The under laws were unhappy and were determined to be heard.

The Ming State penalised insurgents in draconian fashion, and it often took deep resentment and desperation for a peasant to demonstrate against the government. When times were extremely difficult, people migrated in search of work, became monks, sold their possessions, and/or placed their families in servitude. These actions fostered a rebellious attitude from the peasants towards the government. There was a good chance of survival as a rebel and a bandit because a familiar mountain refuge was nearby, government troops and police were far away, and local civil defence forces were disorganised or sympathetic. There was less discontent during the early part of a dynasty because at that time the emperors attended court regularly and ran the country more efficiently. Epidemic violence widely occurred as corruption increased in each of the inner and outer courts towards the end of a dynastic line.

Qing experienced the same problems that Ming had. The first few emperors oversaw a very efficient and involved government. The peace and prosperity of these times was reflected by a rapid increase in population. This marked the first time that Chinese history had witnessed such sustained and continued growth. Although historians share different opinions about the precise number and scope of the expansion, they agree that substantial increase in population occurred between early Qing and the time of the Kangxi Emperor. Before the Qing dynasty, China's population had remained constant at around 20–60 million people. The population of the former Han dynasty (AD 2) was around 60 million, which reduced to 20 million during the later Han dynasty (AD 56). It had recovered to 55 million at 157 AD but reduced again during the unstable periods of Three Kingdoms, the Jin dynasty, and the Southern and Northern dynasties. It recovered once again through the Sui, Tang, and Song dynasties. It reached over 60 million during the Yuan dynasty (1291), and became 64 million and three thousand at Ming.[91]

Not every Qing ruler had the vision of Kangxi and his sense of responsibility. The Qing government after the middle of Qianlong's reign deteriorated rapidly. Government officers no longer harboured idealist ambitions, as did those of previous reigns. All they wanted was personal material gain and the opportunity for their families and servants to improve their well-being. Through a combination of neglect and ignorance, middle Qing governments had no sense of what was going on in the rest of the world, which had become substantially smaller with the development of international trade and the emergence of new economic powers. They underestimated the change in the balance of power between China, which had been held back by her lack of technological advances and political corruption, and her foreign trading partners. They insisted on considering trade as a favour that the Great Chinese Empire granted to their less influential neighbours, and they enacted rigid regulations to control the activity of foreign merchants who could either follow the rules or leave.[92]

Chinese reformers finally started to promote a more open policy during the middle of the nineteenth century.[93] For example, Rong Hong (1828–1912) championed his plans to reorganise the Chinese army, establish a modern military academy and navy college, and establish new vocational schools. In 1863 he suggested a general government reform in order to attract talented councillors. Rong was sent to the United States to purchase industrial equipment. By 1872, he established the newspaper *Hui Bao* to promote Western-style education institutions. He became Chinese counsel in the United States, Spain, and Peru. He even suggested that the government should borrow money to build a navy and hire foreign mercenary armies. He opened a Western-style bank financed by the Guangxu Emperor (1971–1908), with 10 million liang of silver.[94]

Wang Tao (1828–1897), translator and publisher in the Qing dynasty, promoted legal and educational reform. His ideas were prominent in the Hundred Days' Reform.[95] He Qi (1859–1914) went to England to study law and medicine in 1882. He worked as a lawyer in Hong Kong and became a member of Parliament for the legislation division. He helped Sun Yat-sen organise the first Guangzhou uprising in spring 1895 by the Revive China Society, which was based in Hong Kong. This revolt was a failure, however; Sun Yat-sen became wanted by the Qing government and had to leave China. He Qi and Hu Liheng wrote *Xinzheng Lunyi*, which provided systematic and specific reform plans. He Qi suggested that the government should raise salaries of civil servants to eliminate embezzlement of public funds, abolish private contribution (bribes) for official position to promote the best and brightest, establish a system of election and public evaluation for the civil servants, and improve schools to encourage real talents.[96]

On June 11, 1898, Emperor Guangxu announced imperial reform under the encouragement of Kang Youwei and Liang Qichao.[97] He later issued more than one hundred imperial orders to promote political, economic, and cultural reform. He recognised and reduced the number of rulings of administration and purged corrupt regional staff from his court, thus opening the channels for free thought. Various agencies, such as the

Division of Industry, Railways and Mines, were created to improve internal manufacture operations. The financial system was modernised, and technical innovations were encouraged. Educational reform included the abolishment of traditional forms of literary composition (*bagu*), open public schools, sending Chinese students overseas, permitting private publications and newspapers, and establishing publishing houses that specialised in translation.

Chinese imperial law had never enjoyed the popular respect of that of the early modern English. Edicts signed and sealed by an emperor were easily overturned or nullified by an imperial coup d'état. The words, implications, and connotations of Chinese law changed every time that the face of the throne changed.

Guangxu soon realised that his reform policy upset and threatened his mother, the Empress Dowager Cixi (1835–1908), who at the time had the complete control of the Qing court. So he decided to retreat from his position. On September 12, 1898, he secretly wrote to Yang Rei (one of the reformers). He concurred that China was weak and backward, and it needed new policy, but now these changes were beyond the scope of his power. If he proceeded to initiate such sweeping reform, his crown would be in danger.[98] Under pressure, Guangxu also issued secret orders to Kang Youwei and his friends to leave the country as he realised Cixi had the upper hand.

On September 21, Cixi put the emperor under house arrest and claimed that a serious illness had incapacitated him from fulfilling his responsibilities. She rescinded virtually all of Guangxu's reform edicts, executed numerous supporters of Guangxu, and placed a bounty on the heads of the rest of the leaders of the reform movement. According to the official document Her Imperial Instruction, Kang Youwei and his coconspirators were accused of attempting to attack the Imperial Summer Palace to arrest Cixi and harm the emperor. The document also claimed that the insurgent actions were not to reform the law, but rather to disrupt the law, and that their plans could not possibly defend the country because they did not defend the imperial court. The list of charges against the reformers included the organisation of a political party in opposition to the throne, deviation from Confucian principles, and betrayal of the universal law. They were not saints, and their activities were illegal.[99] On the same day, Cixi issued another imperial instruction in the name of Guangxu. The instruction ordered the abolishment all of the new laws and regulations derived from the reform policy of the emperor.[100]

In 1901, three years after the killing of the reformers, Empress Dowager Cixi decided that China needed a reform because change was the only way to sustain the dying dynasty. On January 29, she issued an imperial instruction in the name of Guangxu, the emperor, announcing that the imperial law was going to change.

The instruction-entitled law change (*bianfa*) said that constant laws (*chang jing*) will never change in ten thousand years but administrative laws (*zhifa*) will always change after they have been established. As Confucius put it, exhaustive change paves the way to endurance, and deletion and addition are a common occurrence. Three Cardinal Laws (*sangang*) and Five Customs of Virtues (*wuchang*) are eternal laws that are unchangeable, like the sun, the moon, or the stars. (The three Cardinals are the following: King is the cardinal for his officials, father is the cardinal for his sons, and husband is the cardinal for his wife. The Five Virtues are kindness, righteousness, courtesy, resourcefulness, and faithfulness [*ren, yi, li, zhi,* and *xin*].) Other laws (*ling*), such as this or that instruction, can be changed, like the changing of the strings on a qin (an ancient musical instrument).[101]

Since ancient times, each of the dynasties had its initiatives and reforms according to their needs. When the ancestors of the Qing dynasty established legal systems, they made change as they assessed different situations. They changed laws after they entered Beijing—their systems were made anew and different from what they had in Shenyang (North China); the system changed again and again during and after the reigns of Jiaqing and Daoguang. They gradually changed the old Qing systems during the reigns of Yongzheng and Qianlong. Generally speaking, when laws accumulated, they became stale; when stale, they had to be amended for the sake of strengthening the nation and benefiting the people.[102]

Without sufficient knowledge of Chinese, English readers will have difficulty distinguishing and pinning down the exact meanings of five different words for *law*, other than *fa*, that appear in this passage. They refer to different kinds of laws in different contexts, none of which are used in the sense of the English concept of law, let alone the constitution. *Chang jing* means "way of the world that never changes", which, in this instance, is the closest to natural law in the English sense. *Zhifa* means "law, legal system, legal administration, and method of political rule". *Gang* and *chang* mean "principles," but not exclusively legal principles; they could be moral regulations as well as customs. *Ling* and *fa* mean either "statue" or "decree", as concrete legal rulings. Using different words that refer to law, the document defines the laws and regulations that are subject to reform: what is going to be changed and what is not. The way of the world, which will never change, is the imperial system and its basic principles. The specific method, regulation, and decree can be changed.

This imperial initiative that changes the specific decrees and regulations without touching the imperial system is now defined as *reform*, while the previous reform movement (like that of Kang Youwei's) was designed to change the system—not to reform the law but to disturb the law.

In April 1901 the Qing court established an administration bureau for reform (*Duba zhengwuchu*), which sent ministers and high-ranking officers to investigate and report to the court about how to reform Chinese legal, political, and educational systems.[103]

From the beginning of 1902, the court passed many new regulations and measurements to promote education, economic growth, and commercial activities. It reformed the imperial recruiting system and established a new examination system. In the field of legal reform, it did nothing except for the reorganisation of the established laws and decrees, and the reduction of harsh punishment in criminal courts. The plan was to move gradually towards a parliament by first developing provincial assemblies with the privilege of free discussion and advice, then developing a national assembly with similar powers. After the assembly's members would be developed by experience, full legislative rights would be granted. In 1908 an articulated nine-year program of constitutional reform was announced that included a very full schedule of civil and military changes.[104]

The only important change in this reform was an attempt to restore the political and legal control of the central government. After more than two thousand years of imperial rule, the Qing had established an excellent central control system. Until the middle of the Qing dynasty, the political and legal power was completely centralised in the hands of the emperor. The emperor was the only person who could decide and change the personnel of the regional officers, and grant their very limited powers. The regional officers had no military powers and could not make decisions about any financial, personnel, or legal issues. This situation changed during the middle of the nineteenth century.

During the Taiping Rebellion, the Qing Army, mainly composed of Manchu warriors, had great difficulty dealing with the widespread peasant revolt. The Qing government had to rely on regional armed forces. As a result, the Xiang Army (*Xiangjun*), led by Zeng Guofan, and the Huai Army (*Huaijun*), led by Li Hongzhang, emerged as strong military forces. For their military support, the central government had to give them the title of governor-general, which had both military and financial control. Now the regional officers could ignore the intent of the imperial court and do whatever they pleased.[105]

During the reform, the Qing court attempted to recoup some of the power that it had given up to the regional warlords. It replaced Yuan Shikai with a new marshal to lead the imperial armed forces to regain some military power. It strengthened its hold on the officials responsible for the rail system and mindes.[106] However, these desperate measures had come too late. Regional power had become so strong that many regions demanded autonomy and freedom from the regulations of the central government. The imperial central system became hollowed out as its traditional control based on the respect of the throne, financial stability, and military strength failed. The Qing Empire fell apart and became segregated and controlled by regional warlords.

The Qing dynasty died because neither its words of law nor its swords could maintain order in China. General popular respect of the imperial state evaporated as Empress Dowager Cixi emptied the throne of it roles in the economy and the military. Emperor Guangxu was stripped of his power and acted only as a royal seal that was in the hands of the empress. An empty imperial seal, which was enough to rule China in peace for many years, failed quickly in difficult times of war and internal turbulence.

CONCLUSIONS OF IMPERIAL LAW

Up to the reign of Zhu Yuanzhang, Chinese imperial codes had an inherited form that distanced itself from the words of rulers. This formal consistency underlies the historical continuity of the Chinese legal system, regardless of dynastic change. The final version of the Ming Code (1397) faithfully followed the structure of the Tang Code and was later adopted by the Qing Code.[107]

Zhu's Grand Pronouncement was the first document in Chinese legal history in which the words of an emperor juxtaposed with the words of law. Zhu was the first emperor who claimed that his words had the power to overrule those of the Ming Code.[108] This precedent was expanded only by Mao Zedong, who actually announced that his words not only paralleled the law but were also so superior that they could replace both the legal and moral rules of society.

The increasingly autocratic nature of Chinese states was a historic process during which personal instructions of the ruler or the top administrator carried more and more weight in state affairs. When the words of the ruler were used to override the words of law, in most cases it was a reaction to opponents of the emperor who had crossed legislative or judicial boundaries within the administrative structure. For example, the emperor often dismantled the office of the state bureaucracies when strong ministers attempted (in impression or reality) to override imperial authority. The central administration would assume more responsibility when the imperial house became weak and unable to deal with individual ambition that attempted to manipulate the throne. This delicate balance between the autocratic and the administrative institution formed a highly fluid boundary that allowed overall responsibilities to flow towards the stronger party or individual at any given time. The autocratic nature of the Chinese State has not been rooted in the personalities of its rulers but rather took its form from the inherited linguistic and cultural practice that created and maintained this balance.

China became a land of man rather than that of law because of the failing authority of its ageing language in which its law was written. The administrative authority that originally was intended to strengthen the old language and amend its rustic fences eventually became a means to break the codes of law. Chinese law was efficient only when there was the mouth of the emperor and the hands of a strong administration working together and in unison. The pronouncements of the throne and the chief administrator had various degrees of overriding force to reinforce the law or override the words of law. To clarify the words of law, they could restate the law more precisely and forcefully. They could create an efficient legal administration. But words accumulated too many connotations, and rules became elastic. The emperors and administrators had to use their personal authority and freedom to redefine the meanings of law or to make it serve their own interests. As their words hollowed or replaced the words of law, legal administration became abused and manipulated. Most dynasties in Chinese history often began with emperors who clarified and reinforced the law, and ended with those who dismantled and even abused the law.

CHAPTER 2

WORDS AND SWORDS OF THE REPUBLICAN REVOLUTION

Chinese experience with being a republican state is drastically different from that in the West because of China's cultural and social establishment. Three main characteristics that China has inherited from its imperial past have fundamental influence on the formation and function of its modern legal and political institution.

The first characteristic is that the words of law as positive rules alone are no longer able to regulate and arbitrate social relations in Chinese society because they have lost binding power. Without an external source (divine or secular), words of law—which were and still are able to restrict, balance, and distribute power in the West—are too old and rustic to stand fast, let alone take initiative independently from political authority. Chinese law needs political authority to define its connotations and to guard its boundaries, which have become frayed, highly fluid, and elastic. In times of chaos, armed forces become increasingly important to validate both law and legal administration. And the army, rather than the law, acts as a custodian of social order.

As words of law fail, military action becomes preeminent in the reinforcement of political intent. Eventually, or sometimes immediately, the army usurps the role of making law rather than simply providing guardianship.[1] This creates a state of military law. Hence, anyone capable of seizing power by military coup can gain control of the state and commands to renounce, rewrite, and proclaim new law and new legal administration as they see fit. The new words of law mean absolutely nothing without the support of the military. The struggle for power in China depends almost solely upon the strength of the military establishment that backs the new regime. Similar to medieval Europe, a ruling position could not be secured unless all of the potential rivals were physically eliminated. Moreover, in China, one did not need a royal bloodline to justify rulership; a strong, loyal army would suffice. China's tradition has never established legal status and rights for political opposition. Therefore, Chinese political victory has to be complete and uncompromising in order to eliminate a resurgence of the political dissidents.

The second characteristic is that the real moral force behind Chinese social order is not a body of positive or negative rules, but rather a shared moral code that has been cultivated for more than five thousand years. This code provides basic principles that organise a highly ranked social hierarchy. China has never developed a concept of law that is perceived as abstract and universally and equally applicable to all of its citizens. There are different rules for different people of different social status. There are regulations for the rulers and the ruled. The hierarchy of regulation is specified by nominal title and is ratified by moral principle. All people are morally bound to a specific place within this stratified system, where they have specific positions, benefits, and duties. There is great fear and stigma for one to be classified as being outside of this social organisation (outlaw). This civil order stabilises the society because it allows the reorganisation and resumption of authority during and after military intervention (revolution). After chaos, order is restored, and every individual regains his or her previous place. Life goes on.

Third, the nonlegal (or nonconstitutional) nature of Chinese politics creates a separation of legislative and administrative functions. As a consequence, political authority, military or civil, can kidnap the law, reissue it, and re-patronise the established, generic, and nonpolitical state bureaucracy. Ideological distinctions, which are the foundation of Western politics, have minimum significance in the Chinese political arena. Chinese politics is not concerned with ideas. It is concerned about a strategy (*shu*) that pursues power through the establishment, alteration, and manipulation of personal relations. An emerging political authority, regardless of its ideological background, can recruit millions of well-trained and well-versed intellectuals who willingly offer their loyalty to the new establishment. For these eager recruits already trained in Confucian conformist education, the state (including the ruler of the state), the nation, and their personal identities are one and the same.[2]

The nonideological nature of Chinese politics can be illustrated in the behaviour of many Chinese politicians, both military and civilian. During the first half of the twentieth century, most Chinese politicians considered many different ideologies, including Republican, Democratic, liberal, conservative, and Communist. In most cases, they did not remain loyal to any of these doctrines but used them as tools to enhance their political careers. If a politician committed to a certain ideology, he always quickly invented his own version of it that departed from its orthodox nature. His deviation from the orthodox ideas guaranteed his freedom of action. This type of manipulation of words and ideas, including the words of law, allowed Chinese ideological discourse to become imaginative, and permitted its political influence to become boundless and ruthless.

Chinese law, as a form of language, a method of interpretation, or an institution, is highly personalised. As Chinese law has never established abstract connotations (as does English law), the only restriction that arbitrates and tempers the behaviour of Chinese politicians is the "by-me" laws: individual proclamations interpreted, filtered, and dealt with through personal judgement. Politicians follow different degrees of endorsement (or disregard) to the words of law depending on their status and the influence within the legal system. They need and promote law when they wish to reinforce and stabilise an established position. They ignore it when they feel that they are strong enough to announce new laws that promotes their goals. Law is nothing but an option that can be used, modified, or set aside for some individual's political expediency.

Although it is nonideological, Chinese political legitimacy envelops a high moral standard, and it needs to be righteously implied. This is the reason why the military can only function as a transitional means to overturn or bring down a legitimate political position until civilian order and moral law can resume. The military must eventually surrender to civilian rule because rulership has to be justified in words (moral righteousness or constitution), as well as ratified by the return of legitimate social ranks and titles. The words *to rule* and *to be upright* have the same phonic root in the Chinese language. Several thousand years of tradition dictate that one must be upright (or righteous) in order to rule.

The first half of the twentieth century is the best illustration of these characteristics in China. Sun Yat-sen's ideas of democracy and a republican state failed because he did not have an army strong enough to support and defend his principles. He was not an experienced politician who knew how to control, manipulate, and exterminate his enemies. Chinese politics of the republican state quickly turned from ideas to military action, and from law to anarchy. The concepts of a Republican Constitution and democratic ideals, which Chinese intellectuals dreamed of transplanting from the West, were short-lived. These thoughts were immediately replaced by the constant political and military actions of the warlords. The Northern Expedition, a military attempt to establish new order and establish a modern republic, ended in disaster after the coalition between the Nationalist and Communist parties dissolved. Both sides concluded that they could not secure political control without completely eliminating the other. During the ensuing fifty years, each of the Nationalists under Chiang Kai-shek and the Communists led by Mao Zedong seized control of China. Both of these regimes were single-party states backed up by strong armies, political censorship, and tyrannical social repression.

* * * * *

During the late Qing, the imperial court created the Beiyang Army, the first modern army in China.[3] Originally, the relationship between the state and this army was mainly political. The army was one of the tools, like law, to be used by the emperor to maintain political control. When the Qing dynasty was overthrown of by Sun Yat-sen's Republican Revolution in 1911, the military commanders who had been under effective civil control found that they were no longer bound by any responsible governmental authority.[4] These military commanders became warlords and spent the next two decades attempting to consolidate their control over various regions of China.

The new republican government made efforts to regulate the political involvement of these renegade army officials by establishing a Ministry of Military Affairs in 1912. However, the new government lacked sufficient authority and adequate financial resources to control the warlords.[5] In an attempt to gain the support of these armies, the government had to give formal recognition of the previous military rank that had been established at the end of Qing, and it also offered high-ranking administrative positions to senior officers. These warlords became cabinet ministers, prime minister, or even president of the republican administration.

The career of Yuan Shikai best illustrates the extralegal (or non-constitutional) maneuvering utilised by the warlords.[6] Yuan was first considered the lifesaver of the dying Qing court and later as the guardian of the infant republic. The newly elected government was completely incapable of controlling its military commanders. Yuan was the only person during this time of chaos who could foster a type of military balance, political control, and stability.

Yuan Shikai's power lay in his historic connection with the Beiyang Army. In 1895, when the very existence of the Qing dynasty was threatened, the Empress Dowager Cixi recalled Yuan from his assignment in Korea and commissioned him to organise the army. Yuan selected Feng Guozhang, Wang Shizhen, and Duan Qirui as his assistants.[7] This military organisation was determined by personal loyalty to Yuan and quickly became his personal force.[8] Yuan controlled financing from the Qing court, and with his modern military backup, he quickly became able to demand just about anything he wanted from the desperate Qing court.[9]

When Yuan Shikai was forced to retire after the death of his patroness, Cixi, the Beiyang Army was placed nominally under the leadership of a Manchu officer, who was the direct appointee of the throne. The actual control of the army, in fact, was in the hands of Feng Guozhang and Duan Qirui, each of whom had established a group of loyal subordinate officers. Due to financial considerations, the Qing government decentralised the Beiyang Army.[10] Feng Guozhang commanded the imperial forces in the Hankou area (now Wuhan), and Duan Qirui occupied Beijing. When Yuan Shikai was recalled by the throne to suppress the 1911 Revolution, he once again assumed command of the Beiyang Army.

With the assistance of Duan, who had been loyal to him during his retirement, Yuan Shikai successfully obtained complete control of the Beiyang Army. Yuan now held the balance of power between the Qing court and the republicans. Realising that time was on his side, Yuan took advantage of both sides and manipulated them to increase his share of political power. He initially decided against the possibility of becoming president of the newly proclaimed republic. He also repeatedly declined offers from the Qing court to become prime minister of the imperial cabinet until November 1, 1911. His first act as the prime minister was to demand that Zaifeng, the regent, abstain from political activity.[11] After Zaifeng was resigned from his regency, it was possible for Yuan to construct a predominantly Han Chinese cabinet that was loyal to him.

Yuan could not assemble his cabinet before the Wuchang Uprising of October 10, 1911, which established Sun Yat-sen's republic. By the end of the year, representatives of sixteen out of seventeen Chinese provinces had selected Sun as the first president of the Chinese Republic.[12] However, with his control of the army, Yuan represented a very powerful force within the infant and highly unstable republican state. Yuan demanded more and more political power. The new government had to reluctantly compromise with him. After he fulfilled his promise to the revolutionaries by arranging the abdication of Puyi, the child Xuantong Emperor, he proclaimed himself as the new president of the republic and replaced Sun Yat-sen.[13]

Sun Yat-sen requested that the capital be moved from Beijing to Nanjing.[14] Yuan did like the suggestion because he wished to maintain his strategic military advantage around Beijing. He fabricated a coup d'état in Beijing, and could now claim that he could not leave and lose his military control in Zhili (Hebei Province). Once again, the republicans compromised, and the capital of the new republic was established in Beijing. Yuan was sworn in as president on March 10.[15]

Yuan Shikai did not share the same faith in the democratic process with Sun and his republican friends. As an old and shrewd politician, Yuan knew that those who threatened his leadership the most were his immediate subordinates. After gaining control of the government, he quickly moved to weaken the positions of Duan Qirui and Feng Guozhang. He named Duan as minister of war, a post of great nominal authority that would weaken Duan's contacts with his loyal Beiyang forces. At the same time, he appointed Feng Guozhang as the military governor of Zhili, an office of less glamour but in direct command of Feng's loyal Beiyang officers. Yuan Shikai then immediately turned his attention to the establishment of a new model army, led by the generals of the lower rank, such as Lu Jingtian and Zhang Xun, to strengthen his own position.[16]

Unlike in the West where agreement in writing concludes a military action and political disagreement, Chinese politicians, especially those who are intelligent and shrewd, often utilise words as a shield or temporary cease-fire as they plot to further advance their position or take vengeance on their opponents. Yuan Shikai bribed the republican members in the legislative assemblies, who used to support Sun Yat-sen, and thus was able to undermine Sun's local organisations. In response to this threat, Yuan dissolved both the national and provincial assemblies, and replaced the House of Representatives and Senate with the newly formed Council of State, with Duan Qirui as prime minister.[17]

Sun Yat-sen's Second Revolution, when seven southern provinces rebelled against Yuan Shikai in July 1913, ended in disastrous failure, as Yuan's military might zeroed in on the remnants of republican forces from all sides. Provincial governors with republican loyalties were either bribed or coerced to submit to Yuan. After his victory, Yuan reorganised the provincial governments in such a way that each governor had control of his own army. This institutional change, which consolidated (rather than separated) military, legal, and political power, laid the first foundations for a dictatorship and the subsequent civil war that crippled China for the next two decades.

To further secure control, Yuan Shikai and Duan Qirui ordered Feng Guozhang to move to the Yangtze Valley where the republicans were strongest to suppress the revolt. Feng was appointed commander (*dudu*) of Jiangsu, a southern province. Yuan and Duan now dominated the scene in the North and Beijing. Feng found himself in a strategic position in Jiangsu and was soon able to build up his power in the Yangtze Valley, establishing independence from Beijing.

On December 12, 1915, with his power secure, Yuan proclaimed his reign as emperor of China (*Zhonghua Diguo Dadi*) under the era name of Hongxian (Constitutional Abundance) to begin on January 1, 1916. But before Yuan's constitutional monarchy began, Yunnan's military governor, Cai E, rebelled, and several provinces followed him to rise against Yuan.[18] Cai and Tang Jiyao launched the Republic-Protection Campaign in Yunnan (a southwestern province) to crusade against Yuan. Their army of twenty thousand soldiers defeated Yuan's eighty thousand in Sichuan. Several provinces joined in the fight against Yuan, and the republicans successfully forced Yuan to abandon his imperial dream.

The Republic revolution was based on the idea of establishing a new order that was free of imperial or autocratic authority. The death of Yuan on June 6, 1916, put more stress on the relationship between the constitutional authority of the republican government and military power of the regional commanders. Yuan had represented a balance of an authority that had stabilised Chinese politics, and his death initiated a new round of discontent among the provincial military leaders who had no respect for either the constitution or the elected civilian government.

Military leaders were regrouped and were temporarily united by the succession of the vice president, Li Yuanhong, to the office of the presidency. Li had been selected as the vice president of the new republic during the compromise reached in 1912 between the representatives of the northern group under Yuan Shikai and the southern republicans' Sun Yat-sen. The possibility that a vice president could become president had never been seriously contemplated by the military leaders at the time. When Li Yuanhong did succeed to the presidency in 1916 according to the rules outlined by the constitution, the military commanders considered it an accident that interfered with the normal considerations of seniority within the military hierarchy. As a result, the new president soon found that he had little control over the *dudus*, who continued to see him as a subordinate and as a nominal military commander.[19]

Now, constitutional code and military norm clashed as a civilian officer, who used to have a subordinate military rank, was constitutionally elevated into the highest office in the land. The military commanders considered this to be a blatant challenge and insult to their sense of propriety and order. From that time on, generals who appreciated the realities of their military hierarchy could only look upon the elected offices as lacking in substance and undeserving of their respect. The success of President Li depended upon his ability to elicit sufficient support for the formal institutions of the republican government to counter the power of the military leaders. Li, who had never previously been an outspoken advocate of republican rule, became, as president, one of the most active champions of constitutional law. In a normal legal situation, his support would have come from the Parliament. However, the Chinese Parliament at the time was of little help because it was crippled by the divisions among the republican representatives and those loyal to the warlords.

This sharp break between the constitutional leaders and the military commanders made it impossible for the government to function as a legislative and decision-making institution. To establish a formal and constitutional channel for the government to function, Li Yuanhong decided to appoint Duan as premier and Feng as vice president. Li hoped that, by making this gesture, he would be able to convince the military leaders to adhere to the constitutional rules, thereby strengthening the government and improving his own position. However, it was soon apparent that he had only opened the way for Duan, who already conrolled the cabinet, to dominate the government.

As constitutional method failed to control the military, the president, like many Chinese politicians, turned to guns, hoping that he could meet the threat of the military commanders on their own terms. To strengthen his own military position, he sought to gain the support of the lesser military commanders who were not under the direct influence of the Beiyang Army. He enlisted the support of the same group of commanders that Yuan Shikai used to employ in his efforts to balance the two factions of the Beiyang Army. Li found what he believed to be willing support in Zhang Xun, a general, who had been one of the most active defenders of the imperial family in 1911 and remained loyal to the old dynasty.[20]

The relationship between the president and the premier, Duan, further intensified in light of the issue of China's role in World War I.[21] Duan attempted to use the issue of breaking diplomatic relations with Germany and Austria-Hungary as an opportunity not only to gain the support of the European Allies but also as a means to win over the Parliament, thus weakening the position of President Li. However, on March 14, 1917, Li was able to gain a majority vote in Parliament that opposed China's entry into the war. Duan Qirui, like many Chinese politicians who had failed in democratic involvement, retreated to his speciality: building up military power. He moved his headquarters to Tianjin, thereby strengthening his dominance over the military leaders in the northern provinces. This forced the frustrated Parliament and the president into a degree of unity that had never before been achieved under the republic. In April 1917 the Parliament voted to dismiss Duan as premier; President Li announced the dismissal in May. On June 9 Duan, with the consolidated approval of his army in Tianjin, sent an ultimatum to Beijing threatening to attack the capital if the president did not dissolve the Parliament.

In response to this threat, Li Yuanhong called upon Zhang Xun to transfer his troops to Beijing to protect the government. However, on the night of July 1, 1917, rather than moving to the defence of the republic, Zhang Xun seized Beijing and announced the restoration of the Qing monarchy. He proceeded to move into the Forbidden City and placed Puyi, a young emperor, [22] upon the throne. After this incident, President Li Yuanhong had to be rescued from his assumed protector by Japanese troops and was given asylum. The republican constitution and Li's Parliament died because they finally succumbed to the military strength of various factions that did not recognise the words of law as set out in the constitution.

Puyi's reign as emperor lasted only two weeks, after which time he was allowed to live in the Forbidden City with a small court. Duan waited long enough to create an impression that the restoration was a serious threat to the republic. He also insisted that it was the policy followed by President Li, rather than unconstitutional action, that had made the restoration possible. When he massed his troops and marched into Beijing, Zhang Xun fled. Duan found himself considered to be a hero of the republic.

The restoration of the monarchy radically changed the political atmosphere of North China. The coup d'état and the dissolution of Parliament led directly to the establishment of another republican government: the government of Guangzhou (the capital city of the Guangdong Province). The republican members of Parliament moved to Guangzhou and formed a southern regime that was supported by an army, assembled by Sun Yat-sen. Sun was elected again as president in 1921. From this time on, there was great deal of friction in the relations between the northern warlords and the democratic South.[23]

Duan Qirui was not comfortable playing the role as the defender of the republic. His only alternative to reinstating President Li, his old political rival, was to allow Vice President Feng Guozhang, his military rival, to complete Li's term as president. Feng, backed by his personal following from the old Beiyang Army and his recently developed power in the Yangtze provinces, was ready to demand his own terms for coming to

Beijing to assume the presidency. Before leaving Nanjing, Feng compelled Premier Duan to promote several officers that he chose into the key military positions in the Yangtze area, thus retaining his power base in Central China. Once this demand was met, Feng returned to Beijing.

The old Beiyang Army was now divided into separate factions: one followed the presidency, and the other followed the premiership. Military subordinates became highly politicised and supported the political goals of each of the factions. This transformation from a military to a political grouping established two dissenting groups: the Anhui group (*Wanxi*) under the leadership of Duan Qirui, and the Zhili group (*Zhixi*) of Feng Guozhang.

As a political rather than military entity, the Anhui group was far better organised, but it was little more than a loose association that lacked central leadership and policy. It was dominated by the personalities of Duan Qirui and his immediate lieutenant, Xu Shuzheng.[24] With the military now clearly involved with the day-to-day affairs of civil government, the conflict between Duan's Anhui group and Feng's Zhili group became a contest to gain control the Parliament and the civil bureaucracy.[25] Through the Anhui group, Duan bribed members of Parliament to join the Anhui group and offered to pay them a monthly stipend for remaining in Beijing and voting in favour of his policies. Having bought off the Parliament, Duan was assured at all times of maintaining a quorum and was thus able to thwart the efforts of Feng Guozhang to dissolve Parliament. Such dissolution would have brought about a new election, which Feng Guozhang hoped would change the premiership and insure his reelection in October 1918.

Feng Guozhang and his followers formed their own group, the Zhili group, taking its name from Zhili (now Hebei), the hometown of Feng Guozhang. During the period from 1917 to 1920, the Zhili group was not a clearly defined group capable of united political or military action.[26] It was made up of leaders of the old Beiyang Army who were loyal to Feng and opposed to Premier Duan's authority.[27] Initially, the Zhili group lacked strong leadership and a secure revenue strain that could be utilised for united activities. Having little influence in Parliament, and with its centre of military power in Central China, the Zhili group was unable to act as an effective opposition to the Anhui group.

In October 1918 the Anhui group's control of the government was made even more secure when Xu Shichang[28] succeeded Feng Guozhang as president. Xu was considered a safe civilian candidate by both the Anhui and Zhili groups because he lacked any particular following and was regarded as an old and harmless scholar who could be easily manipulated. By the end of 1918, the Anhui group appeared to be in a position to serve as the first unifying force in China since the death of Yuan Shikai. With a civilian president in its pocket, the Anhui group's control of the Beijing government was undisputed, and it was backed by what appeared to be a sufficient bloc of military commanders to insure that its decisions would be effected throughout Central and North China.[29]

Without the charisma of Yuan Shikai and enough financial resources, the Anhui group's military and political control was limited to the North. The Zhili group's *dujuns* of Central China felt threatened by the Beijing government. Duan Qirui knew that any direct attack on these *dujuns* might lead to a strengthening of the rather weak ties among them. Therefore, he followed a policy of attempting to weaken the position of each of the area commanders separately by means of economic strangulation and administrative control. He gradually reduced the flow of funds from the central government to the provincial areas and limited new appointments in the central provinces.

This policy of control by separation was particularly effective and led to active opposition by the Zhili group and the development of a dynamic leadership within the group. Duan's appointment of Zhang Jingyao (1881–1933) as *dujun* of Hunan stiffened the resistance of *dujuns* in the part of the Central China.[30] Wu Peifu[31] saw this appointment as a threat to his rising power in Sichuan and western Hunan. To react to the Anhui group's move, Wu Peifu began to seek out the support of the Zhili group and, in particular, the assistance of his old commander and tutor, Cao Kun.[32] Cao had been an officer in the Beiyang Army, but he had never clearly sided with either Duan or Feng. However, in 1917, through the influence of Feng Guozhang, he had been given the post of *dujun* of Zhili Province (Hebei), an office of great strategic significance, which he had been able to retain because the Anhui group sought to refrain from pushing him directly into the Zhili group. However, Cao knew that, with the weakening of the Zhili group's power in Central China, the Anhui group would have little reason to tolerate his semi-independent position. When Wu Peifu approached him, Cao agreed to Wu's plan for a campaign against the Duan leaders on the condition that Wu guarantees that he would bring sufficient forces to attack the centre of Anhui group power in Beijing.[33] Wu also approached other *dujuns* of Sichuan, Shanxi, and Hubei provinces, who were equally unhappy with the financial support from the central government, and persuaded them to join with him as military allies against the Anhui group.[34]

By May 14, 1920, Wu was prepared to launch his drive into North China, and he began to move his armies up the Tianjin-Pukou Railway line. In the meantime, he had been successful in recruiting Zhang Zuolin[35] to campaign south of the Great Wall. The unexpected appearance of three divisions of Zhang's troops moving south from Shanhaiguan caught Duan Qirui completely unprepared. On June 6, 1920, Duan ordered his troops in the capital to move to Tianjin to confront the advancing armies of Wu Peifu and Cao Kun. With the appearance of Zhang's Manchurian, or Fengtien, troops, the *Wanxi*'s move was little more than a gesture, and the actual conflict lasted only two days. Duan Qirui retired to his "Buddhist studies" and contemplated his future.

Wu Peifu, with the support of Cao Kun, was able to create a new alignment of power in North China and take over the leadership of the Zhili faction from the warlords of the eastern Yangtze area. To Wu Peifu's surprise, the partnership with Zhang Zuolin brought him an enemy rather than an ally. Zhang realised how much power he had. He had little respect for Wu and openly questioned his judgement. Zhang felt more comfortable with Cao Kun, whom many military commanders looked to as their leader. President Xu Shichang, who had survived the conflict between the Anhui group and the Zhili group, was now able to follow the same policy of playing off the Feng group (*Fengxi*) led by Zhang Zuolin against the Zhili group to keep his own post.

This unstable balance lasted through 1921. The fact that Parliament had not been convened since the defeat of the Anhui group prevented the conflict between the Feng group and the Zhili group from emerging into the open; without Parliament, there was no need to force formal decisions on the issues of particular control between the two groups. However, the Zhili group was unable to indefinitely forestall the reconvening of Parliament, for Zhili group members not only had claimed to be the defenders of the republican form of government but also, by reestablishing Parliament, had hoped to bring back to Beijing the South China government. If they had been successful in accomplishing this, they would have had sufficient strength to neutralise the influence of Feng group.

By the end of 1921, Zhang Zuolin, aware of his weakening influence in Beijing, decided to take things into his own hands—he suddenly proclaimed Liang Shiyi as the new premier. The Zhili group was caught off guard and Zhang made it clear that he was willing to defend his appointment by force of arms. This proclamation sharpened the break between the Zhili group and the Feng group because it compelled all of the *dujuns* to declare their allegiance openly. Wu Peifu was quick to force the issue with every means at his disposal, and in the early spring of 1922 he began to mobilise his armies, calling upon the assistance of the most powerful *dujuns*. He sought aid particularly from Feng Yuxiang, who was at that time *Dujun* of Shanxi. Cao Kun once again refused to accept the active leadership of the Zhili group's military campaign, although he fully supported Wu and took part in directing Wu's campaign.[36]

Zhang Zuolin realised that Wu had yet to cement his support from Cao Kun, who still refused to actively engage his troops until Wu could prove his ability to hold off the armies of the Feng group. Cao moved his troops south in April 1922. Zhang Zuolin moved his troops south from Fengtien, exposing himself to a possible attack by Cao from the latter's headquarters at Baoding. Cao decided to make a gesture; he moved his troops down the Jingjiu Railway line into Shandong, leaving only one division at Tianjin. This maneuver forced Zhang Zuolin to make a rapid withdrawal. Zhang was afraid that Cao was about to move from Baoding and cut his supply lines to his main base in Manchuria while he was engaging Wu Peifu and Feng Yuxiang's troops. However, Cao was not yet ready to march on Zhang. He refused to move quickly enough to cause a major engagement with Zhang at Tianjin. He was uncertain of the ability of troops of the Feng group to mount a more powerful force than that which they had placed in the field. Cao contented to allow Wu and Feng to do the actual testing of Fengxi's strength. Cao, therefore, permitted Zhang to make his escape back into Manchuria but arranged to send his troops into Beijing and Tianjin just as Wu's armies moved up from Shandong. Thus, Cao, although not having to bear the cost and risk of a military campaign, still managed to remain in a position to claim the fruits of victory.[37]

Civilian officers of all ranks were nothing but puppets in the hands of the warlords. As soon as the Feng group returned to Manchuria, Wu Peifu moved swiftly to strengthen his own position at Beijing. First, he shifted Feng Yuxiang to Peking to act as an inspector general of the Chinese military establishment. This uprooted Feng from his power base in Henan Province and replaced the best army in his capital to influence politics there.[38] Wu Peifu then announced that he would march against President Xu Shichang, who had been stubbornly successful in riding out previous actions by playing the warlords of the Anhui and Feng groups against each other.[39] On June 1, 1922, Wu charged that President Xu Shichang had been planning, along with Zhang Zuolin, to restore the monarchy and proceeded to oust him from office. On June 11 Wu called back into office Li Yuanhong, who had been forced from the presidency after the monarchical restoration movement (which temporarily placed Puyi on the throne) of July 1917, as president.[40]

With these manipulations, Wu claimed a position as a supporter of constitutional government, while at the same time he had made sure that the presidential office would be held by a civilian who possessed neither military nor political power. Wu's hope was that this political gesture might serve to bring back republican South China under the control of Beijing.[41]

The warlords of the Zhili group now had achieved sufficient control of the capital. On August 1, 1922, they took the risk of reconvening the "old" Parliament, which had first been formed in 1912 under Yuan Shikai and was dissolved by Zhang Xun in 1917. Wu Peifu was interested in the Parliament because he wanted to bring the regime in the South together with Beijing and eventually legitimise his own political position. The old Parliament included representatives of the Guomindang (GMD), also known as the Kuomintang (KMT), Sun Yat-sen's political party that had the support of the armies in the South.[42] The return of Parliament served as a scoring device capable of reflecting the strength of various groups, and the balance among the *dujuns* became less dependent upon direct military following. Thus, Wu's influence began to decline in Beijing because he had few contacts and little control over the parliamentarians. Now, Cao Kun, as the accepted leader of the Zhili group and the more experienced military-political figure, was able to direct the events in Beijing with a surer hand.

Wu Peifu was faced with two alternatives. On the one hand, he could attempt to enter the arena of political manipulation at the capital, where he had little experience—and, by so doing, probably radically change the alignment in the Zhili group, possibly even causing Cao Kun to join forces with Zhang Zuolin. On the other hand, he could continue to play his role as the most efficient military leader of the Zhili alliance. If this latter course succeeded, his military position would become so secure that he would become the dominant figure in the Zhili group. As long as the Feng group existed as a threat and continued to expand its armies, there was pressure on Wu from all elements of the Zhili group to give his full attention to the field of military affairs. Wu chose to withdraw from Beijing, and so he returned to his military headquarters at Loyang (a city west of Henan) and concentrated on building up his armed forces.

The major problems for the Zhili group after it had gained control of the government were the relations with President Li Yuanhong and the financial difficulties. Li's restoration to the presidency did not have an effect in winning back the South as Wu had wished, although it had helped the new government's appearance of legitimacy and brought about a greater degree of popular acquiescence to its control than the previous regime had enjoyed. Wu's claim, that his reinstatement of

Li was due to his legitimacy as president, had the effect of placing Li under a limited obligation to the Zhili leadership. However, Li was soon seeking to strengthen his own claim, independent of the Zhili group. Li's blocking tactics in the Parliament also frustrated Wu and his backers.

This conflict was intensified by the debate on financial issues. As foreign loans began to dry up, the military would no longer look to Beijing as an easy source of finance for its operation. The problem was further complicated by Cao Kun's tactics of permitting the president to grapple with the insoluble problems of finance while he, Cao, used his influence over Parliament to sidetrack the various proposals advocated by President Li to obtain funds. It was by this technique, of embarrassing the president, that Cao hoped to prepare the way to his own assumption of absolute power in Beijing.

The lack of government funds was felt increasingly by elements of the Zhili group, particularly by those commanders who did not control definite geographic areas from which they could extract revenue. The most desperate of these commanders was Feng Yuxiang, who, with his troops stationed at the capital, had to depend entirely upon funds from government coffers.

Feng Yuxiang's financial problems soon became a threat to the stability of the Beijing government. The government began to have the real fear that Feng's troops might act independently in support of their demands for back pay. There was also possibility that Feng might decide to change his political alliance if he could somehow ensure the sovereignty of his armies. Li Yuanhong was not in a position to pay for Feng's army, even if he could find the money. Li was reluctant to offer funds because he simply could not trust a man who had gained so much support from the leaders of the Zhili group.[43]

Feng met with Cao eight times in Baoding but failed to produce any acceptable financial arrangement. On June 13, 1923, he suddenly seized control of the Beijing Octroi as a source of revenue for his personal armies. The Octroi, which levied a modest tax on certain items entering Beijing, had been established as a direct source of funds for the president's office. Feng's move had the intended effects of obtaining the necessary funds to satisfy his own troops and simultaneously destroying the president's revenue stream. Li fled from Beijing.

Now Feng found himself in much the same position as that which Wu Peifu had occupied in 1922. He had sufficient military power to destroy the presidency, but he lacked the political support necessary to establish even a temporary administration. His actions, rather, had opened the way for his wary mentor, Cao Kun, to assume full control of the government free from the perception of stigma of having perpetrated an armed coup d'état.

Several warlords under the leadership of Wu Peifu argued that Cao Kun should take immediate and direct action by ousting Parliament and establishing the basis for new government. They maintained that, with such direct methods, Cao Kun would gain the free hand necessary to meet financial concerns and establish a sound administration, which could act independently from the existing Parliament, the cabinet, and the presidency.[44]

Cao Kun also needed to placate the Zhili group in Tianjin (the Tianjin clique), led by his brother Cao Ying who had influence within the Parliament system. It is believed that Cao Kun spent nearly US$15 million (in silver) to "win" the election.[45] Payments were made to the members of the House for each session of Parliament that they attended, much in the same manner as the Anhui group had done in 1917. Corruption was so rampant that promises of future subsidisation were offered to legislators dependent upon their voting records. On October 5, 1923, Cao Kun was formally elected by Parliament as president and assumed office on the same day.

Once elected, Cao Kun needed to sort through a myriad of demands from various factions of the Zhili group concerning official political appointments and acceptable rankings. The dispute became so serious that many of Cao's key posts had to remain empty because he did not want to alienate the useful candidates who competed for the more desirable posts.[46] If not for the military threat from the Feng group (Zhang Zuolin) and other powerful warlords, the Zhili group would have completely broken down as they trampled over each other in their quest for the most important administrative positions in the land. Cao Kun also could not ignore the entreaties of the *dujuns* upon whose military power he depended. At the same time, he needed the support of the Tianjin clique to keep Parliament in line. He was caught in an awkward spot, needing the cooperation from both the Zhili group and the *dujuns*. The result was a widening of the division between the capital and the provinces, with Cao Kun reluctantly sanctioning a greater degree of autonomy for the provincial leaders.

Wu Peifu continued to lead the *dujuns* who supported the Zhili group. For the military commanders, the centre of decision making gradually shifted from Beijing to Wu Peifu's headquarters at Loyang, leading to a dilution of Cao Kun's immediate control over this group. With the Beijing government falling under the influence of the Tianjin clique, Wu began to think more and more about unifying China by force. For a military still learning politics, everything he did was motivated by fear. In particular, he feared Zhang Zuolin and the *dujuns* who were seeking to ally themselves with Zhang. Wu's worst nightmare was that Zhang might organise the North for a sudden strike on the capital from Manchuria and enlist the support of *dujuns* located to the south of the Zhili group's centres of power. Thus, this would force Wu into a campaign on two fronts.

Wu's nightmare became a reality in the spring of 1924, when the *Dujun* of Zhejiang, Lu Yungxiang, made overt moves to support Zhang Zuolin.[47] Zhejiang was an important strategic jurisdiction that could control Shanghai. In addition, the foreign interests in Shanghai served to protect the area and deter active military campaigns that might involve their holdings. Ever since the defeat of Duan's Anhui group, Lu's control of Zhejiang had been a constant annoyance to the *Zhixi*. But this annoyance had been ignored until Lu solicited support from Zhang Zuolin and actual plans were initiated to eliminate Lu's power. These plans were coordinated by Ji Xieyuan, a loyal subordinate of Wu Peifu. As *Dujun* of Jiangsu, Ji had long been interested in incorporating the Shanghai into his own sphere and, now, with the backing of Wu, felt strong enough to proceed.

On August 25, 1923, Ji Xieyuan moved his troops out of Nanjing in a drive towards Suzhou and Shanghai. Wu Peifu had counted on a quick victory, hoping that the threat of a combined action by Lu and Zhang would be eliminated and that the main forces of the Zhili group could be kept intact for the major campaign against Zhang. However, at the start of the actual fighting, neither Ji nor Lu was in a position to make rapid gains, and the danger of a costly stalemate soon developed. Wu was forced to order reinforcements from Hunan and Sichuan to assist Ji, and finally he directed Feng Yuxiang to proceed to the support of the Jiangsu *Dujun*. With little hope of receiving anything in return, Feng refused to comply with Wu's orders. Feng did not want to give up the security of his command in the Beijing area. In his opinion, the major conflict was with Zhang Zuolin and the Fengxi armies, and the political future of North China rested on the outcome of this campaign. Thus, it was to Feng's advantage to stay close to the capital if he hoped to improve his political and military influence.[48]

Without Feng's aid, Zhang declared war on Wu Peifu and the Zhili group's government. Zhang Zuolin's first strike was timed to reduce the pressure on Lu, who was now faced with the threat of revolt from dissenters who believed that Ji Xieyuan had far greater resources at his disposal than their own leader. Although Lu was defeated before Zhang Zuolin was able to move his forces south of the Great Wall, the unsettled conditions in Zhejiang and differences over the division of the spoils among those who had fought for Ji served Zhang's purpose in preventing the Zhili group from presenting a united front against him.[49]

Zhang had his wish: Feng Yuxiang decided to betray his Zhili commander, Wu Peifu.[50] Feng thought that he had little to gain and possibly a great deal to lose from the campaign against Feng troops. If the Zhili group's forces won, Wu Peifu would have extended his military domination over most of North China and Feng would be deprived of his control of the capital. Feng began to negotiate with Zhang Zuolin before he left Beijing following Wu's order. However, Feng did not trust Zhang Zuolin and did not support Zhang because a resounding victory by Zhang, who appeared to have great advantages in terms of preparation, equipment, and unified command, would have spelled the end of Feng's ability to maintain his independent military power. Feng determined to fight a war for himself.[51]

On the night of October 22, 1924, Feng began to move his army back to Beijing and, by means of forced marches, covered one hundred miles in thirty-six hours. He immediately took over the capital, imprisoned President Cao Kun, charging him with bribery, and ordered the arrest of the members of Parliament. Wu Peifu, who at the time was in direct command of his troops at Shanhaiguan, did not react immediately to the movement of Feng Yuxiang's army. Rather, he counted on a quick victory over the armies of the Feng group, which would not only check the invaders from the north but would demonstrate to Feng the futility of his plans. However, when Wu's plan did not work out the way that he planned, he was forced to withdraw to Tianjin, where he was able to salvage only his best divisions, which he moved to his headquarters at Loyang.

Now, Beijing had a new master. Feng Yuxiang appeared to be in complete control, defeating the power of the Zhili group and imprisoning the president. Feng could not wait to move his troops into the Forbidden City and end the nominal reign of the boy emperor, Puyi.[52] Feng did not have any noble republican intentions. He hoped that, by his ceremonial action, he would be able to obtain the revenue that was being paid to the deposed emperor's court and gain control over the assets of the palace. To legitimise his occupation of Beijing, he proclaimed that his troops were the first in the history of the republic to serve as a national military establishment rather than as a personal army. He reorganised his militia into the National Army of the Guomindang. Feng also persuaded Sun Yat-sen to come to Beijing and participate in the formation of a new government.

With the collapse of the Zhili group, an even more tenuous balance of power emerged. Feng's position in Beijing was steadily weakened by the maneuvers of Zhang Zuolin. The Feng group's commander moved his troops south from Manchuria, and, instead of stopping at Tianjin to negotiate with Feng on the future plans for the government, he first made certain of his military control of the situation by ordering his armies to proceed south on the Tianjin-Pukou Railway. Zhang now controlled East China from Manchuria to the Yangtze Valley. In addition, he reached an agreement with Duan Qirui and provided the old Anhui leader with a place in the new government. By taking these steps, Zhang hoped to strengthen his bargaining power when he met with Feng.

During November 1924, the three warlords, Feng Yuxiang, Zhang Zuolin, and Duan Qirui, held a five-day conference to plot the future of China. Feng soon discovered that he had little negotiating power beyond his military control of Beijing—the little bit of power that he did have was instable because as long as Zhang Zuolin remained in a position to attack him from Manchuria at any time. Feng even found that his trump card—the promise he had obtained from Sun Yat-sen to negotiate the return of the South to the jurisdiction of Beijing—had been realised by Duan and Zhang, who had both established contact with Sun. The only agreement to come from the Tianjin Conference was that Duan Qirui would be made provisional chief executive, thus leaving the door open for Sun when he made the trip to the capital. Feng and Zhang would maintain a hold over the areas that they occupied and would become chief military leaders of the new regime.

On November 24, 1924, Duan assumed office. He immediately formed a new cabinet, which did not include a single follower of Feng. Unhappy with his share of power, Feng decided to resign his post as inspector general and retire. However, his armies still controlled the capital, and on the night of December 2, he demonstrated this control by placing his troops in such strategic positions that Zhang Zuolin felt it advisable to leave the city and return to Tianjin. Zhang resigned his titles, leaving Duan Qirui to face the hopeless task of keeping Feng and Zhang at bay while he was trying to establish a formal government. The death of Sun Yat-sen on March 12, 1925, ended the thought of the South returning to Beijing and removed Duan's only remaining tool for keeping Feng and Zhang in check.

Feng Yuxiang was now ready to build up his forces and a test the strength of Zhang Zuolin. He organised the northwest as a source of revenue and sought out allies. He found a willing supporter in Sun

Chuanfang,[53] who had previously been allied with Wu Peifu but was unhappy with the reward that he had received for his support. At the time, Sun controlled a part of Zhejiang and was dealing with insurgent remnants of the old Zhili group, and he was concerned with Zhang Zuolin's presence immediately to his north.

On October 17, 1925, Sun Chuanfang began his push northward, conquering Jiangsu and Anhui as he proceeded in the direction of the Shandong Province. Feng had counted on Zhang to move his troops from Manchuria via Tianjin, thus affording Feng the opportunity to move eastward to cut the Fengxi's lines of supply and communication. However, Zhang protected his flank by sending an army into Rehe Province, just as he had done against Wu Peifu the preceding autumn. Feng found that rather than cutting Zhang Zuolin's line of communication, he had instead exposed himself to a pincer movement by Zhang.

Feng, however, had discovered another vulnerable point in Zhang's position. Feng was able to make an agreement with Guo Sungling, who was one of Chang's trusted generals and commanded some of the best of the Fengxi troops. On November 27, 1925, Feng and Guo jointly declared war on Zhang Zuolin. Guo occupied Shanhaiguan and was preparing to move south towards Tienjin. It was now apparent to Zhang Zuolin that the treachery of his subordinate had cut his armies in two, and there was a real danger that Guo would have little difficulty in moving against him.

The hostilities between Feng and Zhang had opened the way for a new axis of power. Wu Peifu, who had been quietly building up his strength in Henan, now began to appear as an attractive ally, especially to Zhang Zuolin. A Wu-Zhang alliance would leave Feng isolated in North China with only the northwest left as an area to retreat to. A Wu-Feng alliance was unlikely because of Feng's betrayal of Wu in 1921 and also because Wu's power was still insufficient, even if used in combination with Feng's armies, to bring about the defeat of the Zhang's forces. Wu's hopes for a return to active political influence outside of Henan depended upon his acceptance of a subordinate position to the only power capable of dominating North and Central China: Zhang Zuolin.[54]

The armies of Zhang and Wu arrived in the capital immediately afterwards and were faced with the problem of organising a government. Although Zhang Zuolin had supported the selection of Duan Qirui as provisional chief executive, it was apparent that Duan, now under pressure of public opposition, would be incapable of establishing a stable regime, even with the full support of Zhang. Zhang, who held military superiority, wanted Wu to appear subordinate and created the Committee of Public Safety to oversee governmental offices. The appointees to this committee were generals of both Zhang and Wu.[55]

The Committee of Public Safety did not function as a stable balance of equals. Zhang, with his superior military power and the resources of Manchuria to support him, was soon dominated. Not only was he able to actively support his generals, but it was soon apparent to Wu's appointees that the security in office depended upon the charity of Zhang. On December 2, 1926, Zhang formalised his military position by declaring himself commander in chief of the reorganised Northern Armies, which were to be known as the *Ankuochun*, or, as it was freely translated, the Tranquility Restoration Army. This move did not eliminate the armies of Wu and Feng, but it did allow Zhang to gain control over a major portion of the national budget for military expenditures. Thus, Zhang could at last supplement his own Manchurian sources of revenue with a portion of the Beijing government's finances, and he was now in a position to consolidate his power and expand his area of control.

By June 1927, Zhang ended the sham of rule by the Committee of Public Safety and inaugurated a dictatorial military government with himself holding the post of *dayuanshuai* (supreme general).

* * * * *

During this period of anarchy, the Chinese warlords were above law and had little respect for the constitution or for an elected civilian government.[56] They spent their entire careers building strong armed forces in order to maintain regional control. They would become involved with civilian government only when they saw the opportunity to dominate, blackmail, and manipulate the administration. The warlords denounced or even threatened parliamentarians as soon as they failed to follow instructions. They knew that, at any given time, they could always march into the capital and oust governmental officers to create another puppet administration. However, the constant reality of armed intervention during this military anarchy made the warlords realise that it was much easier to capture an established order and destroy an administration than to build respectful law and sustainable government. From the death of Yuan Shikai in 1916 until the spring of 1926, there were six different heads of state, some brief imperial restorations, as well as three short periods of a temporary care-taking leadership while official positions were being negotiated. Twenty-five successive cabinets were formed. These rapid political changes reflected the arrogance and limitations of the military rulers, their incompetence as administrators (with a few exceptions), and their inability to effectively communicate with the administrations or electorates.

Warlords were not politically astute. They acted and responded only to other military threats. Their vision was limited to the advancement of their ability to obtain resources from regions and continue to build their military powerhouse. Their talk of unifying China was based upon their desire to tap into the cash cow of the South rather than the formation of an enlightened social democratic state.

As the warlords struggled with each other, social unrest fermented throughout China, and the under laws began to emerge from China's millions of farmers. In a country of agriculture, where 90 percent of the population lived off the land, the line between peasant and soldier could be crossed easily, and the line between soldier and bandit was a matter of intention or definition. At its best, the military was honest and robustly egalitarian; at its worst, it abused its strength and initiated outlaw activities such as lynching, robbery, looting, and worse. In a normal Chinese society, soldiers were at the bottom of the hierarchy after scholars, farmers, and merchants. A popular Chinese proverb sums up this social ranking: "No good iron would be used to make a nail, and no good man would be a soldier". The conceptual barrier between military commander and state bureaucrat was much more solid than any code of law.

In theory, the establishment of a military state is considered illegal according to Chinese cultural and political tradition. This illegality is not a minor legal concept that could be nullified by legislating new code about a rather traditional moral value supported by thousands of years of government activity. Chinese illegality, like the English general concept of law or rights, is a cultural and moral conviction shared by every Chinese mind, including those inside and outside of law. For many centuries, Chinese civil order has been based on written codes; authority to rule had to be justified, sanctioned, and legalised by acceptable words of law. In order to sustain, government needed an active civilian structure that included intellectuals, scholars, and professional bureaucrats. Military was only used within this civil organisation. Written Chinese law also required an authoritative seal to be recognised as authentic and legal. This was the reason why Chinese military leaders repeatedly resorted to the elements of the dying imperial family or Parliament sanction, a pragmatic rather than ideological choice.

The actions of the warlords in the early twentieth century were a historical accident that occurred because a strong civil institution did not immediately form after the collapse of the imperial system. After a few thousand years of civil administration, Chinese law had never been discussed by, debated among, or comprehended by its citizens, but rather it had been revoked, re-announced, reapplied, and administrated by several levels of specifically trained bureaucrats. In a way, it was like the medieval canon law of Western Europe, which was conceived to be externally imposed by God. This law could be applied by different administrators, such as the clergy or the kings (emperors), who were associated with an abstract (or faceless) authority, such as God or Nature. Chinese law, which has never been associated with a sustained godhead, could only be conceivable when associated with a human face—the face of an emperor, a chairman, a president, or a combination of all of them.

In China, political authority possesses neither a godhead nor a divine text, which are perceived as higher and unalienated Word. Word (in Chinese language) has never been capitalised in writing or associated with an abstract origin that defies human understanding, interpretation, and divination. Words have only human, concrete, and therefore alienable origins. Even the words of a saint, such as those of Confucius, are often open to redefinition and reinterpretation. This lack of conceptual abstraction made Chinese law human in nature and fluid in connotation. To preserve social order, an army of civilian bureaucrats was recruited and trained to serve as a human shield to barricade against unauthoritative, chaotic interpretations and administrative corruption. This conceptual fluidity did not appear to be a problem when there was an established political authority, such as an emperor, to define the boundaries of law. It became a serious problem after the imperial system ended and the established social hierarchy was left headless.

There were two social groups under the supervision of the imperial court that attempted to assume the spot formally occupied by the emperor, warlords, and intellectual politicians. The warlords, as a social group, had never transformed into statesmen, as did the Japanese samurais.[57] They struggled for legitimacy and failed repeatedly because forming a civil government required more complex skills, social networks, and intellectual conviction. The institutional barrier between the words of the civilian statesmen and the swords of the military was firmly entrenched in social organisation, as well as the mind and soul of the Chinese people. As a nonpolitical and detached instrument, armies were traditionally utilised and directed to intervene in emergency situations that sometimes threatened the emperor, the state, or the people. The place of the military was on the battlefields, the borders, and the frontiers. The military was required to withdraw as soon as order was restored.

Chinese intellectuals who were trained in Confucian rules were often too bookish and gentleman-like to be politicians, who functioned under a different set of rules. Chinese politicians often refused to follow the archaic law, and only did so if it served their interests; their strategies often were highly pragmatic, yet immoral and illegal. Chinese intellectuals are experts in interpreting, arguing, and applying the rules, but very much like their Western counterparts, they are giants in words but incapable of action. They can conceive new ideas but lack the ability to do anything about them. These salon politicians were left with no audience except themselves. When the words lost the power to restrain social order, their precious moral principles lost appeal with the masses. Nobody was paying attention to their war of words (pen battle in Chinese).

The reality of fifteen years of civil war after the Republican Revolution highly radicalised Chinese culture and its political ideas. It appeared that constitutional law (based on words) had no authority without a strong army. Because words alone could not rule and no one could lead without the ability to fight with bullets and control an army, the Chinese Republican Revolution had to take arms in order to remove the warlords from the centre stage of politics.[58]

The Chinese Republicans realised that it had been naive and unrealistic to assume that Chinese people would instinctively and spontaneously embrace the revolution and its new government. In order to establish a constitutional order, the constitutionalists had to have a superior army. They had learned that a period of military rule was necessary to defend the young and fragile republic. They began to see an army as a revolutionary instrument. The later Northern Expedition, a war to fight outlaw warlords and to unify China, was the result of this military choice.[59]

Sun Yat-sen, the twice-elected president, was among the first to come to this conclusion. In 1917, he wrote to Liao Zhongkai, one of the Guomindang's left-leaning veterans who would later play a leading role in the formation of the National Revolutionary Army (NRA) (*Guomin Geming Jun*), which was controlled by Guomindang.[60] Sun told Liao that he was thinking of writing a book entitled *Plans for National Defence*. Although Sun would never complete the book, his outline indicated that he envisioned a National Defence Army as the guardian of the modern nation. He wanted to turn the whole nation into expert soldiers and spoke of training thirty million basic national defence personnel and ten million experts in the material construction of national defence. He stated that the purpose of the army was to safeguard domestic peace, guarantee constitutional government, and resist foreign aggression. Sun argued that past revolutionary attempts and efforts to save the republic had failed because people believed that action was difficult. This forged a general attitude of hopelessness and, consequently, a passive disposition, as well as a lack of boldness and determination. He called for a new commitment to action and argued that even without certain knowledge, action was possible. Sun's vague vision later became a canonical scripture, sanctioning the idea of an elite national army recruited on the basis of a national military service obligation.[61]

Sun Yat-sen died before he could develop any concrete plans for his vague political ideas. The issue of leadership and direction for the continuing revolution divided the Guomindang. A power struggle ensued between Chiang Kai-shek, who leaned towards the right wing of the Guomindang, and left-wing leader Wang Jingwei.[62] In this power struggle, Chiang was disadvantaged on two important accounts. First, he was ranked relatively low in the party's internal hierarchy, and Wang had succeeded Sun to power as chairman of the national government. Second, the Soviet military advisors who had increasingly important influence with the Guomindang disliked Chiang and preferred to work with Wang Jingwei instead.[63]

Wang Jingwei made a powerful bid to take over Sun's mantle of leadership. On July 1, 1925, at the time of the formal establishment of the national government, he was elected chair of the National Government Council and its Standing Committee. With the support of the Soviets, who were the sole financial and military source of Sun's revolution, Wang took steps to increase his influence over the military force by placing a Communist political commissar in many of the National Revolutionary Army (NRA) troops.[64] Wang removed his most important political opponents and brought in new domestic allies with strong military and financial resources. On January 26, 2006, he met with Li Zongren and Bai Chongxi, the leaders of the Guangxi clique who had established control over Guangxi. Subsequent negotiations led to the incorporation of their forces into the NRA. Wang also formed an alliance with Tang Shengzhi, a Hunan militarist, on February 24, 1926.[65]

Faced with the decline of his influence in the NRA, which he had created, led, and defended throughout his entire career, and his difficulty with the Soviet advisors, whom he could not afford to offend, Chiang decided to launch the Northern Expedition. This military action made it possible for Chiang Kai-shek to rise rapidly in the Nationalist hierarchy.[66]

The Northern Expedition began from the Guomindang's power base in Guangdong Province and consisted of seven armies with a total of approximately one hundred thousand troops.[67] The main targets of this expedition were the three most notorious and powerful warlords of China: Zhang Zuolin who governed Manchuria, Wu Peifu in the central plains, and Sun Chuanfang on the eastern coast. On July 9, 1926, Chiang gave his lecture to his soldiers of the National Revolutionary Army. This force was organised by officers trained in the Huangpu (Whampoa) Military Academy and was equipped with superior Russian arsenals. This army was far better organised than the warlord armies that they faced, for they had good military advisors, better weapons, and commissars from CPC to inspire the soldiers. In addition, the NRA was regarded as a progressive force, representing ordinary people who had been persecuted by the warlords. It received a warm welcome and strong popular support from peasants and workers alike. The NRA marched from the Zhu Jiang River area to Yangtze River in less than half a year, annihilating the main forces of Wu and Sun, and strengthened its force to 250,000 soldiers.[68]

However, The NRA was not a unified army led by a single state or a single party. It was a loose alliance of military interest groups that often were not well integrated internally. As they set out on the Northern Expedition, each army had its own agenda. They had joined the fight not only to defeat a common enemy, but also to seek new territories for recruitment and to raise funds. In Chinese terms, they were sleeping on the same bed while having different dreams (*tong chuang yi meng*).

They all attempted to succeed in the battlefield to increase their own political leverage and diminish that of their arrivals.

Further complicating matters, the Nationalists, the Communists, and the Soviets were all divided among themselves and sought to use developments on the battlefields and political events to weaken the infrastructure of their internal rivals. Such rivalries were played out in a tense atmosphere. Revolutionary triumph seemed within reach, while at the same time imaginations were gripped by fears of the loss of a great opportunity to put China on the right course. There were deep suspicions about the ultimate motivations of comrades in arms.

The forces associated with the Northern Expedition were deeply divided among themselves, and each tried to establish their dominion over events by accumulating military force, establishing new military and financial bases, and developing new sources of symbolic and social power. Many reached for increasingly unorthodox and brutally violent measures in this quest.[69] When the Northern Expedition finally took Beijing in 1928, no one could single-handedly control the situation. The shaking alliance was about to fall apart again. As the old warlords were defeated, new ones emerged and barricaded their newly found territories and bases. Paranoia, intrigue, murder, and brutality became commonplace. The unfortunate harvest of the Northern Expedition was the entrenchment of nasty cultures of violence.

Once in Beijing, Chiang Kai-shek was named generalissimo of all Chinese forces and the chairman (president) of the national government, a post that he held until 1932. However, Chiang's government did not have the control that he wished. It was almost as weak as the government of Sun Yat-sen. According to Sun's plans, the Guomindang was to rebuild China in three steps: military rule, political tutelage, and constitutional rule. The ultimate goal of the Guomindang revolution was to achieve democratic rule, a goal that was not yet feasible in China's current fragmented state. The Guomindang had completed the first step of the revolution through its seizure of power in 1928. Under Chiang's leadership, the Guomindang undertook the next step of Sun's plans, thus beginning the period of political tutelage to prepare China for the final transition to a constitutional democracy.

During the next twenty years, Chiang Kai-shek's administration could not complete the second stage of Sun's plan. Chiang had failed to consolidate and maintain his civil government. Like many reluctant Chinese politicians, he needed the support of a large armed force and had to be wary of insurgent activities. This time, his enemy was not so much the regional warlords, but rather a determined and well-organised political rival, the Chinese Communist Party (CCP).

A temporary truce between the Guomindang and the Communist Party was maintained and balanced by the effort of the Soviet Union, which was the main military and financial patron of the Northern Expedition. The original Soviet strategy was to establish a Communist hegemony by controlling Guomindang institutions through its left wing, which was composed of many CCP members. The agenda of the Chinese Communist Party, however, evolved divergently from that of the Soviets. The Chinese Communists wanted to separate and split Guomindang into right-wing and left-wing factions so that the power struggle would be seen as an internal conflict of the Guomindang instead of between the GMD and the CCP. The Chinese Communists were afraid that a unified GMD would be able to concentrate on fighting against them and that a successful Northern Expedition could lead to a victory for the new warlords, such as Chiang Kai-shek and Li Zongren.

To fight for its own share of power, the Communist Party decided to take arms and organise an independent army of its own. At its Fifth Congress of April–May 1927, Chen Duxiu, head of the Communist Party, announced that the CCP was not strong enough to neutralise Chiang Kai-shek because he embraced a strong military force, the support of a sizeable portion of the GMD, and favourable public opinion. Chen strongly proposed the establishment of an independent army to challenge Chiang. Chen asked the Soviets to divert to the CCP some of the military equipment that they now liberally provided to Chiang Kai-shek so that the CCP could arm the peasantry. The request for arms was denied by Soviet representatives in Guangdong on the grounds, according to Chen, because they believed that it would provoke GMD suspicions and lead the peasants to oppose the GMD.[70]

However, the CCP continued to support the radical peasant movement, a strategy that Chen employed to build social base for the GMD left wing and the CCP. In October 1926 the CCP adopted a Draft Peasant Policy, which stressed that the GMD political power could not endure without a peasant policy that satisfied the demands of the masses. It called for a united front of the GMD and the CCP to coordinate in the countryside and oppose the political power of the evil gentry in the villages.[71]

To advance this plan, Chen Duxiu set up the Peasant Movement Committee of the CCP Central Committee and appointed Mao Zedong as its secretary. Mao had worked in various capacities for the national government in Canton. Wang Jingwei had appointed him acting head of the GMD Propaganda Department and editor of the *Political Weekly*. Mao, like his comrade Zhou Enlai, had been among those who believed that a countercoup against Chiang Kai-shek was possible.[72] As the relationship between GMD and CCP went from bad to worse, the peasant movement revived and rapidly spread in Guangdong. In Hunan, peasant movement work spread to sixty-five counties, where the Communists organised many peasant associations with a membership of 416,000. During the Northern Expedition, many Hunan peasants had obtained arms and gained battle experience.[73]

In his report to the Central Bureau, Mao promoted political movement of poor peasants, whom he believed to be the vanguard of the revolution.[74] Mao Zedong's powerful and convincing argument shifted the opinions of the party about radical movement in the countryside.[75] Mao insisted that revolution was not a dinner party, or literary composition, or painting, or embroidery; revolution was an act of uprising.[76] In fact, uprisings began to take place in provinces where landlords became the targets of vengeance for past wrongdoings. Some landlords were tried by the peasant mob and lynched. Landlords began to mobilise militia to defend their properties.[77] Red terrorism became the dominant strategy of the Communists to fight Chiang Kai-shek.

Violence provoked more and more violence. In Shanghai, the red terror encountered police brutality. In October 1926 the CCP attempted their initial uprising. This action failed, and the Shanghai Communists turned their attention to improve the quality of their pickets and organise military actions. Many Communist pickets had gang backgrounds, and workers were often reluctant to join them. In December Chen called Zhou Enlai back from Guangdong to help with the organisation of a new uprising. On February 18, Shanghai workers went on a massive general strike, partly to fulfil the CCP's political demands but mainly to welcome the NRA forces, which now closed in on the city. Two CCP attempts to translate the strike into an armed uprising petered out quickly due to a lack of military support. However, violence spread and there were many incidents of mob violence, mob trials, and public execution.[78]

A new wave of red terror took place in Shanghai as the Communists began to assassinate suspicious union members, especially foremen, who were believed to be spying on the workers for the government. The Special Committee called for a "citizens' government" in Shanghai that would exclude the GMD right-wing members. An uprising to oust the warlord administration of Sun Chuanfang followed. It also oversaw a programme to restructure pickets into eight battalions with more than two thousand troops. On March 5, Zhou Enlai reported to the Special Committee about military preparations. According to Zhou's report, the CCP could mobilise seven hundred pickets, shock troops, and rally a peasant self-defence corps from the Shanghai countryside. Zhou stated that the CCP had thirteen thousand arms at its disposal.[79]

On March 21, the Third Shanghai Uprising took place. Some three thousand armed pickets attacked police on the streets and seized police stations, while thousands of workers of the General Labour Union went on strike. Chaos quickly spread. Similar to the Second Uprising, mob rule and mass trials of despised plainclothes policemen and hated foremen became flashpoints in an already-explosive situation. In the revolutionary anarchy, all laws—national and international alike—were completely ignored. The Shanghai Communists further discussed plans for a general uprising to take the International Settlement and the French Concession. Disregarding the advice of the Soviets, they organised mass rallies and strikes focused against the British.[80]

Because the CCP insisted on outlaw and non-civil activities, tensions in Shanghai escalated. Warlord forces had left, but Chiang Kai-shek's army could not restore the city to the control of regular NRA forces (as opposed to irregular Communist ones) until March 26.[81] The arrival on April 1 of Wang Jingwei, who had travelled from France via Moscow, provided Chiang a final hope. After meeting Wang on April 3, Chiang Kai-shek issued a telegram stating that from then on he would only concern himself with military affairs and that Wang Jingwei would again take over as chairman of the GMD. Wang and Chen Duxiu issued a joint public statement on the morning of April 5, which called on the CCP and the GMD to work closely together to prevent the enemies of the Republican Revolution from exploiting the conflicts between them.

Anarchy and violence were the product of uncontrollable social tensions that had built up over time. This accumulation occurred because there was not a peaceful means to negotiate and solve the difference of opinions favoured by one side or the other. In cruel power struggles, policy issues were confused and defused with personal rivalries. Most historians, especially the left-leaning Western historians, focused on the Shanghai Massacre when Guangxi forces of Li Zongren, with the support of Chiang Kai-shek, ruthlessly massacred Communist pickets and began the white terror. However, this was not an isolated incident. Violence became epidemic in countless rural towns and villages, as well as in Shanghai and in a number of other cities. By March 30, bloody conflicts had been occurring for a month in Hangzhou. Led by pickets and supported by the General Labour Union, the demonstrators surrounded NRA headquarters, and NRA troops fired on them. On the same day, in Chongqing, the attempt by the garrison commander to prevent a demonstration against Chiang Kai-shek led to a bloodbath when the pickets resisted the army. In Nanchang, on April 2, a CCP–GMD left-wing alliance staged a coup. Some twenty people died, and people's courts condemned several KMD leaders to death. In Fuzhou, a struggle between forces for and against Chiang Kai-shek led to the latter's victory on April 7. In Nanjing, the struggle for power turned bloody on April 10 and 11 after Chiang Kai-shek had sent his own forces into the city. Armed thugs, police, and the military suppressed Left masses.

As the terrorist revolution of the CCP and GMD left wing threatened the existence of Chiang Kai-shek's government, Chiang and his supporters decided to retaliate. In Shanghai, Bai Chongxi began to ruthlessly crack down on the activities of the Communists. He determined to disarm the pickets and keep order at a welcoming rally for Chiang Kai-shek on March 26. A drive for party purification (*qingdang*) in GMD began to expel the leading CCP members from his high offices. This action of the GMD right wing took place because the leaders of Shanghai's business community had pressured Chiang Kai-shek to reestablish order, and they offered financial support. Even the media urged Chiang to act swiftly and ruthlessly. To fight terror with terror, the NRA gave arms and ammunitions to the Green Gang, the notorious Shanghai Mafia, as long as they would support and participate in the crackdown of the Communists.

On April 11, Du Yuesheng, the head of Green Gang, invited Wang Shouhua, the head of the General Labour Union, for dinner and had him murdered. The next day, the Green Gang and Bai Chongxi's troops, with the support of the Settlement and the French Concession authorities, began rounding up pickets. They fired on a rally organised in protest by the General Labour Union. The white terror had begun to accelerate. In the next few months, between three to four thousand CCP members were massacred, as well as thirty thousand of their supporters. Forty thousand more were injured and twenty-five were imprisoned. To completely destroy the organisations and activities of the Communists and left-wing GMD, brutal suppression took place not just in Shanghai but also in Canton, Shantou, Amoy, Ningbo, and various places in Guangxi.[82]

The white terror had left the Communists in an impossible situation, where their physical existence was in a state of uncertainty. They decided to turn radically left. They withdrew from the united front with

GMD and established an independent leadership of their own. They kept their ideological and emotional commitment to the peasant movement, which was their remaining source of actual influence. The party ordered accelerated popular violence by raising an independent army of seventy thousand troops made up of Communists, workers, and peasants.[83]

The Nanchang Uprising on August 1, 1927, was the first major Guomindang-Communist engagement of the Chinese Civil War. The military forces in Nanchang rebelled under the leadership of He Long, and Zhou Enlai attempted to seize control of the city after the end of the first GMD–CCP alliance. The uprising was a military success, while future generals such as Ye Ting, Liu Bocheng, Zhu De, Nie Rongzhen, Luo Ruiqing, and Lin Biao participated.[84] They took Nanchang and acquired great amounts of ammunition and money. But the party was badly organised and divided among its leader about what to do next.

Facing a counterattack from the GMD army, the Communists decided to retreat towards the south to the province of Guangdong. They hoped that they could try to take over the city of Guangzhou while spreading influence to the peasants and workers in that area. He Long, the commander of more than half of the troops that had participated in the uprising, and other commanders, such as Ye Ting and Ye Jianying, strongly opposed this idea. They predicted that the popular support for the Communists in Guangdong was merely a fraction of the huge peasantry support in Hunan where Mao Zedong and his comrades had been working diligently in organising peasantry for many years. They preferred to establish a new Communist base in the border region of Hunan where the newly organised Communist army could be easily resupplied and their troops strengthened by the enlistment of the local populace. He Long also pointed out that marching a thousand miles in the heat of summer would not make sense in military strategy. This move would put a severe strain on the troops.

However, the majority of the leadership vetoed these suggestions, which proved to be more prudent by the result of later historic events. Guangzhou subsequently became the target of the new army. On August 3, the troops pulled out of Nanchang and began the march to Guangzhou. In December 11, 1927, Communist troops, militia, and Red Guard workers launched an uprising in Guangzhou.

The Chinese Communists hoped to make use of a struggle for power in the province between Li Jishen, who hoped to capture the city, and Zhang Fakui. The uprising armies surprised the defending troops, which had move most of their military forces away from the city. The armies initially captured most of the city's police stations, the military headquarters, the railroad station, the telegraph office, government offices, and the treasury by 6:00 a.m., despite a huge numerical and technical disadvantage, and the Communist leadership announced the formation of a Guangzhou Soviet. This Soviet became official when it was ratified at a mass meeting the following day. But the population did not support the uprising and refused to attend mass rallies to give popular legitimacy to the Guangzhou Soviet. After three days of street fighting, looting, vandalism, and arson, a thousand buildings had been destroyed and thousands of bodies lay dead in the street. The Guangzhou Soviet destroyed its chance of success and lost Guangzhou to the huge army of Li Jisheng.[85]

In the resulting battles, many young Communists lost their lives. The Guangzhou Soviet became known as the "Guangzhou Commune" and lasted only a few days at the expense of more than five thousand Communists' lives, with an equal number missing. As a scapegoat, Ye Ting, the military commander, was removed and blamed for the failure, despite the fact that the obvious disadvantage of the Communist force was the main cause and Ye Ting and other military commanders had correctly pointed out the problem. Enraged by his unjustified treatment, Ye Ting left China and went into exile in Europe, and he did not return until nearly a decade later.[86]

After the Guangzhou Uprising, the Communist armies suffered many more defeats in other cities and towns. The troops in Chaozhou and the surrounding area were engaged and defeated by the Nationalist troops. The Communists were separated and went in two general directions:

One group retreated to Shanwei and engaged the Nationalists in guerrilla warfare, and the other went to southern Hunan and eventually joined Mao Zedong's forces.

After the serious defeat that the Chinese communists had suffered, only one thousand soldiers remained as a complete unit, in a regiment. Under the command of Zhu De and Chen Yi, who had faked their names, the remaining regiment sought refuge under a local warlord in Hunan. From this humble beginning, the force eventually grew to a ten-thousand-strong force and went to Jiangxi, later joining Mao Zedong at Jinggang-shan in April 1928.

Other surviving members were much less fortunate; they became fugitives. Zhou Enlai, Ye Jianying, and Ye Ting lost contact with others and fled to Hong Kong with Zhou seriously ill. The three had two pistols with them and were successful in reaching Hong Kong. Nie Rongzhen, the other Communist leader, also successfully escaped to Hong Kong.

He Long went home alone after the defeat. Reduced from an army commander in charge of tens of thousands of men to a beggar, he was not well received by his family except for a few who were already Communists. Soon, He Long would raise another three-thousand-strong Communist soldier force in his native home, but it would soon be wiped out by the Nationalists, with only less than three dozen members surviving. It would take several years for He Long's force to recover again for the third time.[87]

Under laws in China were often unpredictable and unreliable political allies. Even the peasants in other provinces, in whom the Communists had great hope for a faithful ally, did not come out in support of the Communists during the Autumn Harvest Uprising. In Hubei, a bandit leader, whom the Communists had hoped to rely on, betrayed them. In Hunan, Mao was able to cobble together a ragtag force of deserters of some NRA army members, bandits, unemployed miners, local militia, and peasants. An attempt to give rise to peasant uprisings around Chang-sha and then pounce with this force had failed by mid-September. Similar to the experience in Guangdong, Communist forces had to withdraw from several mid-sized cities, for example, Haifeng and Lufeng, after they had seized them and maintained control for a short while. With great military disadvantage, they simply could not afford to engage in a bloody counterattack against the warlords and Nationalist armies.

The Shanghai massacre of 1927 did not lead to the victory of Chiang Kai-shek but rather to the collapse of military unity in the NRA, and the spread of violence in the cities and the countryside made it possible as well as justifiable for the northern warlords to launch a counteroffensive military campaign. The Northeastern Army, headed by Zhang Zuolin and supported by Sun Chuanfang and Zhang Zongchang's substantial Shandong forces, almost captured Nanjing.[88] Facing enemies from both directions, warlords in the north and the Communist uprisings in the south, Chiang Kai-shek's NRA was forced out of North China by the Northeastern Army. This army arrived on the other side of Yangzi River, threatening Nanjing, Chiang's capital.[89]

As a result of these defeats, Chiang Kai-shek announced his "retirement" and left Nanjing, leaving the fraction of soldiers remaining in Wuhan and Nanjing to continue their fruitless negotiation for power and allowing the soldiers from various sides of the warlords to kill each other. Now the struggle for power was between Wang Jingwei and Li Zongren. Li Zongren's victory at Longtan against the National Pacification Army had so greatly increased his power that he did not include Wang Jingwei or Tang Shengzhi in the new leadership organs formed in September. In response, Tang Shengzhi, Wang Jingwei, and Li Jishen formed an alliance in opposition to Nanjing and refused to recognise its legitimacy. Li Zongren's forces then undertook an offensive, which eventually took Wuhan. As the battle went back to square one, nobody could gain complete control or domination, and Wang Jingwei agreed to negotiate with Chiang Kai-shek.

Seeing that all sides had been weakened by the war and exhausted financially, Chiang Kai-shek saw his opportunity to return and pick up the fruit of victory. This had always been anticipated; retirements were often simply one's political strategy to get through a difficult impasse. The minutes of the Joint Conference in Nanjing show that many had anticipated Chiang's return to take charge of the army once unification had come about. Besides, after years of war, no one had any money left because Chiang had emptied the treasury, and the new joint government could not make ends meet.[90]

Back in Shanghai, Chiang Kai-shek settled the unreconcilable dispute by distributing power among various regional commanders. In return for an acceptance of his overall military leadership and the legitimacy of the Nanjing government, he proposed that four Branch Political Councils should be established in Wuhan, Guangdong (Canton), Kaifeng, and Taiyuan and that there would be four Group Armies. Li Zongren was offered the leadership of the Wuhan Branch, Li Jishen that in Guangdong, Feng Yuxiang that in Kaifeng, and Yan Xishan that in Taiyuan. Each would also have under their command one Group Army and serve as its commander in chief. This proved acceptable to the military leaders of all sides. In the terms of this agreement, the Nanjing government formally invited Chiang back on January 1, 1928.[91]

These arrangements were reached during the second phase of the Northern Expedition. Chiang's own forces became the 1st Group Army with 290,000 troops, Feng's formed the 2nd Group Army with 310,000 troops, and Yan's became the 3rd Group Army with 150,000 troops. Li Zongren's Guangxi forces became the 4th Group Army with 240,000 troops. By May 1, the tide of the battle had swung in favour of the NRA forces. As Zhang Zuolin withdrew his forces from North China, the NRA's component armies began to race to Beijing. Yan Xishan[92] arrived first on June 8, 1928, bringing the tumultuous Northern Expedition to a close with the nominal unification of China.

During this period of war and anarchy, only military men could possibly win political battle, which was very much decided by armed force. Chiang Kai-shek was among the handful of military commanders who completed the transformation from warlord to politician. It was true that Chiang Kai-shek commanded a substantial military force; however, many commanders did, too. Chiang's success lies in the fact that he created and maintained a network of military commanders when he was the president of the Huangpu Academy.[93]

Very similar to the relationship between Yuan Shikai and his followers, Chiang's immediate circle of soldiers became and remained an important pillar to Chiang's power base. The presidency of the Huangpu Academy provided Chiang the opportunity to build student-teacher relations with Huangpu's graduates and to train the officer corps of the 1st Group Army. The first group of Huangpu cadets included future favourites, such as Chen Cheng.[94]

Chiang was able to gain the loyalty of the top generals of the various NRA armies who were not considered his "own", such as Chen Mingshu in Li Jishen's 4th Group Army.[95] Chen played a leading role in the occupation of Wuhan. Tang Shengzhi assumed that Chen would support him, as they had collaborated in a reform movement at the Baoding Military Academy. When Tang Shengzhi tried to oust Chiang Kai-shek, however, he found that Chen decided to support Chiang Kai-shek. In fact, Chen Mingshu was in telegraphic contact with Chiang throughout the great crisis of March 1927, the internal crisis between the left-wing group in Guomindang centered in Wuhan and the right-wing group led by Chiang in Nanjing. Chen also supplied detailed information to Chiang on the attitudes of the various generals and politicians in Wuhan.[96]

Chiang Kai-shek's control over appointments as the commander in chief of the NRA was one device he used to foster military networks tied to him and to manage them. Chiang insisted that he personally oversee all of the appointments. He also made sure that any recruitment and incorporation of local militia had to be approved by his headquarters at all times. He carefully watched and sanctioned all of the commanders to be the legitimate heads of their forces. He could withhold promotions of people he distrusted. He did so in the case of Zhang Fakui, who had performed with great merit, as Chiang acknowledged, but whom he, nonetheless, did not want to advance quickly. It seems likely that Li Jishen was pleased with Chiang's efforts to undermine a threat to him.[97]

What distinguishes Chiang Kai-shek from the rest of the military commanders was his ability as an expert politician. His calculated strategy made it possible to strengthen his military and political position by other people's money. He was able to build his military and political networks through his access to substantial financial resources. Chiang had cultivated relations with important financial figures, including Song Ziwen, Kong Xiangxi, and Zhang Jingjiang. These men were a part of the community of rich bankers and businessmen of Shanghai, Jiangsu, and Zhejiang.[98] This is a mutually dependent relationship, as well as an ideological alliance, between Chiang's GMD and his financial supporters. The GMD needed to finance its armies, while Shanghai businessmen needed the military to secure stability—not just to be able to trade, but also to reestablish fiscal order and tax collection on which the loan business of their banks depended.

Chiang demonstrated a high level of political competence as he obtained financial support without compromising his political control. He begged, threatened, bribed, blackmailed, and massaged bankers who had international connections in order to weather his constant financial crisis. He cultivated their faith in him personally as he convinced them that if he lost, then they all would lose; if he could win, then they all were going to benefit. One of the examples of this was the difficult relationship between Chiang Kai-shek and Song Ziwen (T. V. Soong). Song Ziwen used to compete with Chiang for leadership in many occasions. However, an American PhD that gave him the capacity deal with a highly regulated system of the world market did not qualify him for the complex political game of China, which was highly irregular, dark, and ruthless. Song decided to be Chiang's friend rather than opponent. As minister of finance, Song was the paymaster for the Northern Expedition. Chiang Kai-shek needed his help to provide funds to the various armies of the NRA. In August 1926 Chiang acquired 400,000 yuan of campaign funds for the 7th Group Army of Li Zongren. He supported the 6th Group Army of Cheng Qian in a similar way.[99]

Chiang Kai-shek's rise to power was partly the result of his control over substantial military forces. Important, too, were the networks he cultivated in various circles, including the military, Shanghai's financial communities, the underworld, and that of elite families. As Chiang's difficulties in the first months of 1927 illustrate, however, these relationships were tenuous, and support could be and was withdrawn when

Chiang Kai-shek was not doing well militarily. Chiang's success depended heavily upon his ability to prevail on the battlefield, which made him a potential winner in the civil war. However, he would never have been able to continue and eventually win the war without the funds that were available to him. Chiang had a knack for making sudden but decisive military moves, for example, the Zhongshan Warship Incident, also known as the March 20th Incident. Similarly, his decisions to abandon the Wuhan front and move into Jiangxi, and then to not strike north but to instead march into the Lower Yangtze, also radically altered the military situation.

CONCLUSIONS

Fear was the most dominant motivation for both the white terror of Chiang Kai-shek and the red terror of the Communists. Military action and political manipulation were a part of the political conflict for success and survival in Chinese politics, which had no institutional alternative for discourse and compromise. During a time when both GMD and CCP knew that neither of them had the military capacity to completely eliminate the other, each claimed to be a willing ally of the other while simultaneously racing to accumulate enough armed forces to dominate the other. Because they both knew that one could not survive if the other was allowed to become strong enough to take over control, political negotiation and compromise were a means, rather than an end, of the Chinese power struggle.

In the brutal arena of Chinese politics, the winner must be extremely intelligent and shrewd. Winners have to know their own strengths and weaknesses, and recognise if and when to both advance and retreat. Chiang Kai-shek proved to be one of these winners because of his good instinct, swift decisions, and intelligent strategy. Ironically, Chiang shared a great deal of characteristics with his longtime opponent, Mao Zedong. Like Mao, Chiang was an independent thinker who took whatever proved useful to him from various sources of ideas while keeping his own agenda. Like Mao, he did not like the Soviet advisors who looked down on him and sidelined him by supporting more blind-minded and submissive followers. In Chiang's case, Wang Jingwei was the ideal choice of Soviet advisors, as was Wang Ming in Mao's party, the loyal follower to the Soviet policies.[100] Chiang, like Mao Zedong, showed just enough tolerance to the Soviets for his own political course, yet deliberately deviated from their policies.

Like Mao, rather than those ignorant warlords, Chiang was a shrewd politician and statesman, as well as a military commander. He understood how to gain media support and political legitimacy both in China and on the international stage. For decades, Chiang was successful in painting himself as the legitimate successor of Sun Yat-sen's revolution, as well as the only man in China who could bring unity and stability after years of war. If Japan had not invaded China, which prolonged the civil war and forced Chiang to ally with CCP, Chinese modern history would have been very different.

If Chiang Kai-shek's main political ability was weathering a crisis—a state of chaos—and leading that crisis into a state of relative unity and stability, then the political genius of his main opponent, Mao Zedong, was creating a crisis and taking advantage of it in order to overthrow an establishment. The career of the latter is described in the next chapter.

CHAPTER 3

NATIONALIST LAW AND THE COMMUNIST REVOLUTION

Chiang Kai-shek could not build a more democratic, constitutional system, even if he wanted to, after he succeeded in unifying the country by force. His efforts to strengthen national unity and establish legal order were met with constant upheaval that pushed him further and almost perpetually into military and political consolidation.[1]

Chang did not win the war by fighting only. He bribed the warlords, who were convinced that they would keep their army and territory if they agreed to support Chiang's leadership and became partners in his regime. Under these terms, Chiang's government controlled major cities, but the countryside still lay under the influence of the unaligned regional warlords, who were now severely weakened yet still undefeated during the civil war. They were not satisfied by Chiang's insufficient promises of money and weapons, and they refused to submit to the central government. Chiang had no choice but to resolve the issue through military pressure, the only language that soldiers understood. In 1930 Chiang fought against the armies of Yen Xishan and Feng Yuxiang to maintain his military dominance and the legitimacy of his administration. This war almost bankrupted the government and cost nearly 250,000 casualties on both sides. When Hu Hanmin established a rival government in Guangzhou in 1931, Chiang was forced to fight again.[2]

Chiang decided to focus his attention upon the Communist Party, the most resilient and most threatening enemy of his government—an adversary that refused to either be bought or share power with him.[3] However, only a small section of Chiang's army, that which was directly under his personal control, followed his instructions wholeheartedly and participated in the campaign against the Communists. When Chiang surrounded the Red Army that was regrouping in Jiangxi province, he avoided further depletion of his loyal troops by sending the unloyal sections of his army to the front line to fight. He deliberately allowed the Red Army to escape through the warlord-controlled regions in the hope that the warlords would engage the Communists. This plan did not work. The warlords refused to fight the Communists and allowed them to escape, battle-free, through their land. As a result, although Chiang's fifth campaign eventually defeated the Red Army with the help of foreign military advisors in 1934, the Communists survived in the countryside. They marched northward to Yanan through the areas in south and southwest China.[4] In this difficult and long retreat, the CCP lost nearly 90 percent of its strength (in number) but took refuge in a part of North China that was far away from Chiang's personal army and was much less vulnerable to attack.[5]

Chiang's government was weak, both politically and morally.[6] In the 1930s, the Guomindang was a largely military-based party without a political structure. Its huge nominal membership did not lead to great political strength. Between 1932 and 1938, the number of its members more than doubled because many soldiers and civil servants were conscribed to the party as a job requirement or obligation. So the vast majority of the GMD were passive members.[7] The party had neither set ideology nor fixed social base, enjoyed by rural landlords and urban bourgeoisie, whose concerns and interests were sometimes expressed and represented to the government. From time to time, the Guomindang received funding with political conditions. For instance, during the late 1920s, some Shanghai businessmen funded the Guomindang and Green Gang to massacre troublesome trade unionists and suspected communists. The GMD leader, Chiang Kai-shek, also received money on the condition that he would dissolve the GMD–CCP alliance (the First United Front). However, these politically motivated funds were insufficient to support years of wartime expense. To raise more money, the Guomindang and Green Gang simply kidnapped, blackmailed, and extorted Shanghai businessmen. This shortsighted fund-raising technique failed to earn public support for the legitimacy of the GMD's government.[8]

The GMD was widely divided as its disaffected leaders often were overwhelmed by factionalism and regional loyalty. During the 1930–1931 period, they fought with each other in North China for territorial dominance; the anti-Chiang faction of the GMD established the Northern Coalition with several warlords and proclaimed a provisional constitution. These internal squabbles and organisational problems occupied most of Chiang Kai-shek's time and energy; he became too busy to pay attention to anything else.[9] By January 1932, Japanese troops were stationed outside of Shanghai, with two hundred thousand Shanghainese assembled to demand that the Guomindang defend Manchuria. Although he was unwilling and unprepared, Chiang knew that he had no choice but to tolerate active resistance by the media, which championed popular opinion.[10]

For years, Chiang Kai-shek refused to allow any political activity of opposition parties or establishment of limited democracy until the CCP was eliminated. He knew that without a decisive victory over the CCP, he would definitely lose control of the country. He believed that he had to dismantle the Communists and unite the country domestically before he could deal with the Japanese.[11] However, with the Japanese on his doorstep, he had to pretend to defend the country against the foreign invaders because the Guomindang needed popular support to gain legitimacy.

First, he announced a Provisional Constitution for the Period of Political Tutelage. Although this proclamation claimed to be a half step towards fulfilling longstanding demands for constitutional government, this constitution neither legitimised opposition nor legalised opposing political parties. As the GMD was forced to call a National Emergency Conference for April 1932, the well-known educator Cai Yuanpei declared that many able men were being excluded from both the GMD and the administration. The national media also called for a boycott of the conference, and only one-third of delegates attended. Even these delegates demanded a people's assembly. In response, the Guomindang proposed the gradual creation of popularly elected advisory councils in accordance with its concept of a long tutelage in preparation for full democracy.[12]

By 1936, the crisis of Japan's aggression against China became more imminent. The anti-Japanese National Salvation Association (NSA) (*Jiu guo hui*) had begun to call for an end to the GMD–CCP civil war and the formation of a united front against Japan. However, Chiang considered the activities of the NSA as a direct challenge to his authority. So, he arrested the NSA's "Seven Gentlemen" activists: Shen Junru, Zou Taofen, Zhang Naiqi, Sha Qianli, Li Gongpu, Wang Zaoshi, and Shi Liang. Only three NSA radicals escaped arrest, due to their social status—Song Qingling, He Xiangning, and Tao Xingzhi. Song was the wife of the late Sun Yat-sen and He was the wife of Liao Zhongkai. Both women enjoyed nationwide respect as the widows of GMD's founding fathers and early leaders. Their social status and connections provided a unique protection that allowed them to organise and speak out publicly.[13]

Chiang was surprised that these arrests irritated the entire country so much that it actually strengthened the patriotic NSA's popular support. Even Chiang's old and loyal allies, merchants and politicians of Shanghai, backed the patriots. They even visited them in prison to make their stand known publicly and to humiliate Chiang's government. The popular support for the NSA was so overwhelming that it eventually became China's third largest political party. Even important factions and prominent members of the Guomindang wanted to deal with the Japanese menace before tackling the Communists.[14]

Facing this tremendous dissension, Chiang had to appear willing to hold secret negotiations with the Communists to establish a united front against the Japanese.[15] In the meantime, he continued to plan his final assault against his domestic archrivals, the Communists. However, no one in China was concerned about the Communists because the Japanese army was threatening the very existence of the nation. In Xian, Generals Zhang Xueliang and Yang Hucheng, who were ordered to wage the anti-Communist campaign, rebelled and held Chiang hostage, demanding that his administration join with the CCP to repel Japan.[16]

This incident reflected the overwhelming popular support for an anti-Japanese alliance forged from National Salvationists, the GMD factions, the CCP, minor political groups, the media, and the public. After his release, Chiang established an alliance with the CCP. This second period of GMD–CCP cooperation officially began several months after the outbreak of full-scale war with Japan on July 7, 1937. Under popular pressure, the GMD also legalised all political organisations and created a People's Political Council.[17]

Unlike the GMD, which declined from its heyday of the 1920s and early 1930s, the Communist Party went through an extremely difficult time during the same time period. It grew stronger and stronger during the later 1930s, thanks to its constant ideological cultivation and organisational reform. Its organisation and discipline that was moulded and trained in the anti-Japanese war bases eventually won a startlingly swift victory in the Chinese Civil War.[18]

Unlike Chiang Kai-shek, who organised, led, and controlled his troops mainly through personal loyalty, Mao's Communist Party attempted to establish an army that worked as a highly disciplined, effective, and powerful machine fueled by the Chinese version of Marxist ideology.[19] This forced (by circumstance as well as design) a unity of minds, and a strategy transformed an army of rebellious peasants, bandits, and petty intellectuals—who practised anarchism, factionalism, and regionalism in a similar fashion as the GMD army—into a modern political organisation.[20]

The military expansion of the Communist Party was impressive. In 1937 the Red Army had controlled only the barren border region of three provinces after the Long March to Yanan, Shaanxi, Gansu, and Ningxia. The war against the Japanese created a great opportunity for the party to expand its army of only eighty thousand experienced veterans. During the next eight years, the military forces under the leadership of the CCP developed and multiplied tenfold. The People's Militia, over 2 million strong at the time, consisted of village volunteers. The service of the Chinese militia forces was similar to the National Guard in the American states in which normal command rested with local government but special conditions could place militia units under regular army commanders. The party established two more war bases behind Japanese lines and set up many compartments of resistance.[21]

The first of these was the Shanxi-Chahar-Hebei Border Region (*Jin-Cha-Ji*) established in 1938. At the same time, Liu Bocheng's 129th Division swept south and east from the Shanxi hills onto the North China plains, then into Shandong and the China Sea. As it advanced, it dispersed into smaller units, which organised new centres of resistance and coordinated the activities of resistance groups already operating. With this organisation and collaboration between the army and its guerrilla war activities, the CCP unified the entire hills and plains region in the Shanxi-Hebei-Shandong-Henan Border Region (*Jin-Ji-Lu-Yu*) by 1941.[22]

The military political process was repeated and spread elsewhere. In Central China, eight smaller bases grew up around the New Fourth Army. By 1945, nineteen anti-Japanese war bases protecting an estimated population of 90 million were sandwiched in between the Japanese garrisons and points of control in North and Central China. The formation of Red China was dictated by the conditions of war, but its lifeblood was the moral force of Chinese nationalism.

These widely dispersed military forces under the Red Army succeeded in gaining powerful popular support in their command areas. They split the military forces and placed them close to village life. Farsighted policy made this potentially dangerous position not only tenable but also advantageous. The party demanded that Communist troops love the civilians and set a good example of discipline. Unlike the Guomindang army, which looted wherever it travelled, the Communists insisted on paying for their supplies, helping farmers with fieldwork when not fighting, and respecting local government and mass organisations. The party also instructed these small warfare units to live with, and not on top of, the civilians. The Red Army had to establish a trusting and friendly relationship with civil society, for it was the village that fed, hid, and clothed the army, as well as provided informants, replacements, and recruits. The success of Communist policy, coupled with the absence of large-unit positional warfare, made conscription unnecessary. Substantial mass support and participation were pivotal factors in the enlargement of the anti-Japanese war bases and, later on, the Communist victory in the civil war.

During the wartime, the party, the army, and the government shared political power with various legally recognised grassroots organisations at the district level. Trade unions were among them. The North China Federation of Trade Unions claimed 2 million members in guerrilla areas in 1943.[23] There were also women's associations, cooperatives, and peasant salvation associations. When the peasant salvation associations became the chief weapon of the 1946–1947 land revolution, it was said and believed that the government had the right and these associations had the power. The party took over leadership of mass organisations through the work of its member groups (*dang tuan*). Like government, the party was leader; complete organisational independence was not allowed. But mass organisations possessed wide areas of operational independence and acted as the most important sounding boards for popular sentiments. The party was the leader and policy maker, but its power was limited by its need for active popular support. This did not lead to a Western-style democratic rule in the war base organisations. It did, however, make the maximum use of media, propaganda, and indirect controls by political rhetoric, rather than a system of dictation.[24]

After 1937, the Communist Party was rebuilt anew in membership and composition. The party had been virtually destroyed twice during the fifteen years since its birth in 1921—first in 1927, and later in the fall of the Jiangxi Soviets in 1934. The new wartime environment demanded a clear ideology, a winning strategy, and a strong, flexible structure. The striking difference was the absence of a central government through which the party could work its policy. Contact between party and government had to begin at the regional level.[25]

Within the border regions, the party came directly in contact with the areas it controlled. In general, the structure of the party down to the district level (*chu*) duplicated the structure of the government, the various mass organisations, and the military forces. Party control of these groups was exercised as a double structure. On the one hand, party members took the positions of the highest levels of leadership in non-party organisations. On the other hand, groups of party members from the same party pyramid supervised each of the lower levels of these organisations. This method could be illustrated in both mass organisations and armed forces.

The top generals in the Eighth Route and the New Fourth Army—Liu Bocheng, Lin Biao, Chen Yi, and Nie Rongzhen—were all high-ranking party members.[26] As a result, military policy came directly from the party's Central Committee. To further ensure party control of the army, every unit at the divisional, regimental, and battalion level was assigned a political commissioner to share the military leadership. The commissioner functioned both as teacher and leader. As teacher, he was responsible for the political indoctrination, morality, and organisation of the unit's troops. As leader, he divided responsibility with the military commander and passed on all military decisions of possible political significance to party heads. Anxious to strengthen party leadership in the armed forces, the Central Committee ruled in 1943 that the jobs of political commissioners in garrison regiments and battalions were to be held by the secretaries of the area and district party committees. Under the direction of these commissioners, party branches organised at the lowest levels, and the Red Armies became effectively involved in both political and military activities at the grassroots level.

The most important step to establish an organisational unity in the CCP was the rectification movement, a vehicle through which a new line of thought (or "new spirit", in the party's vocabulary) was implanted

into the minds of its members.[27] The word *rectification* was a translation from a two-character word in Chinese, *zheng feng*. *Zheng* is the
abstract form of another two-character word, *zheng dun*, which means
"to correct and reorganise". *Feng* also comes from a two-character word,
zuofeng, which means "working (or living) style". The new combined
word, *zheng feng*, means "to correct style". When *zheng feng* is translated into English, it loses some of its Chinese connotation, in particular,
the conceptual link between ideas, politics, and personal life choices.
The English word *indoctrination* covers only a part of the *zheng feng*
(the ideological part); it abstracts and hollows the meaning of it. *Zheng
feng* is not only about ideological choices, as is Marxism, Leninism,
Stalinism, or Trotskyism, but also concerned about specifying the personal signature that represents the leading ideology. It is an intellectual
debate that determines who has the final say about what Marxism is in
China and how to apply it in the Chinese environment. Unlike in Russia,
where ideological retribution often reflected the power struggle within
the Communist Party, Chinese political struggle began with the naming,
renaming, and rewriting of the words, titles, rules, and ideas. It began by
defining the language in which the law, the history, and the administration would operate. It would not end with a purge or reorganisation, but
continued on to include a general mental and spiritual cleansing of the
masses through its political hierarchy.

On February 1, 1942, more than a thousand party members crowded
into a Yanan lecture hall to hear Mao Zedong inaugurate the Zheng Feng
Movement. In his speech, Mao identified the target of the movement
and launched a broad three-front attack on errors in the style of work
and thought in the party. He pointed out and criticised subjectivism in
thought, sectarianism (separation from the masses) in party relations,
and formalism in literature and art. As he ended his speech, Mao asked
that the audience and the entire party work vigorously to correct their
ways of thought and action.

A week later, Mao and propaganda chief K'ai Feng identified and
elaborated on the evils of formalism in party literature and propaganda
to an audience of eight hundred men and women. As Mao put it, it is

necessary to expose the original form of the monster (formalism): if "old rats are driven out into the street and everyone screams, 'hit them'"—the monsters can easily be exterminated. With these words, Mao's role as keynote speaker for the rectification movement ended, and the reform machinery slowly began to operate.[28]

The first activity noted by the *Liberation Daily* was in the higher level organisations in the Yanan area. Within a month, full discussions and investigations had been concluded in committees, panels, and schools directly subordinate to the Central Committee. Editorials and articles indicated increased activity in March as the Political Academy and the Bao An Military Command reported their reform programmes. The Party School of the Central Committee of the Communist Party was reorganised, and by the end of the month, the movement was in full swing in the Natural Sciences Academy. Finally, on April 3, a formal movement for the entire party was announced in a bulletin for the Central Committee's Propaganda Bureau.[29]

The Propaganda Bureau called for a movement in three parts. The first was a period of study and discussion of two months' duration for all party schools and three months' duration for party committees. After this period, a general examination was to be conducted on the texts of Mao's speeches and twenty other documents. The second period was to investigate party work, and was to be carried out by the grassroots associations and school panels. In the final period, the members of the individual organisations and schools were to draw conclusions on the quality of their comrades' work, then submit reports to higher levels for approval. Incorrigible comrades were to be dismissed from the party, but second and third chances were to be given to the comrades who confessed and showed willingness to reform.

The Zheng Feng Movement was carried out through small study groups.[30] These groups worked their way through the maze of standards set in Reform Documents. Criticism and self-criticism followed on the basis of these codified standards. Self-criticism meant complete public confession and symbolised an allegiance to Mao's standards. Public confession was a major tool of the Zheng Feng reform. Party members were prohibited from discussing national questions outside of the party; yet they were encouraged to spy and report on their comrades' errors. Study meetings and confessionals became the main activity of the Zheng Feng Movement. All of the surviving high officers of the CCP had been subjected to this kind of mental cleansing. Through this activity, they had proved their loyalty and benefited from it as others either refused to do so or did not do enough to meet the standard. For example, Zhou Enlai criticised himself at length before a mass meeting.[31] To implicate this system of control, rules of awards and punishments were established. One form of punishment for deficient leaders was demotion and an assignment of forced hard labour for a definite period in a peasant village.

The Zheng Feng Movement was a licence to invade both the physical and mental space of individuals. The techniques developed to implement thought reform ("washing the brain" as the Chinese also called it) included isolating individuals in "study groups". Under the guidance of a group leader, they studied specified documents to understand key principles. They then had to relate those principles to their own lives in a critical, concrete, and thorough way. Other members of the group put the individual under extraordinary pressure to examine fully his or her most deeply held views, and to do so in the presence of the group. The individual then had to write a full, self-revealing confession. The confession could be rejected several times if it was not thorough or deep enough. Only when a confession was accepted would the writer be drawn back into a position in the group and into the larger society. This humiliating process stripped people of individual thought and ensured state dominance within personal space.[32]

The Central Committee established the law and regulations for this internal cleansing. Liu Shaoqi published *The Intra-Party Struggle* in July 1942 as a set of procedures for the Zheng Feng Movement.[33] He repeatedly warned that excesses of all kinds (unwarranted expulsion from the party, slander, and plotting) were unnecessary as long as the movement was proceeding in an orderly fashion. This view was confirmed by the Central Committee Resolution on "Methods of Leadership" which initiated the second Zheng Feng Movement in 1943. This document maintained that the first year of reform suffered from a plethora of general slogans and a lack of direct guidance by leaders. Decentralisation (the basic war base organisational problem) worked against Yanan's close control of the movement. Yanan kept in touch with its area headquarters by radio transmission of orders, speeches, and *Liberation Daily* editorials, but it was not possible to bring the entire party under a watchful central eye. The object of *zheng feng*, however, was not only physical control of the party's members. Its purpose was to provide intensive indoctrination and training that would allow the party to operate with unanimity in a situation where close administrative control and inspection were out of the question. Nothing was more important in 1942, 1943, and 1944 than the immense amount of time spent throughout the party hierarchy studying the writings that make up the reform documents. The entire party went to school.

After an orchestrated criticism of the foreign (Russian) Marxism and any deviation from the official Chinese line of thinking, the Zheng Feng Movement successfully established the thought of Mao Zedong as the official ideology of the party.[34] After this forceful unification of mind (changing spirit), the party members were reminded of the principles of the CCP: The individual must obey the organisation, the minority must obey the majority, lower echelons must obey higher echelons, and the entire party must obey the basic principles of the Central Committee.[35]

The Zheng Feng Movement was much more than a purge and a political and organisational act. Instead of providing merely a cleansing of the party structure, it was an intellectual and mental exercise that exterminated opposite ideas and ratified the sole intellectual leadership of Mao. The leadership of the CCP had been monopolised by a group of Russian-trained intellectuals following the leadership of Wang Ming, the party's leading Comintern representative.[36] Wang returned from Moscow in 1930 with twenty-seven comrades. In January of the following year, this group led the attack on Li Lisan and immediately assumed the top position in the Central Committee.[37] They controlled the main posts from 1931 until the ascendancy of domestically trained leaders associated with Mao in the 1935–1937 period.

To establish the leadership of Mao and his comrades, the Zheng Feng Movement began to make Marxism speak Chinese rather than Russian. To isolate Wang Ming's version of Marxism and identify it as incorrect, Mao and Liu Shaoqi attacked Wang's formalist, dogmatist, and Menshevik tendencies. These writings became the main documents to guide the movement.[38] From this point on, Wang's writings and all of the non-Maoist writings of the foreign-trained Marxist intellectuals disappeared. After silencing the voice of the non-Maoists, leading policy statements came from Mao, Chou Enlai, and rising theoreticians Liu Shaoqi and Chen Boda.

After the linguistic and ideological rectification movement, an organisational purge followed naturally and represented only one stage in Mao's consolidation of leadership. Mao gained prestige in the 1920s, practical leadership of the party in the mid-1930s, and official leadership when he became head of the Politburo in 1937. His only rival, Chang Guotao, was actually purged as a traitor in 1938.[39] When the Zheng Feng came, Mao had to make sure that foreign-trained leaders were relieved of their positions as principal party spokesmen. Mao also cultivated a public recognition of his position as the righteous leader and promoted his ideas as the only correct interpretation of Marxism. Party documents claimed that Mao's ideas represented the universal truths of Marxism-Leninism within the concrete reality of the Chinese Revolution. Wang and his group had only theory. They were demoted and replaced by leaders who were on the righteous side of Mao.

The Zheng Feng Movement was a pursuit of righteousness in legislation and legitimacy of rulership and was the most important development in Chinese politics since the days of Confucius. "Correct name (or title) makes words flow." This righteousness in Chinese conveys a conceptual spectrum much wider than does the English concept of legal rights. Chinese righteousness is neither bound nor restricted by any previously codified laws or moral principles, either written or custom. Rather, it is about defining the words of law or the authority to define the law. In the particular case of the Zheng Feng Movement in Yanan, the argument was seemingly focused upon Marxism. However, the debate was not concerned about how to understand and practice Marxism and

Leninism according to the original meaning of the Marxist theories and particular writings. It initially centred upon the meaning of Marxism and whose version of Marxism was correct and should be recognised as the guiding light of Chinese revolution. The Marxism of Wang Ming and his Russian- or European-trained colleagues was considered wrong, and it was criticised as formalist, dogmatic, and subjective in an adversarial argument to prove the righteousness of Maoism. Mao did not only win the discourse against his opponents; he also gained the right to define Marxism. He became the mouth of Marxism and Leninism in China. His words became boundless because they juxtaposed those of Marxism. They became one and the same.

Naming (or titling) has been a key component of Chinese discourse as well as political argument for thousands of years. Whoever has the correct name (or title) possesses the right to lead and win the discourse. Therefore, unlike Western legal argument, which wins the case by alignment with the words (a part) of law, Chinese legal argument wins the legal discourse by monopolising the mouth of law (its entirety). Whoever gains the righteous name, which travels beyond the normal boundary of legal language, has the right to defy any established rules and make his own. He also had the opportunity to silence the voice of dissidents.

The greatest theoretic significance of the Zheng Feng Movement was Mao's insistence that Marxism be made Chinese. He gave the Russian phrase "union of theory and practice" a much more creative twist and boundless freedom. Ironically, just like Chiang Kai-shek, who interpreted Sun Yat-sen's theory of people, the value of Marxist theory to Mao was only in its application in the Chinese environment. Otherwise, he could easily discard it and declare it incorrect or inappropriate. He saw Marxism as an "arrow" and the Chinese Revolution as a "target". The principal enemy of the Zheng Feng Movement was the group of dogmatists who loved and worshipped the arrow, but never shot it. After the movement, Mao made himself the subject of worship because he was considered the only one able to decide which of the arrows to use and which to discard. He cultivated a highly disciplined army that would fight any enemy with his chosen arrows.

Compared to Mao Zedong's party constitution, Chiang Kai-shek's law and state were very similar; they both were very Chinese and autocratic. However, unlike Mao's highly defined and specific rules, Chiang Kai-shek's law was weak, undefined, and even chaotic at times. He maintained his authority by personal relationships, police intelligence (including kidnapping, torture, and assassinations), and secret (most often unlawful) services of his immediate loyalties.[40]

Chiang learned from his early career in politics that he could not maintain control without an organisation constructed and built upon personal loyalty. In Chiang's eyes, his success depended entirely upon securing a group of close followers who were totally committed to his idea of one party and one leader (*yige dang yige lingxiu*).[41] As soon as he resumed command of the government in 1932, he transformed the Lixingshe organisation into a major political force. Its members gave their personal vows to protect the party and save the nation (*hudang jiuguo*), and respect the title of leader (*xiaozhang* and *lingxiu*) that Chiang had assumed. Within the closest group of his Guomindang officers, Chiang was confirmed as one of the three undividable identities that this organisation served: leader, party, and nation.[42]

The binding force between Chiang and his closest circle of subordinates was verified in a ritualistic manner, similar to a traditional blood brotherhood. When Chiang Kai-shek organised Lixingshe, the inaugural personal organisation of his immediate followers, Chiang (called leader, *lingxiu*) and his disciples walked to a auditorium that was dominated by a large photograph of Sun Yat-sen. Holding hands, they formed a circle with Chiang. Chiang suggested that the organisation should be named Sanminzhuyi Lixingshe. Then each man pulled out a written oath that he had been told to prepare earlier and stood at attention, facing the portrait of Sun Yat-sen. Raising their right hands, they pledged the following:

> I swear in all my sincerity to practice the Three People's Principles with vigour, to recover revolutionary spirit, to revive the Chinese race, to sacrifice all personal interest, to obey orders, to adhere strictly to secrecy, and to complete the task of revolution

and of building the country. If I breach my oath, I am willing to accept the most severe punishment. I pledge this sincerely.[43]

Each stamped his right thumbprint on the oath, which was stamped with Chiang Kai-shek's seal. The paper texts were then collected by Teng Jie and solemnly burned, just as one would burn paper money for the spirits of one's ancestors in heaven. Holding hands again, they were addressed one last time by Chiang: "I will do my best to lead you. From now on all of you must exert yourselves even harder than before to unite in society, to strive, and to struggle. We will not stop until we achieve our goal. I wish you success."[44] The Sanminzhuyi Lixingshe was thereby, in a ceremony that eclectically drew upon the cultural trappings of the sworn brotherhood and the literati's Confucian examination system, formally established.[45]

Within this highly ritualised organisation, Chiang's personal relations with his subordinates were cultivated by a highly informal and personal language and rhetoric, which created individual bonds between Chiang and his immediate subordinate officers.[46] Here is an example of Chiang's speech:

> Our party and our nation are now in a situation of extraordinary disaster (*weinan*), so I have especially invited you to come and chat, in order to get your individual views. Therefore I deliberately will not adopt formal meeting procedures. My emphasis is on hearing each and every one of you express your own ideas. I put no limitations on the time you may take.[47]

The agenda, or the order of the speakers in a meeting of this kind, often followed the usual practice in the military academy (Huangpu), which allowed the officers from the earliest class and highest seniority to speak first. Unlike the shouting matches in English that were seen in the civilian meetings, Chinese military executives spoke in an orderly sequence and for an equal time period. To demonstrate his personal trust to these commanders, there were no guards posted outside, which was extremely unusual in wartime China. Dai Li, the soon-to-be head of

Chiang's secret police, was armed and would get up now and then to check outside of the room and around the building. He appeared alert, diligent, and composed. According to the recollection of an eyewitness, Chiang Kai-shek listened attentively, while taking notes from time to time using a blue pencil. Occasionally, for clarification, he would quietly ask a question or two, as if he was trying to avoid interrupting the speakers. He seemed calm and patient, which was totally different from his usual stern and commanding attitude, and he appeared to invite comments, letting each presentation run its course. The speeches of the officers lasted four consecutive nights.[48]

When it was Chiang Kai-shek's turn to speak, he did not use bombastic language and sweeping rhetoric to invoke patriotic spirit. He stressed the overwhelming danger that the Japanese posed to the nation. In a matter-of-fact fashion, he described how Japanese militarists had spent fifty years preparing for the invasion of China. Their army, air force, and navy were highly modernised. By comparison, the Chinese army was utterly defenceless.

Chiang made a bleak prediction to his officers: Once conflict would break out on the battlefield, Chinese officers and soldiers in the front lines were hardly able to raise their heads to take aim and shoot, let alone engage in an effective counterattack. All they could do was hold their position and sacrifice themselves. After suffering enormous casualties, they would retreat and pull back. Soon their backs would be against the wall, and they could find no reinforcements for the battlefield. Then they would have no choice other than to sign an unconditional surrender. And once the surrender was signed, China would be lost and the Chinese race would be exterminated.[49]

Chiang went on to describe the helpless situation in China, where it was facing an enemy many times stronger, more efficient, and more modernised. The Japanese army could practically do anything it wished to the defenceless Chinese. Now, what China needed was not empty heroism or passionate self-sacrifice but rather a clear understanding of the situation and the desperate dedication to organise and train a strong army.

He demanded the devotion of his officers to work quickly, thoroughly, and solidly (*ying gan*, *kuai gan*, and *shi gan*).

> In order to improve the results of your efforts, you must all strive to be anonymous heroes (*wuming yingxiong*). You must have the resolution not to care for personal honour, humiliation, gain, and loss. You must dedicate yourself to the salvation of the country wholeheartedly. If you can do that then you will have success.[50]

Chiang Kai-shek told his disciples that he did, indeed, have an army of three hundred thousand men. If his only goal was to be a popular "national hero" (*minzu yingxiong*), without regard for the greater historical consequences of the national crisis, then that ambition was surely not beyond his reach. But his individual honour was nothing compared to the success of the revolution and the safety of the Chinese people. To sacrifice the nation for his personal reputation would betray the souls of the chairman and the revolutionary martyrs, and pass disaster on for posterity.

> All I can do is to sustain humiliation and carry the heavy burden (of public opprobrium)...I will not lightly speak of laying down our lives before we have come to the last critical moment (*guantou*). We will never give up peace until we totally despair of continuing. We must gain time for preparation. And what I mean by the last critical moment, or a time when all hope for peace is completely gone, is the time when the enemy attacks without any consideration of consequences, intending to force us to sign an unconditional surrender and extinguish our country.[51]

With these words, Chiang Kai-shek appeared to have completely won over his audience. Deeply touched by his sincerity, the Huangpu men all rose to their feet to show that they had accepted their lesson respectfully.[52]

Contrary to his apparent trust of his subordinate officers, Chiang, as a military man, had never completely trusted anyone except his very own bodyguards. To ensure his personal security and dominance, he established a Special Service Department and assigned Dai Li, his former bodyguard, as the leading administrator of his personal political force.[53]

This section of the Guomindang closest to Chiang Kai-shek formed a secret organisation that was popularly known as the Blue Shirts; Dai Li was named as its leader.[54] Chiang Kai-shek organised this secret organisation by the same process of moral righteousness and indoctrination used by Mao Zedong, although Chiang called his doctrine *Sanminzhuyi* (nationalism, democracy, and prosperity).

To cultivate necessary moral righteousness and discipline, Chiang demanded that his party give his leadership absolute support by promoting an autocratic concept of state, society, and rulership. In order to establish a unified and strong nation, the Guomindang had to exterminate Communism and uproot the amoral individualism of capitalism.[55] In the name of the Chinese people, Chiang attempted to establish a military dictatorship in which his personal will would be carried out without hesitation.[56]

Ironically, Chiang even promoted a similar connection between a borrowed ideology and its implication, as Mao did. Instead of the metaphor of arrow and target, Chiang quoted the ancient philosopher Wang Yangming and reinterpreted Sun Yat-sen's philosophy of a Republic Revolution as "the unity of knowledge and action" (*zhi xing he yi*). Chiang Kai-shek pointed out that Sun Yat-sen had said "knowing is hard and doing is easy; those who act learn" (*zhi nan xing yi, li xing zhexue*). Chiang, therefore, replaced the core of Sun Yat-sen's theory (*Sun Wen Xueshuo*) with the action plan of the Republic Revolution, Three Principles of the People, national independence, political democracy, and economic security (*Sanmin Zhuyi*). As Chiang reinterpreted Sun's republicanism, the goal and principle of the people disappeared. Chiang insisted that the most important idea of Sun was the unity of theory and action (*zhi xing he yi*). Sun believed that when considering revolution, it was hard to know (if the time was right), but easy to carry out the task. All that was required was to strive hard (*nuli*) and to practice vigorously fairness and rectitude (*lixing gong zheng*), which is what the Doctrine of the Mean intends: "Even the stupid can be enlightened. Even the weak can be strengthened."[57]

Under the same name of unity between theory (knowledge) and action (implication), both Mao and Chiang added and created something of their own. Mao did so by redefining or naming the theory (Marxism in Chinese), while Chiang diverged from Sun's democracy, economic prosperity, and nationalism into a military dictatorship and civil war against his Communist enemy by redefining how to act on Sun's principles. In order to establish a strong state, he had to create a military dictatorship; to allow democracy, he had to exterminate the Communists first; in order to maintain national unity, he had to break the moral law and murder, kidnap, and torture—in the name of action, Chiang's version of Sun's philosophy allowed everything that Sun's Republican Revolution and Constitution deplored.

With this reinterpretation and justification, anything could be done in front of the portrait of Sun Yat-sen and justified by his principles. Kidnapping was conducted on a vast scale; it was a speciality of the secret agents commanded by Dai Li, especially in Shanghai. "Do not let a single Communist escape, even if we have to kill one thousand men by mistake" became the principle of the action of Extermination of Communists. Even the head of the East China District Operations Group (*Huadong qu xingdong zu*) could not remember exactly how many persons he had ordered to abduct and to kill during the years which he was in charge of the division of "secret arrests" (*Mimi daibu*) in the Shanghai area. At the time, Chiang believed that Communists used the International Settlement in Shanghai as their free refuge. By 1937, the secret agents boasted that they could kidnap anybody, anyplace, anytime. Dai Li developed special procedures to avoid media attention and the protest of international organisations that represented human rights.[58]

Torture has a long history in Chinese politics, and it engaged a widespread revival in the Guomindang's prisons of the 1930s.[59] Torture was often used to pressure captives to defect and to reveal the names and addresses of their comrades. Except for a small number of prisoners who actually confessed, the rest underwent daily torture until they died behind lice-ridden sheds. They had never seen a judge or appeared in court. Without any legally appointed interrogation officials present, the torture was conducted by a special guards unit (*jingwei*) under the supervision of a section chief, inspector, or deputy brigade head. There was no one to prevent the torturers from horribly maiming or killing the captives. One survivor of the Guomindang prisons put it this way: "You only have people in good walking condition upon entry. You seldom have people in good walking condition on their way out."[60]

The scenes of torture are well documented. For example, the interrogation room in the Shanghai Station lockup was traversed by a thick joist. Hemp ropes were suspended from the heavy wooden beam. The end of one of these was tied to the thumbs of the prisoner, whose hands were tied behind his back. At the shout of "Lift up!" (*diao*), the rope was yanked and the person was lifted off the floor. At first, the victim was left with his tiptoes touching the ground, and the rope was tied to a hook while the interrogation continued. After several minutes, the victim's face would be covered with perspiration. If there was no confession at that point, then the torturers would shout, like lectors in a traditional yamen, announcing the next level of judicial punishment, "Pull!" (*che*), and the prisoner would be hoisted clear of the floor, his weight suspended entirely from his thumbs. While the wretch's entire body broke out in sweat, the interrogators would sit in relaxed positions, smoking cigarettes while they watched the tormented writhe in pain. If the prisoner still refused to talk, the pain usually made him pass out. Then, the body was taken down and doused with cold water until the victim recovered consciousness and could be hoisted again. Usually, one session of hanging was enough to get the prisoner to reveal all that he knew.[61]

If hanging (*diao*) was not enough, then the *Juntong* torturers moved on to "fry the ribs" (*chao paigu*). Again, the prisoner was hung from the beam on his tiptoes, and his legs were tied together to keep him from kicking. The victim's clothing was stripped away and his back was pressed against the wall. One of the interrogators would don thick leather gloves and then slowly squeeze down on the ribs, moving the gloves up and down the flanks. This created friction and put pressure on the internal organs. Although prisoners who survived this torture might feel internal pains for a long time afterwards, the agony at the time of the ordeal was not sufficient to cause unconsciousness. Interrogators favoured this technique for precisely this reason until much later, when they learned how to use magnetos for torture.[62]

Some prisoners preferred death rather than torture. They simply struck back at their tormentor who would obligingly find enough anger to beat the victim to death. Most inmates refused to talk, and during interrogation an extremely small percentage of them survived to tell the horrifying stories of routine torture.[63] One survivor recollected that during the interrogation, the administrator suddenly had an iron door in the wall opened. Out of the adjoining torture cell came a dazzling glare of light and the reek of blood, shed by the inmate's battered assistant, who had also been captured by the secret police.

> A torn, bleeding body was lying on the concrete floor with heavy fetters on its ankles. Blood was still dripping from the motionless body. Several hair-chested men stood over him holding gory whips. One of them picked up a brown leather jacket and with a hideous laugh tossed it towards the unconscious man.
> …
> There was the sound of whips whistling through the air and thudding on naked flesh…The man in the swivel chair straightened up and lit a cigarette. Slowly blowing out smoke rings, he listened to the cries, the faintest hint of a smile playing around his lips. To him the screams of the torture were like music. He was used to this life. A lull in the groans and shrieks, and a feeling of emptiness and fear would overtake him. Without interrogations under torture, he would have lacked a sense of his own existence and power.[64]

Though Chiang had achieved status abroad as a world leader, his government was deteriorating under the pressure of political corruption and economic bankruptcy. In his diary, on June 1948, Chiang himself painfully admitted that the Guomindang had failed, not because of external enemies but because of disintegration and rot from within; and it was this, more than any alleged foreign intrigue, that contributed to his defeat.[65] The war had severely weakened the Nationalists both in terms of resources and popularity, while the Communists were strengthened by successful political strategy and guerrilla organisations extending throughout rural areas. The Nationalists initially had superiority in arms and men; but their lack of popularity, the heavy infiltration of Communist agents in the nationalist government, and apparent disorganisation soon allowed the Communists to gain the upper hand. Chiang's generals eventually pocketed at least US$30 million of American aid from 1945 to 1949, but as much as US$3 billion in arms and equipment, given by his American supporters who tirelessly pressured Congress, ended up in the hands of Mao's army.[66]

CONCLUSIONS

In the time of chaos, Chinese politics took military form where the fates of both potential winner and loser would be decided by an armed struggle instead of a battle of words. As the legal and moral establishment went to ruin and the old social boundary collapsed, political competition for control became a contest of forces and resources to gain the upper hand in lawmaking, and it become the voice of authority. Chiang Kai-shek won the contest with the above-law society, warlords, international bankers, and intellectual politicians who had connections with the old society. Mao won the contest within a much wider spectrum of Chinese society by motivating and organising the under laws to overthrow the established social hierarchy upon which Chiang's government was based.

Both Chiang and Mao were among the few Chinese politicians who are able to activate and influence the people both within and outside of law. Chiang had a special talent that allowed him to reach out to the affluent and the Western-educated politicians who had connections to foreign capital. This was crucial for his strategy of civil war and political career. Mao's success stemmed from his capacity to harvest and focus a huge amount of human capital: the peasants, who represented over 90 percent of China's population. Mao's vivid and highly colloquial use of language could touch both the ignorant and the educated. He made himself the hero of under laws.

Unlike their predecessor Sun Yat-sen, both Chiang and Mao were ruthless strategists who not only abolished the old legal establishment and established new laws, but also reinforced them with vigour and eliminated the outlaws against their regimes. They shared a deep understanding of the codes and functions of the Chinese legal and moral laws that regulated social behaviour, yet were cynical enough, and had the nerve and detachment, to refuse to be bound by them. They both were highly gifted political rhetoricians who could utilise and manipulate words creatively, cruelly, and ruthlessly. Chiang was a master of mental and physical terror who would rather kill a thousand men by mistake than allow a single Communist to escape. Mao was an expert in verbal manipulation and mental terrorisation. He not only refused to keep his words ("eating one's own words" in Chinese) like a gentleman, as often did Chiang, but also managed to become the word, which motivated generations of men and women to fight for him and defend him before and even after his death.

China was not like Japan, as Chiang had wished. With its much longer civil tradition, China could not be controlled by guns, even imported and modernised guns. Mao's achievements and his cruelty went far beyond those of Chiang Kai-shek. Chiang maintained his leadership by silencing his oppositions; Mao did so by forcing his agenda, manipulating minds, and castrating individual spirit. Mao could make his opponents surrender willingly and he could convince them to celebrate defeat as winning. Mao's attempt to control and dominate did not stop at behaviour. It extended to attacking the weaker mind and destroying its spirit. This level of abuse substantially increased after the CCP became the ruling force of China. Now, Mao was the ruler and his words were the real fountain of law. His immense skills in building organisations and political structure brought order to China but became the cause of his own decline after he pushed the boundaries of his personal power beyond the successful system that he had built.

CHAPTER 4

COMMUNIST PARTY AS LEGISLATOR AND ADMINISTRATOR

In 1949, through military advance rather than popular support (as the Communists have claimed), Mao Zedong and his Communist Party became the new legislator for China. The government immediately abolished existing laws of the Guomindang and established a socialist legal system. In the early 1950s, the Communist government passed a number of regulations, including laws on marriage, land reform, and corruption. This legal system experienced a brief period of popular support from 1954 to 1956. The Constitution, which included a Bill of Rights, was announced. Four levels of courts were established in accordance with the Constitution and organic laws: the Supreme People's Courts, the Higher People's Courts, the Intermediate People's Courts, and the Basic People's Courts. Courts were subordinate to the National People's Congress (NPC), but they were of the same rank as the State Council, military, and procuracy. The courts were intended, at least on paper, to enjoy functional independence. The Ministry of Justice (MOJ) was also created, law schools were opened, and law journals began to appear.[1]

The glorious days of law came to an abrupt end with the anti-rightist movement in 1957, when party politics took over the legal system. Many in the legal community challenged the Chinese Communist Party's monopoly of law and called for greater judicial independence. They suggested that party policies should be transformed into laws and that the courts should be responsible for deciding cases on their own without party interference and in accordance with the law. The party responded to this challenge by labelling the judges, lawyers, and legal academics as capitalists and rightists, and the party persecuted them or reassigned them to labour camps and countryside posts. After this political inference, law became a political tool to serve the political goals of the party.[2]

In the People's Republic, the Communist Party was the single legislator and had never been challenged until recently. During the Mao era, the party's role in day-to-day governance was extremely intrusive. To ensure control over government operations, the party structured its organisation to parallel the government administration at all levels. The real authority resided with the party; government officials answered to their party counterparts. Party cells were also established within government entities and other work units by recruiting the elite officers. The party placed a great deal of emphasis on thought control and reinforcing the party line.[3]

The struggle for political control internalised after the CCP silenced any possible opposition outside of the party. According to the party's Constitution, the chairman had enormous power to direct its members and determine policies; however, he had only one vote during election of the central committee, which was organised by its constitutional rules. Voting was the only mechanism through which the party organisation evolved and regenerated. To be a legitimate legislator, one had to win the internal discourse and conviction of its majority. Mao Zedong emerged as the most influential leader of the CCP after defeating his primary rivals because he had persuaded the majority of the party that his ideas were the correct policy of the Chinese Revolution.

Compared to Sun Yat-sen and Chiang Kai-shek, Mao was much better prepared to be a national leader and state legislator. Unlike Sun, who possessed only a superficial understanding of the Western democracy and legal system, Mao and his comrades spent thirty years studying Marxism, in both theory and practice, in their quest to find a meaningful way to incorporate these theories in China. They gained substantial experience in government during the war period. Mao and Chiang Kai-shek shared the qualities of political sharpness and shrewdness. However, Mao was an original thinker and political visionary, rather than merely a military commander or statesman.

Mao knew that to achieve his political ambition he needed a modern and highly disciplined party. An organisation based upon traditional Chinese brotherhood or personal loyalty alone would not be enough to deal with his modern and complex China. He had a deep and thorough understanding of Chinese history, its culture, and its intricate political strategy.[4] His ideological cultivation, rectification, and propaganda established him as the sole legislator within the Communist Party years before it took power. By the Seventh Party Congress of the CCP in 1945, Mao Zedong's position as the dominant leader had been fully consolidated, a result of his persistent work within the party since the later 1920s. Not only was he reconfirmed as the supreme authority in both of the party and military leadership hierarchies, he also had created a group of leaders, his future bureaucrats, who completely supported his vision.[5]

The early history of the Communist Party illustrates that the main issue for the Communist leadership had never been whether Marxism should be the guidance of the Chinese revolution. Rather, it concerned whose interpretation of this foreign theory should be recognised as the valid and correct option, as well as how to create a coherent ideology that would satisfy various party factions. The first condition to create leadership legitimacy was to unify the language that translated and interpreted Marxism into Chinese. Mao Zedong was not by any standard the best and the most knowledgeable of Chinese Marxist theorists, and his theoretic knowledge and adaptation often appeared to be limited, rigid, and overly simplified. However, he was the most gifted storyteller and rhetorician, and he was able to make his version of Marxism rise above those of his opponents and comrades. Mao's words had the power to navigate easily between theory and practice, reality and illusion, legality and morality, and right and wrong. This superior usage of language made his words sharp enough to penetrate (people's minds), hard enough to overpower (his opponents), and soft enough to move and irritate. His words, like skilful hands, could massage and manipulate his followers however and whenever he wished.

Chinese political argument and persuasion do not triumph by reaching out and seeking compromises from diverse opinions by breaking conceptual barriers, as does the Western discourse, because it was an older, more complex, and extremely precise yet fluid language. Chinese discourse has to deliberately build up a seemingly impenetrable boundary from one that is vague or even nonexistent. Western politicians rally along conceptual lines such as capitalism, Socialism, liberals, and conservatives; Chinese political authority has to navigate through various connotations of these ideas to identify and build a distinct connotation and reasoning that will successfully negate its opponents.[6]

In absence of ideas based on unalienated texts or abstract notions of justice, political authority in modern China emerges only through a verbal justification that produces a moral righteousness. This moral righteousness (like the Western ideas of liberty, law, and democracy) serves as a foundation for political organisation, policy, and propaganda. This righteousness legitimises political authority, and it justifies any political movement that designs to overthrow an established authority. Chinese politics always begins and ends with a battle (rather than alliance) of words: words to rally troops, to organise a party, to establish a regime, as well as to repress opposition.

The battle of words that is designed to destroy opposition begins with creating a verbal (or symbolic) opposition (or ideological enemy), with which an ideological difference can be identified and through which political campaign can be launched. The opposition is deliberately created by encouraging individual or unofficial expression that makes it easy to identify "incorrect" ideas or "incorrect" interpretations of a correct idea (in this case, Marxism). This process, known as "exposing one's thoughts", was used at the beginning of all of Mao's political movements. It was used to create and isolate the target of criticism and justify a soon-to-come political attack. Then, as the political attack was launched, it became focused and was repeated with campaigns against these ideas through a deliberately exaggerated and adversarial argument.[7] The next step was to create the enemy of the organisation by attacking the words and ideas of the opposition. The owners of these opposite ideas became the official enemy of the initiator of the discourse. Dissenters were scandalised, denigrated, or even imprisoned.

The righteous theory not only owns the argument. It also gains political power by defeating opposing opinions and forcing them to surrender. This smothers the very intent and courage for dissenting voices to arise. After silencing all the oppositions, whoever speaks the final words becomes the mouth of the law. Every time throughout this cruel political process, Mao Zedong succeeded and entrenched himself as the mouth of the law and the hands behind legislation.

The best example of this verbal and political mechanism is the rectification movement (*zheng feng*), which began in Yanan, was repeated during the second half of the 1950s and early 1960s, and was developed and refined to its extreme during the Cultural Revolution.[8] Unlike Western legislation—which interprets law by identifying the original wording and intent of the code, reviews codified cases, and considers written law as guidance for future legal issues—the Constitution of the Chinese Communist Party was rewritten whenever there was a personnel change in its leadership. There was no barrier or unalienated conceptual line between the established code of law and new legislation. Both were written and could be rewritten over and over again as political situations allowed.

Mao wrote new law by reinventing history and thus validating his ideological and moral opinions. He became the ultimate guarantor of justice by redefining law as and when he required. After defeating the opposition that he had just created, his prize in winning moral leadership was the power and prestige to override the judgements of his subordinates and those who preceeded him. His voice after this cruel battle of words was always single-minded, extreme, exclusive, and self-righteous. For example, the reconstruction of an official history of the CCP gave a prideful place to Mao and his supporters in China's revolution while dismissing his opponents, the Russian- or European-trained Marxist theorists.[9] By cultivating this adversarial and instrumental version of history, Mao established new laws and invented new morality for his party.

Unlike in the West, Chinese law has never stopped at sanction of social behaviour; it has a strong tendency to internalise and invade the civil and psychological space of its citizens. During the Yanan Rectification Movement, people were bombarded by official documents. More than twenty texts were selected to serve as a core curriculum. These documents set the template for the inner-party struggles against evil heresies such as subjectivism in study, sectarianism in party work, formalism in propaganda, and rules for self-cultivation. These rules were not simply announced and applied. Everyone involved had to submit with his or her heart and soul and participate in this grand discourse. There was no escape or place to hide. All party members had to reveal their personal experience, their most private thoughts, and reinterpret their entire lives according to the party standard. Through this conceptual inversion, everyone's private lives were reinterpreted and judged by the collective guidelines; individuals were reinvented and forced to be openly and willingly committed to the common course and discourse of the revolution. This method of mental torture and spiritual castration was adopted time and again after 1949. It reached extremes of cruelty and barbarism during the Cultural Revolution.

The public confession and self-salvation were often further secured by a form of mental and physical terrorism, where the few daring dissents who refused to bow to authority and participate in the exegetical bonding were tried without a court, interrogated without legal representation, beaten, or simply murdered. Caught between the fear of exclusion or personal harm and the glory of supporting a righteous course of revolution and the implied opportunity to rise in political status, the majority submitted. The party always apologised for its cruelty and brutality against unfortunate individuals and eventually rehabilitated them after a political movement. Most times, rehabilitation came too late and was too little to compensate for the wrongly convicted and executed. However, this political movement that was designed to terrorise often effectively silenced dissenting voices and unified minds by will or by force. The assumed future rehabilitation created an illusion of a regained righteousness for the people whose spirit was destroyed by the political movements.[10]

Unlike in the former Soviet Union, ideological and political manipulation was the main method of control within the Communist Party, and physical terrorism was only used as secondary means.[11] In the historic context of civilised repression, physical terrorism became rampant only during the Cultural Revolution after Mao failed to win the majority with his words alone. Ironically, Kang Sheng, the head of the secret police of the Communist Party, became Mao's primary weapon to once again silence the opposition.[12]

Another very important aspect of the CCP's internal struggle, a part of its policy after 1949, was the systematic discrimination against intellectuals.[13] Mao and his party saw intellectuals as a main group of dissidents that supported many unofficial (even opposing) ideologies. Within the party's ideological foundation, upon which its political righteousness was built, nonintellectual dissidents could only exercise limited influence at the local level of leadership. This posed no threat to the central control system. However, with their ability to independently read, analyse, and especially write and publish deviant or opposing opinions about the official party line, intellectuals as a group were politically threatening.

Until the end of the 1940s, the majority of party members were illiterate peasants and the urban poor who would have taken anything that came out of the mouth of Mao Zedong as genuine and orthodox Marxism. However, the intellectuals read and compared the original meanings of Marxist writings and the CCP's self-righteous claims and discovered the discrepancies, contradictions, and even errors of these claims. Most importantly, intellectuals detested the discrepancy between the party's political rhetoric and its actual behaviour, and between the words of its leaders and their actions. In a system without public scrutiny, the eyes and mouth of the intellectuals became the only thing that the party had to monitor to maintain its winning image and political legitimacy.[14]

Every opposite opinion about Mao's policy came from another intellectual (often an intellectual who had a better formal education and Marxist training) who believed that Mao's thought had deviated from orthodox Marxism. For example, as the CCP made its extravagant claims of egalitarianism between officers and ordinary men, and between men and women, intellectuals (including the best literary writers of contemporary China) in Yanan wrote to expose the discrepancy between what the party claimed and what it practised. They pointed out the different entitlements allowed between those within and those outside of party control—in particular, the habitual and unequal access to (and use of) food, uniforms, shelter, and women. Wang Wei asserted that in a society in which equality is a chief moral claim, the principle on which the nature of truth itself is to be re-rendered, transformed, and redeemed cannot—indeed, must not—be compromised by such hypocrisies. Intellectuals were the only people who dared to confront the party with its own claim of righteousness and its hypocrisy.[15]

To maintain the party's ideological monopoly and its moral rights, the loud voice and the sharp pen of the intellectual group could not be tolerated. The intellectuals had to be sacrificed for the sake of party unity. Wang Wei was labeled as a "Trotskyite Spy" and a member of a five-person antiparty gang. (This accusation was officially revoked forty-nine years later by the CCP.) He was the only one of this group who refused to admit his mistake. He was refused the right to resign or redeem. Wang's execution terrified many dissident intellectuals and writers and forced them to surrender to official policy. As long as one acknowledged and apologised for his mistakes (against the party) and was publicly convicted (without a trial), he or she would be excused from personal harm or execution. He would be accepted again by Mao as a humbled, defeated, and rehabilitated comrade.[16]

Most of the surviving CCP members during the Yanan movement had experienced the same kind of intellectual terrorism, including prominent statesmen Zhou Enlai, Liu Shaoqi, and hundreds of others who later benefited from the repeated purges and became distinguished administrators of Mao's government. They survived because they had realised that in the universe of the Chinese Communist Party, there was room for only one sun, and that was Mao Zedong. If they wanted to be a part of the righteous movement, they had to dim down and only reflect Mao's light, until perhaps they, someday by seniority, become the sun themselves.

The organisational unity and ideological purity of the CCP faced a new challenge after it became a ruling party, which brought immense responsibility. Party rectification was now an integral part of the overall consolidation of national power and become the central feature of the early years of the People's Republic. Military success and the crumbling of organised resistance shifted leadership energies from seizing power to government organisation and administration. The most pressing task was social and economic recovery from the dislocations of civil war.[17]

The campaign against Gao Gang and Rao Shushi was the first major leadership challenge for the new government, and was mainly an internal affair.[18] Gao and Rao were accused of forming an alliance and conspiracy against the party (*fan dang*), even though no specific documents were produced and no trial was conducted. The conviction was announced by Mao Zedong himself, who headed an enlarged meeting of the Politburo. Mao claimed that Gao and Rao had established a second headquarters of the CCP in Beijing that shadowed his.[19] Of course, opposing Mao and his leadership was a crime against the party and the nation as well. No one could survive this charge.

Gao Gang might have survived if he would have repented and admitted his mistakes, but he killed himself. Rao Shushi was openly unrepentant and persisted with his attack upon the party. Both were formally expelled from the CCP. As a result of the fall of Gao and Rao, Lin Biao and Deng Xiaoping became members of the Politburo.[20]

After of the Gao–Rao incident, the party specified several strict disciplinary actions against dissenters, including expulsion from the party for those who deliberately carried out factional splitting activities, led an independent kingdom, undermined party unity and collective leadership, and refused to repent. The party continued this round of struggle and the ensuing new law without advising the general public. Mao Zedong was in a very comfortable controlling position, although he was disturbed by the plot of a few. Gao and Rao could not really challenge the central committee because the latter enjoyed a broad policy consensus at the time. The Gao-Rao independent kingdom was neither large nor airtight; only about two dozen government and military officials had been affected by this purge.[21]

In fact, Mao was so confident that he thought it was the time to deal with other internal problems within the party. In the spring of 1956, the slogan "Let a Hundred Flowers Bloom, a Hundred Schools of Thought Contend" (*baihua qifang, baija zhengming*) initiated a new rectification campaign. Unlike the anti–Gao-Rao movement, a closed-door exercise where indoctrination was carried out through self-criticism among party members, the innovations of the Hundred Flowers departed from all of the former procedures. It opened the door for non-party organisations, and even the general public, to participate. Unlike the early rectification movement where non-Communist participation was optional, Mao now invited criticism from outside of the party. He even went so far as to advocate that each province should have two newspapers, one run by the party and another run by the non-Communists, to engage in mutual criticism.[22]

The initial goal of the movement was to make internal adjustments to ensure that the party was competent to lead a vast and complex state. The Communist bureaucrats disappointed Mao with their lack of ideological direction and analytical intelligence and skills. There were many problems within the ruling elite, including red tape, buck-passing, overstaffing, and overlapping of organisations. Under Mao's prodding, an effort to eliminate such tendencies was launched in the winter of 1956–1957 through a retrenchment of personnel and an organisational drive. Closely related to this structural obesity were overcentralisation and administrative rigidity. In his speech "On the Ten Great Relationships", Mao stressed the need for greater local initiative while the major reports to the Eighth Congress criticised central departments for overly elaborate regulations binding lower level authorities and ignoring special conditions.[23]

This movement activated an unexpected level of popular criticism directed at the CCP that claimed to be the liberator and saviour of the Chinese people and that had taken popular support for granted. Comments of intellectuals from all professions revealed manifold aspects of sectarianism and the depth of resentment it stirred. Party cadres were accused of considering themselves made of "uncommon stuff" while looking down on non-party people as knowing nothing of politics. These prejudices were not limited to those with proven revolutionary achievements; even newly recruited party members would suddenly take on an air of superiority upon being granted membership. As a result, friendly interaction between party and populace became rare, and many intellectuals felt that "high walls" and "deep moats" had been placed between the party bureaucrats and the non-Communist majority members whom they claimed to represent. While some admitted that intellectuals bore some blame for this situation due to their arrogance, the dominant view was that the fault lay primarily with the elitist and exclusiveness of party members. As Mao pointed out, it was up to party leaders to dismantle the walls that separated the people who were inside and outside of the party.[24]

Corruption and preferential treatment exacerbated this estrangement between party bureaucrats and ordinary citizens as party members were conferred many advantages. Citizens complained of special dormitories and dining halls, which had been set aside for bureaucrats and "aristocratic schools" established for the education of their children. Within the government bureaucracy, complaints were made that the rate of promotion for party members was much more rapid than for non-party cadres, despite the better qualifications of the latter. Similarly, when administrative discipline was imposed, party members allegedly received lighter penalties than their non-party colleagues for comparable misdeeds. Favouritism in personnel matters extended beyond individual party members to their wives and relatives.

The crucial source of tension between the party and non-party bureaucrats was a struggle for power. As Mao Zedong spoke favourably of great democracy (*ta min chu*), which included not only mass movements under the CCP's control but also strikes and demonstrations against unresponsive bureaucrats, he put the state bureaucracy under the microscope of popular scrutiny. The CCP was accused of monopoly and abuse of power.[25] As Mao's Hundred Flowers and rectification policy led to the embarrassment of many party administrators, it encountered increasing internal opposition. Party officials, including the highest level immediately under Mao, had reservations about the Hundred Flower movement.[26]

Mao dealt extensively with political leadership and announced that there would be a rectification movement the following year to be aimed at subjectivism, sectarianism, and bureaucracy. As his administrators revealed their insecurity in their power positions and their fear that democracy would get out of hand, Mao assured them that he was aware of a "right opportunist wind" and an "antisocialist tide". Yet, he reaffirmed the Hundred Flowers policy while he called for the forceful refutation of "harmful" statements, as well as the prohibition of "counterrevolutionary" utterances. However, Mao—this time under internal pressure—did not even mention mutual supervision or advocate radical departures in rectification procedures. His position became conducive to a markedly cautious approach.[27]

The tone and tide of the politics began to change after Mao's new speech.[28] Official newspapers began to express concerns about the expected erosion of political criteria, and satiric literature became more popular at the expense of party-line works praising Socialism. This pushed Mao's originally relaxed attitude towards non-Communist oppositions and drew sustenance from his comments about getting rid of the weeds in the flower garden. The allowed criticism against party bureaucrats now was associated with an intention to attack and condemn the entire Communist system. The media began to attack the "right revisionist", a term from another of Mao's writings, which levelled criticism of the doctrinism and bureaucratism that Mao had originally set to rectify.[29]

In an attempt to restrict popular criticism against the party, the media also published selected "personal" opinions or stories that attacked individuals who had championed the voice of discontent. By 1956, the legal means used to publicly demonstrate against leadership, such as popular gatherings, strikes, and parades, became illegal. These methods appeared to promote chaos, which could be exploited by counterrevolutionaries, and advocated taking grievances to party leaders for a solution rather than appealing directly to the masses. These opinions of the media were at variance with the view expressed by Mao in both November and January that strikes were not only legal but also, when reasonable, they helped by pointing out shortcomings. However, the chairman had also stated that disturbances were not to be encouraged and unjustified ones should be criticised. In any case, by emphasising the use of regular party channels for redress of grievances, the media tacitly opposed more liberal interpretations of Mao's instruction, which could justify the Hundred Flowers and mutual supervision policies.[30]

In June 1957, an anti-rightist struggle (*fanyu douzheng*) replaced the Hundred Flower movement. Mao bowed to party consensus for a rebuff of intellectual critics, which was a major turnabout from his spring position, but the chairman negotiated this shift without apology or apparent embarrassment. He undertook key initiatives, not only in readjusting the CCP policies towards rightists, but also in commencing a rectification campaign against the rightists during the summer of 1957. In spite of differences that may have existed earlier, and whatever loss of prestige Mao may have suffered from his first major policy "miscalculation" of the post-1949 period, the party rallied around him once again as he opted for a more orthodox course.[31]

The anti-rightist phase of the rectification movement was essentially defensive in strategy and tone. Official arguments sought to refute rightist views and to restore party control, which was believed to have been weakened by the Hundred Flowers movement. This was used as a political defence for Mao's approach of using non-party criticism to correct the errors of the party members who deviated from Mao's policy. To maintain his political righteousness and gain party consensus, Mao now called for a confrontation with the rightists who had challenged the leadership of CCP.

The reason why Mao had to modify his position was that he had begun to face a challenge from his own administrators. At the CCP's 8th

Congress in September 1956, Mao's prestige suffered when the "Thought of Mao Zedong" was omitted from the party's Constitution, which reflected a consensus within the party. It was a collective decision for Mao to retreat to the "second line" of party leadership, shedding duties and functions, and thus allowing Liu Shaoqi and his other colleagues to gain experience and prestige in senior leadership roles.

Mao was not happy about this decision, although he openly agreed with it. He became very sensitive about the perception of his leadership. In early 1957 he deliberately leaked out his resentment by comparing himself to a leading character in a well-known Chinese opera. He said that now he was growing too old to play the star's part well; he hinted that he soon might accept a subordinate role. In April 1959 Mao had a change of heart (or asserted his original resentment) about his retirement plan, which would hand over the state chairmanship to Liu Shaoqi and hasten his retreat to the second front within the Politburo Standing Committee. The logical step would have been for him to exchange the CCP chairmanship for the honorary chairmanship of the 9th Party Congress in 1961.

The Third Plenum in fall 1957 marked a fundamental turning point in the history of modern China, as the first steps towards new economic policies—known as the Great Leap Forward (or simply, the Great Leap)—occurred in 1958. The rectification and purge taken following the Third Plenum was closely linked to the new economic strategy. Now a further redefinition of the party's Constitution took place in accord with the needs of the Great Leap. For the first time, policy differences became a central issue in party rectification. Although Mao was able to build a strong majority in favour of the Great Leap in policy councils, the previous consensus was now shattered, and many officials entertained severe reservations as China plunged down an uncharted economic path.

As policy differences also tended to become more matters of basic approach than questions of timing or degree within a commonly accepted framework, the viability of both established procedures of inner-party debate and traditional rectification measures came under increasing pressure. At least in this early stage of the Great Leap, Mao and other

party leaders had considerable success in their efforts to retain traditional approaches and methods in dealing with different opinions. In the
case of the highest ranking official who was apparently affected, Chen
Yun, neither formal discipline nor informal criticism was applied—a
tacit admission of the right of party leaders to hold minority opinions.
Nevertheless, Mao's growing concern in this same period with the inevitable inner-party splits and assertions—that his projected retirement
from the state chairmanship did not mean political abdication—implied
an awareness that conditions were changing, which might preclude both
the party unity required for mild rectification and the completion of his
graceful withdrawal to the "second line".[32]

The rectification process after the Third Plenum had both successes
and failures. In a sense, rectification was too successful. Together with
other political pressures, it silenced critics and energised vast numbers of cadres to work long hours in the pursuit of ambitious economic
goals. But in so doing, the seeds of future crisis were sown for both the
rectification process and the political system in general. The alacrity
with which party members as a whole took up the Great Leap program
impaired moderating influences and led to excesses that hastened the
collapse of the strategy. Also, with high-level officials suffering career
setbacks, at least in part, for their views, the policy process began to
lose some of its former vitality. As the deficiencies of the Great Leap
Forward became increasingly clear, the already frayed leadership unity
would be further shaken while those who inevitably were blamed for
the Great Leap's shortcomings would be progressively demoralised.
From this perspective, the successes of rectification in late 1957 and
1958 were hollow victories.[33]

The CCP became divided again by the summer of 1959. This time
there was not a clear-cut opposition, such as radical-conservative division,
but a more complex configuration of forces wherein even major pro-
ponents of the Great Leap saw the need for change. Under the pressure
of reality and the sustained reaction in the party, Mao was willing and
indeed eager to make adjustments but steadfastly refused to alter the
basic thrust of his initiatives. In effect, he tried to have it both ways.

He denounced exaggerated production figures while at the same time still demanded higher rates of growth than any country had ever achieved. Previously, when mass mobilisations led to excesses, the collective response of the party leadership was to call for a halt and tend to the accumulated problems in a fully articulated consolidation phase. The "anti-reckless advance" measures of 1956 were an example of this. These measures, with Mao's reluctant assent, marked an end to the first attempt of the Great Leap Forward. In 1959, however, Mao was unwilling to opt for the full-fledged consolidation suggested by his majority colleagues. Instead, he refused to redress imbalances while insisting on his mass mobilisation.

Mao Zedong's hesitation and ambivalence of the economic policies had disastrous results. The Great Leap led to a severe economic and social crisis. Its confirmation and implication also eroded the established Constitution of the party. The severe strains centred on the increasingly erratic role of Mao himself. By 1959, instead of retiring gracefully, Mao was playing a leading role in readjusting the policies of the Great Leap and the people's communes. Mao repeatedly violated the government of collective leadership and attempted to develop an "individual style" independent of the Politburo's direction.

From July to August 1959, the enlarged session of the Central Politburo of the Chinese Communist Party and the Eighth Plenum of the Eighth Party Congress met successively at Lushan in Jiangxi to correct the mistakes in economic development. On July 14, Peng Dehuai, at the time a member of the Politburo and also the defence minister, wrote Mao Zedong a letter in which he affirmed the achievements of 1958, saying that the general line of the party's economic policy was correct. Peng also analysed the mistakes made during 1958 and, at the end of the letter, expressed his hopes that

> we systematically assess the results and lessons of our work during the second half of the year past. Our aim is to make clear the right and wrong of things, raise high our thought, and not set out to blame individuals.[34]

Many party leaders expressed their support to Peng's criticism, which greatly irritated Mao Zedong. He decided to override collective leadership by demanding the disgrace of Peng Dehuai.[35] The right to air dissenting views in party forums had been an established principle and had never been explicitly challenged, but it was now effectively withdrawn in Peng's case. The immediate result was that other leaders unconnected to Peng were no longer willing to risk stating their reservations about official policies, a development that had painful consequences for the policy-making process.

At the same time, collective leadership was emasculated. The collective decision making in the CCP had always been dependent on Mao's forbearance. But now, for the first time, he was presenting his administrators with an ultimatum: to choose between Peng and himself. The party, a loose, unstable, and often weak collective without him, had to back off. This incident completely changed the party's Constitution, which had been established due to the political custom of the past thirty years. It began to be reorganised according to a simple declaration of loyalty rather than according to a discussion and careful weighing of diverse views. The party also turned away from persuasive measures. More and more dissident administrators were sanctioned, disciplined, or even dismissed after the Lushan Conference.[36]

Another example of organised aggression against the rights of the minority is the case of Chen Yun, the then vice chairman of the CCP. Chen Yun was the PRC's fifth-ranking leader in 1957. He was a major architect of the anti-reckless advance policies initiated in mid-1956. These policies—with their emphasis on gradual growth, balanced development, and material incentives—were the antithesis of Mao's Great Leap programme. Consequently, Chen was attacked by Mao and Liu in the Congress of 1958. Chen's proposal on administrative decentralisation and increasing agricultural production clashed with Mao's policy, and it was never published. He soon lost his position as the leading vice premier and the party's spokesman on economic affairs. While no formal disciplinary measures were taken against him, Chen's power clearly began to wane as the Great Leap strategy unfolded. Although Chen made frequent ceremonial appearances in late 1957 and 1958, his economic functions were now minimal. In September 1958, he was removed (*mian zhi*) from his major operational post as minister of commerce. As a part of this removal or reorganisation, Chen was appointed head of the newly formed State Capital Construction Commission, but this body never became active. While Chen continued to make infrequent appearances and was still listed in his Politburo and vice premier positions, by 1959 he was virtually silent on the economic issues he had dominated in the early and mid-1950s.[37]

This time, the most effective weapon to silence the opposition was to identify the expression of dissenting views as personal opposition to Chairman Mao. On this conceptual ground, any policy switch that Mao initiated could be an omen of organisational discipline and purge.[38] As Mao overrode the Constitution and silenced opposite views by organisational punishment and personal politics, he changed the very nature of discourse within the party. From this point on, to encourage consensus and party unity, policy difference and reservations could not be presented except in Mao's own words because no one was allowed to dispute Mao's words. As the officials realised that they could be disciplined solely for their opinions, the only means to express distinct views was to use Mao's words to contradict his other words and to disagree with him by pretending to be loyal to him personally.

The harshness and increasingly autocratic nature of the 1959–1960 campaign again underlines the relationship of leadership unity to disciplinary methods. Party unity, which had been forged during the early 1940s and sustained first with revolutionary success, was now severely strained. With Mao suspicious of his old comrades and foreseeing another twenty to fifty years of class struggle to guarantee the victory of the correct line, some coercion was inevitable. Moreover, leaders at lower levels who strongly backed the Great Leap strategy now had both the opportunity and need to deal harshly with those who opposed their views. With such divisions deepening, rectification was becoming less a method for reform and more a tool for purge.

The policy shift at the top deeply confused and divided the party members, especially at the lower levels of organisation, who had no idea what was going on in Beijing. Post–Great Leap China was a mess. The people's communes were abandoned. Massive economic and social projects closed down. Public grievances skyrocketed. In such circumstances, persuasive measures through the normal chain of command were insufficient. The party centre had to send work teams and peasant organisations to enforce rectification. The administrators who had enthusiastically or otherwise implemented the Great Leap were now severely castigated for pushing the masses too hard and violating objective realities, while in public, the leadership refused to admit that the Great Leap itself had been at fault. Thus, genuine enthusiasts balked at the new policies, while other officials were bitter for being blamed for the failure. For both groups, the leadership's credibility and righteousness had been severely damaged.

Severe economic deprivation, widespread social malaise, and antisocial acts on a significant scale created a lawless chaos and severe demoralisation in the grass roots of the party. Many local legislators became outlaws and engaged in corruption, robbery, and rape. As there was neither law nor judicial administration to judge and police the behaviour of the ruling party, their remaining popular support dwindled. The populace held the local leaders—who did nothing except apply instructions of the Central Committee—responsible for the hardship caused by the excesses of the Great Leap. This popular alienation of local administration led to harsh disciplinary practices, and the externally imposed work teams further demoralised the party members.

The unsuccessful attempt to reassert the rectification approach was only one aspect of a broad effort to restore traditional party norms. Mao stood at the forefront of this effort. He emphasised party unity, the rights of minorities to air their views, and the binding nature of collective decisions. In this period, he also went beyond rectification to promote a "reversal of verdicts" on rightist opportunists who had suffered unjustly in the preceding years. This effort promoted organisational rather than policy criteria for determining right and wrong. Factional ties to Peng

Dehuai's "conspiracy" (which still remains a contentious matter) were held culpable, but holding the same views as Peng was now excused as being perfectly permissible under the principle of minority rights.

Not everyone bought into Mao's efforts to smooth over the previous hostility and abuse of minority rights. One the one hand, many of the falsely accused still harboured resentment of past injustice and expressed their bitterness surrounding the reversal of verdicts. They were not willing to forget and forgive their tormentors who remained in authority. On the other hand, those who had passed the verdicts on the accused resented and resisted the new relaxed policy. They still defended the use of work teams to enforce policy and, in some instances, to invoke harsh sanctions. Generally, the post-1957 period saw a clear linkage between policy positions and political fortunes. This was in sharp contrast to the early and mid-1950s, when the losers of policy debates normally stayed in office to implement the programs they had opposed. The most dramatic case was Chen Yun, who had faded from prominence in late 1957 following his apparent objections to the emerging Great Leap strategy. Chen became a crucial economic decision maker in 1961 and particularly 1962, only to fade again from the scene following Mao's mid-1962 intervention.

The identification between personal opinions, personal loyalty, and political status made the idea of impersonal law impossible to achieve. Despite Mao's repeated declaration to encourage free debate, many leaders, eyeing the recent past, held back. No one would risk his position to announce his disagreement with Mao. No one would tell Mao the truth that he refused to hear. While Mao had withdrawn from active policy making for much of the 1960–1962 period, he still occupied the pivotal position. Not only was his assent necessary for the adoption of major policy readjustments, but also other leaders found it necessary to calculate the chairman's reactions before formulating their own positions.

The effort to silence dissenting views muted them, but it did not stop their existence. Repeated rectification movements to pursue consensus also failed. During the 1962–1965 period, the CCP found itself in deep division again. No strong consensus existed on a clearly defined course of action as in the early and mid-1950s and even, to a lesser extent, during the initial phase of the Great Leap.

During the Socialist Education Movement, Mao and his administrators, including his chosen heir, Liu Shaoqi, appeared to pursue separate approaches. Mao attempted to give the Socialist Education Movement an orientation of broad social reeducation, emphasising class struggle both at the outset of the campaign in early 1963 and from the start of 1965 when he reasserted his control over the movement. In contrast, different configurations of party leaders diverted the campaign from Mao's orientation towards more practical matters ranging from cadre corruption to immediate production tasks. Even when party leaders spoke about the class struggle, they meant party guidance rather than mass initiative in resolving the struggle.

Mao negotiated his position with his subordinates. From 1963 to late 1964, Mao endorsed the different views that were dominant at successive stages of the movement: first, a mild approach represented by Peng Hen until the first half of 1964, and then a much harsher policy launched by Liu after mid-1964. Subsequently, at a key series of meetings in December 1964 and January 1965, Mao reacted both to problems created by Liu's policies and to the issue of rural economic development that, almost by accident, had become linked to the Socialist Education Movement. As a result, he rejected much of Liu's approach and endorsed a shift to a milder campaign similar to that advocated earlier by Peng Zhen. At this time, however, the chairman added some provocative, albeit poorly understood, elements to the movement's guiding principles.[39]

The divergence of Mao's policy and that of his administrators, especially Liu Shaoqi (which can be traced back to the mid-1950s), became more apparent. On the question of economic development, especially capitalism in Chinese development, clear differences separated their theoretical systems. Liu Shaoqi believed that, after the Chinese Communist Party assumed power, a certain degree of capitalist growth should be allowed. As early as 1949, Liu said the following: "Capitalism is not developed in China. Under specific historical conditions, capitalism is progressive. Today's capitalism in China is progressive and not retrogressive."[40] Liu believed that China's capitalism was in its youth and that it was just the right time to develop its historical and positive role.[41]

Although both Mao and Liu thought that China should go through a transition from New Democracy to Socialism, they differed about how rapidly this transition should occur. In the early 1950s, Liu thought that it would take a decade or two for China to put Socialism into practice, and only after a fairly long period of "fortifying the New Democracy".[42] Mao wished to shorten the transitional period. To realise swiftly the great ideal of communism, he insisted upon the quickest way to push ahead with Socialist revolution and reconstruction. At the beginning, though, such differences in thought between Mao and Liu were not serious. What was important was that in party policy, Liu Shaoqi stood firm with Mao Zedong.

The apparent unity of policy between the two men can be seen in the second half of the 1950s, when Liu Shaoqi proposed the "General Line of Constructing Socialism" on behalf of the party. The General Line (*zongluxian*) that originated with Mao, the Great Leap Forward, and the people's commune movement came to be called the Three Red Banners (*Sanmian Hongqi*). In 1958 the Central Politburo of the Chinese Communist Party, meeting in an enlarged session at Beidaihe, passed the resolutions of "Mass Steel Production" and "Mass Organisation of People's Communes". The Congress announced the following: "It seems that the appearance of Communism in our country is no longer a distant event. We must actively use the People's Commune movement as a means of finding a substantive transition to communism."[43] At the Beidaihe meetings, there was no public disagreement between Mao Zedong and Liu Shaoqi.

The discipline of Peng had silenced internal opposition, but by early 1960 it became apparent that large-scale adjustment of the economy was necessary. In early 1961 the Ninth Plenum of the Eighth Party Congress was called, and Mao Zedong refused to recognise his mistakes and proposed another investigation and study movement, suggesting that 1961 be a year for investigation and seeking truth from facts. Responding to this call, Liu Shaoqi returned to his native town, Ningxiang County of Hunan Province, to do field investigation. This was the time when Liu began to change his views about the Three Red Banners, recognising that the difficulties came primarily from human shortcomings and mistakes in work rather than from natural disasters. Moreover, Liu believed that the Party Central Committee ought to assume the major share of responsibility for errors. He came to realise that much of what Peng Dehuai had written was valid.

However, Mao Zedong never changed his view about the Three Red Banners. He believed that the economic hardships did not come from his economic policies, although there were some technical mistakes concerning the policy implication. He insisted that the Three Red Banners was correct policy. Thus, in 1959 he said that, to protect the Three Red Banners, China must war with the rest of the world, including large numbers of domestic opposition and sceptics within the party. He labelled the opposition to the Three Red Banners "revisionism", and he also pointed out that Liu Shaoqi committed a serious right deviant mistake regarding the Three Red Banners.

Believing that the economic hardships came from policy mistakes, Liu Shaoqi, then in charge of daily affairs in the Central Committee, adopted in 1962 a series of measures to change the situation. Seeing that Chinese finances were seriously in deficit and that commodities' supply and demand were far apart, he proposed that China was in an extraordinary period and pressed for a restoration of overall balance. At the same time, he worked for the rehabilitation and redress for those sanctioned during the post-1958 political movements. All of these actions elevated the esteem in which Liu Shaoqi, president of the country and deputy chairman of the Party Central Committee, was held.

The rise of Liu Shaoqi increased the frustration of Mao Zedong, who knew what a majority meant to his own powerful position. Within the Chinese Communist Party, it was already established that the highest party official could lose his enormous power by losing the support of the majority. Leaders such as Chen Duxiu (1879–1942), Qu Qiubai (1899–1935), Li Lisan (1899–1967), and Wang Ming (1904–1974) all lost their positions in this way.[44] In 1962 Mao Zedong discovered that because of errors during the last half of 1958, his influence was in jeopardy.

To protect himself, Mao decided to create a discourse to discredit Liu Shaoqi, who had served as his official successor for years. At the September 1962 Tenth Plenum of the Eighth Party Congress, Mao raised the motto "Never Forget Class Struggle", aimed at Liu's various measures—"contract production" (*baochan daohu*), "the trend of going it alone (as opposed to collectively)" (*dan'ganfeng*), and "reversing verdicts" (*fan'an*). As Mao did not clearly indicate who was the enemy (inside or outside of the party) and how to translate this slogan into party policies, his Politburo colleagues simply ignored and resisted his suggestion through obstruction and noncompliance.[45] Besides, Mao's ambiguous definitions of social contradiction could be read and interpreted differently.

After the Tenth Plenum, a movement for urban and rural Socialist education (*chengxiang shehui zhuyi jiaoyu yundong*), centred on the call to hold tight to the class struggle, was launched throughout China. As it always had been, this argument about class struggle was artificially created by Mao to discredit Liu. In fact, Liu Shaoqi had never expressed ideas distinct from that of Mao on the subject. Liu had regarded the situation of class struggle as serious at the time and had adopted rather left-leaning measures during the movement. However, he opposed viewing the nature of the movement for Socialist education as only "two lines" and the struggle of only "two classes". He also did not agree with Mao that the object of the movement was "the capitalist-readers wielding power within the party", a label that Mao routinely gave to his opponents.

From December 15, 1964, to January 14, 1965, the Central Politburo held its national working sessions in Beijing to study and assess questions about the urban and rural Socialist education movement. The meetings resolved to call this movement the Four Clean-Ups (*siqing yundong*)—cleaning up politics, economics, organisation, and thought.

Mao attended only a few of the meetings. Deng Xiaoping suggested that Mao should rest and advised Mao not to attend a general working session that Deng chaired. Mao, however, insisted on attending and making a speech about the nature of the Four Clean-Ups movement (the goal of this movement was to cleanse the politics, economy, organisation, and ideology of the Communist Party). He said that its basis was the contradiction between Socialism and capitalism. At this point, Liu Shaoqi interrupted Mao and challenged him. Liu said that many contradictions cross one another. There was the contradiction of the Four Clean-Ups and the Four Uncleans, and there was the contradiction of the inner party and the outer party. Things were complicated. It was much better to solve contradictions as they came up. Mao was not happy to be challenged in public like this. At the meeting the next day, Mao fought back. He openly expressed his resentment and claimed that his rights to attend the party meeting and to express himself had been violated. Certain people did not want him to attend the meeting and did not want him to speak.

Playing this role as a victim, Mao spoke and gained the sympathy of those in attendance. After the meetings, some people criticised Liu Shaoqi directly for being disrespectful towards Mao Zedong. Liu then offered self-criticism during the party cell meetings (*shenghuohui*) of the Politburo. Still not satisfied, Mao indicated that the Liu Shaoqi question was not one of respect or disrespect, but one of principle between revisionism and anti-revisionism. He labelled Liu a reactionary element that had sneaked into the party. As Liu was Mao's successor-apparent, Liu had to be removed.

CONCLUSIONS

From the founding of the PRC to the Cultural Revolution, China was a republic without a constitution and was a country that claimed to belong to the people. But the people's voice had never been heard. Until 1949, the ruling party had been guided by relatively well-defined principles of limited and centralised democracy. During the next seventeen years, the party's Constitution deteriorated from collective democracy into an organisation controlled by personal autocracy.

In a language void of abstract meanings and extratextual authority, legal and political authority in China always needs an arbitrator to weigh its diverse opinions and balance the distribution of interests and power. Mao had to play this role before the CCP took power of the state within the scope of existing norms. The party's Constitution was challenged when the CCP became the ruling party. It had to be rewritten through experience, discourse, and persuasion.

During the first decades of the republic, Mao was in complete control as he enjoyed a wide range of support from within as well as outside of the CCP. However, as his opinions proved to be incorrect or as they had difficulty in capturing the support of the majority, especially among his inner circle, he became frustrated. Mao's administrators began to develop their own ideas. They began to question Mao's authority in policy making and deviated from his ultra-left views. At this time, the unity between Mao, the state, and the party began to crack.

In order to maintain ideological control and organisational unity of the party, Mao deliberately utilised the ambiguity inherent in the Chinese language to widen the spectrum of consensus and to make radical policy change possible whenever needed. As he departed from the established norm and encountered opposition, he could turn around by simply emphasising another aspect of his plans that had not yet been emphasised or prioritised, without losing any of his personal authority.

Although this ambiguity guaranteed Mao's position as the final arbitrator to determine a balance between opposite tendencies, it left increasing room for his administrators to take discretion in interpreting Mao's ideas. As these ideas pushed outside of his originally intended scope of meaning, people began to put their words into Mao's mouth and claim authority in Mao's name. It became a game to question or even challenge Mao and his ideas with one's own words.

By the mid-1960s, Mao's authority was challenged and his leadership was not nearly as strong as it had been in the previous decade. He, in fact, had lost control. He lost his support after several fatal political movements, during which his words functioned as the law and the direction for the country. His bureaucrats demanded rule of the majority rather than dictatorship. They wished that Mao would let them to do their jobs.

Mao's written words became overly used and abused and lost their binding power. His administrators increasingly used his words to justify their own positions against other words of Mao that they did not like. Multidimensional interpretation had made Mao's argument flexible enough to be constantly riding the tide of political discourse and at the same time made the argument indecisive and meaningless.

Mao had two choices: He could accommodate the party majority, or he could break his own rule. Realising that the majority of his Politburo colleagues and his handpicked successor were no longer loyal to his leadership, he chose the latter route because he still believed in his own ultimate power. He could fight the majority, create a new one, and rise to power again; he did it before, why not again? Mao launched the Cultural Revolution to create his own majority and maintain control.

On the eve of the Great Cultural Revolution, Mao assessed the situation in China. He believed that Liu Shaoqi had set up a "command headquarters," opposing him at the top, and that Liu had wide support. Mao believed that at least one-third of the leadership authority throughout the country was in the hands of people he could not trust. Thus, he decided that he had to go after the bosses of the lower cadres belonging to the Four Uncleans. In his eyes, most of the art and literature associations and societies had already "fallen in with revisionism", and the schools "were all run by capitalist-class intellectuals".[46]

In the fall of 1965, the Central Committee held working sessions in Beijing, during which Mao attempted to test the political atmosphere by asking the members of the Central Committee what they would do if revisionism appeared in the party. Worried that he belonged to the minority in the Politburo and the Central Committee, Mao requested that his words be passed down to all the provincial party secretaries, thus allowing them to oppose the revisionist Central. To protect his own power, Mao had to rely on followers from lower levels of administration who supported his vision to create a new majority.[47]

CHAPTER 5

WORDS OF MAO AND LAW
IN THE CULTURAL REVOLUTION

In October 1966, as the Cultural Revolution was under way, Mao indicated that the revolution was a shock that the party needed.[1] Mao had been thinking and planning for years about this nationwide civil chaos.[2] It was designed to overthrow the administrators, who had deviated from his vision and created a majority in the Politburo that had its own independent agenda and was able to challenge the chairman's authority. At this point, the party's Constitution, which Mao had spent decades building and by which he had established his own leadership, became an obstacle in the way of attaining of his political goal. Like many politicians in Chinese history, Mao believed that law was useful and deserved respect only when it served political purposes. He would be willing to endorse the law and to abide by it only if the words of law favoured him. Otherwise, he would not hesitate to change the law, announce new law, and create a new administration for the implication of his new law. Mao Zedong had decided to deliberately break the establishment and create a new one that would be loyal to his ideas. For this, rectification would not be radical and efficient enough. It had to be a revolution. In a popular revolution, he could activate hundreds of millions from the under-law populace to attack the established system (including the law itself), and once again he would become the fountain of law and the leader of a new and righteous administration.

The Cultural Revolution swept away the fragile structure of the party's Constitution and leadership. This structure was designed to depend on personal authority and could function only when Mao personally endorsed it.[3] As soon as Mao withdrew his support and attempted to create a replacement composed of his loyal followers from the lower local levels of the administrators, the party, as well as the entire government, fell apart because they were codependent and essentially one and the same.

Mao utilised ambiguous language and shifting policies to maintain his position as supreme legislator. As long as the words and their connotations of the chairman required clarification and redefinition, Mao's mouth, as well as his written words, had to remain the premier fountain of the law. This ambiguity did not only give him the freedom to change his position whenever he chose but was also used to conceal his real political intentions. The majority of the CCP's leaders, who had made a career out of figuring out what Mao intended to mean and what he actually wanted from each of his ambiguous and two-dimensional instructions, were led to believe and constantly hoped that they might be able to persuade Mao to both change his mind and be won over by the majority. During the first decade of the republic, Mao had left the impression that he could be persuaded by the pressure of the collective leadership and party consensus.

Mao Zedong surprised them again when he appeared in person and announced his policy of the Cultural Revolution. He spoke directly to the Red Guard, his new and favourite political instrument. They had neither concept of law nor respect for anyone else except Mao, the "red sun" in their hearts. With only a few words, Mao destroyed the entire legal and political establishment of China. With Mao's red book in their hands, the Red Guard became the organised mob that would dispose (*xiao mie*) of anything Mao desired and murder anyone with or without their leader's permission.[4]

With his voice and public recitation of his words, Mao announced his new plan to create a lawless state. He became the legislator of a non-law society and the god of nonreligious believers. The revolution appeared to be a super democracy (or anarchy, depending on the definition) involving populace in all walks and stages of life. It was created by a modern emperor who vowed to defeat his court, the ruling majority of the CCP, which he believed had adopted a disloyal and revisionist attitude.[5] In this new legislative attempt, Mao decided to establish a new order by simply announcing the law himself and distancing his supreme authority from his detractors.

Mao's law did not work as well as he had hoped. The revolution did not conclude with a new order; rather, it pushed China onto the edge of a civil war. It failed to work, not because of the loyalty or lack of it from his followers, but because the ambiguity of Mao's words had created an increasing gap between his words and their connotations, as well as between his divine law and its various perceivable interpretations. They were not specific and had lost their precision. They became solely dependent to Mao's voice for meaning, direction, and effect. The conceptual distance that Mao created to pursue his political goal extended much further than he had anticipated. As Mao took power from his newly proclaimed law, the ambiguous nature of these words lost their precise meanings. Furthermore, they had no meaning at all without his immediate clarification of the specific connotation that he intended. He eventually lost control of how much distance his own words would travel and what they would do; he lost control of those who claimed to be his disciples and yet pursued their own agendas in the name of his words. By the end of the Cultural Revolution, the crusade had lost its godhead. Mao's words, divine and mighty as they might be, had lost meaning and had become an imperial seal that could be used to justify rather than sanction political actions of various kinds. At the end of Mao's life, he must have felt that people wanted him to die sooner, so they could use and abuse his words more freely. But by then, his mighty words would have lost their original voice, intent, and meaning.

When the Cultural Revolution began, many in the CCP, including high-ranking officers who had been through war and repeated rectification movements during the past decades, did not comprehend its shifting directions. Many more could not have anticipated that young people— sometimes even their own children, lacking of life experiences but emotionally charged—would be willingly recruited as frontline militia for the cause. Worst of all, Mao, who appeared to be a champion of party democracy, certainly stopped communicating with the Politburo, whom he believed had betrayed him. He made his real or pretended intentions known only by his inner circle of extremely left individuals (his inner court, so to speak) leaving the rest of the party veterans living in constant fear. The government administration at all levels was under attack, and the entire state system panicked and became paralysed.[6]

To dismantle the entire system led by Liu Shaoqi, Mao Zedong concentrated his efforts on the administration of Beijing. From April 9 to 12, 1966, the Party Central Secretariat held meetings, during which Kang Sheng (a member of Mao's super-left circle) conveyed the content of the several conversations Mao had with him at the end of March and listed for criticism the series of mistakes committed by Peng Zhen, the mayor of Beijing.[7] The editor in chief of *Red Flag*, Chen Boda (another member of Mao's inner court), exposed and criticised Peng Zhen's series of crimes in the arena of political actions from the democratic revolution to the time of the Socialist revolution.[8] As the result of these meetings, a circular was created that thoroughly criticised the mistakes of the "February Outline of the Five-Person Group". They established a Documents Drafting Group for the Cultural Revolution and reported to Mao Zedong and the Standing Committee of the Politburo for approval.

From April 16 to 26, Mao chaired the enlarged meeting of the Standing Committee of the Politburo and unreservedly criticised the "anti-party crimes" of Peng Zhen. The committee made a decision to abrogate the "February Outline of the Five-Person Group", to dismantle the Five-Person Cultural Revolution Small Group, and to organise a new Cultural

Revolution Small Group. Mao Zedong also repeatedly and severely criticised Peng Zhen:

> [The Beijing mayor] cannot be penetrated even with a needle and is impervious to one drop of water. Peng Zhen wants to reform the Party with his own worldview, when in reality things develop in just the opposite way. He has prepared the conditions for his own downfall. Not everyone learns from the lessons of history. Such is the law of class struggle, not to be swayed by the will of ordinary people. We must call on various regions to oppose whoever makes a disturbance at the Central.[9]

On May 1, during the annual celebration of International Labour Day, Peng Zhen did not make public appearances. His descent marked the first signpost of the Cultural Revolution and the ensuing administrational shuffling. From May 4 to 26, the enlarged sessions of the Politburo of the Chinese Communist Party convened. Liu Shaoqi chaired the meetings as Mao was away from the capital; Kang Shoeing was responsible for reporting to Mao. The main subject of these meetings was the exposure and discussion of the question of the "antiparty gang plot" of Peng Zhen, Lou Ruining, Lou Dingy, and Yang Shangkun.[10] Yang Shangkun was the first to be attacked. At the time, Yang, the director of the Central Office of the Party, was accused of the crime of setting up listening devices behind the back of the Party Central Committee. In fact, tape-recording the formal speeches and conversations of the top leaders had been an established custom and was approved by the Central Committee and by Mao himself.

The next target of the Cultural Revolution was Luo Ruiqing, the chief of the General Staff of the People's Liberation Army who was in charge of the daily work of the Central Military Commission. The attack on Lu Dingyi, the head of the Party Propaganda Department, followed soon after. Lu's attacker claimed that Lu did not publicise Mao Zedong Thought with enough zest and efficiency. They accused him of the crime of being the behind-the-scenes manipulator of counterrevolutionary anonymous letters. Peng Zhen, a member of the Party Central Secretariat and first secretary of the Beijing Party Committee, was the only "predictable" target because of his public disagreement with Mao Zedong as a result of Mao initiating a campaign to criticise Peng's deputy mayor, Wu Han. Peng Zhen was charged with the crime of building an independent kingdom within the party.

The enlarged meetings of the Politburo insisted on a conspiracy of the four and charged them with organising an antiparty gang. For Yang Shangkun, there was the added crime of leaking large amounts of classified intelligence; it was also said that his relationship with the likes of Luo Ruiqing was out of the ordinary. Lin Biao, who had been suspicious of Luo's intention to override him, made special efforts during the meetings to exaggerate the "reactionary nature" of the so-called Peng-Lu-Luo-Yang Gang.[11]

These accusations were aimed at the entire state and party establishment. The people who were under attack were, at the time, in charge of key mechanisms of the state, of political and military authorities, and of the command post of ideological lines. They were accused of engaging in systematic dissention and disorder. Luo Ruiqing was in charge of military power. Peng Zhen seized much power with his role in the Party Central Secretariat. Lu Dingyi was the commander of the cultural and intellectual fronts. Yang Shangkun specialised in classified information, intelligence, and communication. These administrators were believed to work under a certain kind of conspiracy to overthrow Mao's leadership. In this assumed coup, they appeared to seize control of two vital components: The first was public affairs agencies—newspapers, broadcasting stations, writers, the cinema, publishers—all of which engaged in intellectual work. The capitalist class in its subversive activities also began with intellectual work, confusing the thought of the people first. The second was the military, to seize the weapons. Thus, the civil and the military complemented one another—the one harnessing the media, the other grabbing the gun barrel—and together they could engage in counterrevolutionary actions. With votes occurring when needed and armies ready to attack when called for, this group could achieve anything—a political coup in a meeting or a military coup on a battlefield.[12]

From this point on, anything could be linked to class struggle or opposition to Mao and his thought. History, as well as life itself, became highly magnified and exaggerated. Anyone's action could be reimagined and fabricated by distortion, insinuation, and false accusation. Within this highly agitated environment based on adversarial language and extreme reasoning, any friendship, as well as any professional or social association, could be interpreted as some sort of antiparty gang or counterrevolutionary organisation.[13] Revolution of this sort was a game whose goal and target had already been set, while only moral justification needed to be found (or fabricated). Extreme language and adversarial reasoning provided the means to create this justification.

Wu Han, the deputy mayor of Beijing, a writer and historian who wrote a historic play by party commission, was accused of attacking Mao Zedong and attempting to reverse the verdict of Peng Dehai's case. He was kicked around like a football, with the schools and various other activist units of Beijing taking turns to try him in public meetings. His home was ransacked, and he was severely beaten. In 1968 he was accused of being a traitor and was arrested. After undergoing unrelenting tribulation in jail, he took his own life.[14] Like Wu Han, many intellectuals were scandalised, imprisoned, tortured, and murdered. Many burned all of their writings to remove any potential evidence (or excuse) for political abuse and personal harm.

Mao's ultimate target was Liu Shaoqi; however, he had to find a legitimate way to dismantle Liu because Liu had been the president of the People's Republic of China for the past eight years. To crush Liu Shaoqi would require removing a large number of high-ranking officials who had been loyal to Liu for years. Most importantly, Mao would need a majority vote to remove each and every one of them from the Party Central Committee. Mao had to cultivate a highly intricate strategy to attack and bury one while keeping the rest in good faith and in line, so that his remaining opponents would not form a unified front against him. This separation, which was the oldest strategy to challenge a majority, had to be perceived as uncalculating and benevolent on a personal level. Mao needed to make every member of the Party Committee believe that if he sided with him in this purge of attacking others, or at least did not oppose the attack, that he would be spared scrutiny and become trusted again.

Mao utilised two main corporators to initiate his organised chaos, each of which had a distinct function: One was in charge of the cultural and media front, while the other was in charge of utilising the army. The former disturbed and dissented against the establishment, and agitated the general populace to attack specific targets, while the latter stabilised and excised control if things got out of hand. Mao began construction of his inner court with a few members of the Central Committee who were sympathetic towards the Cultural Revolution. Mao also handpicked several administrators from local and lower levels of administration for their support for his ultra-left policies. Mao called this new organisation (inner court within the court) the Small Group of Cultural Revolution in the Central Committee. According to the party's Constitution, this was an illegal organisation—as it was conferred power outside of the Central Committee—but was nonetheless granted an authority and a status that were equal or even higher than those of the Committee.[15]

The Red Guard was a political instrument created by Mao's desire to break all of the established laws, both legal and moral, within the Chinese society. Red Guard members were running about smashing everything that was old, beautiful, Western, or historic, and they were swearing to completely upset the status quo. During the summer of 1967, the Cultural Revolution was spreading like wildfire and factional strife was intensifying. It became a convenient ploy to fabricate cases of class revenge and to organise political campaigns for individual benefit. To destroy someone, it was only necessary to label him as a landlord, rich peasant, counterrevolutionary, bad element, and/or rightist. Any ordinary organisation could set up its own "Supreme Court of the Revolution" and pronounce illegal sentences upon those whom it considered as an enemy or a threat to the revolutionary cause. Gradually, the circle of victims of the revolutionary mob included more and more party members, Youth League members, poor and lower middle-class peasants, and demobilised soldiers. There were many methods of execution, including hacking by sword and beating with a rifle. People were burned to death, buried alive, drowned, and strangled. Among the cruellest tortures were chopping off heads, gouging out eyes, cutting off ears and noses, cutting open stomachs, slicing off breasts, and breaking limbs. Thousands of people were executed without a legal court or trial.[16]

Mao was not personally worried about this lawless disorder because he had delegated to Lin Biao, his handpicked successor, the responsibility of leading the army of millions, while he observed the revolutionary destruction. The movement of Red Guard activities stopped as swiftly as it had begun as soon as their historic function was achieved. Mao sent the entire generation of youth to the countryside where they were supposed to be educated by the communes' peasants rather than counter-revolutionary professors. Young people were instructed by Mao to serve the revolutionary cause without independent thought, like a soldier in the army, a small piece in the machine of the revolution.

With calculated ambiguity, Mao's words directed when, where, and how his armies of words and military forces function—to attack, to march, to restrain, or to retreat. The army of words was composed by his loyal intellectuals who attacked anyone or anything that Mao had named, or even hinted or gestured at, as insight. They not only read Mao's actual words but also skillfully reinterpreted them where necessary to exhibit the depth of their personal loyalty to Chairman Mao's ideas. During the revolutionary chaos, military control was a traditional form of transition between two civilian governments and between two forms of laws.

Mao's grand strategy of chaos determined the fates of the stars of the Cultural Revolution: when and how much to let them to shine, and when to shoot them down. The various fates of the high-ranking officials of the CCP illustrate Mao's strategy of deception and manipulation through his autocratic (or manufactured) democracy and illegal (non-collective) legislation.

There were mainly four types of victims of Mao's political game: the blind, the brave, the flexible, and the opportunist. The first type of officials often were outspoken and yet were deceived. They saw neither the connection between their personal misfortunes within the larger political context nor the hands behind it. They failed to recognise what was intended and what was coming next, and they failed to find the discrepancies between what Mao said and what Mao actually did. Although they openly disagreed with Mao, they still had faith in his role as a leader who could make mistakes and who would change his mind through persuasion if they remained and proved to be loyal to him. Identifying with the righteous course of revolution and Mao's charisma, they believed in this persona, which he had created for his own political gain.

Peng Dehuai, who had the purest heart and the noblest intentions, was the earliest example of the loyal and the blind.[17] After Peng was attacked and removed from his post during the Lushan Conference, he kept his faith in Mao and asked for the opportunity to continue working for the party. His wish was granted. At the end of the Cultural Revolution, Peng was still hoping that Mao would change his mind and revoke his antiparty verdict.

During the revolution, Peng was diagnosed with advanced colon cancer. His relatives were now allowed to visit him. After the direct intervention of Zhou Enlai, the hospital operated and the condition was relieved for a short while. Then, Peng's left side became paralysed and he could not sit up. In November 1973, half a year after the operation, it was discovered that the cancerous cells had spread because of neglect and error during the cure. After the summer of 1974, Peng's condition turned critical. The cancer had spread to his lungs and brain, causing excruciating pain. Under instruction of the ruling lefts, the hospital refused to give any painkillers to him, yet Peng fought the disease with lofty faith. Under this condition, Peng repeatedly said the following: "I have never feared death. My case is not cleared yet. I want to live; I want to see Chairman Mao...History is impartial,...it will evaluate me accurately." From October on, he lapsed into frequent comas. During his few lucid moments, he would shout loudly, "I have not opposed Chairman Mao! I have not colluded with foreign countries!"[18]

Tao Zhu had a similar faith in Mao's persona.[19] In early November 1966 Tao did not know that Mao himself was behind the campaign against Liu Shaoqi and Deng Xiaoping. When he saw a number of posters against Liu Shaoqi and Deng Xiaoping, Tao spoke his mind, without careful thinking, that he did not approve of the way that the Red Guard treated Liu. He stated that he believed that it was wrong to either call Liu an enemy or promote Liu's downfall. He reminded them that Liu was still the president of the country, a standing member of the Politburo—Tao noted that Liu might have made some mistakes, but he should be treated justly and gently.

Tao Zhu's words upset the students, and they refocused their attention to Tao, calling him an "emperor protector". They swarmed along the streets near the Central Propaganda Ministry with posters that accused Tao of opposing the party, Socialism, and Mao Zedong Thought. Tao did not realise or even sense the connection between the action of students and the leftist gangs in the Central Committee headed by Jiang Qing and supported by Mao himself. Tao worked on as usual, labouring diligently night and day.

Tao did not know that a plot to attack him was in the making. On December 20, 1966, Qi Benyu, a writer and member of Mao's inner court, published a letter that circulated among mass organisations telling them that it was all right to mention Tao Zhu in big-character posters and to attack him. In fact, Tao was one of the direct leaders above Qi Benyu. Moreover, Tao did not know the content of the letter, and even afterwards he did not realise what it really meant. With Qi's attack behind his back, Tao's situation was worsening very quickly.

To keep Tao in the dark, Mao expressed his sympathy to Tao. At the expanded meeting of the Standing Committee of the Politburo, Mao commented that Tao Zhu had been working very diligently and responsibly. Mao even openly criticised Jiang Qing for being too harsh and temperamental. Mao suggested that it was against party rules to freely criticise someone like Tao, a standing member of the Politburo whose supposed error in direction and line had not even been formally discussed by the Central Committee. To keep Tao on his side, Mao even asked Tao to stay behind and spoke with him in person for more than an hour, which was an important favourable gesture. Once again, Mao criticised Jiang Qing, saying that she was narrow-minded and not accommodating of others, and asked Tao Zhu not to take her words and actions too much to heart.

Tao was overjoyed, thinking the problem concerning him was not so serious after all and that he had the blessing of Chairman Mao.

Ten days later, however, the representatives of mass organisation demanded that Tao Zhu see them immediately, threatening to fast if he failed to do so. Tao Zhu, already confused by their attitude towards him, complied reluctantly. The minute that Tao appeared, the organisation commanded that Tao answer their questions. That night, under hostile questioning, Tao became angry and protested loudly against the members of the organisation that intended on seizing him. On December 31, some ninety Party Central Propaganda Department Red Guard members released their big-character poster titled "Tao Zhu Is Practising the Liu-Deng Capitalist Reactionary Line", which detailed Tao's transgressions at the ministry.[20]

On January 1, 1967, a joint editorial of the *People's Daily* and *Red Flag*, "Carry the Proletarian Cultural Revolution to the End", pointed out that 1967 should be the year to open a frontal attack on the small group of capitalists wielding power within the party (*dangnei zou zibenzhuyi daolu dang quanpai*).[21] Encouraged by the editorial, several hundred thousand people from more than twenty institutions of higher learning in Beijing gathered at Tiananmen Square for a "Denounce Liu Shaoqi and Deng Xiaoping" parade meeting. A "Letter to the People of the City" was read, as well as a list of the twenty great crimes of Liu Shaoqi. The publicity network that would eventually topple Liu and Deng had been established. Plans for Tao Zhu's demise were being formulated as well.[22]

On January 2, 1967, the *People's Daily* carried Yao Wenyuan's article "Criticising the Reactionary Two-Faced Zhou Yang". Though the article was aimed at Zhou Yang, the timing of its appearance showed it to be a refractive device for criticising Tao Zhu. Using popular double meanings such as "it is imperative to recognise two-faced types", the article made it clear that far more important people than the "two-faced" Zhou Yang were yet to be ferreted out. On the same day, certain units in Beijing convened a Liaison Committee for Criticising the New Representative of the Liu-Deng Line, Tao Zhu, and infiltrated the Party Central Propaganda Department by setting up a committee office there. Slogans of

"Down with Tao Zhu" and "Tao Zhu is China's biggest royalist (emperor protector)" appeared everywhere in the Propaganda Department.[23]

Chen Boda also pointed out that Tao Zhu did not carry out the proletarian revolutionary line represented by Chairman Mao. He was, in actuality, the faithful follower of the Liu-Deng line. He was an advisor of the Central Small Group, but he had never consulted with the extreme left, who were in charge of the revolution and sought to negate the Central Committee.

On the night of January 4, 1967, the "Down with Tao Zhu" slogan spread by radio to all parts of China, followed in its wake by slogans and pamphlets carrying the same message as well as the various commentary made during the reception of the rebel troops. A crowd of more than three thousand people representing about thirty organisations rushed towards the Ministry of Propaganda to "grab and struggle with" Tao Zhu.[24]

From this point on, Tao Zhu (along with Liu Shaoqi and Deng Xiaoping) was considered to be one of the primary targets of the Cultural Revolution. Liu-Deng-Tao criticism took place in all organisations and groups around the country. Tao Zhu became labeled not only as a traitor, but as a focal point of all the incorrect thoughts. For publicity reasons, pictures of Liu Shaoqi and Deng Xiaoping were run during the reporting of the decisions of the Eleventh Plenum of the Eighth Party Congress. This became one of the crimes of Tao Zhu. The following are other crimes attributed to him: To maintain standards of China's athletes, he had voiced Rong Gaotang's three proposals for maintaining training periods for athletes during the Cultural Revolution, and he had asked the Ministry of Public Health to keep up with its good work. He had authorised the Ministry of Propaganda to continue sale of Liu Shaoqi's book *On the Cultivation of Communists*, which was considered evidence for Tao's crime of shielding Liu Shaoqi. All in all, Tao's every action in connection with the Cultural Revolution was deemed wrong.

Some members of the Central Small Group manipulated public sentiment. For instance, Jiang Qing and Chen Boda in particular received workers from the Xinhua News Agency, telling them that Tao Zhu had previously fabricated a photograph showing Mao Zedong and Liu Shaoqi together and that, with provincial and municipal press coverage, the photograph created deleterious influences. The anti–Tao Zhu efforts had become so pervasive that the time had come for Mao to make known his own views.[25]

On January 8, 1967, the Party Central Committee called an emergency meeting to discuss the Tao Zhu situation. Mao changed his tone completely; now he said that the Tao Zhu issue was serious. Tao Zhu had been introduced to the Central Committee by Deng Xiaoping. Mao also discussed his "initial feelings" about Tao Zhu. He told the party that he thought Tao was dishonest. Deng Xiaoping, however, had vouched for Tao Zhu. Prior to the Eleventh Plenum, Tao Zhu had resolutely carried the Liu-Deng line.

Liu Shaoqi was the best example of a brave victim of Mao Zedong's purge who refused to admit to the crimes of which he was accused—and of which he did not, in fact, commit—during the Cultural Revolution. The brave opponents often encountered the most cruel and severe treatment during Mao's political purge. Most of these people killed themselves rather than surrender; but Liu Shaoqi had decided to live on and to fight to the end. After repeated torture and physical abuse by the Red Guard, Liu still resisted, insisting that he had never opposed Mao Zedong Thought, although he might have at times disobeyed it. He had never opposed Chairman Mao, although he might have disagreed with him over details. He also insisted that he was the elected president of the country and that he had his constitutional rights.[26]

However, without a real law, there were no rights even for the president of the state. Once the Red Guard had the permission to invade Liu's private residence, to separate him and his family, and to threaten to arrest his wife, Liu asked to meet with Mao Zedong. Within a week, Mao agreed to see Liu for a conversation. Mao's first words were very personal. He asked how Liu's daughter was doing. Liu's daughter had recently had an accident and was recovering in the hospital. Mao was always sincere, gentle, and considerate in personal dealings with his victims, as if he was trying to smooth over the bad feelings and almost as if there was nothing unhappy between them.

Unlike Peng and Tao, Liu did not take Mao at face value. He did not beg for acceptance or take solace in Mao's apparent personal concern. Liu admitted that he had made some mistakes and that he was willing to take sole responsibility for transgressing the revolutionary line. He offered to resign the presidency, his membership on the Standing Committee of the Party Central Committee, and his directorship of the editorial committee of the Selected Works of Mao Zedong. He said that he was willing to retire with his wife and children to farm the land and become an ordinary citizen. Liu's words sent Mao into a ponderous, chain-smoking silence.[27] Mao hated the idea of allowing his opponent to resign; he could not quit—the party had to expel him and claim righteous victory!

Mao realised that Liu was not going to back down like so many of his previous victims. Liu refused to be seen as a live target and sacrificial loser. During the upcoming Ninth Party Congress, Mao decided to place Liu in solitary detention. Liu did not know that on September 13, 1967, his children would be driven out of the presidential residence and his wife would be arrested, jailed, and tortured.

However, to legitimately dismiss Liu Shaoqi, the party, now controlled by Mao's extremists, needed evidence to convict Liu for his accused crimes. In an attempt to obtain evidence that Liu Shaoqi had defected after being arrested in 1927, they detained Ding Juequn, who had worked underground for the party with Liu Shaoqi forty years earlier, and pressed him to confess. On September 3, 1967, Ding Juequn could not provide any incriminating material against Liu Shaoqi. He admitted that Liu Shaoqi worked in the provincial labour union and that he worked in the municipal party office. They had no special relation except for their working relationship. He could not lie about a man who was still alive, and he had to tell the truth of the matter. This useless confession was far from the evidence Jiang Qing and her cohorts had hoped for. Swearing to not stop until they reached their goal, Jiang Qing and her cohorts used every horrible measure to compel Ding Juequn to finally comment against his will. The following day, he recanted and stated that none of what he had said was true. He had lied while he was threatened.

On September 25, Ding Juequn wrote a letter, directed especially towards those who interrogated him, claiming that his statement had no regard at all for the truth. He wrote it only for the sake of completely criticising Liu Shaoqi. Even such evidence that had no regard at all for the truth was treasured highly by Jiang Qing and the others as ammunition with which to bombard Liu Shaoqi.

In 1929, during a textile strike, Meng Yongqian and Liu Shaoqi had been detained at the police station. Because nothing was found relating them directly to the strike, they were released on bail. It was impossible that they were turncoats under arrest or had anything to do with traitors or labour thieves. However, Jiang Qing and the others still wanted to use Meng Yongqian as a witness to prove that Liu Shaoqi was a turncoat and traitor. Meng Yongqian was isolated for interrogation. A month passed, and Meng Yongqian confessed nothing. Kang Sheng then ordered the interrogators to continue and keep pushing Meng in a small-scale meeting of criticising to make him submit.

Xiao Meng, the head of the Liu Shaoqi and Wang Guangmei Special Investigative Committee, recounted that ten of the investigators interrogated Meng around the clock for the entire day without a break. They surrounded him, talking to him all at once and threatening and intimidating him. After they did everything they could to bring pressure on him, Meng Yongqian still refused to confess. After being interrogated this way for seven days in a row, Meng finally, against his will, admitted that he and Liu had betrayed the party while under arrest.

However, Meng Yongqian soon recanted his confession and wrote several statements to explain that he had fabricated all of those utterly groundless confessions. These retractions were withheld and never reported by the investigation committee, who desperately needed the evidence even if the evidence was known to be incorrect. The Special Investigative Committee forced Meng Yongqian to tear up five of his retractions on the spot and threatened that if he made any more comments on the facts surrounding the 1929 betrayal, he would be punished as an active counterrevolutionary.

While the party busied itself "discovering" (rather, manufacturing) evidence against Liu Shaoqi in 1968, he suddenly developed a high fever. And due to belated medical attention, he contracted pneumonia and was near death. The person in charge at the Party Central General Office at the time informed the medical staff that because the Central Committee was about to hold a meeting on Liu Shaoqi, they could not let him die. Liu needed to be alive when the party expelled him. He had to be a living target during the Ninth Congress! Thus, doctors were dispatched to save him. When the doctor told the authority that Liu had to be hospitalised, permission was not granted. The doctor suggested removal of the posters and slogans hanging in his room to reduce psychological agitation, but once again permission was denied.

Liu recovered, but he had become too weak to get out of bed. He was haggard and thin, and his hair and beard were long and unkempt. No one washed or changed his clothes; no one helped him with toilet activities. His leg muscles had atrophied from his long periods of being bedridden. His body was covered with bedsores. In such a helpless state, Liu was still watched day and night by guards observing renewed vigilance for fear of suicidal actions. They even tied down one of his legs tightly with gauze strips to keep him in place.

From October 10 to 30, 1968, the Twelfth Plenum of the Eighth Party Congress was held in Beijing. Among the Central Committee members and their alternates, those who were branded as traitors, spies, associates with foreign countries, and party renegades numbered over 70 percent of the total and were denied the right to attend the plenum. Of the ninety-seven Central Committee members of the Eighth Congress, only forty could now attend the Twelfth Plenum. If these members were allowed to attend the meeting constitutionally, Mao Zedong and his left-wing followers would have been in the minority. However, it would defeat the very purpose of the revolution aimed at attacking the majority by dismissing the established constitution. The revolution eliminated more than half of the committee members, and the total number (forty) of members who were allowed to attend the Plenum did not even qualify as a quorum for any resolution. Nevertheless, the plenum was held, resolutions were adopted, and alternative members were elected. Mao Zedong again ignored the Constitution, which stated that whenever there are vacancies in membership, the Central Committee Alternates Committee will fill them subsequently. He created an artificial majority by selecting ten alternate members from among those who supported his Cultural Revolution. Mao manufactured his majority to pass his own resolutions.[28]

The purpose of the Twelfth Plenum was to prepare for the convening of the Ninth Party Congress and to resolve the expulsion of Liu Shaoqi from the party. Mao chaired the meetings, and on the question of the Cultural Revolution, he said, "This Great Proletarian Cultural Revolution is entirely necessary and extraordinarily timely in fortifying the dictatorship of the proletariat, preventing the restoration of capitalism, and building socialism".[29] To reduce opportunity for sudden opposition during the meetings, small groups were formed and each was instructed to make concerted efforts to attack the principals of the February Adverse Current—Chen Yi, Ye Jianying, Li Fuchun, Li Xiannian, Xu Xiangqian, and Nie Rongzhen.

Mao's fear was not unfounded. Many Central Committee members were determined to fight. As Tan Zhenlin had once put it, "I will struggle to the end, whether it means getting beheaded, jailed, or expelled from the Party".[30] Mao successfully silenced the expected opposition by simply denying their rights to attend the Congress. To block the influence of other important party figures, the plenum also criticised the usually right-leaning Zhu De, Chen Yun, and Deng Zihui.

The Twelfth Plenum of the Eighth Congress had one important agenda: the matter of Liu Shaoqi. Entitled *An Investigative Report on the Crimes of the Traitor, Spy, and Renegade Liu Shaoqi*, the report was the work of the Central Special Cases Investigative Group controlled by Jiang Qing, Kang Sheng, and Xie Fuzhi. It had been completed after many brutal acts to extract information, and it highlighted confessions under duress, quantities of fabricated evidence, and deliberate contrivances of accusatory materials. Within this mass of material, there was not a single word to suggest Liu Shaoqi's innocence before proof of his guilt. Because of the special conditions whereby selected existing Central Committee members were excluded from attending and those who did attend risked vilification and criticism, when the investigative report was passed and Liu Shaoqi was "permanently expelled" from the party, no one reacted. All were criticised in turn for this lack of reaction and were forced to agree with the report. The meetings followed majority rule, which approved the report and the permanent expulsion of Liu Shaoqi from the Communist Party.[31]

Zhou Enlai was the most prominent Chinese leader who adopted a flexible strategy against Mao's policy of the Cultural Revolution while apparently following the chairman's instructions. To remain politically influential and maintain a position to deter violence and abuse, Zhou said many things that were contrary to his own convictions, but at the same time, he attempted to save his colleagues who were completely stripped of their constitutional rights. Zhou's survival strategy was to demonstrate constant agreement (or at least avoid conflict) with Mao's policy and utilise his superb ability to self-criticise and apologise if he was challenged by Mao's extreme followers.

In September 1966 Zhou openly endorsed the Cultural Revolution and pledged to support Mao.[32] As he waved the red book of Chairman Mao in his hands, he risked constant challenge and self-incrimination. But he did everything in his power to limit the damage that it was done to the country and its innocent citizens.

Zhou was a superb diplomat and had the extraordinary ability to defuse difficult situations and offer satisfactory compromising solutions.[33] At one time, some of the Red Guard discovered that there was a problem with the traffic lights. Red, the colour of revolution, meant stop and hence served to obstruct the progress of the movement! They pointed out that this was nothing less than blasphemy.[34] Another colour was needed. At the height of the revolutionary fever when members of the Red Guard were the angels sent by their god (Mao), no one dared to stand against them and deny this absurd and ignorant demand. Fortunately, Zhou was able to prevent a logistical disaster by engaging the Red Guard in a rather humorous discussion.

When a few self-appointed "most revolutionary" members of the Red Guard suggested changing the colour of traffic lights, Zhou responded,

> I already heard about this suggestion a few days ago, and I really envy your excellent revolutionary spirit. I went to ask my driver and some other comrades, and they told me that the distinguishing feature of the red light is that no matter if it is day or night, clear or foggy, it can be seen from afar. The green and yellow lights are not like that, and under certain conditions they are not very visible. It is precisely for this reason that, all over the world, the red light is used as a stop sign: to ensure the safety of drivers by reducing the risk of a collision.[35]

Zhou paused briefly and went on: "Can we agree on the following, that the red light is the light of revolution that guarantees the safety of all revolutionary activities?"

"Agreed!" The Red Guard members were convinced.

Zhou continued, "So it is okay for me to say that continued use of red as a stop sign is meant to guarantee the safety of the revolutionary activities."

The strategy of Zhou under Mao's shadow was to be diplomatic and to surrender to his wishes rather than challenge him. First, by displaying unconditional loyalty, Zhou had never given Mao an impression or excuse of suspicion that he was a threat to Mao's dominance. Second, Zhou cut ties with anyone who Mao was attacking and sided with Mao regardless of his personal opinions and feelings. After assuring Mao and his newly promoted left-wing leaders that he appeared to support the chairman and the policies of the Cultural Revolution, Zhou would work quietly and personally, and he attempted to both modify Mao's extreme policies and minimise their damaging consequences.[36] With his shrewd strategy (comparable to that of Mao Zedong in depth and vision), Zhou became the only officer whom Jiang Qing had wished to expel from office during the Cultural Revolution but had failed to do so.

Zhou was busy stabilising the overall situation and defending the safety of the other "convicted" administrators. For example, when members of the Red Guard stormed Zhongnanhai (the central office and residence of the central administrators) several times a day, shouting and threatening to nab Liu Shaoqi, Zhou had to come out to calm the crowd. He implored wave after wave of the Red Guard day and night to observe civility in their demonstrations. Once, when more than a hundred people came shouting and streaming through the front gate, Zhou rushed to the spot and said to them sternly, "Zhongnanhai is the home of the Party Central. It cannot be stormed. If you must storm, you'll have to step over my body!" On this occasion, Zhou's enormous prestige in the eyes of the people saved Liu from immediate harm.[37]

Mao's political shuffling during the Cultural Revolution created great career opportunities for many ambitious politicians who had been buried inside of a highly structured and seniority-based system. A rising star of the revolution needed to possess three distinct characteristics: First, he had to have good political instincts to predict the unpredictable—much like a good sailor, he had to know the direction of the wind and establish a plan to sail through it. Second, he needed to study and meditate on every letter of Mao's words and determine Mao's intention in each and every single moment. Third, he had to correctly clarify and specify what Mao's deliberate omissions and ambiguities were so that he could push Mao's idea to its ultimate limit. If someone possessed all three of these characteristics and was adept at predicting Mao's intended meaning, he would be considered loyal to the revolution.

It was always a risky business to read and predict Mao's intentions. As Mao often reinterpreted his own words to serve his strategic thinking and made unexpected personnel shuffling, his followers could suddenly find themselves in the wrong side of the policy, under close scrutiny of the Red Guard, or even became the sacrifice of an abandoned idea. For many, this swift change could jeopardise their careers and transform them overnight from a valued revolutionary to an antirevolutionary, and flip their life from heaven to hell.

During the 1967–1968 period, two power groups emerged from the chaos of the Cultural Revolution: Jiang Qing and the members of her Central Cultural Revolution Small Group (CCRSG), and Lin Biao and his generals. They both became instruments of Mao Zedong's strategy, as well as his scapegoats.[38]

Jiang Qing (Mao's wife) saw the Cultural Revolution as a surprising opportunity to realise her long-repressed political ambition. Jiang's political ambition was well-known in the inner circle of the CCP since the Yanan period when she pressured Mao and the party to accept her as first lady since she was pregnant with Mao's child. She married Mao Zedong (who was still married at the time) with the condition that she would never interfere with the politics of the party and the government. The Central Committee of CCP also ruled that Liu Shaoqi's wife, Wang Guangmei, would be the public hostess for the Republic of China. Jiang Qing loved the limelight and was deeply embittered by her enforced exclusion. She angrily resented Wang Guangmei and the collective leadership of the central committee that forced her into the shadows.[39]

During the next thirty years, she endured this nonpublic and quiet life while swallowing all of the humiliation and embarrassment that ensued from Mao's constant incidents of womanising. But she did not focus her anger and frustration on Mao, her god of salvation, but instead upon Mao's administrators who had set and insisted upon the limits of her political activity.

Mao Zedong had rarely taken Jiang more seriously than any of the many women who were attracted by or submitted to his charisma and power. Although a notorious womaniser, Mao had never let his personal relationships cloud his political judgement. He did what he did because he knew that he could get away with it. His social misbehaviour never jeopardised his position in the party and government. After all, Chinese emperors historically had thousands of women waiting to serve them in the palace. Why not the same for the chairman? Jiang never carried influence in Chinese politics in, before, or after the establishment of the republic because Mao did not allow it.[40]

During the Cultural Revolution, Mao allowed Jiang Qing to emerge because it served his purpose. No one had more passionate hatred towards Mao's colleagues and more enduring motivation to bring down Mao's administrators than Jiang Qing. She could stir and burn her enemies, and she was willing to destroy by any means—legal, illegal, moral, and immoral. Jiang's accomplishment on behalf of Mao during the Cultural Revolution proved that his calculations and expectations were accurate. Jiang Qing manipulated her association with Mao and rode the powerful wave for a ride that she had dreamed about for her entire life. Millions were affected by her actions.

Mao allowed Jiang Qing to reinvent herself into an important political figure when he decided to bring down the administrative establishment.[41] Jiang started the Cultural Revolution with a reinterpretation of the historical drama *Hai Rui Dismissed*. Hai Rui was a Ming officer who served the Jiajing Emperor, a cruel and unenlightened monarch. Hai Rui risked death by writing to his emperor about the corruption of the state and the hardship of the people. For this criticism of imperial rule, Hai Rui was dismissed and imprisoned. In 1959 the damage caused by the Great Leap Forward and the people's commune movements had angered most Chinese. The Party Central Committee met in Shanghai, and some participants were severely critical of the widespread fear of speaking the truth, and they promoted telling the truth about party policies and their consequences. Mao Zedong sensed the resentment and advocated learning from Hai Rui. The chairman spoke forthrightly, stating that many insincere and false statements had been the result of pressure from above and that one should learn from the spirit Hai Rui. Hai Rui had dared to speak the truth, but no Hai Rui existed in the CCP at the moment. During one of the meetings, Mao even told a Hai Rui story, saying that although Hai may have criticised the emperor, he was after all loyal to him. Later, Mao advised that one could learn from Hai Rue's unbending character and forthright courage to speak out. He directed historians to study the story of Hai Rui.

With Mao's blessing, Wu Han, a Ming history specialist, wrote and published an essay entitled *Hai Rui Upbraids the Emperor* (*Hai Rui ma huangdi*). More publications of the topic appeared and a few historic dramatisations were performed throughout the country. At the expanded working session of April 1962, Mao Zedong further urged everyone to speak out and conduct what he called a "Let's be frank" session (*chuqihui*), a general reflective discussion of the shortcomings and mistakes of party work since 1958. On June 16, 1962, Peng Dehuai wrote a letter of some eighty thousand words to Mao and the Party Central Committee, declaring that he had never organised any "antiparty clique" within the party, nor was he involved in collusion with foreign countries. He then requested the party organisation to examine his case thoroughly. During this more relaxed political atmosphere, when party administrators expressed their honest opinions, Mao realised how unpopular his policies were.

To maintain his absolute control of legislative power, Mao floated the issue of class struggle within the party during late September 1962. He spoke of the need to speak of class struggle every year, every month, and every day, and of the importance of identifying class struggle within the realm of ideology. To initiate an attack on the establishment from the realm of culture, Mao decided to let Jiang Qing and her extremely left-wing colleague act on his behalf. Jiang Qing attempted but failed to open up criticism against Wu Han in Beijing. She left secretly for Shanghai to look up Zhang Chunqiao, at that time the alternate secretary to the Shanghai Municipal Party and head of its Propaganda Department, to criticise Beijing's shortcomings from his post in Shanghai. In early 1965, with the support of the Shanghai Party secretary, Ke Qingshi, Zhang Chunqiao and Jiang decided that the essay should be written by Yao Wenyuan, a member of the editorial board of the Shanghai magazine *Liberation*. They also decided to keep the matter a secret from the Party Central Committee, especially Premier Zhou Enlai. Once the article was completed, Mao read it and sent Jiang Qing to Shanghai to publish it.[42]

In November 1965 Shanghai's *Wenhui Bao* prominently ran an article by Yao Wenyuan entitled "Criticising the New Historical Drama Hai Rui Dismissed from Office" (*Hai Rui baguan*), which announced the beginning of the ten-year Cultural Revolution.

On that day, Jiang Qing became an important member of Mao's inner court, whose mission was overthrow the administration led by Liu Shaoqi and destroy its key members politically as well as spiritually.

Her Central Small Group took the leadership of the Cultural Revolution and dismissed the entire legal and governmental system. The Central Small Group attacked, or encouraged attacks on, every single statesman or stateswoman in the CCP using illegal investigation, torture, interrogation, and false conviction.

Lin Biao was the rising star and beneficiary of the massive purge of the Cultural Revolution. Lin reached his powerful position by recognising an opportunity to advance his position and formed a shortcut to gain Mao's trust and respect. He promoted the public worship of the chairman's persona. Lin spoke of the divinity of Mao's words and ideas in order to discredit and bypass Liu Shaoqi, Zhou Enlai, and many others during the eight years following 1958. Wrapping himself within the flag of Mao Zedong Thought and waving the little red book of Mao's quotations, he leaped over his enemies and competitors and rose to the power position second only to that of Mao.[43]

Mao and Lin Biao first met in 1928 when Mao was withdrawing into his mountainous guerrilla retreat in Jinggangshan and Lin was a young officer in Zhu De's army. As commander of the First Army Column in the Jiangxi Soviet, Lin apparently became pessimistic about ultimate victory. In 1930 Mao sent his young friend a letter, which was later publicly released as "A Single Spark Can Start a Prairie Fire". During the Long March, Lin's health began to fail, and when they arrived in Yanan, Mao gave him a rest from active command of troops and made him the head of the Red Army Academy. At the outbreak of the war with Japan, Mao began to set Lin and Peng Dehuai against one another and deliberately slighted Lin by giving Peng command of the First Red Army. During the civil war, Lin commanded the victorious 4th Group Army (of a million soldiers), which had fought throughout the country during the civil war. It liberated large regions occupied by the Guomindang from North China to the most southern tip, Hainan Island. Mao, however, sent Peng Dehuai rather than Lin Biao to command Lin's troops in Korea and lead the Chinese army of volunteers. After this campaign, Peng was recognised as the ultimate hero of the armed forces. Lin Biao, in spite of impressive achievements, remained subordinated to Peng Dehuai. It was only at the

Eighth Plenum of the Eighth Central Committee in August 1959, during which Peng was finally purged, that Lin was made Minister of Defence and thus assumed command of the People's Liberation Army.[44]

So far, there was nothing very special about Lin Biao's progression, neither within the party nor his relationship with Mao. Mao had similar relationships with many of his subordinates. Lin rose swiftly only after he had expressed his unshakeable faith in Mao's leadership during the time that the chairman was facing a serious challenge from Peng Dehuai and many members of the Central Committee. Lin Biao seized the opportunity to split the top of the leadership and proposed the following: that all believe in the party and trust Chairman Mao, that only the Central Commitee and Chairman Mao were accurate, and that only Chairman Mao could claim to be a great hero. At a meeting of high commanders of the PLA, Lin Biao energetically promoted the cult of Mao. He announced that study of the writings of Comrade Mao Zedong was the most efficient way to learn the concepts of Marxism-Leninism and that the writings of Mao Zedong were easy to learn, and once learned could be put to use immediately.[45]

Lin Biao believed that his future depended upon Mao Zedong. After Mao was threatened by the challenge of Peng Dehuai and others in the party centre, he became impervious to criticism and suggestions, and favoured those who fawned on him. After a study of Mao's behaviour, Lin concluded that in order to gain the trust of Mao, he needed to both agree with Mao all of the time on all issues and keep a high posture of leaning to the left. He adopted Ye Qun's (his wife) advice: to curry favour above, one should always wear a slightly smiling face and should always be ready to respond, to extol, and to report good news. Lin developed a strategy to handle Mao. He believed that it was important to grasp Mao's live thought, place the things he wanted done on the daily agenda, and always come away from him with his requests and go to him with reports. In other words, a person had to meet every one of Mao's wishes to cultivate Mao's trust and thus create conditions for promotion.[46]

This outstanding plan that extolled the cult of Mao Zedong paid off handsomely for Lin's career, especially during the Cultural Revolution's storm of massive purge. He climbed quickly within the power ranking of the CCP and became the official successor of Mao Zedong.[47] However, Mao never completely trusted Lin. He was aware of Lin's ambition and his organisational activity in the armed forces, and he was wary that Lin could create his own following.[48]

By September 1970, the Mao-Lin conflict became public when Lin and his generals pressured Mao Zedong to agree upon their agenda. After Liu Shaoqi's death in 1969, Lin Biao was eyeing the position of president of the People's Republic. Mao thought otherwise. During his own presidency, Mao had suggested that Liu Shaoqi succeed him. Mao had not been pleased because Liu actually exercised his presidential power and challenged his authority. Now, Liu was gone. Mao did not want another Liu Shaoqi to share power with him at the top. In March 1970 Mao put his proposal for constitutional change on the agenda of the Fourth National People's Congress and suggested that no president be appointed for the state. No one dared contradict him after seeing what had happened to Liu Shaoqi. All expressed agreement with his suggestion of dispensing with the presidency. Lin Biao was dissatisfied about this decision, as it had destroyed his personal dream. In April 1970 Lin proposed that a president be named and that Mao be this president, which would have left Lin as successor. The next day, Mao decided that he could not take on this position again. Lin's suggestion was inappropriate.

Lin Biao did not agree with this ruling. On the eve of the Second Plenum of the Ninth Party Congress, which had the task of preparing the convening of the Fourth National People's Congress, Lin Biao and his generals attempted to use the plenum to reopen the case for a national presidency. In an intimate conversation between Ye Qun and Wu Faxian in July 1970, Ye complained about what was going to happen to Lin Biao if a national president was not set up. How he was going to be placed within the party structure? Meanwhile, Chen Boda, Huang Yongsheng, Ye Qun, Li Zuopeng, and Qiu Huizuo enthusiastically circulated remarks that Lin Biao was an uncommon genius, a revolutionary teacher and leader of the same rank as Marx, Engels, Lenin, and Stalin. In addition, as the litany went, the three great aides for Marx, Lenin, and Mao

Zedong were Engels, Stalin, and Lin Biao respectively; and Lin Biao was the most glorious aide of all. This media statement was intended to prepare for Lin Biao's seizure of the highest power. Mao reported to the Plenum of the Ninth Central Committee that seven military commanders, including Lin Biao, had launched a surprise attack on him by reversing Mao's order that the new state constitution should not include the office of head of state or state chairman.

Again, Mao deemed this incident to be a struggle between two headquarters, which was the same language that he had used to initiate the purge of Liu Shaoqi and his colleagues. By this time, Lin's usefulness as commander of the armed forces and as a gun to shoot Mao's opponents had ended. He was now Mao's target.

Many historians and political analysts have stated that Mao was oblivious of Lin's ambition and that this inner circle revolt had caught him by surprise. Nothing could be further from the truth. Mao was constantly wary of Lin but needed to wait for him to act. Mao now had the proof and justification that he needed and made Lin's indiscretion public: "First they concealed things, then they launched a surprise attack…They certainly had a purpose in doing all that." According to Mao, he had urged Lin and his gang six times that he did not want to establish a state chairman and he did not want to be the chairman. "My words aren't even worth a sentence; they aren't worth anything," Mao complained.[49] With these words, Mao signalled the beginning of the fall of Lin Biao.[50]

Like his wife and her colleagues, Mao used Lin as a tool to discredit and dismantle the administrators in the Liu camp.[51] The choice of Lin had less to do with his accomplishment for the party than with traditional function of the military in Chinese politics.[52] Chinese military plays an important yet temporary role when civilian government is weak or unstable. Mao knew from the beginning that he was creating a disorder to bring down the establishment; disorder was a means rather than an end for him. To establish an alternative order that would serve his political vision, law and order had to ultimately prevail. The army was extremely important for dealing with chaos. Knowing that his cultural avant-garde had a very limited social and institutional foundation in the government organisation, he needed military support, which would provide enough time to build a new regime and repress the possible reemergence of his opponents.[53]

The PLA played a leading role throughout the Cultural Revolution. With Lin Biao as military support, Mao was able to overrule the majority of the party leadership in 1966, turning the nation drastically to the left. Yet when the Maoist Red Guard tried to seize power from the party and government organisations in 1967, a majority of the local PLA collaborated with their civilian colleagues to suppress the young rebels in spite of Mao's personal blessings given to their revolutionary radicalism. Lin's appointment guaranteed a purge in the PLA in which the majority of commanders who supported Liu's administration were replaced by Lin's generals.[54]

Mao was in complete control as he allowed the power and influence of the army to expand. Lin's influence reached its peak during the Ninth Party Congress in 1969. His troops could establish and maintain stability and security during the organised disruptions. Although the PLA acquired substantial political status in the centre and in the provinces' popular campaigns, it did not directly challenge the political sovereignty of the party. In spite of his enormous status in the armed forces and in the party, Lin never attained the party's chairmanship. When Lin and his generals acted out against Mao, they themselves would soon be purged. The alleged coup never materialised. The struggle for domination between Mao and Lin ended when Lin perished as his military jet suspiciously crashed in Mongolia in 1971. His followers were subsequently purged, and the PLA was reorganised to root out Lin's influence.[55]

During this final struggle with Lin, the civilian administration, which had been severely criticised during the Cultural Revolution, supported Mao. It blamed Lin for the chaos. Zhou Enlai contributed a great deal to suppress Lin and his officers; even Jiang Qing remained at Mao's side. Mao miraculously survived another coup and never had the need to apologise for supporting Lin in the first place.[56]

With Lin gone, Mao could use him as a scapegoat for errors of the Cultural Revolution and for all the crimes that the fanatics had committed against the masses. At the funeral of Chen Yi, a marshal of China who was also a victim of the Cultural Revolution, Mao explained to the widow that Lin Biao had wanted to push out all of the senior officers, such as Chen. These words of Mao were passed to Chen's children. Mao made similar sympathetic remarks about many of the older administrators, including Deng Xiaoping, and rehabilitated them one after another making it possible for them to resume their respective offices.[57]

The Cultural Revolution finally concluded on October 6, 1976. For China, the movement remains a colossal catastrophe in which human rights, democracy, the rule of law, and civilisation itself were unprecedentedly violated. Tens of millions of innocent people, including many in high office, were attacked and maltreated. According to a Xinhua News Agency report, during the trial of Jiang Qing and others in November 1980, some 34,800 people were persecuted and killed. This figure is probably an extremely conservative estimate. The culture was devastated, and the economy almost collapsed. For ten years, republican politics based on the People's Congress system was virtually destroyed; instead, an autocratic system crowned by Socialism was erected.

During the Cultural Revolution, Mao Zedong controlled the legislative, judicial, and administrative powers; his quotations and all of his directives had the force of law. With this highly personal legislation, Mao could overwhelm and eventually defeat his majority colleagues by proclaiming new law and setting broad agenda.[58]

Mao's superb ability to control law, legal administration, and the entire political establishment lay in his exceptional gift of using and abusing the Chinese language. His powerful speech and poetic imagery overwhelmed and overruled written words. Unlike most Western and Chinese writers who hide behind their words and only dream of changing the world, Mao was an orator whose speech could agitate, motivate, and activate the minds as well as the hearts of millions. His omnipotent spoken words shook and destroyed the entire establishment based on written words, including those that he authored. Mao called the words of law and administrative language "crab" (*piwen*), and he was always confident that his moving rhetoric and vivid poetic imagery could erase meaningless paper words.

He was correct. The majority of Chinese people did not understood Marxist theories and legal philosophy, but they did respond to Mao's passionate call to express their grievances and misfortunes with officialdom, and speak bitterness (*suku*) against its officers to dismantle the establishment led by Liu Shaoqi. He had enlivened the Chinese political vocabulary with a host of vivid phrases; he spoke of the enemy as "man-harming vermin" (*haijen jing*), "monsters and freaks" (*niuguei sheshen*, lit., bull monsters and snake spirits), and "poisonous weeds" (*ducao*). With this name-calling, he orchestrated a public outcry and created a real continuous storm that was saturated with hatred and despisement to eliminate his enemies. To aggravate popular rage into a war that "bombarded the headquarters", Mao successfully transformed China into a political drama that physically removed the party majority.[59]

With his well-calculated and controlled aggression against the establishment, Mao enacted a new oral law, the law of Mao Zedong. It was a "by-me" law in which his words, ideas, and personality became the ultimate line that differentiated between legal and illegal, and between right and wrong. It became a religion with a speaking god and his bible. He was a god and a prophet who did not cease speaking until the moment that he died. He completely silenced all of the dissenting voices and killed all of his false deciphers before they could challenge him. However, as history has often illustrated, a godhead and a god's words could never rule and exist at the same time for very long. Man had to die and be remembered, reimagined, and worshipped as a god. When a man tried too hard and too early to become a subject of worship, he lost his very legitimacy to become divine.

This was exactly what happened to Mao Zedong. Exploring the ambiguity of language had won him the political battle against his opponents, but the repeated use and abuse of his words also worked against his will and capacity to control. He could burn all of the books and eliminate all of the thoughts from other people, and even murder those who dared to have independent ideas, but he failed to completely sanctify his own words. This failure had little to do with Mao Zedong as a thinker, writer, and legislator. Rather, the Chinese language and civilisation are too old, complex, and rustic to remain meaningless forever. Written words had long ago lost the magical power that was inherent and perceived in younger languages. The elasticity of Chinese language—which has survived countless repressions and manipulations, and gave enormous freedom to its speakers, writers, and thinkers—simply could not be nullified and monopolised by politics. Chinese civilisation has never worshipped words, human or divine, because its words alone have never been able to exercise arbitrary and controlling power without the mouth and hands of a living ruler. In the grander battles between politics and culture, and between control and freedom, the latter of each always has the last say.

The biggest tragedy of Mao's legacy was that after his death, his words lost their living power; they were repeated only under symbolic and ceremonial context. They lost not only their prestige but also their precise meanings and connotations after ten years of intensive reinterpretation and exploration by everyone, including Mao himself. Competitive use, reuse, and abuse quickly diluted Mao's highly original and distinct ideas. They eventually lost their intended meanings and binding power because they could be made to mean anything one would like them to mean, and they could justify any thought except that of Mao Zedong.

CHAPTER 6

LAW, UNDER LAW, AND ABOVE LAW IN CONTEMPORARY CHINA

The China of the last days of Mao Zedong was at the edge of civil war as its social order was barely held up by the dying ruler. Naturally, the Chinese politics unfolded in a dramatic manner after the death of Mao in September 1976. Hua Guofeng, a relatively junior member of the old hierarchy, became the new leader, arranged by Mao's instruction. Within a month after Mao's departure, Jing Qing, Zhang Chunqiao, Wang Hongwen, and Yao Wenyuan, the most powerful figures in Chinese politics during the Cultural Revolution, were deposed in a bloodless coup. They were renamed as antiparty gang of four by a coalition of the party's old guard supported by key military leaders.[1]

Without Mao Zedong, the new leadership was immediately confronted with the problem of a breakdown of social order in many provinces that resulted from frequent and unexpected policy and personnel change. Labour unrest as well as sabotage of production and transportation were widespread. Sometimes, armed conflicts between rival factions broke up and made tens of thousands of civilians lose their lives throughout the country. It took the new leader many months to deal with public chaos, and public order was not restored until mid-1977, after harsh security measures were adopted.[2]

However, inner-party disorder quickly took its turn as political discourse became chaotic and impossible to resolve after Mao's voice, which had been the only arbitrary directive for the past decade, was silenced. Although Hua Guofang insisted on a much more rigid interpretation and implication of Mao Zedong Thought, Mao's words were received very differently after he was gone. Everyone could put his words into Mao's mouth, and now Mao's words could be made to mean anything. No one could pronounce Mao's words with the same authority and effectiveness because no one had the same personal charisma that Mao did and no one in the party had the authority to pin down the assumed meanings of Mao's words. Without Mao Zedong in person, no one could demand the same total and blind acceptance of everything associated with Mao—not even Hua Guofeng, Mao's official successor.[3]

In order to establish an authority in the name of Mao and defeat his political rival, Hua insisted that one sentence uttered by Chairman Mao exceeded the wisdom of ten thousand sentences of someone else. On February 7, 1977, in a joint editorial carried by the *People's Daily*, *Hongqi*, and the *People's Liberation Army Daily*, Hua announced a rally slogan, "Follow Mao's wishes" (*liangge fanshi*). This doctrine suggested to resolutely support whatever decisions Chairman Mao had made and to unflinchingly obey whatever instructions Chairman Mao had issued. This famous slogan was Hua's reaction to the popular demands to exonerate the participants in the Tiananmen incident of 1976 and to reassess the event, meaning, and consequence of the Cultural Revolution.[4] It was also Hua's self-defence to override the overwhelming power of the majority of old guards in the party who were defeated by the Cultural Revolution and who were eager to reemerge after Mao's death.

No matter how hard Hua attempted to associate Mao's words with his own authority, his words as well as the words of official media meant hardly anything without the god himself. Explosive political situations quickly got out of hand. The resolution that was passed by the Central Committee of the CCP under his leadership was quickly overturned by later decisions after the old guards regained majority. Without the presence of Mao, Mao's words lost its magic. They lost their precise meaning and primacy to override the new laws and consensus of the new legislators. As no single person had the authority to legislate and exercise leadership, party politics became a game of numbers again; old factions that had been exposed and defeated by Mao during the Cultural Revolution reemerged with a vengeance in the spring of 1977. Some Politburo members and provincial leaders soon formed a coalition and began to pressure Hua to rehabilitate Deng Xiaoping, the most senior and able politician after Mao. Hua finally gave in to their demands and agreed to Deng's rehabilitation, which was officially announced by the Third Plenum of the Tenth Congress, convened during July 1977.[5]

The reemergence of Deng Xiaoping changed the very nature of political conflict within the CCP centre. It changed from a struggle for the supremacy (authority) of words, presented in Hua's insistence on Mao's words, to a struggle for the loudest (most numbered) volume of words, those of the real majority of its members. The competition became one that was not so much for how close a leader was to Mao Zedong and the assumed meanings of Mao's words as it was for how many votes a leader could gather in the Central Committee to support his ideas. Hua quickly lost the majority votes as his supporters kept being removed from their voting positions and many old guards of the CCP, who were eliminated and had suffered during the Cultural Revolution, reemerged.[6]

To completely defeat and oust Hua, Deng's first strategy was to separate Mao's words from his person, Mao's ideas from their implications, and his statement from reality. Deng humanised Mao and changed the way in which Mao was perceived.

By October, it was clear that Deng had been able to undermine Hua's leadership by reinterpreting Maoist doctrine. Deng declared that not everything that Mao had said or done was necessarily always right. In this fashion, Deng was able to imply that in governing China, it was more important to apply ideologies flexibly than to adhere dogmatically to Mao's exact words and ideas. Pragmatism became more valid and significant than dogmatism in judging political issues. In early December 1978 Deng set the tone of the forthcoming Third Plenum of the Eleventh Party Congress by stating, "If a party, a country, a nation approaches everything dogmatically, applies rigid thought, and is superstitious, then its vitality will stop. The party and the state will collapse."[7]

The political implication of Deng's theory would shake the very foundation of Hua's leadership, which was entrenched in Hua's association with Mao. Hua had a personal directive written by Mao that appointed him as Mao's successor. There was no one in the CCP who could defeat Mao when he was alive; in his death it became much easier to fight his ghost and twist his words, words without a live utterance. By separating words and their meanings and doctrine from practice, Deng took power and authority from the words of a dead man. He also took power from the current leaders whose authority was based on Mao's words. Deng began to build and cultivate a new kind of authority, the authority of the party majority. Unlike Mao, who had to go outside of the Party Central Committee—or even outside of the party—to create a new power base, Deng's power base was the few hundred surviving members of the old guards who helped Mao establish the new China but who were purged and overthrown by the Cultural Revolution.

Deng gradually gained a majority within the central committee and scored a major victory on several important issues at the Third Plenum held in December 1978. First, he regained personnel and organisational control by sending three more of his supporters to the Politburo. They were Deng Yingchao, Hu Yaobang, and Wang Zhen.[8] Although Hua Guofeng was the party's chairman, the vice chairmen now included Ye Jianying, Deng Xiaoping, Li Xiannian, Chen Yun, and Wang Dongxing, who were more senior and more experienced than Chairman Hua. Deng's supporters became department heads of the party's General Office, such as the heads of the Departments of Organisation, Propaganda, and of the United Front Work. The party also created a Central Discipline Inspection Committee, with Chen Yun as first secretary.[9]

With his pragmatism to fight Mao's extremely left principles, Deng reversed the verdict, legitimacy, and self-righteousness of the Cultural Revolution. The plenum under Deng's leadership also set the precedent of rehabilitating leaders who had been personally vilified by Mao. Peng Dehuai and Tao Zhu were exonerated posthumously, and several other surviving leaders (including General Huang Kecheng and Chen Zaidao) were readmitted to the Central Committee as full members.[10]

In September 1979 at the Fourth Plenum of the party's Eleventh Congress, Deng accomplished more to extend his power base. Twelve more recently rehabilitated administrators who had been disgraced during the Cultural Revolution were elected as members of the Central Committee. Two important allies, Zhao Ziyang and Peng Zhen, were also promoted to the Politburo.[11]

By early 1980, Deng had gained enough organisational control to allow him to take on his opponents. At the Fifth Plenum, Hu Yaobang and Zhao Ziyang were elected to the Standing Committee of the Politburo. More important, Deng finally succeeded in removing from the Politburo the four major figures who had benefited in the Cultural Revolution and its ruthless purge: Wang Dongxing, Wu De, Ji Dengkui, and Chen Yonggui.[12] With these moves, Deng had gained a clear majority in both the Politburo and its powerful Standing Committee, isolating Hua Guofeng in both organisations.[13] Shortly afterwards, Zhao Ziyang replaced Hua Guofeng as premier. With his power in the Politburo greatly strengthened, the Deng group was in a much better position to promote his economic reform policies.

Meanwhile, Deng and his colleagues made great efforts to reorganise the leadership from the ministerial to the local levels. First, they discontinued the military domination of regional politics by replacing the commanders of China's eleven military regions in 1980. By this strategy, they regained the direct control over local administrators. By the end of the year, they completely stripped Hua Guofeng of power by forcing him to yield his party chairmanship to Hu Yaobang, and his Military Affairs Committee chairmanship to Deng. To validate this decision, the Politburo adopted a resolution criticising Hua's doctrine of the "two whatevers". By now, Deng had eventually fulfilled his plan to overthrow Hua and to take control on the national level.

If Deng had to restore democracy within the party, which was his main instrument to purge Mao's followers, he had no intention of extending this democracy outside of the ruling party. After Deng's return to power, he faced a major challenge from the public that threatened the legitimacy of the Communist government. Deng and other Communist administrators always took the premise of one-party dictatorship for granted. According to this premise, the ruling party that had the earned the rights to rule (*zuo jiangshen*) by winning the civil war (*da jiangshen*) had the obligation to impose stringent requirements upon its members to strengthen ideological training and organisational control, as well as insure the fulfilment of its political mission. The party would never allow its authority or the validity of its ideology to be questioned or challenged by anyone outside of the party, especially political dissidents and agitated intellectuals. Only the party had the capacity to rectify its own mistakes, only the party had the authority to interpret its ideology, and only the party had the power to legislate.

This premise came under severe criticism as soon as Deng returned to power. The immediate cause for the outburst of dissension was the popular demand for the exoneration of participants in the Tiananmen incident of April 5, 1976, which the party had condemned as a counter-revolutionary movement. In early October 1978 Wu De was removed from the Beijing municipal party leadership. Then, on November 15, 1978, the Beijing Municipal Party Committee officially excused the incident and exonerated its participants. Although the exoneration was originally intended to placate the administrators, it actually provoked more fundamental criticism from the intellectuals and educated young people outside of the party. The dissidents put up big-character posters, which appeared in an area in Beijing that subsequently came to be called the "Democracy Wall". The posters and discussions along the Democracy Wall often drew crowds of several thousand people every day.

On December 5, 1978, Wei Jingsheng posted an article on the Democracy Wall entitled "The Fifth Modernisation". In it, he argued that the party's four-modernisation program was viable only when accompanied by a concomitant political modernisation, by which he meant democracy, civil liberty, and human rights for all Chinese people. His article triggered a torrent of criticism against the party, its ideology, and its leadership.[14]

In front of such vehement criticism, Deng Xiaoping's initial reaction was to counsel and calm the party. In a speech presented on December 13, 1978, Deng pointed out that there was no need to be unreasonably or overly alarmed by a few discontented people making trouble at the Democracy Wall. He expressed his confidence that the approval of the Tiananmen incident could only increase the party's popularity in public. He said that the masses should be allowed to express their opinions or criticisms without provoking overreaction from the government. He criticised those who were eager to conduct political investigations of the critics, warning that this kind of suppression must cease. Finally, he said that the people's judgement must be trusted and their democratic rights must be protected through laws.[15]

According to Deng's attitude, the official Chinese press also initially consoled forbearance by the masses. It urged them to appreciate the value of national unity and social stability, to direct their energy towards economic development and modernisation, and to not be consumed by bitterness about the past politics. But in the spring of 1979, demonstrations and even riots by young people broke out in Beijing, Shanghai, Yunnan, and other parts of the country. They attacked or occupied public offices of the party and government. They also conducted sit-ins and fasts, blocked traffic, encouraged people to participate in demonstrations, and caused serious disruptions of production and the social order.

If Mao Zedong was alive, he might have appeared in person to make a speech to calm the populace. He would have been able to weather the storm by his sharp directives or humour. Deng Xiaoping was not Mao Zedong, who exercised great personal authority and wide enormous political power; Deng was a leader of a coalition.[16] He was also afraid of the crowd, especially an agitated and angry crowd, which must have reminded him of the chaos and panic of the Cultural Revolution. He was an expert in party politics, not a popular rhetorician. He believed that his historic job was to restore the unity and stability under the leadership of the CCP, which had been turned upside down by the Cultural Revolution. He would do anything to get these back.

Within weeks, Deng's attitude towards the dissident movement changed completely. As the dissidents had attracted an increasing following, they began to appear to be a fatal threat to the legitimacy of one-party rule and the state. In early 1979 the situation got worse. Fu Yuehua led ten thousand peasants from four provinces in street demonstrations in Beijing to demand better living conditions and work permits. On February 5 and 6, about twenty-five thousand people demonstrated in Shanghai, occupying the railway station and blocking traffic. Unlike Mao, who faced the challenge head-on by directly talking to the officers who alleged to be a part of the planned military coup to eliminate the chairman, Deng became paranoid. He was convinced that the dissidents' objective was to derail the party's four-modernisation program. He suspected them of having secret organisations throughout the country, as well as links with Taiwan and other foreign powers. As a result, Deng determined to suppress them.[17]

The party quickly took action, including tanks and soldiers with real ammunition, to crack down on the dissidents because, like Mao, Deng had the support of the PLA. The first weapon of the regime was to pass laws to restrict political activism. In March 1979, the municipal party organisations of Beijing and Shanghai introduced new regulations to ban all antiparty and counterrevolutionary wall posters. Soon, other cities also enacted laws to force the closing down of the democracy walls, which had grown in number since the creation of the first Democracy Wall, throughout the country. Armed with a new regulation and party directive, a wave of arrests of prominent activists of the democratic movement took place. Their publications were forced either to stop circulation or to go underground. The most celebrated case was the arrest of Wei Jingsheng in March and his trial in October 1979 in a Beijing municipal court. The court sentenced Wei to fifteen years of imprisonment for treason and counterrevolutionary behaviour.[18]

To justify the suppression of the democracy, the party decided to change the law again. Deng personally labeled the young activists of democracy as antisocialists and recommended the removal of the four guaranteed freedoms of speech (big blooming [of a hundred flowers], big contending, big debate, and big-character posters) from the Constitution of the People's Republic of China.[19]

At the time when Deng's authority was challenged, he behaved exactly the same as Mao Zedong did. Neither hesitated to crush the dissidents with the bat of law that was rewritten and renounced according to political needs. Before they gained the majority support in the party, they appeared to be more liberal and supportive to democracy, which might have worked to their favour because relaxation might have helped their causes. However, as soon as the democratic movement spread, Deng, like Mao, changed his tone. He increasingly emphasised party leadership and control, and he opposed any democratic gesture. In the face of attacks from outside of the party, he could not admit the validity of the dissidents' complaints about the party's shortcomings, even though Deng had previously criticised some of these same issues himself. The assault by outsiders made it necessary for him to defend the party, if only to strengthen his own position within it and not give his opponents any excuse to depose him.

Ironically, however, it was Deng who ultimately benefited from this crisis. The democracy movement provided him with a greater opportunity to enhance his status within the party as a resolute leader. When other leaders were hesitant regarding how to react, Deng decisively advocated harsh, swift, and repressive measures.

The CCP's overreaction to democracy derived from its deep fear. It was afraid that the democracy movement of the educated and young would attract industrial workers. The Chinese leaders particularly worried about this possibility because they had already witnessed the disruptive impact of the Polish Solidarity movement. They saw the potential that Chinese dissidents could take the same strategy to joint industrial workers and create a Chinese Solidarity movement. Although Deng's harsh treatment of the dissidents might have caused him to lose prestige in the public eye, he definitely gained status within the party as he demonstrated his ability to lead the party through a major political storm.

Like many Chinese politicians, Deng had never trusted the words of law, even those of his own laws. To secure the implications of his law, he needed an organisation to stand behind his words. In 1980 and 1981, Deng speeded up the rehabilitation (*pingfan*) movement. He needed more administrators on his side, not only at the party centre, but also at provincial and local levels, which were still occupied by people whom he could not trust. All of those who used to work for Mao and Mao's followers had to be stripped of their positions. If Deng was to impose his own political agenda in the nation, he needed to rebuild his network of supporters, and the only people he could trust were the old comrades he had worked with before the Cultural Revolution and were deposed with him in the ensuing power struggle. By the end of 1982, the party's Organisation Department reported that about three million administrators had been rehabilitated throughout the country. Party membership was restored to more than 470,000 after the return of the administrators, who had been unjustly expelled during the Cultural Revolution. The erroneous punishments given to another 120,000 members were annulled. According to the official reports, tens of millions of administrators and ordinary citizens who had been implicated in fabricated political crimes were cleared of their charges.[20]

With a strong sense of mission to restore the pre–Cultural Revolution order, Deng fulfilled his wish to have a unified national leadership in September 1982 when the party's Twelfth National Congress was convened. Like many CCP leaders of the past, Deng had to rewrite the history as well as the law of the party to validate his victory and legitimatise the change. The Congress passed a new Party Charter, which effectively removed many provisions associated with Mao and his policies, such as class struggle, continuous revolution, and recurrent cultural revolutions. It also abolished the position of party chairman; so Hua Guofeng was driven out of the top echelon. New party institutions were reconstructed again. Hu Yaobang was made the general secretary. The leadership had finally achieved a complete independence from the shadow of Mao.[21]

Soon, however, Deng was surprised to find that the Cultural Revolution was not the only problem that he had to struggle with. The reversal of the verdict of the Cultural Revolution did not solve the numerous problems that were exposed during the chaotic period. Both the party and the citizens he encountered were not the same after a ten-year, extremely cruel and bitter conflict. The party administrators became demoralised and cynical, and their misconduct provoked increasing public discontent. The public who had exposed too many dark sides of the ruling party had lost their faith for the system. By the late 1970s, a crisis of lack of confidence of major proportions had pervaded Chinese society and its citizens.

The criticism directed towards the CCP went far beyond the limits that were tolerated by Deng's leadership. The demand to change did not stop at the Cultural Revolution and Mao's legacy. Some posters denounced Mao as a dictator and the Cultural Revolution as a fascist reign, and advocated an unequivocal repudiation of both the Cultural Revolution and Mao Zedong Thought, as well as a wholesale rehabilitation of all victims of previous political campaigns since 1949. Many even rebuked Deng Xiaoping for having betrayed his democratic pledges and for having become a dictator himself. The posters called upon citizens to protect their own political rights against the encroachment by the party and the state.[22]

If the inner struggle of the CCP had been about who should be the controlling leader, then now the very legitimacy of the Communist rule was under attack. Public writings challenged some of the most sacred doctrines of the Communist Party and its state. They expressed doubts about the validity of Marxism, the superiority of Socialism, and the trustworthiness of the Communist regime. They rejected the principle of single-party leadership. Others suggested that, according to the track record, the Communist Party had forfeited its legal right to rule in China.[23]

The public now demanded the guarantee of civil rights, a free press, freedom of assembly and association, and even free competition between Communists and non-Communist political parties through a nationwide electoral process. Many were particularly impressed by the human rights policy of the United States and drafted a "Human Rights Declaration" for China. Some even appealed to U.S. President Jimmy Carter to monitor the abuse of human rights in China, which was an ultimate insult to the Communist government.[24]

As the public expressed a higher and stronger demand for the integrity of the ruling party, the disciplinary problems of CCP became multiplied, ironically, and worsened since the death of Mao Zedong. Their god was dead; there was neither law to follow nor morals to respect. Even the official argument of blaming the Gang of Four for everything that went wrong in China was no longer convincing. The death of Mao and darkening of his legacy erased the self-righteousness of the CCP, the self-respect of its members, and the validity of its official ideology. As the party lost its morale and self-righteousness, corruption became rampant. Party membership transformed from moral and political commitment to a license to be above law and a credit card to pursue whatever one desired to purchase.

Within the conventional toolbox of the Chinese Communism, there was nothing except for the rectification movement and self-criticism to discipline its organisation. So, the Central Committee quickly revived a few old documents and regulations and drafted a few new rules, hoping that the problems would go away after the usual official propaganda campaigns.[25] However, these measures proved to be ineffective because of the decline of party discipline and morale. The sickness of the organisation had gone far beyond its capacity of self-policing. If the party could not discipline itself, who would?

By the beginning of 1982, the widening scope of economic crimes persuaded the leaders that the party's organisational framework was itself defective. As the misconduct no longer involved just individuals but often groups of individuals interconnected by shared interests, it became extremely difficult even to find out the truth about the extent of criminal activities. Cases of misconduct now implicated a large number of administrators who would form a tight pact to protect one another. Very often, even the local leading administrators whom the party centre had designated to investigate these cases were either direct participants of such criminal activities or were bribed to keep their mouths shut. Many leading administrators were reluctant to offend anybody and chose to ignore the illegal activities of their subordinates. In some instances, whole work units engaged in illegal activities from top to bottom and then tried to justify such activities as measures to promote the collective welfare of their units.[26]

Ironically, at this time, the CCP came to a realisation similar to that felt by Chiang Kai-shek at the end of the 1940s: Internal crime and corruption were responsible for defeating the party, not its political opposition. The situation worsened to the point that even the official press of the CCP was allowed to publicly acknowledge that the extent of corruption, smuggling, theft of public properties, and embezzlement of public funds had become far worse in both scope and severity than similar activities at the height of the anticorruption campaigns of 1952.[27] These campaigns and subsequent political movements failed to curb economic crimes and stop corruption. This eventually led to the Cultural Revolution. On January 5, 1982, Chen Yun warned the party,

> I suggest that we deal sternly with those who have committed serious economic crimes. Impose prison terms on several of them or even execute them. We should carry out this policy sternly and stick to it, and publicise it in the newspapers. Otherwise, we will not be able to rectify party discipline.[28]

In February, the leaders decided to launch a campaign specifically aimed at smashing illegal commercial activities—the National People's Congress passed a resolution about punishing economic criminals.[29] Finally, the party and the state jointly decided to get tough with the criminal activities that were committed mainly by party administrators.

To promote the campaign against crimes, the party now vowed to employ severe punishment, including the death penalty, against the perpetrators, regardless of their rank or seniority in the party. But the party sought to give the perpetrators a last chance to confess their crimes before a deadline in exchange for a reduced penalty. The party also required lower level party organisations that were plagued by serious ideological, political, or organisational shortcomings to undergo reorganisation, and it threatened to totally disband those organisations with excessive problems. Aided by an intense propaganda barrage, the party and government obviously expected this campaign to be sufficient to arrest the decline of the party's prestige. Through these measures, the party finally elevated the task of combating poor discipline to the status of a "campaign", albeit a narrowly focused one.[30]

It soon became obvious that the laws and directives of the Party Central Committee meant nothing in the deft ears of the misbehaving members who were not intimidated by the party's dire warnings. Nobody stepped forward to admit guilt before the announced deadline to seek leniency. The few economic criminals who got caught were "flies" rather than "tigers" in the crime rings.[31] Meanwhile, administrative corruption and misconduct continued unabated. In fact, the major cases involving higher ranking perpetrators were even more immune from prosecution. Leading administrators often came under tremendous social pressures or material inducements to cover up the crimes of their subordinates or prevent their prosecution. If they were unable to stop the investigation and prosecution, they would resort to delaying tactics, hoping that the superior organisation would simply lose interest in pursuing the cases because of the difficulty and time consumption that they had created.

Since there was no functional division between the legislators and administrators, even when the higher court persisted and succeeded in establishing evidence for criminal deeds, the lower level administrators could still reduce the originally harsh sentence and even allow the criminals to go free. They could always find a clause or two in the regulation to justify their actions, such as that the criminals had voluntarily cooperated with the authorities, offered thorough confessions, and/or made sincere gestures of contrition, among other reasons.

The old concept and method of *zheng feng* failed miserably, and so did the party disciplinary system. It appeared that a more offensive campaign and even a new purge were needed. In 1983 the party finally decided to purify its organisations at various levels by throwing three types of administrators out of office.[32] The first type was people who gained power as a result of engaging in rebellious and violent activities during the Cultural Revolution. They closely followed the Lin and Jiang gangs, were involved in factional strife, and had since been promoted to become leading administrators. The second type was those who had espoused the ideological line of the Lin and Jiang gangs, and who had continued to oppose the official party line after 1978. The third type was those who had committed criminal acts like beating, torture, causing injury or death, smashing public properties, and looting.[33]

However, without specific and regulated procedures and well-defined levels of the court system, this resolution was very difficult to apply to the vast party organisations that just came out of the gigantic turmoil of the revolution. The party resolution did not make the distinction between the leader and follower of the crimes in a time when violent acts were committed indiscriminately and on a massive scale. When many people could be blamed and prosecuted, with or without proof, the illegal investigation became an opportunity for factional vengeance and warfare.[34]

The party also realised that if the term *three types* was applied too literally, it could cause widespread panic in all ranks, and it would make everyone feel threatened. To avoid this situation, the party announced that the rectification was directed primarily against the ringleaders who had planned, organised, and led criminal acts during the Cultural Revolution and not against their followers, especially if the latter had not opposed the new leaders since 1978. By virtue of this clarified distinction, the party had hoped to isolate the factional leaders from their followers. It was believed that once the former group was neutralised, the capacity of the latter to do harm would be substantially reduced. In reality, the line between the factional leaders and followers had to be drawn by the leaders themselves, who were often in control of the administration. They could easily convict other people for the criminal activities that they themselves had committed and escape from verdicts and punishments. All the criminals had to do was pick one or two of their subordinates as scapegoats to satisfy the Central Committee while the organised criminal activities went on.

In late 1983 the CCP reported that the majority of the three types had been exposed and expelled from the leadership of the national- and provincial/municipal-level organisations. It also pointed out that a sub-stantial number of them were still well hidden and entrenched in the county and lower levels, in economic enterprises, and in auxiliary administrative organisations. They vowed that the party should not rest until the purge had been thoroughly carried out all the way down to the local level. Otherwise, such elements could resurface to cause problems even after a hibernation of ten to twenty years.[35]

By December 1984, Bo Yibo was able to report that some 50 percent of people identified as one of the three types had been dealt with since the beginning of the rectification campaign.[36] Thus, shortly after the Third Plenum of the Twelfth Party Congress, Deng showed his confidence. He believed that he finally had a mature Party Central Committee leadership that could handle things with deliberateness. He mentioned not only Hu Yaobang and Zhao Ziyang among the second echelon but also a number of younger people in the State Council and the Party's Central Committee as very capable members of the third echelon, whom he could trust to get things done right.[37]

However, the leaders who had suffered a great deal in the Cultural Revolution refused to stop. The task of exposing and removing the three types was pursued with a thoroughness that bordered on vengeance. Just like the Mao period, once people were categorised as antirevolution-aries, they were immediately crucified and removed from office without a legally scheduled investigation or court procedure. The people who were labeled as three types were instantly dismissed from office and expelled from the party. It was as cruel as it was in the Cultural Revolu-tion, where mercy was rarely shown to the underdogs of politics. By the mid-1980s, it was believed that the ideology of the three types was destroyed, as well as their factional organisations; any realistic hope of their return to power had completely vanished.[38]

Even with this determination and thoroughness, the party became helpless to control corruption, which remained a constant headache. There was no legal distinction between political and criminal crimes, and between accusations, proved evidence, and lawful verdicts, because there was no institutional division between the legislator, the judge, and the legal administrator in a single-party system. Even with the establishment of a censorial Disciplinary Committee, criminals who had connections in various levels of party administration would not change their behaviour except to add one more organisation to bribe and to influence. They were untouchable because they knew that the administration could not expose them because it would require convicting themselves. Therefore, criminal activities went on as if nothing had happened.

CCP members and administrators could get away with anything except politically challenging the system, which would immediately earn them the title of "antirevolutionary". As long as one got along with the administrators in power and had connections within the current system, one could be an above law. One Chinese saying states that "one person in the family becomes an officer, even his chickens and gods fly with him". It became clear that party membership had turned into a license to pursue material gain and privileges to earn favours for one's family, relatives, and friends. Party power became a lucrative position where one could issue by–me laws whenever he or she chose. With this position, one could sell anything—especially things that belong to the public—within one's power, including college admission, employment opportunity, legal status of city residence, and even a certain verdict in court room.

The worst of all was the fact that the administrators and party members had already acquired the habit of trying every conceivable way to circumvent the party's regulations and disciplinary measures. They could reinterpret public law as their own by-me laws, and they got away with crimes. For instance, as the Central Discipline Committee made it illegal to use public funds to build expensive housing for party members in February 1983, the members quickly found loopholes in the new regulations so that they could use public funds to subsidise the members' purchases or constructions of their own residences. Since living spaces in China were distributed (rather than sold) not according to family sizes but rather based on official ranks, leading administrators not only grabbed huge living spaces for themselves but also often hoarded several apartments for their children and grandchildren as well.

Without an efficient legal administration, officials' misconduct and corruption accelerated in both scale and frequency. Illegal economic activities, complex in nature, became routine operations for some public agencies. The leaders and administrators were the ones who masterminded these illegal activities, which were participated in by most of the staff, and conducted under the pretext of carrying out reform or promoting employee welfare. A large number of public organisations took advantage of the party's new policy of encouraging economic entrepreneurial activities to form private companies, even though the laws had specifically forbidden them to engage in profit-making activities. These "attaché-case companies", as the Chinese called them, were all phantom companies because their capital, production facilities, warehouses, vehicles, and so forth were all taken from the government at no cost. Company employees were all bureaucrats who drew salaries from the state but conducted company business during their regular office time. Children of prominent leaders often played key roles in these attaché-case companies, and influential and well-connected retired administrators were retained as consultants or board members. As the administrators and staff members became stockholders of their private companies, their official and commercial roles became indistinguishable, but the company's profits would be split only among themselves. When losses were incurred, however, they would shift the cost entirely onto the public organs. In less than a year from the fall of 1984 to mid-1985, more than twenty thousand such commercial enterprises had sprung up.[39]

As law stood forceless in front of these illegal activities, the forms of misconduct became more inventive and sophisticated, even as the rectification campaign was being carried out. Companies could purchase commodities from the state at centrally controlled prices and resell them in the open market for substantial profits. Commodities like steel, automobiles, chemical fertiliser, colour television sets, bicycles, and woolen fabric were in short supply in the 1984–1985 period. The reason for this was that many producers of these commodities told the government that they were unable to fulfil production quotas set by the state while they actually supplied their products to their own phantom companies to sell in the market for much higher prices.[40]

With connections among the party administrators, tax evasion and document falsification became common practices in China. Large quantities of merchandise were written off as gifts or free samples from their producers while, in fact, they had been sold to evade taxes. Producers who had earned foreign currencies from the sale of their products concealed their revenues from the state so that they could sell the currency in the black market for higher prices. State and collective enterprises sometimes lent their business licenses, contract forms, and bank account numbers to criminal elements for a fee. Factories often sold high-grade products through their own outlets while delivering their inferior products to the state's distribution system. State- and collective-owned enterprises also concocted schemes to sell or transfer resources or merchandise to cooperative or private economic entities at concessionary terms on the pretence that they were helping these less advanced forms of economy, but they actually were splitting the profits with them.

Without specific laws to regulate commercial activities or a legal system to deal with these crimes, cases of fraud, deception, and swindling began to mount. By late 1985, the official newspaper of the party acknowledged that there had been a notable increase in the frequency of major cases of economic irregularities. The perpetrators of such schemes usually were able to enlist leading party or state administrators to be their partners and swindle money from other gullible customers (usually other public agencies), sometimes amounting to millions of renminbi.[41] Some of the public agencies whose leaders were unfamiliar with economic activities often entrusted their business operations to charlatans who advertised their connections with high-ranking officials, as well as their ability to open doors and make deals.

In this new atmosphere of economic free-for-all, many people, especially people who had official positions to control money and power, acquired an expectation to be paid off. Public agencies routinely demanded commissions, kickbacks, or service charges for services they rendered. Because there was never any division between law and business and between law and politics, politicians had divided judicial space among themselves where they could make their own laws. An increasing number of organs of the party, state, military, and economic enterprises converted their public authority into an economic asset and exploited it to enrich themselves. Every public service agency had the potential of becoming a "hegemon" who could hold the people hostage and demand a ransom. As these agencies were located on the basic level and away from the party's disciplinary control, they could do practically anything they pleased, and the under-law populace was totally helpless.[42]

The illegal activities became legalised and permitted because the administrators and party leaders perpetrated their schemes with the support or acquiescence of their colleagues and subordinates in the government and court. To retain the latter's loyalty and collusion, bureaucratic agencies and economic enterprises concocted numerous excuses to pay hefty bonuses out of public funds, ranging from cash to uniforms and household wares (e.g., washing machines, refrigerators, and television sets).

In China, illegal activities often developed as quickly as the law and regulations did. As soon as the law was announced, loopholes were discovered, illegal means to get around it were found, and so a "legal" way was established to legitimate the illegal activities. Some units of government or government-run enterprises were even more creative in finding pretexts to pay their leaders and staff with large amount of public funds. Some paid a "walking fee" to those who walked to their workplace. Some leaders were paid an "organisation fee" for doing their office work. Some state-owned organisations paid out more than a million renminbi to their staff to compensate for their working on weekends during the previous twenty-seven years.

A substantial number of public agencies and state-owned companies also established contact with criminals or oversaw businessmen engaging in bribery, hoarding, smuggling, black marketeering, evasion of taxes and customs duties, manufacturing of counterfeit medicine and liquor, sale of pornographic materials, and prostitution.[43] Some of these activities were highly organised and conducted on a truly grand scale, and involved a network of colluding administrative organisations over many districts and provinces.[44]

The reason why Chinese economic and commercial activities became a lawless chaos lies in the fact that the CCP granted itself an above-law status. Just like in the Mao period, laws and constitutions were made to control political enemies; the politicians who were lawmakers and administrators were beyond the rule of law. Now, it became normal for the party administrators to take bribes, and embezzle public funds and properties; party members could realistically get away with any misconduct except for antiparty activities.[45] With the licence to obvert rules, CCP members accounted for an inordinately large portion of the official statistics of crimes. For instance, they represented 25 percent of the economic criminals prosecuted by the city of Beijing in 1985 and 36 percent of them in 1986. Nationwide, one out of every four economic criminals in 1986 was a member of the Chinese Communist Party.[46] These numbers appear particularly significant when one considers that party members constituted only 4 percent of China's population.

The law became even weaker and less effective when it came to dealing with the illegal activities of high-ranking administrators of the CCP and their children, who had personal and social connections with lawmakers and judicial administrators. By the early 1980s, incidents of misconduct involving high-level leaders and their children had multiplied substantially. Many of them had abused power to gain access to the state's confidential economic data for personal speculative use, to establish liaisons with overseas businessmen, to set up secret bank accounts in Western countries, or to sign exclusive deals to import or export certain commodities (ranging from minerals to weapons). Through this shortcut to wealth, they quickly became an important part of China's emerging entrepreneurial class. The children of high-ranking administrators, who had suffered during the Cultural Revolution because of their family background, now took advantage of the system with a vengeance. Now was the time to harvest and to be compensated for what they had lost. Now their parents had been rehabilitated, and they could fly with them again; they, in turn, also became above laws. They had no fear because they knew that the system had to look the other way because their parents were the ones who made the law. They knew that they actually had the authority to make or break the careers of judges and legal administrators. If the party had been serious about launching an exhaustive investigation into their activities, it could have found a staggering amount of wrongdoing at the top. This would have created intense conflict within the leadership and could possibly have caused significant economic confusion and instability, neither of which the party wanted or could afford.[47]

If the above-law officers occasionally got tough, there would be an outburst of denunciations and threats from a leader against high-level abuses of privileges, but no concrete action would follow. In most cases, there was a conspiracy of silence on this subject. If a high-ranking leader's misconduct was detected, tremendous pressure would be marshalled to let him go free. Since corruption was an organised actitivy, the organisation to which this individual was associated would do its best to reduce the legal consequence of his or her actions. The organisation would hire lawyers and motivate politicians to come to the defence of this individual. To control the damage that might spread to others, especially the real leaders and beneficiaries of the illegal actitities, the organisation would attempt to convince the court that the accused was a first-time offender and that leniency in sentencing would be appropriate. Ignorance of the law was often successfully used as a secondary argument for special consideration of exceptional treatment.[48] Therefore, in the eyes of the criminals, the possibilities of material gains appeared much higher than any legal consequences.

The misconduct at high-level administration had gained wider and more immediate circulation; the party was no longer able to conceal them from the public. By 1985, high-level corruption had become the number one complaint of the public. During the remainder of 1985, the party made increasingly open and threatening denunciations hoping to control the worst wave of economic crime, but to no avail. Finally, the party mounted a new major offensive at the beginning of 1986. Between January 6 and 9, some eight thousand leading administrators from the national party, state, and military organs, as well as the municipality of Beijing, were summoned to hear a series of denunciations delivered by top party and government leaders against high-level wrongdoing.

At the January 9 session, General Secretary Hu Yaobang, after reciting a long list of misconduct by high-ranking administrators, said, "For a long period of time, there has been a tendency within our party to put the blame on lower levels whenever the party encountered problems, instead of looking for causes among the leading organs". This was a perversity that must be corrected. Hu called upon

> the party organs of national agencies...to set examples for perfecting internal party life, overcoming [organisational] weakness and laxity, promoting healthy criticism and self-criticism, paying heed to the voices of the masses, and accepting the supervision of the people and lower-level organs.[49]

The Central Discipline Inspection Committee also declared that the top administrators should assume personal supervision and responsibility over the drive to eradicate erroneous party style, and that the party would prosecute several major cases of economic crimes involving high-ranking people in 1986 to show its determination. The special commentator of the *People's Daily* issued a specific warning to high-ranking administrators and their children to not test the resolve of the national leaders. He said,

> Our party does not allow the existence of 'special party members' who place themselves above party rules. As long as a rule has been violated, we do not care whether you are high-ranking cadres, or children of high-ranking cadres, or famous people. We will sternly prosecute you.[50]

Unfortunately, the overall results of this much-publicised offensive against corruption were disappointing. To the Chinese public, it was "great noise of thunder with very little rainfall". From January 1986 until the official termination of rectification in June 1987, only a handful of middle-level criminals were convicted and prosecuted. In the cases involving children of powerful party leaders, the latter had either retired or died. Not one current high-ranking officer's child had been touched, including any children of Deng Xiaoping himself, although their notorious illegal activities were well-known by the public. A few more incumbent officials were given unspecified forms of intra-party sanctions.[51]

The highest ranking administrator to receive expulsion from the party, public disgrace, and full criminal prosecution during the entire process of rectification was the governor of Jiangxi Province. He was accused of a moral offence and the embezzlement of over half a million U.S. dollars. The party claimed that its investigation concluded in success by giving punishment to 74 army officers on the provincial level and 635 members on the district division level. But these cases hardly scratched the surface of the problem of high-level misconduct and corruption. They were hardly adequate to soothe the cynicism of the party or the masses.[52]

If the party was frustrated, then the public was outraged. The Tiananmen Square incident was but a mere reflection of the people's moral outrage, resentment towards the CCP's leadership, and frustration with the quality of political life in China. It became obvious that the most serious danger to Chinese politics came from the CCP's own moral and organisational decay. By the early 1980s, the party had virtually lost its sense of mission and its reason for existence. Its organisational sinews had atrophied, its style of work had degenerated dangerously, and its prestige had plummeted. The conventional measures of its internal rectification campaign that aimed at correcting its widespread problems did not accomplish much. The party had nothing to congratulate itself except for driving its political opponents, the three types, out of the organisation, which was used as an excuse for overlooking the real problem: the rampant corruption and economic crime of the old guards themselves.[53]

The decline of CCP's prestige also led to the erosion of its official ideology based on Marxist, Leninist, and Maoist political theories. Moral righteousness has always been a cornerstone of Chinese political legitimacy, since "to rule" and "to be upright" in the Chinese language have the same phonic origins. This has partially been the reason why Chinese rulers throughout history have a common tendency to sincerely or superficially worship Confucianism as actual or ceremonial guidance.

This moral righteousness works the same way for Chinese rulers as does the Christian God or ideal of democracy for Western politicians. The ruling class needs to be perceived as being morally righteous in order to justify their position of rulership. Mao's notorious Cultural Revolution acted under the name of the glorious fight of Socialism against capitalism. People were motivated and excited about it, at least at the beginning. Deng's pragmatic theory of "good cat" (any cat is a good cat as long as it can catch the rats) defeated not only Maoism but also the very idealistic tendency to be morally rightous, which has been an important part of Chinese literary and political tradition.[54] A widespread cynicism increasingly discredited Deng's own version of Socialism, which he needed and decided to maintain to justify the rule of the CCP.

To at least superficially maintain the integrity of the system and to gain public consensus, the CCP could divorce itself from Maoism by condemning the Cultural Revolution, but not Socialism, even after it decided to take the road of capitalist development. To deny Socialism would defeat the moral purpose of the very existence of the Communist Party, let alone the right to rule. More importantly, the CCP could not claim to be a liberal or conservative party, as do the political parties in the West, because it did not allow democracy, freedom, and civil rights. A capitalist political system would immediately vote the CCP out of office.

Therefore, the CCP was stuck in-between opposite political theories, creating a dilemma whereby it could not go either way whole-heartedly. The party could take capitalism only as an economic system, without its democracy and legal obligation and responsibility to its citizens. This theoretical and political inconsistency became evident to all as the increasingly widening gap between the rich and the poor that resulted from capitalist development dimmed the dreams of social equality.

The CCP leaders did not understand the capitalist system enough or refused to recognise that democracy and law are the cornerstones of the social order in the West, where competitive individual and group interests can be openly debated, mediated, and regulated. The impersonal language of law, which has the binding power of the social behaviours of its citizens as well as that of its government, keeps the order and prevents anarchy. China's social order has been maintained by an iron fist of a dictator (or a group of dictators) and their emotional manipulation, love or fear, if necessary. It was destined to fall apart after the iron fist was lifted up; the country was left in chaos because there were no alternative means to control illegal aggression and aggression against public interests, especially the interests of the under laws. The discrepancy between the high moral claim of the Communist Party and the immoral, even criminal, activities of its members became more and more apparent, and the public became more and more disgusted and outraged.

The first expression of this crisis of faith and distrust that marked the beginning of the deepening sense of alienation by China's educated people was the Democracy Wall movement, as well as the underground organisations and publications of 1978–1979. By 1980, a significant cultural change began to manifest itself on college campuses. Complaints were heard more frequently about how the paths of life under Communist rule had become progressively narrower. Towards the end of the year, college students began to fight for the right to have free elections on campuses.

The anti–spiritual pollution campaign of 1982–1983 that was launched by the Party Central Committee did little to intimidate the college students. Unrest on individual campuses increased in both scale and frequency. On September 18, 1985, students combined their personal grievances and intellectual discontent with patriotic sentiments and successfully created a sizeable following of nonstudents in public demonstrations. In 1986 college students were disappointed by the lack of progress in the promised political reforms and went into the streets again. Student demonstrations spread to many major cities during the fall of 1986 and the spring of 1987. But their demands were met with an open and official crackdown. Deng reaffirmed his support for the four cardinal principles and denounced the student activities as manifestations of bourgeois liberalisation. Deng's words only led a brief hiatus; student unrest regained its momentum in 1988.

The confidence of college and university students in the party and its ideology slid even further. Many of them became intensely interested in political alternatives to the Chinese system as self-organised political activi-ties, such as discussion groups and democracy salons, mushroomed. Many well-known advocates of liberal ideas made public speeches on campuses in favour of private ownership, political pluralism, and leadership reforms.[55]

Later, in 1988, many educated people in China were anticipating major disturbances during the forthcoming anniversary of the May Fourth Movement in 1989. While they wanted to use the commemora-tion as a vehicle to express their discontent against the party and the government, the CCP tried desperately to contain it as a purely patri-otic historical event without contemporary political overtones. During the fall of 1988 and spring of 1989, students and intellectuals of all age groups became bolder every day in their expressions and activities. They made open criticisms against official public policies and party leaders, signed petitions for the release of political prisoners, and issued public demands for the redress of the party's past mistakes. But before May 4 arrived, former general secretary Hu Yaobang's death occurred in mid-April. This introduced an additional emotional dimension to the escalating confrontation between the party and the intellectuals.[56]

The party under Deng, like that under Mao, had never had good rela-tions with China's intellectuals. On the contrary, that relationship dete-riorated rapidly during the decade, and the party eventually alienated virtually all of the important groups of China's educated population. When the Democracy Wall movement began in the late 1970s, its fol-lowers consisted primarily of urban educated youths that were embit-tered by their experience during the Cultural Revolution. But their bold tactics and radical messages actually shocked and scared the mainstream intellectuals, who still wished to cooperate with the party and hoped that the rehabilitated leaders would give them the chance to do so. Many of them regarded the Democracy Wall protesters as "troublemakers" and were not sorry to see them imprisoned. But it did not take long for the majority of these intellectuals to lose faith in the party's reforms and become disillusioned.[57]

However, Chinese intellectuals alone could not pose any direct threat to the party's dominant role in the society, even with their deep and palpable grievances against the party's dictatorship. The CCP had a long history of oppressing intellectuals and denigrating free liberal education. Since the Mao period, it has suppressed and crucified many dissident intellectuals without endangering its own rule.[58] The average Chinese was not inspired by ideas of democracy, nor did he care much about the principle of separation of powers. The party's failure to enlist the support of educated people could create serious difficulties in its ability to manage and develop the Chinese society and economy, but this would not threaten the party's control. Even the occasional outbursts from educated people in favour of educational reforms were not enough to galvanise the general population to join forces with them.

The CCP, like the imperial governments of the past, has never failed to attract a few ambitious intellectuals to serve the party as its lips and tongue and run the official media; working for the Communist Party was the only and the most lucrative career choice for Chinese scholars and students of arts for the past thirty years. The student demonstrations and related activities by people in the fields of arts and literature before 1989 remained ineffective because their political slogans were too intellectualised to strike a responsive chord among the masses. The demonstrations of April–June 1989, however, were different. The students became able to relate their political agitation for democracy and freedom to concrete conditions of life that ordinary Chinese had to endure in their daily existence, and to stimulate their indignation.[59]

This time, the students could articulate the strongly felt grievances of Chinese people from all walks of life and convince them to participate in the protest. Soon, the demonstration substantially increased in both scale and intensity; it spread from a few thousand in previous years to a million in Beijing alone. The demonstrations also expanded to many other cities throughout China in 1989. After the mid-1980s, the Chinese people had become increasingly disgusted with the corruption and abusive conduct of the party administrators, the dishonesty and incompetence of the ruling party and government, and the continued domination of the party's old guards over Chinese life. They repeatedly witnessed and were shocked again and again by how the conduct of party members and administrators violated even the most rudimentary standards of fairness and justice, as well as minimal political decency.

The repressed anger of the Chinese people only needed a trigger to erupt into open conflagration, and the death of Hu Yaobang was conveniently utilised for that purpose. Thus, the demonstrations began with profuse eulogies to Hu Yaobang but quickly turned into a massive display of banners denouncing the corruption and abuse of privileges, and advocating the overthrow of senior administrators. The shared resentment against Chinese corruptive politics under the party's leadership made it possible for the educated people to forge a solidarity with the industrial workers, older intellectuals, ordinary urban residents, and even members of the party and state organs whose conscience had been insulted by corruption and crimes.

Ironically, at this time the reputation of the Communist Party was not any better than that of Jiang Kaisha's Guomindang before it was overthrown and kicked out of the mainland. The only difference was that the Communist Party now did not have a strong opposition party to challenge and battle it after many years of physical and ideological repression. Having neither a political opposition nor public scrutiny was partially the reason why the above-law corruption in the CCP went wild while the administrators became careless and fearless. The behaviour of the party members and administrators went through drastic changes before and after Mao's death. During the first decade of Communist rule, when Mao exercised fundamental control of the leadership building and launched a rectification movement almost every year, party membership was often associated with rectitude, honesty, and discipline. The Cultural Revolution disillusioned the party members after being crushed into the under-law section of the society. As they witnessed the ruthlessness, arbitrariness, and fickleness of political power, they concluded that they should grab power aggressively and exploit it to the hilt while they could. In the late 1970s, the rehabilitated administrators set new examples of unscrupulous self-seeking and self-aggrandising conduct that surpassed anything that had ever existed in the party's history.[60]

If Mao Zedong plunged his administrators from the above-law heaven to the hell of the under laws for his political agenda, Deng Xiaoping elevated them back to the position of unlimited power for his need to organise a majority coalition. He did not know that they who had been to hell were now different men and women. They were no longer the idealists who would sacrifice their lives for the revolution (to be a Communist was a capital crime before 1949); they had completely lost faith in their god (Mao) and his ideology (Communism). They became worshipers of money and absolute political power. Many things became more important to them than the party's integrity, such as properties, material possessions, living space, club memberships, the welfare of their children, and personal importance. They could care less about the party's reputation because the party did not care about them when they were jailed, tortured, and stripped from all rights.

The hell that the under laws experienced made them learn the hard way that life was short and one had to make the most of it. They decided to turn their backs on the spirit of dedication, the sense of mission, and the personal vow that they took when they joined the Communist Party, and so they became free from all public obligations and pursued personal interests. Their misbehaviour and corruption became their vengeance against the Cultural Revolution, and they laughed at the law. Refusal to retire, which meant losing all of the privileges and benefits, made them a liability to the party and its political agenda.

Once an underdog himself, Deng understood all this cynicism and vengeance against law, which he believed to be the least of his concern. In the early 1980s, Deng concluded that his leadership had been consolidated with the appointment of Hu Yaobang as general secretary and Zhao Ziyang as prime minister.[61] Hu fully shared Deng's vision for achieving rapid economic progress, as evidenced by his frequent reference to the "takeoff" concept. Hu was also more genuinely concerned with the health of the party and was particularly disturbed by the party's discipline problem and the retirement of the old guard.

On the question of discipline, Hu seemed genuinely repulsed by the widespread corruption and abuse of privileges. His own lifestyle was simple and frugal, and he was very sympathetic to the hardship of life on the grassroots level. During his tenure as general secretary, Hu made more personal inspection tours around the country than any other senior administrator. He personally read many letters of complaint from ordinary citizens and attended to the correction of many cases of injustice. Hu believed that the corruption of unscrupulous administrators should be classified as an antagonistic contradiction and should be punished without mercy. By late 1985, Hu had become so impatient with the lack of progress of the rectification campaign that he resorted to the dramatic step of assembling eight thousand administrators in early 1986 to issue them a stern warning against misconduct. Hu made a valiant but futile effort to take personal charge over the party's rectification campaign, and he threatened to punish high-ranking offenders.

On the issue of the party's relations with the intellectuals, Hu's attitude was far more relaxed. He enjoyed a good reputation among intellectuals, many of whom trusted his sincerity and goodwill towards them. It was during Hu's tenure that the party experimented with the practice of inviting prominent scholars to present seminars to party and government leaders inside of the Zhongnanhai compound. In contrast to his harsh denunciation of party members' misconduct, Hu characterised the criticisms and liberal ideas espoused by intellectuals as nonantagonistic contradictions, because they were meant to help the party and therefore should be respected or at least tolerated. He often refused to take repressive measures against outspoken intellectuals as suggested by the old guards.

Although he had popular support outside of the party, Hu soon became a minority in the Party Central Committee because of his strong effort to enforce law and to cleanse the party of corruption, especially his unconcealed enthusiasm for the real retirement of senior administrators, including Deng Xiaoping. Hu now appeared to be threatening and offensive in the eyes of the old guards who held majority in the party centre. Those who were interest seeking and overly sensitive about their own self-importance, those who refused to retire, and those who held fast to the belief that the party's authority should never be allowed to be questioned formed a coalition against Hu. Hu, the only party administrator who had an ardent desire and sincere drive to make the party good enough to deserve popular support, was terminated in January 1987.[62]

Like Mao Zedong a decade ago, the the collective dictatorship of the party needed an administrator who would not interfere with its dominance in policy control. They picked up Zhao Ziyang as the acting general secretary. Zhao appeared to be a technocrat who showed very little interest in party organisation, or he was smart enough to not show interest in this sensitive department after seen what had happened to Hu Yaobang. Zhao actually preferred to be the prime minister, not the general secretary, of the party. As a nonpolitical administrator, Zhao, like Zhou Enlai, managed to not pose any threat to the establishment. Zhao made himself known as a technical man with a lifelong career in economic affairs. His earlier careers in the provinces (Guangdong and Sichuan) and his elevation to the central government after 1978 had all been predicated on his reputation as an able manager of economic development. Therefore, he found it easy to share Deng's goal of economic growth, and so he proceeded to prove how innovative he could be about it.[63]

Having learned from Hu's mistakes, Zhao compromised with the collective dictatorship by bending the law and even allowing its illegal asset of power. Zhao had never showed any sign of impatience with the ageing administrators who continued meddling in party affairs, but he tried very hard to keep them out of the economic realm as much as possible by paying them well to keep silent during the major decision-making process. Instead of straightforwardly urging Deng's prompt retirement, Zhao actually supported the highly irregular secret arrangement to give Deng virtual veto power over the Politburo's major decisions shortly after the Thirteenth Party Congress. This was the veto power that even Mao Zedong was not allowed to have. If Mao would have had that power, he probably would not have had to launch the Cultural Revolution to fight the majority. Zhao also flattered the several ageing administrators with high prestige and high-paying positions to make peace with them rather than deciding to push aggressively for their complete withdrawal from politics.[64] Zhao also turned a blind eye to high-ranking corruption,

although he paid lip service to the need to tighten party discipline. Therefore, he blended in easily with the majority attitude and was considered a
safe person for the office of prime minister. His own lifestyle was flashy
by Chinese standards, and his sons were widely rumoured to have prof-
ited from illegal commercial activities. Predictably, once the rectification
campaign was concluded, he was content to return to the normal state of
affairs, while in fact he presided over a period of even steeper decline of
the party's discipline.[65]

On the question of the party's relations with the intellectuals, however, Zhao's position deviated from the norms of the old guards. His
preoccupation with economic development probably made him more
appreciative of the value of intellectuals and more tolerant of different
opinions. He was the first Chinese leader to have successfully utilised
the "think-tank" format by enlisting the services of a number of well-
educated and well-trained young professionals as advisors. He was also
quite open-minded towards Western economic theories and often invited
both overseas Chinese scholars and Western economists to suggest ways
to accelerate China's economic growth rates.

Being uninterested in the task of party building, Zhao probably was
not loathe to let the party take a backseat and allow the technocrats to
run China's economy. In this connection, he might indeed have been
influenced by an elitist view towards politics, which raised doubt about
his commitment to uphold the critical political importance of the party or
his adherence to the four cardinal principles. It is not accidental that the
concepts of the separation of party and state and the adoption of objective criteria to manage the civil-service system both received extensive
publicity under Zhao's leadership.

The liberal and tolerant tendency presented in Zhao struck the nerves
of the old guards, who out of ignorance or paranoia were afraid of bourgeois liberalism. The fear that had played an important role in Hu Yaobang's dismissal actually accelerated during Zhao's stewardship over
the party. Dissident views had no difficulty finding their way into print.
People like Fang Lizhi got away with increasingly sharp attacks against
the party, the ideology, the political system, and even individual leaders.

Starting in late 1988, many more Chinese intellectuals threw caution to the wind and signed public letters taking positions on one issue or another in clear contravention of the party's policies. Long before the spring of 1989, several movements had been underway to turn the commemoration of the forthcoming seventieth anniversary of the May Fourth Movement into a political indictment of the present regime and to seek a complete rejection of the party's verdict on the anti-rightist campaign of 1957.

The senior administrators saw these trends as alarming because they fundamentally threatened the four cardinal principles and Deng's personal status. Deng had been deeply involved in persecuting the intellectuals during the anti-rightist campaign. In the eyes of the senior leaders, Zhao was responsible for being ineffectual and indecisive in arresting these dangerous trends. They considered Zhou to be a champion of bourgeois liberal tendencies in the fields of arts and literature, although all Zhao did was negotiate a compromise between the old guards and young professionals.

In the midst of these problems, the Chinese economy also had begun to show signs of serious trouble. The inflation rate had reached 30 percent or more in some major cities, and approximately 20 percent throughout the entire country. A difference over economic policies began to develop between Zhao Ziyang, who favoured the continuation of bold reforms, and Premier Li Peng and Deputy Premier Yao Yilin, who preferred to follow Chen Yun's advice to retrench and revive centralised control over certain key sectors. This economic debate inevitably also poisoned Zhao's relationship with some elder leaders of the party.

When the unrest began in the spring of 1989, Zhao perceived it as a threat to his economic program, while the old guards perceived it as a challenge to the four cardinal principles and their right to rule. Zhao downplayed the points of confrontation between the demonstrators and the party, hoping that some gestures of conciliation from the party could placate the former and return the situation to normal as quickly as possible. But the senior leaders were gripped with the fear of a disastrous loss of face if the party should ever give in to popular pressure and chose instead to handle it as a last-ditch defence of the party and Socialism. This fundamental difference in their perceptions of the nature and danger of student movements in 1989 eventually produced another break and shuffling in the ranks of the Politburo.

The frequent personnel crisis that the CCP encountered during the 1987–1989 period demonstrates that the real legislative power in China remained in the hands of the old-guard collective created and led by Deng Xiaoping. The younger executive, Hu, and Zhao could function only if they followed the instructions of the dictatorship and did not cross the boundaries that the latter had set. Just like Liu Shaoqi and Lin Biao, who were purged by Mao Zedong when they were perceived as threatening, both of Deng Xiaoping's general secretaries found themselves in untenable situations as their administration went beyond the original intention or pretended intention of the policies of the dictatorship. In both Mao and Deng's systems, the party legislative (individually or collectively controlled) dictated the office of administration. If any administrator dared to enforce the law beyond the boundaries that had been set by the legislative, even he did not do more than the letter of the regulation for fear of provoking retaliation and endangering his position, eventually losing his job as an administrator. Compared to Liu Shaoqi, Hu and Zhao had much less experience and hardly any power base or time to create their own power base in the central organisations They had much less power and influence. Therefore, the fates of their administrations had to rely on the dictatorship, and each fell out of favour as soon as the dictator withdrew its support.

The main difference between Deng and Mao Zedong was fact that Deng Xiaoping was a reluctant dictator who practiced dictatorship because neither he nor any other of Chinese politicians of the old generation knew any alternative to rule. He did what he had to do to end the misery of China that was caused by the policies of the extreme left. He used his personal charisma to restore peace, unity, and stability that China badly needed after the chaos of revolution. However, Deng knew the limitation of Chinese dictatorship after seeing what had happened after Mao died. In his remaining days, Deng was searching for an alternative to the familiar way, although he faced tremendous internal resistance.[66]

To transform China from an ageing institution of dictatorship to a country ruled by law was a much more difficult task than Deng Xiaoping had ever imagined. In December 1978 Deng Xiaoping, in his pivotal address to the Communist Party Central Committee meeting that set the course for China's reform movement, called for the government to draft a law on factories that would help reform China's chronic, money-losing, state-owned enterprises. Armed with Deng's public endorsement, a senior party economic planner in charge of enterprises set straight to work drafting the law and hammering out a consensus policy among the government ministries, unions, party officials, and legislators concerned with the project. Finally, the bill that China's top leader called for was passed into law—*ten years later.*

To hammer a consensus in words without an effective involvement of personal authority appeared to be extremely difficult, if not impossible. In March 1989 Zhao Ziyang, then the Communist Party's general secretary, addressed a briefing session for key delegates to the annual meeting of China's legislature, the National People's Congress. Zhao told the attendees, all of whom were loyal party members, that the top leadership wanted that year's meeting to show unity and obedience to Central Committee directives. But when the piece of legislation most important to Zhao came up for discussion and vote (a bill designed to give the southeastern Shenzhen Special Economic Zone greater freedom to enact experimental laws, promoting economic reform), there was terrific debate and resentment among the delegates. Led primarily by legislators and officials from Guangdong province (where Shenzhen is located), over 40 percent of the delegates present either voted "no" or abstained on the resolution, which then limped embarrassingly to passage.

If the consensus was hard to reach, personnel shuffling had to be adopted to impose authority. In autumn 1997 Jiang Zemin, Zhao's successor as the party's general secretary, anxious to secure his position after the paramount leader Deng Xiaoping's death, skillfully maneuvered to remove his chief rival Qiao Shi, one of Hu Yaobang's personnel, from the organisational positions that made him a threat. Over the past decade, Qiao had occupied several of the cornerstone posts in China's Communist power hierarchy, including head of party organisation and personnel, overseer of party discipline, and chief of internal security and intelligence. The most important of all was his position as chairman of the Standing Committee of the National People's Congress, which threatened Jiang Zemin's authority as the former "rubber stamp" of the legislation.[67]

In recent years, the National People's Congress has, from time to time, voted down proposed State Council amendments to its own draft laws, and some members of NPC's Standing Committee have specifically voted down two of the party-approved draft laws. It seems that the days before 1979, when NPC would hear a brief summary of a bill, move to an immediate vote, and then invariably pass it unanimously, have gone.[68]

However, it is a mistake to identify Chinese separation of power of legislation and administration with that of the laws in English. The former is a designed and monopolised power, while the latter is an institutionalised competition for power.[69] Both are seemingly defined by their constitutions, yet these languages create different legal structures. While all political parties (both the winner and loser in a particular election) are under the rule of English law, the above-law position of the Communist Party was pretext (constitutionalised) in the Chinese law. The Chinese Constitution passed on January 17, 1975, stipulated that the National People's Congress is the supreme state institution under the leadership of the Chinese Communist Party. The chairman of the Central Committee of the Communist Party commands the armed forces of the entire country. The Constitution vested the party and the party leader with full authority; the party leader actually controls the supreme power of the state. The 1982 Constitution affirms in its preamble adherence to the four basic principles, namely, Socialism, the People's Democratic Dictatorship, Marxism-Leninism and Mao Zedong Thought, and the leadership of the CCP.[70]

The reason why the ruling party has the rights to both lead the Congress and define the ideological foundation of the state is because the party has the authority to write and rewrite the law. This supervision on legislation made separation of power institutionally and constitutionally impossible. The attempt to make a clear distinction between the functions of the state and those of the party is bound to fail, as does "one's attempts to fly by pulling his own hair". In other words, as long as the CCP has the above-law position—which determines who will sit in the Congress; what law is going to be written and announced; what should or should not be the law; how and when a law should be enacted, abolished, or rewritten; and who is going to administer the implication of law—Chinese law will remain a showcase and puppet in the hands of the ruling party.

There were three similarities between the law of Mao and that of Deng, although they pursued entirely different political and organisational policies. One was the fact that inner-party democracy was an instrument to be adopted rather than a law binding the personal authority of the Communist leaders. Second, democracy outside of the party was reluctantly permitted and utilised only when interparty politics were needed and allowed. Third, each insisted on the absolute control of the CCP, who had the real power of legislation and military leadership.

CONCLUSIONS

China's struggle for order, law, and social stability after the Mao period was led by Deng Xiaoping. As a member of Mao's generation of Communists and as a victim of the Cultural Revolution, Deng blamed Mao and the revolution for China's misery, not the party dictatorship. He believed that as long as the party recovered from its destruction and chaos, and focused on economic development, China would be on its way to peace and prosperity; people would be happy ever after. Deng never realised and could not admit to himself that the above-law position of the ruling party was the definitive challenge that impeded Chinese modernisation. He was limited in his vision because he was still part of the old guard of the party and thought that all he needed to do was re-announce the law, as Mao and scores of emperors before him had done.

Based on this assumption, the first thing he did after he returned to power was not try to bring the party under the letter of law; rather, he insisted on the absolute authority and supremacy of the CCP over the law, the state, and the society.[71] Therefore, it is only logical for Deng to ruthlessly crush the democratic movement and oppress the young dissidents. Just like Mao, for Deng, law and democracy were instruments rather than goals of political dominance. At any time, his law was ready to prosecute political crimes and denounce them as being sponsored by the foreign interests. His law, written and rewritten as politics allowed, was willing to sanction any dissidents as "bourgeois liberalists", "imperialist spies", or counterrevolutionaries who desired to overthrow the leadership of the CCP.[72]

Deng's plan to restore unity within the Communist Party and to regain public faith in its leadership failed. The China that Deng left was a country ruled by a collective dictatorship that legislated and administered, yet could not even govern itself. Each faction of this collective had its own by-me laws that legislated distinct and unequal rights and privileges to different individuals and social groups according to one's personal relationship with a particular legislator. Compared to the China that Mao Zedong left thirteen years ago, the key issue has changed from who was going to be the next dictator to rule the country to how the collection of factional and local dictatorial legislators get along with each other (without resorting to military conflict) and gain a consensus to distribute power and wealth. These factions would unite to fight the under laws outside of the party if the outsiders posed a challenge to them; they would ignore or fight each other for supremacy among themselves when the outside threat became suppressed and disappeared.

In thousands of years, there has never been any Chinese law in abstract and impersonal language that has been distinct from and above political power. Mao and Deng were neither the first nor the last rulers who exercised dictatorship. The difference is that Mao manufactured anarchy to maintain his dictatorship, while Deng preferred dictatorship to fight anarchy to achieve order. Neither of the men trusted in the words of law without political interference, yet Mao deliberately erased the law in order to replace it with his own words. Deng, however, took dictatorial politics to safeguard the order that he believed might fall apart too soon and too easily for his plan of economic development to come to fruition.

Deng's realisation of the limits of party dictatorship, his reluctance to push it to ultimate cruelty, and his desire to search for a non-autocratic means to govern opened a new horizon for the following generations of Chinese politicians who have the ambition to lead China away from the actions of its past.

CHAPTER 7

CONCLUSIONS

The law in the People's Republic of China still does not possess an independent binding power as is understood in the English laws, which enjoy the respect of all of its citizens. Chinese law was dictated solely by the Communist Party and administered only under its surveillance. It is a hollow (without a soul) and weak (without teeth) law that can only voice what the party wishes or reflects in its politics and interests. The party, whether represented by an individual or a collective, has failed to discipline itself through rectification movements, chaotic revolutions, or harsh criminal procedures because it is above the law of the land and free from the scrutiny of the public. As long as the ruling party and its members detain this position of above law, an impersonal and nonpolitical law in the Western sense can never prevail.

China, in its five-thousand-year history, has never had a law that has worked without the interference of the politics of words or the influence of arms, or that has worked without an emperor or a group of administrators who functioned as its custodian. Law, as an institution, has played the role of mistress for a ruler or a ruling organisation (a faction

of the society) rather than as a template that has been determined, negotiated, composed, and cultivated by the collective wishes of its citizens.
Collectively, the Chinese people have never had the right to express
opinions, discuss rules, or change the words of law. The law has been
defined and announced by the above-law rulers, no matter what title
they held and regardless of their ideological beliefs or political claims.
Law has been enacted, interpreted, and administrated within a small
spectre of specified and ranked privilege rather than within a broad
range of equal rights. Legislators have always looked after themselves
from a place above the law while vast portions of society remain outside of legal protection.

During the latter half of the twentieth century, China was governed by a
dictatorship of one form or another, sometimes a dictatorship with a single
dictator or a group (party) of dictators. The Cultural Revolution illustrated
the tragedy of a single dictatorship; Deng Xiaoping's regime proved the
failure of a collective dictatorship. Deng's two able administrators, Hu
Yaobang and Zhao Ziyang, could not survive the internal conflict even
before Deng's death. This clearly indicated that Deng had difficulty in pursuing his agenda without making major compromises to the majority old
guards. Deng's failed attempt to discipline the party provided further evidence that he did not have an absolute control of the party, even though it
rallied around him during the national emergency that surrounded the trials of the Gang of Four. After the old guards regained power under Deng's
watch, the party fell apart and the CCP had to utilise military resources to
repress social resentment and popular unrest.

Autocratic rule is deeply rooted in the highly complex social networks of China. Words, such as the abstract words of law and ideas that
they represent, can never succeed without personal connections, which
provide the infrastructure of the society. A discourse can never carry the
day unless an army of administrators who have invested their personal
interests and status are there to prop it up. To force a consensus, a leader
has to bring in his own followers and create a loyal personnel base. Deng
had to help the old guards regain power. Hu Yaobang had to promote his
old subordinates into the Party Central Committee and entrust them with

the most powerful positions. Jiang Zemin had to purge Hu's people and replace them with those of his own.[1]

This is why factionalism has been a constant phenomenon of Chinese politics. Organisation is a necessary instrument for political activities in China as it is in the West. However, the relationships within and between organisations are very different. Factionalism, the opposite of unity, has emerged from an authoritarian context where law allows only one group to be considered legitimate; other organisations or even associations are considered illegal and unrighteous. In China, the concept of unity does not mean a coalition based on ideological compromise and shared interest. Rather, it means elimination of opponents through mental and physical suppression. Any organisation begins as a faction and is an under law (has no legal status). It must constantly escape from the persecution of the above laws and fight for its survival. After an organisation obtains power, the first thing it must do is publicly condemn factionalism, because otherwise individuals in that organization may use this strategy to overthrow positions of others.

Therefore, political organisations and their activities have to carry different names, take a different attitude towards law, and have different legal status determined by whether they were in power or out of it. An emerging party that has yet to obtain a legitimate position would advocate for democracy before it obtained power. As soon as it becomes the ruling party, it comes to worship law and order. It immediately becomes less interested in democracy because it sees democracy as an instrument that a rival could use to overthrow its newly established legal order. Deng Xiaoping encountered challenges to his radical reform policies. Hu Yaobang was ousted because he attacked his opponents too hard and too soon before he could replace his own people on every level of the administration. The old guards ousted him before he could replace them. They dismissed Hu, the party's general secretary, illegally without the consent of the Plenum of the Central Committee, which was required according to the Party Charter. This was the same illegal procedure by which many Communist administrators were purged during the Cultural Revolution.

The fall of Hu Yaobang and Zhao Ziyang revealed the weakness of a collective dictatorship led by Deng Xiaoping. Without Mao's charisma and ruthless strategies, Deng Xiaoping's law was weak, and inefficient at best, as it battled with a small group of angry old men who were pushed into political retirement against their will. They had refused to fade away; they insisted on holding onto power, which served nothing except their personal interests.

It will be a long time before China has a law detached from political rhetoric and personal connotation—a law that would regulate the entire society without exception for social privilege or political favour and a law that would extend its protection to the rights of every ordinary citizen. Law has to be able to draw an impersonal, nonpartisan, and unshakeable line, which cannot be altered and abused by anyone, especially the politicians and party leaders. Along the way, Chinese people must learn to respect the words of law and defend them vigorously.

NOTES

INTRODUCTION

1. Please see similar limitations described by Professor B. S. Jackson about early Biblical Law in Hebrew (up to the time of Ezra). Jackson 1989, 187.
2. Kuhn 1970; Wakeman 1966; Chesnaux 1972, 1973; Naquin 1976, 1981; V. Y. C. Shih 1967; Michael 1964, 1971; Esherick 1976, 1987; Chiang Siang-tseh1954; Graff 2002, 227–251; Gray 1990, 138–204; Crowell 1983, 319–354; Ownby 1996; Li Wenzhi 1948; Parsons 1957, 1970; Perry 1980; Tong 1991; Chu Fang 1998.
3. Tanner 1999; Fewsmith 1994; Lubman 1999, 2005; Townsend and Womack 1986; Chang Ta-kuang 1987; Dicks 1989; Di Guiseppe 1990; Domes 1985; Hsia and Johnson 1986; Keith 1994; Pye 1971, 1981; Saich 1991, 1996; J. T. Dreyer 1993; Ogden 1992; Lieberthal 1995; Wang Yaping 2004; O'Brien 1990; P. B. Potter 1994a, 1994b; Bernstein 2000; Bian 1994.
4. Cheng Li 2001; Mulvenon 1997; Shambaugh 2002.
5. Wakeman 1995, 2003; Leutner 2002; C. M. Lewis 1976; Twitchett and Fairbank 1978.
6. Chi 1976, 1982; Fu Chunyang 2007; Fung 2000; Lary 2007; Fenby 2003.
7. Zhang Guotao 1972, 1991; Twitchett and Fairbank, 1983.
8. D. J. Anderson 1973; Byron and Pack 1992; Chakrabarti 1998; M. Goldman 1981; Cheek 1989a, 1989b, 1992a, 1998.
9. Bian 1994; Hao and Johnson 1995; Wu Haimin 1990; Yang Liguang 1996; Yan Shi 1998; Liu Shengrong and Dan Wei 2001.
10. Chen Guidi 2004; Yang Yonghua 2005; Liu Shengrong and Dan Wei 2001; Yan Shi 1998.
11. Bian 1994; Gold 1985; Guthrie 1997, 1998; Keister 2004; Wank 1999; Yan Yun-Xiang 1996; M. Yang 1994.

CHAPTER 1

1. Sharron Gu 2006, 76–107, 158–189.
2. Hu Houxuan 2000, 2001a, 2001b, 2003; Chang Kwang-chih 1980.
3. Hetzron, 1997; Falaschi 1988; Lipinski 1997; Rabin 1991; Freedman 1992; Mahmūd Alī Ghūl 1993; Houston 2004.

4. Sáenz-Badillos 1993; Kutscher 1982; Hoffman 2004.
5. Cua 1978; Peerenboom 1993a; 2002a, 29–36; Hulsewe 1955; Graham 1989; MacCormack 1990; McKnight 1987, 1992; McKnight and Liu 1999; Bernhardt and Huang 1994; P. C. Huang 1996, 2001; Leng 1967; Victor Li 1971, 1978; Tay 1987, 1990; Lubman 1999; Alford 1999; Cai 1999; Orts 2001; DeBary and Lufrano 1999–2000; Hall and Ames 1999; Tu 1993; Neville 2000.
6. Hochstrasser 2000, 1–39, 111–149; Benditt 1978; Friedrich 1958, 84–91; Cairns 1949, 250–267; Penner 1987; Duyvendak 1974; Needham 1956, 2:518–544; Bodde 1957,709–727; Bodde and Morris 1973; Chu T'ung-tsu 1961; Hulsewe 1955; Peerenboom 1990,1993b, 2002a, 34–36; Turner 1989; Tomohisa Ikeda, 2005.
7. Needham 1956, 214–215; Hall and Ames 1987; Peerenboom 1990a; Wang Hsiao-po and L. Chang 1986; Schwartz 1985, 249.
8. Geoffry McCormack 1996; McKnight 1987, 1992; McKnight and Liu 1999; Bernhardt and Huang 1994; P. C. Huang 1996, 2001; Shaochuan Leng and Palmer 1967; V. H. Li 1971, 1978; Tay 1987, 1990; Lubman 1999; Alford 1999; Cai Dingjian 1999; Peerenboom 1990a.
9. Baker 1979; Tiefer 2004; Clayton 1992; Limbaugh 2001.
10. Pye 1971, 3–12.
11. Pye 1971, 132–153; Jiang Weiguo 1978; Liu Zhi, 1972; Liu Chang 2007; Worthing 2007.
12. Sharron Gu 2006, 158–192; McKnight 1987, 122–124; Peerenboom 2002a, 36.
13. McKnight 1987, 112–113; 1992, 62–65; Jinfan Zhang, Zhang Xipo, and Zeng Xianyi 1981.
14. Bodde and Morris 1973; McKnight 1987, 1992; Chen Gu-yuan 1935; Jinfan Zhang, Zhang Xipo, and Zeng Xianyi 1981; Qian Mu 1969; Wang Jieping 1982; Metzger 1973.
15. Sharron Gu 2006, 158–189.
16. Hulsewe 1955, 1981; Duyvendak, 1974; Gao 1980; Bodde 1986; Qian Mu 1973, 1969.
17. Hulsewe 1955, 1981, 1985; Bodde 1986; D. Cao 2004, 2007a, 2007b; Duyvendak 1974; DeBary 1998; Uchida 2005; Kern 2008.
18. *Han Shu* 1995, 10, 15b; 19A, 4a–5b; 19B, 48a–b; 39, 4b–5a; *Hou Han Shu* 1923, 24, 6b–7a; 27, 5b–6b; 29, 4b; 36, 3a–4b; Qian Mu 1982, 4–5; Wang Yu-ch'uan 1949, 144–179; Hulsewe 1955, 14; Ku Pan 2:23; Bielenstein, 1954–1967, 3:119–128, 151–153; 1980, 5–12, 143–144.
19. *Hou Han Shu* 1923, 1B, 19a–b; Bielenstein 1980, 12–13.

20. *Han Shu* 1995, 11:8a; 19A:4b; 19B:51a; *Hou Han Shu* 1923, 1B:7a; 19a–b; Bielenstein 1980, 12–17, 145–147.
21. Bielenstein 1980, 143.
22. *Hou Han Shu* 1923, 44, 74:6a; 146–147.
23. Dubs 1944, 1:8–9; Bielenstein 1980, 96, 146.
24. Dubs 1944, 2:23; Wang Yu-ch'uan 1949, 145–179.
25. *Han Shu* 1995, 10:15b; 19A:5b; 19B:48a.
26. Bielenstein 1980, 11–12.
27. Qian Mu 1982, 37.
28. Qian Mu 1982, 37–40.
29. Qian Mu 1982, 41–42.
30. Qian Mu 1982, 67.
31. Qian Mu 1982, 71.
32. Farmer 1995, 33–47; Langlois 1988, 118–719; Taylor 1976; Huang Chang-chien 1977.
33. Farmer 1995, 49–50; Hucker 1985, 72–74.
34. Wu Han 1972, 251–252; Farmer 1976, 71–86, 100–104; 1995, 100–113; Dreyer 1982; Hucker 1985, 13–14.
35. Jiang Yonglin 2005, xli, xci, xlvi; Farmer 1995, 150–223; Yifan Yang 1992; Hucker 1978, 44–46.
36. Zhu Jianhua 1994, 11; Jiang Yonglin 2005, lxxx; Farmer 1995, 64–80.
37. Zhang Dexin and Mao Peiqi 1995, 745–951; Yang Yifan 1988, 195–452; Shen Jiaben 1929, 1783–1896; Huang Chang-chien 1977, 2:155–207; Farmer 1995, 69–73.
38. Yang Yifan 1988, 45–57, 252, 337, 419.
39. Shen Jiaben 1929; Yang Yifan 1988.
40. Shen Jiaben 1929.
41. Yang Yifan 1988, 41–76.
42. Zhang Dexin and Mao Peiqi 1995, 387–410; Farmer 1995,118; Jiang Yonglin 2005, lxxxii–lxxxiii. I have made minor changes in the translation.
43. Wang Hongxu 1962, 72.1b.
44. Hucker 1969, 46.
45. *Hou Han Shu* 1923, 78, 108:4a, 7a–b; Bielenstein 1980, 150–151; Wang Yu-ch'uan 1949, 144–169.
46. Farmer 1995, 49; Qian Mu 1982, 97.
47. Wang Hongxu 1962, 74:24a–32a; Hucker 1961, 10–12, 55–58; Ding Yi 1983; Crawford 1961, 115–148.
48. Wang Hongxu 1962, 95; Ding Yi 1983; Anderson 1990.
49. Qian Mu 1982, 97.

50. McMorran 1979, 133–66.
51. Qian Mu 1969; Silas H. L. Wu 1970, 86; P. H. Huang 1996, 502–515; Bartlett 1991, 2–3.
52. Bartlett 1991, 1.
53. Silas H. L. Wu 1970, 509–511.
54. Bartlett 1991, 4.
55. Bartlett 1991, 171.
56. Bartlett 1991, 173, 350–351; Millward 1998, 2004; Perdue 2005.
57. Bartlett 1991, 194.
58. Mair 1985, 325–357; Chu T'ung-tsu 1961, 309.
59. G. Jer-lang Chang 1978a; Übelhör 1986, 371–388.
60. Andrew and Rapp 2000, 49–58.
61. Hsiao Kung-chuan 1960, 186; Andrew and Rapp 2000, 58–59.
62. Spence 1974; Spence and Wills 1979; Wakeman 1985.
63. Hucker 1966.
64. Liang Qichao 1941, 35; Hucker 1951, 1966, 2:225–226, 242; Creel 1970, C. Hsu 1965, 92–96; Chu T'ung-tsu 1961, 242–266; Metzger 1973, 235; Hsieh Pao Chao 1925.
65. Waley 1949, 41–43; Feifel 1961, 30–33; E. Hung 1997, 24.
66. Qian Mu 1982, 72.
67. Qian Mu 1982, 73–74.
68. Gao I han 54–56; Kracke 1953, 33–37; Qian Mu 1982, 59–62; Hucker 1966, 17–18.
69. J. Liu 1959, 1962.
70. Kracke 1953, 31; Hucker 1966, 21.
71. Ko Shaomin 1988, 57:1a–8b, 85–91; Ratchnevsky 1937–1985, 153–180.
72. Hucker 1966, 25.
73. Hucker 1966, 26–27.
74. Hucker 1966, 6; Jacobini 1991, chap. 7.
75. Hucker 1966, 27.
76. Hucker 1966, 289–290.
77. Hucker 1996, 184–185, 192–195.
78. Qian Mu 1982, 76.
79. M. M. Anderson 1990, 256–257; Metzger 1973, 433–435; S. H. Wu 1967, 1970; *Qingkuo Xingzheng Fa* 1906, 2:4:4:195.
80. Di 2002, 5–16.
81. Hu Shi 1924, 142; Yang Guo 1996.
82. Sheng Langxi 1934, 63–67; Hayashi 1958, 7–9; Meskill 1969, 150–151.
83. Sheng Langxi 1934, 43; Hu Shi 1924, 142–145; Meskill 1969, 152.

84. Li Xinda 1995; Qian Maowei 2004; Tian Jianrong 2004; Xue Ruizhao 2004; Yang Xuewei, Sun Peiqing, et al. 2004; Sun Peiqing and Li Guojun 1995; McMullen 1988.
85. Qian Mu 1982, 111–112.
86. Qian Mu 1982, 138–139; Fang Hao 1954, 1:104; Qian Mu 1956, 2:423.
87. R. Brown 1997.
88. Qian Mu 1982, 124.
89. Li Ji 1953, 1:35a; Peerenboom 1990b, 309–329.
90. Kuhn 1970; Wakeman 1966, 2003; Chesnaux 1972, 1973; Jen Yu-wen 1973; V. Y. C. Shih 1967; Michael 1964, 1971; Chu Wen-djang 1966; Chiang Siang-tseh 1954; Weller 1994; Naquin 1976, 1981.
91. Liang Fangzhong 1981, chart 1.4–11; Yin Yingzhang, 1985, 2:490.
92. Qin Guojing 1996, 235–238.
93. Lin Zexu 1985, 2:568; Cameron 1931; Wright 1957; C. M. Lewis 1976; Hsiao Gungchuan 1975; Purcell 1974; Ownby 1996.
94. Rong Hong 1915, 88–97, 119–120, 147–177.
95. Wang Shounan 1999, 133–144; Wang Tao 1984a, 1144–1145; 1984b, 858–860.
96. Wang Shounan 1999; Wang Tao 1984a; *Guangxu* 1955, 576–838.
97. Alitto 1979; Tang Xiaobing 1996; Chang Hao 1971; Chang P'eng-yüan 1964, 1972; Ding Wenjiang 1958; Ding Wenjiang and Zhao Fengtian 1983; P. C. Huang 1972; Liang Qichao, 1936, 1941, 1959, 2000; L. E. A. Ma 1990; Min, Kuhn, and Brook 1989; Kang 1967.
98. *Qing Shigao* 1960, 2:464.
99. Ding Wenjiang and Zhao Fengtian 1983, 146.
100. Qinghua 1998, 1247–1248; Yuanzhang 1988.
101. Zhu Shoupeng 1958, 4: 4601.
102. Zhu Shoupeng 1958, 4: 4601.
103. Zhu Shoupeng 1958, 4:4655–4771.
104. Zu Yuhe, Ouyang Junxi, and Shu Wen 2004, 28–39.
105. Peng Yuxin 1958, 8–9; Wang Yanan 1981, 162–163.
106. Zu Yuhe, Ouyang Junxi, and Shu Wen 2004, 47–49; Gugung-Bowuyuan-Ming-Qing-Danganbu 1995, 2:713–746.
107. Jones 1994; Wu Tan 1992.
108. Hucker 1969, 1971, 1985; Wu Han 2000.

CHAPTER 2

1. The pursuit of a military career was highly stigmatised according to Confucian tradition. As the popular saying describes, "No good man wants to be a soldier, just as no good steel would be used in making a nail." In Chinese society, all the best and brightest pursue learning and and look down upon a military career. Personal armies had been apparent during most periods of Chinese history, and especially during the periods between dynasties. It was a major factor in the fall of many dynasties. Eberhard 1950, 102–105; Pye 1971, 32–35.

2. Chen Gujia 1997; Lee 2000; Walton 1999; Cheek 1992a, 1992b; Goldman, Cheek, and Hamrin 1987; Qian Maowei 2004; Tian Jianrong 2004; Xue Ruizhao 2004; Yang Xuewei, Sun Peiqing, et al. 2004; Sun Peiqing and Li Guojun 1995; Gong Pengcheng 2007; Tian Gang 2005; S. Chan 2004; Li Guowen 2004.

3. Lo Ergang 1984, 1997; Bales 1937; Wen Gongzhi 1930, 1:39–60; Shen Jian 1937.

4. Hatano 1994; Bonavia 1995; Waldron 1995, 161–180, 277–278.

5. Lujun Bu 1916, 1:1–2; Pye 1971, 12; Li Xuezhi 2004.

6. J. Chen 1967; Fang Ke 2003; Young 1977; Satō 2005; Wen Fei 2004c; Hou Yijie 1994; Wu Changyi 2001; Liao Yizhong 1997.

7. Wen Fei 2004; Wen Gongzhi 1930, 1:1–14, 39–60; Shen Jian 1937.

8. Whitson and Huang 1973, 13–20; Pye 1971, 39–60.

9. Bales 1937; Hail 1927.

10. Reid 1935, chap. 12 and 13; Bland 1912; Wen Fei 2004.

11. Chen Zongshun 1987; Ling 1988.

12. Sun Yatsen 1981–1986, 1:544–579; Chen Xiqi 1991, 610–618; Zu Yuhe, Ouyang Junxi, and Shu Wen 2004, 330–338; Liew 1971; Cao Yabo 1982, 1:209–392; Schiffrin 1970; Sherman 1968, 120–125.

13. Sun Yatsen 1981–1985, 1:544–576, 2:102–107, 302–303; Chen Xiqi, 1991, 601–615, 656–685; Hu Hanmin 1969; Pu Yi 1987, 41–43; Bai Jiao 1966, 23–26; Zu Yuhe, Ouyang Junxi, and Shu Wen 2004, 413–441; Spence 1974, 277–278.

14. Sun Yatsen, 1981–1985, 2:102–106, 302–303; Chen Xiqi 1991, 656; Sherman 1968, 132–143.

15. Fu Zhengyuan 1994, 153–154; Zu Yuhe, Ouyang Junxi, and Shu Wen 2004, 428–441.

16. Wen Gongzhi 1930, 1:8; Pye 1971, 15; Nie Leng 1994; Liu Wangling 1975; Wang Yungao 2004; Lu Juntian 1987.

17. Li Liejun 1996; Zhu Zongzhen and Yang Guanghui 1983, 2:762–785; Zu Yuhe, Ouyang Junxi, and Shu Wen 2004, 476; MacNair 1931, 34–35; Hornbeck 1916, chap. 5 and 6; Pye 1971, 15–17; Wen Fang 2004.
18. Lin Yi 1987.
19. Zhang Jungu 1971; Shen Yunlong 1972; Pye 1971, 16, 137; MacNair 1931, 37–38.
20. Nie Leng 1994; Zhang Guangan 1973; Pye 1971, 16–18.
21. Xu Guoqi 2005, 81–113; La Fargue 1937.
22. Pu Yi 1996; Lu Yongyan 2006.
23. MacNair 1931, 48; Pye 1971, 18–20, 60–94; Wen Gongzhi 1930, 1:8–9.
24. Dong Yao 1995.
25. Vinacke 1922, 141–147; Linebarger 1938, 155–160.
26. Wen Gongzhi 1930, 1:11–29; *China Year Book* 1912–1939.
27. Wen Gongzhi 1930, 1:11–29; Pye 1971, 19.
28. Ding Huayong 1989; Zi 1988; Shen Yunlong 1979.
29. Pye 1971, 18–19.
30. Wen Gongzhi 1930, 1:11.
31. Guo Jianlin 2006; Wen Fei 2004a; Dong Yao 1995; Wu Tingxie 2007.
32. Wen Fei 2004; Diyi Tushuguan 1924.
33. Wen Gongzhi 1930, 1:11; Wen Fei 2004; Pye 1971, 21.
34. Wen Gongzhi 1930, 1:11; Feng Yuxiang 1930, 1:7.
35. Hu Yuhai 2005; Wen Fei 2004b; Xu Che 2004; Chen Chongqiao, Hu Yuhai, and Hu Yuzheng 1991; Wen Gongzhi 1930 1:49–100.
36. Wen Gongzhi 1930, 2:118.
37. Wen Gongzhi 1930, 2:115–132.
38. Feng Yuxiang 1930, 30.
39. Shen Yunlong 1979.
40. MacNair 1931, 52–53; Pye 1971, 23.
41. Pye 1971, 60–76.
42. Vinacke 1920, 156–157; Pye 1971, 24.
43. Feng Yuxiang 1930, 2:57–59; Pye 1971, 24–26.
44. Pye 1971, 25–26.
45. MacNair 1931, 54.
46. Pye 1971, 96–113.
47. Wen Gongzhi 1930, 2:181.
48. Feng 1930, 2:96–102.
49. Pye 1971, 77–94; Lou and Fu 1924.
50. Feng Yuxiang 1930, 2: 111–115; Pye 1971, 27–29, 39–45.
51. Wen Gongzhi 1930, 2:180–205.

52. Aixinjueluo 2004.
53. Wang Xiaohua 2000; Wen Fei 2004f.
54. Pye 1971, 32–35.
55. Wen Gongzhi 1930, 1:166.
56. Pye 1971, 133.
57. For a detailed comparison of Chinese and Japanese history, please see my forthcoming book *Rising Sun and Fading Moon*, chap. 5.
58. Van de Ven 1991, 9–54; 2003, 65–72; Waldron 1995, 280; Dirlik 1989, 61–73; 1991.
59. Jiang Kefu 1987; Guo Taifeng 2004; Zeng Xianlin 1991; Huang Xiurong 1992; Van de Ven 2003; Jordan 1976; Wilbur 1984; Schwartz 1957.
60. Chen Fulin 1990.
61. Sun Yatsen 1981–1986, 5:570–572; Van de Ven 2003, 68–69.
62. Zhang Cixi 1999; Iechika 2005; Ye Yang 1999; Cui 2003; Zhang Liang-shen 1998; Wen Shaohua 2007; Lin Kuo 2001b.
63. Van de Ven 2003, 97–98.
64. Wilbur and How 1989, 2:602–609; Jin Chongji 1988, 100–114.
65. Li Zong ren 1979, 136–140; *Jiang Jieshi Nianpu*, 529–540; Jordan 1976, 72–73; Van de Ven 2003, 97–98.
66. Van de Ven 2003, 104; Wilbur and How 1989, 1:255–265.
67. Wilbur and How 1989, 2:620–621; Jiang Kefu 1992, 254–288; Van de Ven 2003, 105.
68. Jordan 1976; Issacs 1938; Wilbur 1984; Wilbur and How 1989.
69. Waldron 1995.
70. Jacobs 1981, 211–212; Saich 1996, 233.
71. Van de Ven 2003, 112.
72. Jin Chongji 1996, 99–119.
73. Van de Ven 2003, 151–153.
74. Schram 1992, 2:426–427.
75. Schram 1992, 2:426–430; Wilbur 1984, 644–648; S. Smith 2000, 130–188; Van de Ven 2003, 114–118.
76. Saich 1991, 2:201.
77. Wilbur 1984, 344–348; Van de Ven 2003, 170.
78. Smith, 130–164.
79. Smith, 173–187; Van de Ven 2003, 180–182.
80. Smith, 187–189.
81. Wilbur and How 1989, 1:399–400.
82. Van de Ven 2003, 191–198.
83. Wilbur 1984, 648–681; Schwartz 1964, 67; Van de Ven 2003, 109–111.

84. Duan Yusheng 1989; Huang Lin 2007; Liu Bingrong 1999; Li Lie 1996; Wang Xilan 1997; Zhu De 2003; Jin Chongji 2000; Nie Rongzhen 1983; *Nie Rongzhen Zhuan* 1994; Huang Yao 1996; Lin Qingshan 1988, vol. 1; Gu Yongzhong 2007.
85. Wilbur 1984, 173–196.
86. Shi Shiming 2001; Zhongshan Daxue 1979; Cheng Jin 1997.
87. Schwartz 1964, 63.
88. Wen Fei 2004d.
89. Jordan 1976, 126–137; Chang Shih-ying 1997, 147–180.
90. Nanjing Guomin Zhengfu 1993, 35–37; Chang Shiying 1997, 2:154–180; Li Zongren 1979, 23.
91. Li Zongren 1979, 242–245; Liu F. Fu 1956, 12–14.
92. Luo Chunpu 2004; Wang Xiang 1999.
93. Williamsen 1975; *Huangpu Jianjun Shi* 1955; Wen Wen 2006.
94. Liu F. Fu 1956, 12–13.
95. Jiang Ping and Luo Kexiang 1993; Zhu Zongzhen and Wang Chaoguang 1996.
96. Chen Yan 1996.
97. Van de Ven 2003, 124–126.
98. Chen Boda 1947; Yu Liang 1955; Chen Tingyi 2004; Zhang Jianzhi 2004; Yang Zhesheng 2001; Wu Jingping 1992; Yang Jing 1999.
99. Chen Liwen 1991; Wu Jingping 1998; Coble 1980; Seagave 1985.
100. Ishikawa 2006; Yao Jinguo 2006; Barrett and Shyu 2001; Bunker 1972; Li Kuo 2001; Van de Ven 2003, 98–105; *Jiang Jieshi* Nianpu 1994, 528, 536–537.

CHAPTER 3

1. Strauss 1998; Sutton 1980; Li Yong and Zhang Zhongtian 1995; Xu Xiaoqun 1997; Fang Yonggang 2007; *Jiang Jieshi Nianpu* 1994; Zhang Xiuzhang 2007.
2. Luo Chunpu 2004; Zhu Jianhua 1994; Feng Yuxiang 1930, 1947, 1949, 2004; Zhou Yu'e and Chen Hongmin 1994; Hu Hanmin 1969; Pye 1981, 128–130; Strauss 1998; Sutton 1980; Sih 1970; Yan Xishan 1997.
3. Snow 1961b; S. Smith 2002; Stranahan 1998.
4. Jeans 1992; J. P. Harrison 1972; Coble 1980; Eastman 1984, 1991; Wilson 1977a, 1977b, 1991; Sih 1970; G. T. Yu 1966; A. N. Young 1971; Yan Xishan 1997; Ai Fei 1984; Sheridan 1966; Zhou Yu'e and Chen Hongmin

1994; Hu Hanmin 1969; Sutton 1980; Li Ping 2006; Jocelyn and McEwen 2006.

5. Snow 1961b; Eastman 1984, 1991; Salisbury 1985; Byron and Pack 1992; Wilbur 1984; Li Ping 2006; Jocelyn and McEwen 2006.
6. Chi 1982; Crozier 1976.
7. Wang Cheng 1982, 27; Groot 2004, 3–4; M. B. Young 2004.
8. Eastman 1990, 243–245; Coble 1980, 10–12, 30–38; Dirlik 1989, 989–990; Groot 2004, 4–5; Van de Ven 1996, 1997; Wakeman 1995.
9. Geisert 2001; Hsiung and Levine 1992; Eastman 1990, 1991; Waldron 1995.
10. Fitzgerald 1989, 113–116; Eastman 1990, 160; Fenby 2003; Jordan 2001.
11. Deng Yuanzhong 1984, 112–118.
12. Eastman 1990, 160–163; Fitzgerald 1989; Groot 2004, 3–4; Fewsmith 1985; E. S. K. Fung 2000; Xu Xiaoqun 2000; Yeh 1990.
13. Zhou Tiandu 2002, 2006; Taofen 2000; Ma Zhongyang 1997; Lin Difei 1999; Jiang Ping 1999; Chen Fulin 1990; Hung Chang-tai 1994.
14. Jeans 1992, 140–144; Chien Tuan-sheng 1950, 357–358; C. Johnson 1962; L. Li 1994; Linebarger 1941, 175; Groot 2004, 8–9; Jiang Tao 2005; Chen Fulin 1990.
15. Garver 1988, 43–46.
16. Wu Tienwei 1976; Zhang Xueji 1996; Li Yibin 1998; Yang Han 2007; Wu Changyi 2001; Hao Jiangsheng 2004.
17. Jiang Tao 2005.
18. Compton 1952; Belden 1970; Lindsay 1950.
19. Chang Jui-te 1993; *Guomin Zhengfu Junzheng Zuzhi Shiliao* 1996; Furuya 1981; Jiang Kefu 1987, 1992.
20. Chesnaux 1972, 1973; S. Smith 2000; Huang Li 1999; Wang Shiyi 1992; *Zhongguo Gongchandang Shigao* 2006; *Zhongguo Guomindang Dangwu Fazhan Shiliao* 1999–2000; Yi Yang 2004.
21. Compton 1952, xix–xxi; Van de Ven 2003; Hsiung and Levine 1992; Rosinger 1944; Wen Gongzhi 1930; Zhang Xianwen and Fang Qingqiu 2001; Shum 1988; Van de Ven 2000.
22. Rosinger 1944, 132–142; Compton 1952, xx–xxii; J. Chen 1965, 1979; Chen Yung-fa 1986.
23. Wales 1949, 226.
24. Compton 1952, 16–35.
25. Huang Li 1999; S. Smith 2000; He Husheng 2006.
26. Li Pu 1997; Zhao Jianguo 2001; Wang Xilan 1997; Luo Yingcai 1996; Luo Laiyong and Zhou Junlun 2001; Cai Renzhao 1994.
27. Apter 1994; Chen Yung-fa 1994; Saich 1995; Cheek 1998.

28. Mao's speech delivered on February 8, 1942, as cited in Compton 1952, 33.
29. Compton 1952, 1–8.
30. Barnett 1967; J. W. Lewis 1963; Townsend 1969, 174–176; Lifton 1961.
31. *Zhou Enlai Nianpu* 1998.
32. Lieberthal 1995, 50; Teiwes 1979, 32–38; J. A. Cohen 1968.
33. Liu Shaoqi 1984, 1991.
34. Compton 1952, xxxix; Wylie 1980.
35. Compton 1952, 156–160.
36. Cao Zhongbin 1991; Zhou Guoquan 2003.
37. Li Sishen 2005; Li Zhiying 1994; Wu Baopu and Li Zhiying 2007.
38. Compton 1952, 33–53, 255–268.
39. Lu Haijing 2003; Zhang Guotao 1991.
40. Chang Jui-te 1993; Chen Boda 1947; M. Hsia Chang 1985; Fei Yunwen 1985; Ma Lie 2007; Jiang Shaozhen 1994; Lin Kuo 2001a; Ma Chi 2007; Shen Meijun 1996; Shen Zui 1962, 1979; Shen Zui and Wen Qiang 1980, 1983, 1984; Fewsmith 1985; Wakeman 2003; Cheng Yiming 1979a, 1979b, 1980; Chung 2000; Chen Feng 2006.
41. Zhang Weihan 1992, 79–151; Xiao Zuolin 1960, 38–39; Chi 1976, 1982; Chiang Kai-shek 1957; Iechika 2005.
42. Deng Yuanzhong 1984, 113; Wakeman 2003, 55–56.
43. Gan Guoxun 1979, 37, as cited in Wakeman 2003, 62.
44. Yuanhong Deng 1984, 119, as cited in Wakeman 2003, 62.
45. Gan Guoxun 1984, 36–37; Deng Yuanzhong 1984, 118–130; M. Hsia Chang 1985, 41–42; Wakeman 2003, 61–62.
46. Chen Feng 2006; Wong Yuan 2003; Chiang Kai-shek 1984, 1985.
47. Deng Yuanzhong 1984, 35, as cited in Wakeman 2003, 57.
48. Gan Guoxun 1984; Wakeman 2003, 56–97; Deng Yuanzhong 1984, 35–37; M. Hsia Chang 1985; Chen Jingbao and Chen Yanping 1991; Chen Weiru 1988; Chen Yung-fa 1986, 1994; Deng Baoguang 1986.
49. Gan Guoxun 1984, 36–37; Wakeman 2003, 60.
50. Deng Yuanzhong 1984, 117; Wakeman 2003, 61–62.
51. Shen Meijiun 1996, 171; Wakeman 2003, 57–59, 413.
52. Deng Yuanzhong 1984, 118–119.
53. M. Hsia Chang 1985; Chen Weiru 1988; Chen Yun-fa 1986, 1994; Deng Baoguang 1986; Shen Zui 1962, 1979, 1983.
54. Wakeman 2003, 55–96.
55. M. Hsia Chang 1985, 130; Fewsmith 1985, 178; Wakeman 2003, 85–86.
56. Xiao Zuolin 1960, 30–44; Wakeman 2003, 86–87.

57. To make the translation flow better in English, I have made some changes in the quotations. Deng Yuanzhong 1984, 119; Wakeman 2003, 61–63.
58. Shen Meijuan 1996; Fei Yunwen 1985; Shen Yuan 1991; Dai Li 1984; Jing Shenghong 1989; Wakeman 2003, 157–159.
59. Bao Zhenyuan 1998; Jin Liangnian 1991.
60. Shen Zui 1984, 74–75; Luo Guangbin and Yang Yiyan 1977.
61. Shen Zui 1984, 75; Wakeman 2003, 163–164.
62. Shen Zui 1984, 75–76; Wakeman 2003, 164–165.
63. Luo Guangbin and Yang Yiyan 1977.
64. Luo Guangbin and Yang Yiyan 1977, 176, 108, as cited in Wakeman 2003, 162.
65. Liu Hong 2001; Ye Yonglie 2002.
66. Van de Ven 2003, 133.

CHAPTER 4

1. Peerenboom 2002a, 43–45.
2. Leng Shaochuan and Palmer 1967.
3. Peerenboom 2002a, 45.
4. One can trace and understand Mao's strategic thinking and method from his original interpretation and political manipulation of Chinese history. Mao 1969–1971, 1981, 1987–1998, 1991.
5. Teiwes and Warren, as cited in Saich 1995, 339–387; 1996; B. Yang 1986, 235–271; Hu Sheng 1994; Woody 1989, 168–169.
6. For a systematic comparative study of the forms of language and history of ideological discourse and political authority, see my forthcoming book, *Word Prophet*.
7. Saich 1995, 221; Madsen 1986; Zhang Guotao 1972, 2:427–429, 350–360; Selden 1971, 7–10; Holm 1992, 77–96; Cheek 1984b, 25–57.
8. Selden 1971; Wylie 1980; Apter 1995, 193–232; Compton 1952; Price 1927; Holm 1991, 79–102.
9. Schram 1969, 1992; Levenson 1965.
10. Apter 1995, 189–234; Seybolt 1986.
11. Mao, "Resolution on Certain Questions in the History of Our Party" on April 1945, included in Mao Zedong 1981, 3:177–225; J. P. Harrison 1972, 212–218; Teiwes 1979.
12. Cheng Min, 1993; Byron and Pack 1992; Ding Longjia and Ting Yu 1999; Faligot and Kauffer 1989; Lin Qingshan 1985.

13. Goldman 1967b, 1978a, 1978b, 1981, 2002; Goldman, Cheek, and Hamrin 1987.
14. MacFarquhar, Cheek, and Wu 1989, 39–49; Doolin 1964, 12–17.
15. Apter 1994, xv–xvii.
16. Apter 1994, xviii–xxviii.
17. Barnett 1964; Vogel 1969; Teiwes 1978; 1979, 105–165.
18. Nakajima 1977; Teiwes 1979, 105–176; Bridgham 1970a, 206–208; Ma Weian 1999; Shi Dongbing 1994; Zhang Yuwen 2000.
19. Mao 1981, 5:161–163; Schurmann 1971.
20. Teiwes 1979, 183; Wenxian Zhongyang 2005; Su Tairen 2004; Yang Bingzhang 2004; Lin Qingshan 1988; Hu Ping 1988.
21. Teiwes 1979, 202–208; Ma Weian 1999.
22. Teiwes 1979, 240.
23. Mao Zedong 1981, 1:67, 2:92–108; Teiwes 1979, 213–215, 237; MacFarquhar 1960; 1983a, 57–90.
24. Mao 1967, 2:105.
25. Teiwes 1979, 263–264.
26. Mao 1981, 5:342–348; Teiwes 1989, 242–254; Mac Farquhar 1960; 1974, 193–219, 226–229, 285; 1983, 375–389; Solomon 1971, 304.
27. Mao 1967, 2:73–77, 84–86; 1981, 5:353, 358–359, 370; Teiwes 1979, 231–232.
28. Teiwes 1979, 233.
29. Goldman 1967, 179–186; MacFarquhar 1974, 179; Teiwes 1979, 232.
30. Mao 1981, 5:344–345, 373–374; 1967, 2:74–75; Teiwes 1979, 233–234.
31. Teiwes 1979, 275.
32. Mao 1981, 2:179, 268–69; Teiwes 1979, 383.
33. Teiwes 1979, 381–383.
34. *Xinzhongguo jishi* 1986, 263.
35. Peng Dehuai 2002; Ji Xue and Zeng Fanhua 2000; Liu Songmao 1998; Zheng Qi 1998; Wang Chengguang 1996.
36. Teiwes 1974b, 1978; 1979, 384–440; Dittmer 1977b; Terry 1976, 796–806; Joffe 1975; Ahn 1972, 97–100; Vogel 1969, 229–230; Charles 1966; Dittmer 1977a; Bridgham 1970a; Ding Wang 1969; Wang Chengguang 1996.
37. Zhu Jiamu 2000; Sun Yeli 1996; Teiwes 1979, 342–343, 491–492.
38. Teiwes 1966, 1971, 1974a; 1979, 377–380.
39. Teiwes 1979, 494.
40. Liu Shaoqi, speech at Beijing cadres meeting, May 19, 1949, as cited in Teiwes 1979, 6–7.

41. Liu Shaoqi, speech at Tianjing industrial and commercial circles discussion session, April 25, 1949, as cited in Teiwes 1979, 7.
42. Liu Shaoqi, speech at study session of democratic personages of the Chinese People's Political Consultative Conference, May 13, 1951, as cited in Teiwes 1979, 7.
43. Teiwes 1979, 7; Lieberthal 1987, 293–359.
44. Liu Yongmou and Wang Xingbin 2005; Uhalley 1988; Liang Huakui 2005; Zhou Guoquan 2003.
45. Teiwes 1979, 493.
46. For Mao's directives on art and literature work on June 27, 1964, see *Xinzhongguo jishi* 1986, 354.
47. Jin Qiu 1999, 201–204.

CHAPTER 5

1. Solomon 1971, 476.
2. Chen Boda, as cited in Ye Yonglie 1992, 14; Schoenhales 1996, 3.
3. Woody 1989, 169–171.
4. Lin Jing 1991; Hunt 1988; Jiang Pei 1994; Liu Binyan 1990; Schoenhales 1996.
5. Snow 1972, 17.
6. Schoenhales 1996.
7. Potter 2003; Li Haiwen 2003.
8. Chen Boda 2005; Ye Yonglie 1993a; Zhou Guoquan 1993.
9. Yan Jiaqi and Gao Cao 1996, 33–34.
10. Chen Qingquan 2006; Yang Shangkun 2001a, 2001b; Huang Yao 1996; Shu Yun 2005.
11. Yan Jiaqi and Gao Cao 1996, 186–187.
12. Yan Jiaqi and Gao Cao 1996, 34–35; *Xinzhongguo jishi* 1986, 399.
13. Yan Jiaqi and Gao Cao 1996, 35–37.
14. Su Shuangbi 1984; Yan Jiaqi and Gao Cao 1996, 23–38.
15. *Renmin Ribao* [People's daily], August 8, 1966. References to *Renmin Ribao* hereafter *RMRB*.
16. Ding Xiaohe 2006a; Mi Hedu 2005; Gong Xiaoxia 1995; Lin Jing 1991; Rosen 1982; Yan Jiaqi and Gao Cao 1996, 377–390; Wang Xuewen 1969.
17. Peng Dehuai 1984, 1990, 2002; Domes 1985a.
18. Yan Jiaqi and Gao Cao 1996, 214.
19. Quan Yanchi 1991; Zheng Xiaofeng 1992; Xu Zifang 1981.
20. Yan Jiaqi and Gao Cao 1996, 118.

21. *RMRB*, January 1, 1967; *Hongqi* 1967, no. 1.
22. Yan Jiaqi and Gao Cao 1996, 119.
23. MacFarquhar and Schoenhales 2006, 102; Yan Jiaqi and Gao Cao 1996, 119; Schoenhales 1996.
24. Yan Jiaqi and Gao Cao 1996, 119.
25. Yan Jiaqi and Gao Cao 1996, 119–120.
26. Liu Pingping, Liu Yuan, and Liu Tingting, "A Fresh Flower of Victory for You—Remembering Our Father Liu Shaoqi," *Lishi zai zheli chensi*, 1:27–30, as cited in Yan Jiaqi and Gao Cao 1996, 154–156.
27. Yan Jiaqi and Gao Cao 1996, 117; Dittmer 1998, 109–118; Jin Qiu 1999, 207–208; Zhang Xiaolin 1993, 152–153.
28. Yan Jiaqi and Gao Cao 1996, 157–159.
29. "Communiqué of the Twelfth Plenum of the Eighth Party Congress," *RMRB*, November 2, 1968, as cited in Yan Jiaqi and Gao Cao 1996, 160.
30. Gao Wenqian 2007, 155; Yan Jiaqi and Gao Cao 1996, 160–162; Wang Dongxing 1997.
31. Yan Jiaqi and Gao Cao 1996, 159–164.
32. Schoenhales 1996, 27.
33. Lin Qing 1991; Gao Wenqian 2007, 131–148.
34. Schoenhales 1996, 331–332.
35. Yu Xiaoming, "Quxiao hongdeng de zhenglun," *Dixue de tongxin—Haizi xinzhong de wenge*, as cited in Li Hui and Gao Lilin 1989, 293–295; Schoenhales 1996, 331–332.
36. Xia Shuzhang and Wang Shujun 2002; Barnouin 2006, 244–257; An Jianshe 1995; Cao Yingwang 2006; Chen Yangyong 2006; Guo Hongjun 2006; Liu Wusheng 2000; Hu Changming 2005; Jiang Mingwu 2004; Li Ping 2001; Gao Wenqian 2007, 157–167.
37. Yan Jiaqi and Gao Cao 1996, 155.
38. Jin Qiu 1999; Bonavia 1984; Bridgham 1973; P. H. Chang 1973; Chien Tieh 1972; Ginneken 1972; Goldstein 1991; M. Y. M. Kau 1975; Li Tianmin 1971, 1973, 1978; Lin Qingshan 1985, 1988; Robinson 1971a, 1972; Shao Yihai 1988a, 1988b, 1988c; Teiwes 1984, 1990, 1993; Teiwes and Sun 1996; Wang Zhenghua 1995; Wu Tienwei 1983.
39. Pye 1976, 212–213; Rice 1972, 30–66, 102–104; Snow 1972a, 250–251; Chen Changfeng 1959, 8; Yang Zulie 1970, 333–334; Terrill 1999; Witke 1977.
40. Lawrance 1991; Pang 2002; Shi Haoming et al. 2006.
41. Terry 1976; Yan Jiaqi and Gao Cao 1996, 334–355; Ye Yonglie 1993b; Liu Yuen-sun 1967.

42. Yan Jiaqi and Gao Cao 1996, 23–27.
43. Jin Qiu 1999; Yan Jiaqi and Gao Cao 1996; Bonavia 1984; *Lin Biao Zhuanji* 1970; Chien Tieh 1972; Fessler 1967; Ginneken 1972; Bridgham 1973; Brugger 1978; Liu Yuen-sun 1967; Shao Hua 2003; Li Tianmin 1973; Lin Qingshan 1988.
44. T. W. Robinson 1971b, 1972; Salisbury 1985, 188–192; Snow 1961b, 135–160; MacFarquhar 2006, 333–336.
45. Lin Biao 1967, 1988; Jianghua 1988; Teiwes 1996; Wang Zhenghua 1995; Yan Jiaqi and Gao Cao 1996, 180.
46. Lin Biao tongzhi 1967; Lin Biao zai jundui ganbu dahui shang de jianghua 1988; Yan Jiaqi and Gao Cao 1996, 179; Wang Zhenghua 1995; Teiwes 1996.
47. *Zhongguo Gongchandang Lichi Zhongyao Huiyi Ji* 1983, 2:236–237, 483; Yan Jiaqi and Gao Cao 1996, 194–196, 303–304.
48. Yan Jiaqi and Gao Cao 1996, 285–301.
49. "A Summary of Chairman Mao's Talks to Responsible Local Comrades During His Tour of Inspection," *Chinese Law and Government* 5 (3-4) (winter 1972–1973): 35–38, as cited in Yan Jiaqi and Gao Cao 1996, 308.
50. Yan Jiaqi and Gao Cao 1996, 308–309; Li Rui 1989; Liu Huinian, Zhao Qi, Xu Xinhua, Zhou Cilin, and Yang Jinzhou 1980.
51. Li Tianman 1978.
52. Chu Fang 1998.
53. Chu Fang 1998, 280.
54. Chien Yu-shen 1969; Chuan Tsun 1972; Li Ke and Hao Shengzhang 1988; Parrish 1973.
55. Wang Dongxing 1997; Tumen and Xiaosike 2003; Jin Qiu 1999; Bridgham 1973; Bonavia 1984; Shao Hua 2003; Wang Wenzheng 2006; Wu Runsheng 2006; Ginneken 1972; M. Y. M. Kau 1972–1973, 1975; M. Y. M. Kau and Perrolle 1974; Shao Yihai 1988a, 1988b, 1988c.
56. Yan Jiaqi and Gao Cao 1996, 318–319.
57. Yan Jiaqi and Gao Cao 1996, 453.
58. Teiwes and Sun 2007; Oksenberg 1977.
59. Pye 1976, 232–239.

CHAPTER 6

1. Wang Zhang Jiang Yao zhuan an zu 1976–1977; Ding Wang 1976, 1977, 1979; Ye Yonglie 1993c, 1993d, 1997; Li Tianmin 1982; P. H. Chang 1989.

2. Domes 1985a, 140–142; Chi 1991, 1–3.
3. Ye Yonglie 1997; Li Tianmin 1982; Ding Wang 1976; P. H. Chang 1989.
4. Chi 1991, 2.
5. Domes 1985, 146–147; Ye Yonglie 1997.
6. Chi 1991, 4–5; Deng Xiaoping 1984, 1:35–36, 133; Domes 1985b, 162–163.
7. Deng Xiaoping 1983, 133.
8. Tang Fei 2005; Tian Guoliang 1989; Chen Liming 2005; Jin Feng 1993; Yang Zhongmei 1988; Zhao Wei 2004; P. H. Chang 1989.
9. *Dangde Shiyijie Sanzhong Quanhui Yilai Dashiji* 1987, 1–14.
10. Huang Kecheng 1994; Chen Zaidao 1988; Zheng Bo 2001; Domes 1985, 162–163.
11. Zhao Wei 1989; Li Wenhai 2003; P. B. Potter 2003; Domes 1985, 169; Chi 1991, 5–6; P. H. Chang 1989, 30–42.
12. Wang Dongxing 1993, 1994, 1997; Wu De 2004; Yingguan 1996.
13. Domes 1985, 170–171; Chi 1991, 5–6.
14. Butterfield 1982, 406–434; Fraser 1980, 199–271; Goodman 1981; Seymour 1980; Wei Jingsheng 1997; Holzman 2005; Chi 1991, 7–9.
15. Deng's speech, "Jiefang sixiang, shihshih qiushi, tuanjie yizhi xiangqiankan," in *Shiyijie Sanzhong Quanhui Yilai Zhongyao Wenxian Xuandu* 1987; Deng Xiaoping, as cited in *Shiyijie Sanzhong Quanhui Yilai Zhongyao Wenxian Xuandu* 1987, 18–33; Chi 1991, 8.
16. P. H. Chang 1989, 122.
17. Deng's speech, "Shixian sige xiandaihua bixu jianchi sixiang jiben yuanze," March 30, 1979, in *Shiyijie Sanzhong Quanhui Yilai Zhongyao Wenxian Xuandu* 1987, 44–61; Domes 1985a, 160; Chi 1991, 7.
18. Wei Jingsheng 1997.
19. Chi 1991, 7–8.
20. *RMRB*, July 22, 1983, p. 1; Chi, 1991, 11–13.
21. Deng Xiaoping, as cited in *Shiyijie Sanzhong Quanhui Yilai Zhongyao Wenxian Xuandu* 1987, 398–410; Chi 1991, 18–19.
22. Wei Jingsheng 1980, 29–30; Deng Xiaoping, as cited in *Shiyijie Sanzhong Quanhui Yilai Zhongyao Wenxian Xuandu* 1987, 44–61, Chi 1991, 27–29.
23. *RMRB*, November 30, 1983, p. 1; Deng Xiaoping, as cited in *Shiyijie Sanzhong Quanhui Yilai Zhongyao Wenxian Xuandu* 1987, 44–61.
24. Deng Xiaoping's speech, "Shixian sige xiandaihua bixu jianchi sixiang jiben yuanze" [To achieve modernisation, it is necessary to insist on the four principles], March 30, 1979, in *Shiyijie Sanzhong Quanhui Yilai Zhongyao Wenxian Xuandu* 1987, 44–61; Niming 1979, 72–75.

25. Deng Xiaoping, as cited in *Shiyijie Sanzhong Quanhui Yilai Zhongyao Wenxian Xuandu* 1987, 336; Chi 1991, 34–36.
26. *RMRB*, April 20, 1982, p. 1; Chi 1991, 37–38.
27. Chen Yun 1984, 245; Deng Xiaoping 1987, 336.
28. Chen Yun 1984, 245–246; Chi 1991, 38.
29. Deng Xiaoping's speech, "Guanyu yanchen yanzchong pohuai jingji de zuifan de jueding" [The decision about punishing the dangeous economic criminals], in *Shiyijie Sanzhong Quanhui Yilai Zhongyao Wenxian Xuandu* 1987, 422–429; Deng's speech, "Jianjue daji jingji fanzui huodong" [Resolutely attack economic criminal activities], April 10, 1982, in *Shiyijie Sanzhong Quanhui Yilai Zhongyao Wenxian Xuandu* 1987, 357–359.
30. Chi 1991, 37–39.
31. *RMRB*, February–March 1982.
32. *RMRB*, editorial, October 14, 1983, p. 1; Chi 1991, 46.
33. *Hongqi* 1983, 2–11; Chi, 1991.
34. *RMRB*, November 13, 1984, p. 5; Chi 1991, 47.
35. *RMRB*, December 21, 1983, p. 1; Chi 1991, 48.
36. *RMRB*, December 23, 1984, p. 1; Chi 1991, 48–49.
37. *RMRB*, December 23, 1984, p. 1; Chi 1991, 49.
38. Chi 1991, 50.
39. *Hongqi* 1986, no. 5, pp. 8–10; 1985, no. 19, p. 40; Chen Yun 1984, 309–310; *RMRB*, January 26, 1985, p. 1.
40. Chi 1991, 175.
41. Notice by the Central Discipline Committee on December 18, 1985, in *RMRB*, January 15, 1986, p. 1; Chi 1991, 175.
42. *RMRB*, May 29, 1986, p. 1; Chi 1991, 175–176.
43. Chen Yun 1984, 309–310; *Hongqi* 1985, no. 19, 40.
44. Chen Yun 1984, 310, 389; Chi 1991, 176.
45. *Dang de Jianshe* 1986, no. 7, 21.
46. *Xuexi yu Yanjiu* 1986, no. 4, 29–30; Chi 1991, 207.
47. Chi 1991, 208.
48. Zhang Yun, as cited in *Hongqi* 1986, no. 10, 13–14; Chi 1991, 208.
49. Zhang Yun, as cited in *Hongqi* 1986, no. 10, 9 and 14; *RMRB*, January 11, 1986, p. 1; Chi 1991, 209.
50. *RMRB*, February 3, 1986, p. 1; Chi 1991, 209.
51. *RMRB*, May 28, 1987, p. 1; see also *RMRB*, March 4, 1986, p. 1.
52. *Zhongguo Nianjian* 1988, 70; Zhang Yun, as cited in *Hongqi* 1986, no. 10, 3–14; Chi 1991, 210.

53. Chi 1991, 211.
54. Deng Xiaoping 1983, 259–260.
55. *RMRB*, June 28, 1989, p. 1; Chi 1991, 260.
56. Chi 1991, 260–261.
57. Hao Zhidong 2003; Ding Xiaohe 2006; Fewsmith 2001.
58. Thurston 1988.
59. Chi 1991, 261–262.
60. Chi 1991, 262.
61. Chen Liming 2005; Tang Fei 2005; Shambaugh 1984.
62. Chi 1991, 264.
63. Chi 1991, 264–265.
64. P. H. Chang 1989, 137.
65. Chi 1991, 264–265; Zhao Wei 1989.
66. Wenxian Zhongyang 2005; Yang Tianshi and Xie Chutao 2005; Pu Xingjue 2005; Yang Jisheng 1998.
67. Gao Xin 1995.
68. Tanner 1999; Pye 1981, 328–329; Chi 1991, 180–181; Saich 1981, 120–122; Domes 1985a; J. T. Dreyer 1993; Ogden 1992, 184, 236–237; Lieberthal 1995; Lubman 1982, 1995, 1999; Lubman, Diament, and O'Brien 2005; O'Brien 1989, 1990b, 1994c; P. B. Potter 1994a, 1994b.
69. Zhao Suisheng 1996.
70. *Zhonghua Renmin Gongheguo Fagui Huibian* 1956, 1979–1984; Lindsay 1976, 291–311, 328–336; *Constitution* 1978; Constitution 1982; Zhang Jinfan 2004a; Cai Dingjian 2004; Xia Xinhua 2007.
71. Chi 257–258; Moody 1989, 165–202.
72. *RMRB*, overseas edition, September 11, 1989, p. 2, October 10, 1989, p. 1, October 12, 1989, p. 2; June 28, 1989, p. 1; Deng Xiaoping's speech to new members of the Politburo Standing Committee, June 16, 1989, reprinted in the *World Journal*, July 15, 1989, p. 31; Chi 1991, 258–259.

CHAPTER 7

1. P. H. Chang 1989, 127.

BIBLIOGRAPHY

Ackerman, B. 2000. The new separation of powers. *Harvard Law Review* 113:633–696.

Ah Cheng. 1984. Shazi [The idiot]. *Wenhui yuekan* 10:38–41.

———. 1985. The chess master. Trans. W. J. F. Jenner. *Chinese Literature* (Summer): 84–131.

———. 1990. *Three kings: Three stories from today's China.* Trans. B. S. McDougall. London: Collins Harvill.

Ahern, E. M. 1981. *Chinese ritual and politics.* Cambridge, U.K.: Cambridge University Press.

Ahn, Byung-joon. 1972. Ideology, policy and power in Chinese politics and the evolution of the Cultural Revolution, 1959–1965. PhD diss., Columbia University.

———. 1976. *Chinese politics and the Cultural Revolution: Dynamics of policy processes.* Seattle: University of Washington Press.

Ai, Fei. 1984. *Yan, Xishan.* Shijiazhuang: Hebei Renmin Chubanshe.

Aixinjueluo, Yuyan. 2004. *Modai Huangdi Lisi Jishi* [The record of the last emperor]. Ed. Jia Yinghua. Beijing: Renmin Wenxue Chubanshe.

Alford, W. 1984. Arsenic and old laws: Looking anew at criminal justice in imperial China. *California Law Review* 72:1180.

———. 1986. The inscrutable occidental? Implications of Roberto Unger's uses and abuses of the Chinese past. *Texas Law Review* 64:195.

———. 1990. "Seek truths from facts"—Especially when they are unpleasant: America's understanding of China's efforts at law reform. *Pacific Basin Law Journal* 8:177.

———. 1993. Double-edged swords cut both ways: Law and legitimacy in the People's Republic of China. *Daedalus* 122:45.

———. 1995. Tasseled loafers for barefoot lawyers: Transformation and tension in the world of Chinese legal workers. *China Quarterly* 141:22.

———. 1999. A second Great Wall? China's post-Cultural Revolution project of legal construction. *Cultural Dynamics* 11:193.

———. 2000. Exporting "the pursuit of happiness." Review of *Aiding democracy abroad: The learning curve*, by Thomas Carothers. *Harvard Law Review* 113:1677.

———. 2001. *Of lawyers lost and found: Searching for legal professionalism in the People's Republic of China.* Unpublished manuscript presented at the Rule of Law and Group Identities Embedded in Asian Traditions and Cultures Conference, UCLA School of Law, January 19–20.

Alitto, G. S. 1979. *The last Confucian: Liang Shu-ming and the Chinese dilemma of modernity.* Berkeley: University of California Press.

Allee, M. A. 1994. Code, culture, and custom: Foundations of civil case verdicts in a nineteenth-century county court. In *Civil law in Qing and Republican China*, ed. K. Bernhardt and P. C. C. Huang, 122–141. Stanford, CA: Stanford University Press.

Almond, G. 1994. Foreword: A return to political culture. In *Political culture and democracy*, ed. L. Diamond, v–vii. Boulder, CO: Lynne Rienner.

Ames, R. T. 1994. *The art of rulership: A study of ancient Chinese political thought.* Albany: State University of New York Press.

Ames, R. T., and P. D. Hershock. 2006. *Confucian cultures of authority.* Albany: State University of New York Press.

An, Jianshe, comp. 1995. *Zhou Enlai de Zuihou Suiyue, 1966–1976* [Zhou Enlai's last years]. Beijing: Zhongyang Wenxian Chubanshe.

An, Tai Sung. 1972. *Mao Tse-tung's Cultural Revolution.* New York: Pegasus.

An, Zuozhang. 1982. *Qin Han Nongmin Zhanzheng Shiliao Huibian* [A collection of historical materials on peasant wars in the Qin and Han dynasties]. Beijing: Zhonghua Shuju.

Anderson, D. J. 1973. Kang Sheng: A political biography, 1924–1970. PhD diss., St. John's University.

Anderson, M. M. 1990. *Hidden power: The palace eunuchs of imperial China*. Buffalo, NY: Prometheus Books.

Andrew, A. M., and J. A. Rapp. 2000. *Autocracy and China's rebel founding emperors*. Oxford, U.K.: Rowman & Littlefield.

Ansley, C. 1971. *The Heresy of Wu Han*. Toronto: Toronto University Press.

Antony, R. J. 1988. Pirates, bandits, and brotherhoods: A study of crime and law in Kwangtung Province, 1796–1839. PhD diss., University of Hawaii.

———. 1993. Brotherhoods, secret societies, and the law in Qing dynasty China. In *"Secret societies" reconsidered: Perspectives on the social history of early modern South China and Southeast Asia*, ed. D. Ownby and M. S. Heidhues, 190–221. Armonk, NY: M. E. Sharpe.

Apter, D. E. 1985. The new mytho-logics and the spectre of superfluous man. *Social Research* 52 (Summer): 269–307.

———. 1994. *Wang Shiwei and "Wild Lilies": Rectification and purges in the Chinese Communist Party, 1942–1944*. Armonk, NY: M. E. Sharpe.

———. 1995. Discourse as power: Yan'an and the Chinese revolution. In *New perspectives on the Chinese Communist Revolution*, ed. T. Saich, 193–234. Armonk, NY: M. E. Sharpe.

———. 1987. Mao's Republic. *Social Research* 54 (4): 691–729.

Ayers, W. 1960. Chang Chih-tung and educational reform in China. PhD diss., Harvard University.

Bachman, D. 1985. *Chen Yun and the Chinese political system.* Berkeley: University of California Press.

———. 1991. *Bureaucracy, economy, and leadership in China: The institutional origins of the Great Leap Forward.* Cambridge: Cambridge University Press.

Bai Chongxi. 1989. *Bai Chongxi Xiansheng Fangwen Jilu* [Record of interviews with Mr Bai Chongxi]. Taibei: Zhongyang Yanjiuyuan Jindaishi Yanjiusuo.

Bai, Jiao. 1966. *Yuan Shikai yu Zhonghua Mingguo* [Yuan Shkai and Chinese Republic]. Taibei: Wenhai Chubanshe.

Bailey, C. N. 1982. *On the Yin and Yang nature of language.* Ann Arbor, MI: Karoma Publishers.

Baker, H. D. R. 1979. *Chinese family and kinship.* New York: Columbia University Press.

Balazs, E. 1954. *Le Traité juridique du "Souei-chaou."* Leiden: E. J. Brill.

———. 1964. *Chinese civilization and bureaucracy: Variations on a theme.* Trans. M. Wright, ed. A. Wright. New Haven, CT: Yale University Press.

Bales, W. L. 1937. *Tso Tsung-t'ang: Soldier and statesman of old China.* Shanghai: Kelley & Walsh.

Bao, Zhenyuan. 1998. *Zhongguo li dai Kuxing Shilu* [A history of cruel penalties in Chinese dynasties]. Beijing: Zhongguo Shehui Chubanshe.

Bar-Asher, M., and S. E. Fassberg, eds. 1998. *Studies in Mishnaic Hebrew.* Jerusalem: Hebrew University Magnes Press.

Barme, G. R. 1992. Wang Shuo and *liumang* hooligan culture. *Australian Journal of Chinese Affairs* 28:23–64.

———. 1999. *In the red: On contemporary Chinese culture.* New York: Columbia University Press.

Barme, G. R., and Frederick C. Teiwes, eds. 1968. *Ssu-Ch'ing: The socialist education movement of 1962–1966.* Berkeley: University of California Press.

Barnett, A. D. 1964. *Communist China: The early years, 1949–55.* New York: Praeger.

——. 1967. *Cadres, bureaucracy, and political power in Communist China.* New York: Columbia University Press.

——, ed. 1969. *Chinese communist politics in action.* Seattle: University of Washington Press.

——. 1974. *Uncertain passage: China's transition to the post-Mao era.* Washington, DC: Brookings Institution.

Barnouin, B. 1993. *Ten years of turbulence: The Chinese Cultural Revolution.* New York: Kegan Paul.

Barnouin, B., and Yu Changgen. 2006. *Zhou Enlai: A political life.* Hong Kong: Chinese University Press.

Bartke, W., and P. Schier. 1985. *China's new party leadership.* Armonk, NY: M. E. Sharpe.

Bartlett, B. S. 1991. *Monarchs and ministers: The grand council in mid-Ch'ing China, 1723–1820.* Berkeley: University of California Press.

Barrett, D. P., and L. N. Shyu, eds. 2001. *Chinese collaboration with Japan, 1932–1945: The limits of accommodation.* Stanford, CA: Stanford University Press.

Baum, R., ed. 1968. *Ssu-Ch'ing: The socialist education movement of 1962–1966.* Berkeley: University of California Press.

——. 1975. *Prelude to revolution: Mao, the party, and the peasant question, 1962–66.* New York: Columbia University Press.

——. 1986. Modernization and legal reform in post-Mao China: The rebirth of socialist legality. *Studies of Comparative Communism* 19:69.

———. 1993. The road to Tiananmen: Chinese politics in the 1980s. In *The politics of China 1949–1989*, ed. R. MacFarquhar, 340–471. New York: Cambridge University Press.

———. 1994. *Burying Mao: Chinese politics in the age of Deng Xiaoping.* Princeton, NJ: Princeton University Press.

Baum, R., and F. C. Teiwes. 1968. Liu Shao-ch'i and the Cadre Question. *Asian Survey* 8 (4): 323–345.

Baum, R., and A. Shevchenko. 1999. The "state of the state" in post reform China. In *The paradox of China's post-Mao reforms*, ed. M. Goldman and R. MacFarquhar, 333–362. Cambridge, MA: Harvard University Press.

Beattie, H. J. 1979. *Land and lineage in China: A study of T'Ung-Ch'Eng county, Anhwei, in the Ming and Ch'ing dynasties.* New York: Cambridge University Press.

Belden, J. 1970. *China shakes the world.* New York: Monthly Review.

Benditt, T. 1978. *Law as rule and principle.* Stanford, CA: Stanford University Press.

Benton, G. 1975. The second Wang Ming line. *China Quarterly* 61:61–94.

Bergere, M. 2000. Reforming confession law British style: A decade of experience with adverse inferences from silence. *Columbia Human Rights Review* 31:243.

Bergere, M., and J. Lloyd. 2000. *Sun Yat-sen.* Stanford, CA: Stanford University Press.

Berman, H. 1983. *Law and revolution.* Cambridge, MA: Harvard University Press.

Bernhardt, K. 1992. *Rents, taxes, and peasant resistance: The lower Yangzi region, 1840–1950.* Stanford, CA: Stanford University Press.

———. 1999. *Women and property in China, 960–1949.* Stanford, CA: Stanford University Press.

Bernhardt, K., and P. Huang. 1994. *Civil law in Qing and Republican China*. Stanford, CA: Stanford University Press.

Bernstein, T. 1977. *Up to the mountains and down to the villages*. New Haven, CT: Yale University Press.

——. 2000. Farmer discontent and regime responses. In *The paradox of China's post-Mao reforms*, ed. M. Goldman and R. MacFarquhar, 197–219. Cambridge, MA: Harvard University Press.

Bernstein, T., and Xiaobo Lu. 2000. Taxation without representation: Peasants, the central and local states in reform China. *China Quarterly* 163:742.

Bian, Yanjie. 1994. *Work and inequality in urban China*. Albany: State University of New York Press.

Bianco, L. 1971. *The origins of the Chinese revolution, 1915–1949*. Trans. M. Bell. Stanford, CA: Stanford University Press.

Bielenstein, H. 1954–1967. The restoration of the Han dynasty. Published in three parts. *Bulletin of The Museum of Far Eastern Antiquities* 1954, 26: 1–209; 1959, 31: 1–287; 1967, 39: 1–198.

——. 1980. *The bureaucracy of Han times*. Cambridge: Cambridge University Press.

Billingsley, P. 1988. *Bandits in Republican China*. Stanford, CA: Stanford University Press.

Birch, C., ed. 1995. *Scenes for mandarins: The elite theater of the Ming*. New York: Columbia University Press.

Bland, J. O. P. 1912. *Recent events and the present policies of China*. London: William Heinemann.

Bo, Yibo. 1991. *Ruogan Zhongda Juece yu Shijian de Huigu* [Review of several important decisions and events]. 2 vols. Beijing: CCP Party School Press.

——. 1992. *Lingxiu, Yuanshuai, Zhanyou* [Leaders, marshals, and comrades]. Beijing: Zhonggong zhongyang dangxiao chubanshe.

Bodde, D. 1954. Authority and law in ancient China. *Journal of the American Oriental Society.* Suppl. no. 17.

———. 1957. Evidence for the "laws of nature" in Chinese thought. *Harvard Journal of Asiatic Studies* 20:709–727.

———. 1963. Basic concepts of Chinese law: The genesis and evolution of legal thought in traditional China. *Proceedings of the American Philosophical Society* 107:375.

———. 1979. Chinese law of nature: A reconsideration. *Harvard Journal of Asiatic Studies* 39:139–155.

———. 1986. The state and Empire of Ch'in. In *Cambridge history of China 1: The Ch'in and Han Empires, 221 BC–AD 220*, ed. D. C. Twitchett and J. K. Fairbank, 20–102. Cambridge: Cambridge University Press.

Bodde, D., and C. Morris. 1973. *Law in imperial China: Exemplified by 190 Ch'ing dynasty cases (translated from the* Hsing-an hui-lan*), with historical, social, and juridical commentaries.* Philadelphia: University of Pennsylvania Press.

Bol, P. K. 1982. Culture and the way in eleventh century China. PhD diss., Princeton University.

———. 1990. The Sung examination system and the Shih. *Asia Major* 3 (2): 149–167.

———. 1992. *"This culture of ours": Intellectual transitions in Tang and Sung China.* Stanford, CA: Stanford University Press.

Bonavia, D. 1984. *Verdict in Peking: The trial of the Gang of Four.* New York: Putnam.

———. 1995. *China's warlords.* Hong Kong: Oxford University Press.

Bond, M. H., ed. 1988. *The psychology of the Chinese people.* New York: Oxford University Press.

Bowie, R. R., and J. K. Fairbank, eds. 1965. *Communist China 1955–59: Policy documents with analysis.* Cambridge, MA: Harvard University Press.

Brandt, C., B. Schwartz, and J. K. Fairbank. 1958. *Stalin's failure in China: 1924–1927.* Cambridge, MA: Harvard University Press.

——, eds. 1967. *A documentary history of Chinese communism.* New York: Atheneum.

Bray, F. 2000. *Technology and society in Ming China (1368–1644).* Washington, DC: American Historical Association.

Bridgham, P. 1967. Mao's Cultural Revolution: Origin and development. *China Quarterly* 29 (January): 1–35.

——. 1968. Mao's Cultural Revolution: The struggle to seize power. *China Quarterly* 34 (April): 6–37.

——. 1970a. Factionalism in the Central Committee. In *Party leadership and revolutionary power in China,* ed. J. W. Lewis, 203–235. Cambridge: Cambridge University Press.

——. 1970b. Mao's Cultural Revolution: The struggle to consolidate power. *China Quarterly* 41 (January): 1–25.

——. 1973. The fall of Lin Piao. *China Quarterly* 55 (July–September): 427–449.

——. 2004. *Bringing the party back in: How China is governed.* Singapore: Eastern Universities Press.

——. 2006. *The Chinese Communist Party in reform.* London: Routledge.

Brodsgaard, K. E., and Zheng Yongnian. 1973. The fall of Lin Piao. *China Quarterly* 55 (July–September): 427–449.

Brokaw, C. J. 1991. *The ledgers of merit and demerit: Social change and moral order in late imperial China.* Princeton, NJ: Princeton University Press.

Brook, T. 1994. *Praying for power: Buddhism and the formation of gentry society in late-Ming China*. Cambridge, MA: Harvard University Press.

———. 1999. *The confusions of pleasure: Commerce and culture in Ming China*. Berkeley: University of California Press.

———. 2003. *Geographical sources of Ming-Qing history*. Ann Arbor: University of Michigan Press.

———. 2005. *The Chinese state in Ming society*. London: Routledge Curzon.

Brook, T., and B. M. Frolic, eds. 1977. *Civil society in China*. Armonk, NY: M. E. Sharpe.

Brook, T., and B. T. Wakabayashi, eds. 2000. *Opium regimes: China, Britain, and Japan, 1839–1952*. Berkeley: University of California Press.

Brose, M. C. 2000. Strategies of survival: Uyghur elites in Yuan and early-Ming China. PhD diss., University of Pennsylvania.

Brown, K. 2006. *The purge of the Inner Mongolian People's Party in the Chinese Cultural Revolution, 1967–69: A function of language, power and violence*. Folkestone, U.K.: Global Oriental.

Brown, N., and J. S. Bell. 1998. *French administrative law*. Oxford, U.K.: Clarendon Press.

Brown, R. 1997. *Understanding Chinese courts and the legal process: Law with Chinese characteristics*. Boston: Kluwer Law International.

Brugger, B. 1978. *China: The impact of the Cultural Revolution*. Canberra: Australian National University Press.

Bullard, Monte. 1985. *China's political-military evolution*. Boulder, CO: Westview Press.

Bunker, G. 1972. *The peace conspiracy: Wang Ching-wei and the China War, 1937–1941*. Cambridge, MA: Harvard University Press.

Burchett, W. 1973. Lin Piao's plot—The full story. *Far Eastern Economic Review* 20 (August): 22–24.

Burns, J. P. 1989. *The Chinese Communist Party's nomenklatura system.* Armonk, NY: M. E. Sharpe.

——. 1994. Strengthening central CCP control of leadership selection: The 1990 nomenklatura. *China Quarterly* 138 (June): 458–491.

Burns, J. P., and S. Rosen, eds. 1986. *Policy conflicts in post-Mao China: A documentary survey, with analysis.* Armonk, NY: M. E. Sharpe.

Bush, H. 1949–1955. The Tung-lin Academy and its political and philosophical significance. *Monumenta Serica* 14:1–163.

Butterfield, F. 1982. *China: Alive in the bitter sea.* New York: Times Books.

Byron, J., and R. Pack. 1992. *Claws of the dragon.* New York: Simon and Schuster.

Cahill, J. 1995. *The painter's practice: How artists lived and worked in traditional China.* New York: Columbia University Press.

Cai, Dingjian. 1995. Constitutional supervision and interpretation in the People's Republic of China. *Journal of Chinese Law* 9:219.

——. 1999. Development of the Chinese legal system since 1979 and its current crisis and transformation. *Cultural Dynamics* 11:135.

——. 2002. The function of the People's Congress of China in the process of law implementation. In *Implementation of law in the People's Republic of China*, ed. Chen Jianfu, Li Yuwen, and Jan Michiel Otto, 35–54. The Hague: Kluwer Law International.

——. 2004. *Xianfa Jingjie* [Detailed interpretation of the Constitution]. Beijing: Falü Chubanshe.

Cai, Renzhao. 1994. *Zhongguo yuanshuai Nie Rongzhen* [Chinese Marshal Nie Rongzhen]. Beijing: Zhongyang Dangxiao Chubanshe.

Cai, Shangyi. 1994. Dangqiang Xingzheng Fuyi Shao de Yuanyin ji qi Duice [Reasons for and responses to the low number of administrative reconsideration cases today]. *Jingji yu Fa* 5:24.

Cairns, H. 1949. *Legal philosophy from Plato to Hegel*. Baltimore: Johns Hopkins University Press.

Cameron, M. 1931. *The reform movement in China*. New York: AMS Press.

Cao, D. 2004. *Chinese law, a language perspective = Shuo fa*. Aldershot: Ashgate.

——. 2007a. Interpretation, law and the construction of meaning: collected papers on legal interpretation in theory, adjudication and political practice by International Roundtable for the Semiotics of Law (2004: Lyon, France). Dordrecht, Springer.

——. 2007b. *Translating law*. Clevedon, U.K.: Multilingual Matters.

Cao, Lüning. 2005. *Zhangjia Shan Hanlü Yanjiu* [Zhang Jiashan's research of Han law]. Beijing: Zhonghua Shuju.

Cao, Siyuan. 1997. Shinian Lai Zhongguo Pochanfa de Lifa yu Shishi [Legislation and implementation of China's bankruptcy law during the last ten years]. *Dangdai Zhongguo Yanjiu* 2:55.

Cao, Yabo. 1982. *Wuchang Geming Zhenshi* [The accurate history of Wuchang revolution]. 3 vols. Shanghai: Shanghai Shudian.

Cao, Yingwang. 2006. *Zhou Enlai Jingli Jishu* [The record of real life of Zhou Enlai] Shanghai: Renmin Chubanshe.

Cao, Zhongbin. 1991. *Wang Ming Zhuan* [A biography of Wang Ming]. Changchun: Jilin Wenshi Chubanshe.

Cass, V. 1999. *Dangerous women, warriors, grannies and geishas of the Ming*. Lanham, MD: Rowman & Littlefield Publishers.

Center for Chinese Studies, ed. 1970. *Lin Biao Zhuanji* [Collected materials on Lin Biao]. Hong Kong: Zi lian Press.

Central Committee of Chinese Communist Party. 1981. *Guanyu Jian-guo Yilai Dangde Ruogan Lishi Wenti de Jueyi* [The resolution on several questions about our Party's history since the establishment of the PRC]. Beijing: Six Plenum of the Eleventh Central Committee, June 27.

——. 1989. *Shierda Yilai Zhongyao Wenxian Xuanbian* [Selection of the important documents since the Twelfth Party Congress]. 2 vols. Beijing: Remin Chubanshe.

Chakrabarti, S. 1998. *Mao, China's intellectuals and the Cultural Revolution.* New Delhi: Sanchar Publishing House.

Chamberlain, H. 1998. Civil society with Chinese characteristics. *China Journal* 39:69.

Chan, A. 1985. *Children of Mao: Personality development and political activism in the Red Guard generation.* Seattle: University of Washington Press.

Chan, A. S. 1982. *The glory and fall of the Ming dynasty.* Norman: University of Oklahoma Press.

Chan, A., S. Rosen, and J. Ungar, eds. 1985. *On socialist democracy and the Chinese legal system: The Li Yizhe debates.* Armonk, NY: M. E. Sharpe.

Chan, Hok-lam. 1999. *China and the Mongols: History and legend under the Yuan and Ming.* Aldershot: Ashgate.

Chan, J. 1995. The Asian challenge to universal human rights: A philosophical critique. In *Human rights and international relations in the Asia-Pacific region,* ed. James T. H. Tang, vii–xii. New York: Pinter.

——. 2000. Thick and thin accounts of human rights: Lessons from the Asian values debate. In *Human rights and Asian values,* ed. O. Bruun and M. Jacobsen, 66–81. London: Routledge.

——. 2002. Moral autonomy, civil liberties, and Confucianism. *Philosophy East and West* 52 (3): 281–310.

Chan, S. 2004. *The Confucian Shi, official service, and the Confucian analects*. Lewiston, NY: Edwin Mellen Press.

Chan, Wing-tsit. 1954–1955. The evolution of the Confucian concept *Jen. Philosophy East and West* 4:295–319.

——. 1964. The evolution of the neo-Confucian concept of Li as principle. *Qinghua Xuebao* 2:123–148.

——. 1967. Neo-Confucianism: New ideas in old terminology. *Philosophy East and West* 17:15–35.

——, ed. 1986. *Chu Hsi and neo-Confucianism*. Honolulu: University of Hawii Press.

——. 1987. *Chu Hsi: Life and thought*. Hong Kong: Chinese University Press.

——. 1989. *Chu His: New studies*. Honolulu: University of Hawaii Press.

Chang, Ching-yu, ed. 1983. *The emerging Teng system: Orientation, policies, and implications*. Taipei: Institute of International Relations.

Chang, Chun-Shu, and S. H. Chang. 1998. *Crisis and transformation in seventeenth-century China: Society, culture, and modernity in Li Yu's world*. Ann Arbor: University of Michigan Press.

Chang, Chung-li. 1955. *The Chinese gentry; studies on their role in nineteenth-century Chinese society*. Seattle: University of Washington Press.

——. 1962. *The income of the Chinese gentry*. Seattle: University of Washington Press.

Chang, David Wen-wei. 1989. *China under Deng Xiaoping: Political and economic reform*. New York: St. Martin's Press.

Chang, G. 1999. What does the rule of law mean in China? *China Law and Practice* 13 (6): 33–35.

Chang, G. Jer-lang. 1978a. Local control in the early Ming 1368–1398. PhD diss., University of Minnesota.

———. 1978b. The village elder system of the early Ming dynasty. *Ming Studies* 7:53–72.

Chang, Hao. 1971. *Liang Ch'I-ch'ao and intellectual transition in China, 1890–1907.* Cambridge, MA: Harvard University Press.

———. 1987. *Chinese intellectuals in crisis: Search for order and meaning, 1890–1911.* Berkeley: University of California Press.

Chang, J., T. Lawton, and S. D. Allee. 2000. *Brushing the past: Later Chinese calligraphy from the gift of Robert Hatfield Ellsworth.* Washington, DC: Freer Gallery of Art.

Chang, Jui-te. 1993. *Kangzhan Shiqi de Guojun Renshi* [The personnel system of the National Army during the War of Resistance]. Taibei: Zhongyang Yanjiuyuan Jindaishi Yanjiusuo.

Chang, Jung. 1991. *Wild swans: Three daughters of China.* New York: Simon and Schuster.

Chang, Kuo-t'ao. 1971. *The rise of the Chinese Communist Party, 1921–1927.* 2 vols. Lawrence: University Press of Kansas.

Chang, Kwang-chih. 1980. *Shang civilization.* New Haven, CT: Yale University Press.

Chang, M. Hsia. 1985. *The Chinese Blue Shirt Society: Fascism and developmental nationalism.* Berkeley: University of California Press.

Chang, P. H. 1973. *Radicals and radical ideology in China's Cultural Revolution.* New York: Columbia University Press.

———. 1975. *Power and policy in China.* University Park: Pennsylvania State University Press.

———. 1983. *Elite conflict in post-Mao China.* Baltimore: University of Maryland School of Law Occasional Papers/Reprint Series in Contemporary Asian Studies, No. 2, 55.

——. 1987. China after Deng: Toward the 13th CCP Congress. *Problems of Communism* 36 (3): 30–42.

——. 1989. Institutions in Flux. In *Chinese politics from Mao to Deng*, ed. V. C. Falkenheim, 117–138. New York: Professors World Peace Academy.

Chang, P'eng-yüan. 1964. *Liang Qichao yu Qingji Geming* [Liang Qichao and the late Qing revolution]. Taipei: Academia Sinica, Institute of Modern Chinese History.

——. 1972. *Liang Qichao yu Minguo Zhengzhi* [Liang Qichao and politics in Republican China]. Taipei: Shihuo Press.

Chang, Shelly Hsueh-lun. 1990. *History and legend: Ideas and images in the Ming historical novels*. Ann Arbor: University of Michigan Press.

Chang, Shih-ying. 1997. Longtan Zhanyi de Pingjia yu Fansi [Evaluation of and reflections on the Longtan Battle]. *Zhongguo Junshi Xuehui Jikan* II:147–180.

Chang, Ta-kuang. 1987. The making of the Chinese bankruptcy law: A study in the Chinese legislative process. *Harvard International Law Journal*, 28 (Spring): 333–372.

Chauncey, H. R. 1992. *Schoolhouse politicians: Locality and state during the Chinese Republic*. Honolulu: University of Hawaii Press.

Cheek, T. 1981. Deng Tuo: Culture, Leninism and alternative Marxism in the Chinese Communist Party. *China Quarterly* 87:470–491.

——. 1984a. *Contracts and ideological control in village administration: Tensions within the "village covenant" system in late imperial China*. Paper presented at the 36th Annual Meeting of the Association for Asian Studies, Washington, DC.

——. 1984b. The fading of wild lilies: Wang Shiwei and Mao Zedong's Yan'an talks in the first CPC rectification movement. *The Australian Journal of Chinese Affairs* 11:25–58.

———. 1983–1984. The politics of cultural reform: Deng Tuo and the retooling of Chinese Marxism—Editor's introduction. *Chinese Law and Government*, 16 (Winter): 3–30.

———. 1986. Orthodoxy and dissent in People's China: The life and death of Deng Tuo 1912–1966. PhD diss., Harvard University.

———. 1989a. Redefining propaganda: Debates on the role of journalism in post-Mao China. *Issues and Studies* 25 (2): 25–50.

———. 1989b. Textually speaking: An assessment of newly available Mao texts. In *The secret speeches of Chairman Mao: From the Hundred Flowers to the Great Leap Forward*, ed. R. MacFarquhar, T. Cheek, and E. Wu, 84–90. Cambridge, MA: Harvard Council on East Asian Studies.

———. 1990. Studying Deng Tuo: The academic politician. *Republican China* 15 (2): 1–15.

———. 1992a. *Broken jade: Deng Tuo and intellectual service in Mao's China*. Colorado Springs, CO: Department of History, Colorado College.

———. 1992b. From priests to professionals: Intellectuals and the state under the CCP. In *Popular protest and political culture in modern China: Learning from 1989*, ed. J. N. Wasserstrom and E. J. Perry, 124–145. Boulder, CO: Westview Press.

———. 1996. *The names of rectification: Notes on the conceptual domains of CCP ideology in the Yan'an rectification movement*. Bloomington: Indiana University Press.

———. 1998. *Propaganda and culture in Mao's China: Deng Tuo and the intelligentsia*. New York: Oxford University Press.

Cheek, T., and T. Saich, eds. 1997. *New perspectives on state socialism in China*. Armonk, NY: M. E. Sharpe.

Chen, Boda. 1947. *Zhongguo Sida Jiazu* [The four grand families of China]. Hong Kong: Changjiang Chubanshe.

——. 2005. *Chen Boda: Zuihou Koushu Huiyi* [Chen Boda: Last memoir]. Hong Kong: Huanqiu.

Chen, Changfeng. 1959. *Gensui Mao Zhuxi Changzheng* [With Chairman Mao on the Long March]. Peking: Zuojia Chubanshe.

Chen, Chongqiao, Hu Yuhai, and Hu Yuzheng. 1991. *Cong Caomang Yingxiong Dao Da-yuanshuai—Zhang Zuolin* [From grassroot hero to general: Zhang Zuolin]. Shenyang: Liaoning Renmin Chubanshe.

Ch'en, Ch'un. 1986. *Neo-Confucian terms explained* [The Pei-his tzu-I]. Trans. W. Chan. New York: Columbia University Press.

Chen, Feng. 2006. *Jiang Jieshi de chu shi wei ren* [Chiang Kaishek's personal politics]. Beijing: Tuanjie Chubanshe.

Chen, Fulin. 1990. *Sun Zhongshan Liao Zhongkai yu Zhongguo ge ming* [Sun Yatsen and Liao Zhongkai and Chinese revolution]. Guangzhou: Zhong Shan University Press.

Chen, Gongshu. 1941. *Yingxiong Wuming: Beiguo Chujian* [Anonymous heroes: Weeding out traitors in North China]. Taibei: Zhuanji Wenxue Chubanshe.

——. 1943. *Lanyishe Neimu* [Inside story of the Blue Shirts]. Shanghai: Guomin Xinwen Tushu.

Chen, Guidi, and Chun Tao. 2004. *Zhongguo nongmin diaocha.* [An investigation on Chinese peasants]. Beijing: Renmin Chubanshe.

Chen, Gujia. 1997. *Zhongguo Shuyuan Zhidu Yanjiu* [Study of Chinese academic system]. Hangzhou: Zhejiang Jiaoyu Chubanshe.

Chen, Guyuan. 1935. *Zhongguo Fazhishi* [A history of Chinese legal system]. Shanghai: Shangwu.

Chen, Hua. 1992. *Zh Enlai he Tade Mishumen* [Zhou Enlai and his secretaries]. Beijing: China Media and Television Press.

Chen, J. 1965. *Mao and the Chinese revolution*. London: Oxford University Press.

——. 1967. *Yuan Shih-K'ai, 1859–1916.* Liverpool: George Allen & Unwin.

——, ed. 1970. *Mao papers: Anthology and bibliography.* London: Oxford University Press.

——. 1972. *Yuan Shih-k'ai.* Stanford, CA: Stanford University Press.

——. 1979. *The military-gentry coalition: China under the warlords.* Toronto: University of Toronto-York University Joint Centre on Modern East Asia.

Chen, Jack. 1976. *Inside the Cultural Revolution.* London: Sheldon.

Chen, Jianfu. 1999. Market economy and the internationalisation of civil and commercial law in the People's Republic of China. In *Law, capitalism and power in Asia,* ed. Kanishka Jayasuriya, 58–79. London: Routledge.

——. 2002. Mission Impossible: Judicial efforts to enforce civil judgments and rulings in China. In *Implementation of law in the People's Republic of China,* ed. Chen Jianfu, Yuwen Li, and J. M. Otto, 85–112. The Hague: Kluwer Law International.

——. 2008. *Chinese law: Context and transformation.* Leiden: Martinus Nijhoff.

Chen, Jianfu, Yuwen Li, and J. M. Otto, eds. 2002. *Implementation of law in the People's Republic of China.* The Hague: Kluwer Law International.

Chen, Jieru. 2006. *Wo yu Jiang Jieshi de Qinian zhi Yang* [Mrs Chen Jieru's memoir]. Beijing: Tuanjie Chubanshe.

Chen, Jin. 1991. *Mao Zedong de Wenhua Xingge* [The cultural character of Mao Zedong]. Beijing: Zhongguo Qingnian Chubanshe.

——. 1993. *Mao Zedong zhi Hun* [The soul of Mao Zedong]. Changchun: Jilin Renmin Chubanshe.

Chen, Jingbao, and Chen Yanping. 1991. A sketch of China's secret service—Past and present. *China Forum* 1 (12): 1–14.

Chen, Lifu. 1994. *Storm clouds over China: The memoir of Ch'en Li-fu, 1900–1993.* Ed. S. Chang and R. Myers. Stanford, CA: Hoover Institute Press.

Chen, Liming. 2005. *Hu Yaobang Zhuan* [A biography of Hu Yaobang]. 2 vols. Hong Kong: Xiafei'er Chuban Youxian Gongsi.

Chen, Liwen. 1991. *Song Ziwen yu Zhanshi Waijiao* [Song Ziwen and wartime diplomacy]. Taibei: Guoshi Guan.

Chen, P. Heng-chao. 1979. *Chinese legal tradition under the Mongols: The Code of 1291 as reconstructed.* Cambridge, MA: Harvard University Press.

Chen, Pengren, Qiao Baotai, et al., eds. 1999–2000. *Zhongguo Guomindang Dangwu Fazhan Shiliao.* Taibei: Jin dai Zhongguo Chubanshe.

Chen, Qingquan. 2006. *Zai Zhonggong Gaoceng 50 Nian: Lu Dingyi Chuanqi Rensheng* [Fifty years in high position of China: A biography of Lu Dingyi]. Beijing: Renmin Chubanshe.

Chen, R. 2004. *The execution of Mayor Yin and other stories from the Great Proletarian Cultural Revolution.* Rev. ed. Ed. N. Ing and H. Goldblatt. Bloomington: Indiana University Press.

Chen, Shaozhou. 1992. *Liu Shaoqi zai Baiqu* [Liu Shaoqi in the white areas]. Beijing: Chinese Communist Party History Publishers.

Ch'en, T. H. 1960. *Thought reform of the Chinese intellectuals.* Hong Kong: Hong Kong University Press.

Chen, Tingyi. 2001. *Sun Zhongshan Dazhuan* [A long biography of Sun Yatsen]. 2 vols. Beijing: Tuanjie Chubanshe.

——. 2004. *Songshi Sanxiongdi: Sange Yangboshi yu Minguo Jingji* [Three song brothers: Three foreign PhDs and Chinese economy]. Beijing: Dongfang Chubanshe.

Chen, Weidong. 2001. *Xingshi Susongfa Shishi Wenti Diaoyan Baogao* [Report on the problems in implementation of criminal procedure law]. Beijing: Zhongguo Fangzheng Chubanshe.

Chen, Weiru. 1988. Wode Tewu Shengya [My career as a spy]. In *Tegong Zongbu: Zhongtong* [Secret service headquarters: Central statistics], Zhang Wen et. al, 142–188. Hong Kong: Zhongyuan Chubanshe.

Chen, Wenmin, Hualing Fu, and Yash P. Ghai. 2000. *Hong Kong's constitutional debate: Conflict over interpretation.* Hong Kong: Hong Kong University Press.

Chen, Yan. 1996. *Jiang Jieshi he Li Jishen* [Chiang Kai-shek and Li Jishen]. Changchun: Jilin wen shi chu ban she.

Chen, Yangyong. 2006. *Kucheng Weiju: Zhou Enlai zai 1967* [Handling the crisis: Zhou Enlai in 1967]. Chongqing: Chongqing Chubanshe.

Chen, Yun. 1984. *Chen Yun wenxuan (1949–1956)* [Selected works of Chen Yun]. 2 vols. Beijing: Foreign Language Press.

——. 1986. *Chen Yun wenxuan (1956–1985)* [Selected works of Chen Yun]. 2 vols. Beijing: Foreign Language Press.

Chen, Xiaoming. 2007. *From the May Fourth Movement to Communist Revolution: Guo Moruo and the Chinese path to communism.* Albany: State University of New York Press.

Chen, Xiqi. 1991. *Sun Zhongshan Nianpu Changbian* [Long chronology of Sun Yetsen]. Beijing: Zhonghua Shuju.

Chen, Yi zhuan bianji zhu, ed. 1991. *Chen Yi zhuan* [A biography of Chen Yi]. Beijing: Dangdai Zhongguo Chubanshe.

Chen, Yung-fa. 1986. *Making revolution: The communist movement in eastern and central China, 1937–1945.* Berkeley: University of California Press.

——. 1994. Reconsidering the "Yan'an Way": From rectification to cadre-screening and spy-hunting. Paper presented at the annual meeting of the Association for Asian Studies, Boston, March 25–27.

Chen, Zaidao. 1988. *A memoir.* Beijing: Jiefangjun bao Chubanshe.

Chen, Zhili. 1991. *Zhongguo Gongchandang Jiandangshi* [A history of the Chinese Communist Party]. Shanghai: Renmin Chubanshe.

Chen, Zhimai. 1935–1936. Impeachments of Control Yuan: A preliminary survey. *Chinese Social and Political Science Review* xix: 331–366, 515–542.

Chen, Zilong et al., eds. 1997. *Huang Ming jing shi wen bian* [The August Ming dynasty's writings on statecraft]. Beijing: Beijing Chubanshe.

Chen, Zongshun. 1987. *Modai Huangfu Zaifeng* [Last regent: Zaifeng]. Ha'erbin: Heilongjiang Xinhua Shudian.

Cheng, Chung-ying. 1983. Metaphysics of Tao and dialectics of Fa. *Journal of Chinese Philosophy* 10:251–284.

Cheng, Jin. 1997. *Tie Jiangjun Ye Ting* [Ye Ting, iron general]. 2 vols. Beijing: Zhongguo Xiju Chubanshe.

Cheng, Li. 2000. Jiang Zemin's successors: The rise of the fourth generation of leaders in the PRC. *China Quarterly* 161:1.

———. 2001. *China's leaders: The new generation.* Lanham, MD: Rowman & Littlefield.

Cheng, Min. 1993. *Dangnei Dajian* [Internal spy]. Beijing: Tuanjie Chubanshe.

Cheng, Shu-de. 1931. *Zhongguo Fazhishih* [A history of China's legal institutions]. Shanghai: Huatong Shuchü.

———. 1965. *Jiuchao Lükao* [A study of the penal statutes of nine dynasties] 2 vols. Taipei: Taiwan Shangwu.

Cheng, Shuwei, Sun Qimai, and Wang Guangyuan. 2003. *Jiang Jieshi Mishi* [The secret documents of Jiang Jieshi]. Taipei: Fongyun Shidai.

Cheng, Yiming. 1979a. *Cheng Yiming Huiyilu* [Memoirs of Cheng Yiming]. Beijing: Qunzhong Chubanshe.

———. 1979b. Wen Yiduo bei Ansha de Neimu [The inside story of the murder of Wen Yiduo]. *Guangdong Wenshi ziliao* 23:197–202.

———. 1980. Juntong tewu zuzhi de zhenxiang [The truth about the special services organization of Juntong]. *Guangdong Wenshi Ziliao* 29:186–281.

Chesnaux, J. 1972. *Popular movements and secret societies in China, 1846–1950.* Stanford, CA: Stanford University Press.

———. 1973. *Peasant Revolts in China, 1840–1949.* New York: Norton.

Chi, Hsi-sheng. 1976. *Warlord politics in China, 1916–1928.* Stanford, CA: Stanford University Press.

———. 1982. *Nationalist China at war: Military defeats and political collapse, 1937–45.* Ann Arbor: University of Michigan Press.

———. 1989. Disciplinary problems and the CCP's rectification campaign. In *Chinese politics from Mao to Deng*, ed. V. C. Falkenheim, 139–164. New York: Professors World Peace Academy.

———. 1991. *Politics of disillusionment: The Chinese Communist Party under Deng Xiaoping, 1978–1989.* Armonk, NY: M. E. Sharpe.

Chiang, Kai-shek (Jiang Jieshi). 1957. *Zongtong Zhexue Yanlu Jingbian* [Selected works of philosophy by President Chiang Kai-shek]. Taibei: Zhonghua Wenhua Chubanshe.

———. 1984. *Xian Congtong Jiang Gong Quanji* [Complete works of late President Lord Chiang Kai-shek]. Ed. Zhang Qiyun. 3 vols. Taipei: The University of Chinese Culture.

———. 1985. *Zongtong Jianggong Sixiang Yanlun Congji* [The complete collection of Mr. President Chiang Kai-shek's thought and speech]. 40 vols. Taipei: Zhongguo Guomindang Zhongyang Wciyuanhui.

Chiang, Siang-tseh. 1954. *The Nien Rebellion.* Seattle: University of Washington Press.

Chien, Tieh. A study of a document concerning the Lin Piao incident. *Issues and Studies* 8 (June 1972): 38–56; (July 1972): 87–95; (Aug. 1972): 51–60; and (Sept. 1972): 41–46.

Chien, Tuan-sheng. 1942. War-time government in China. *The American Political Science Review* 36 (October): 859–872.

——. 1950. *The government and politics of China.* Cambridge, MA: Harvard University Press.

Chien, Yu-shen. 1969. *China's fading revolution: Army dissent and military divisions, 1967–1968.* Hong Kong: Center for Contemporary Chinese Studies.

Chong, Woei Lien. 1996. Mandkind and nature in Chinese thought: Li Zehou on the traditional roots of Maoist voluntarism. *China Information* 11 (2–3): 138–175.

——, ed. 2002. *China's Great Proletarian Cultural Revolution: Master narratives and post-Mao counternarrative.* Lanham, MD: Rowman & Littlefield.

Chow, Ching-wen. 1960. *Ten years of storm: The true story of the communist regime in China.* New York: Holt, Rinehart and Winston.

Chow, Kai-wing. 1994. *The rise of Confucian ritualism in late imperial China: Ethics, classics, and lineage discourse.* Stanford, CA: Stanford University Press.

Chow, Tse-tsung. 1960. *The May Fourth Movement: Intellectual revolution in modern China.* Cambridge, MA: Harvard University Press.

Chu, Fang. 1998. *Gun barrel politics: Party-army relations in Mao's China.* Boulder, CO: Westview Press.

Chu, G. 1977. *Radical change through communications in Mao's China,* Honolulu: University of Hawaii Press.

Chu, G. C., and F. L. K. Hsu, eds. 1979. *Moving a mountain: Cultural change in China.* Honolulu: University of Hawaii Press.

Chu, Kung, and Peng Teh-huai. 1968. *The case of Peng Teh-huai 1959–1968*. Hong Kong: Union Research Institute.

Chu, R. 1967. An introductory study of the White Lotus sect in Chinese history. PhD diss., Columbia University.

Chu, T'ung-tsu. 1961. *Law and society in traditional China*. Paris: Mouton.

Chu, Wen-djang. 1966. *The Moslem rebellion in northwest China, 1862–1878*. The Hague: Mouton.

Chuan, Tsun. 1972. The Lin Piao incident and its effect on Mao's rule. *Issues and Studies* 8 (February): 21–28.

Chung, Dooeum. 2000. *Elitist fascism: Chiang Kaishek's Blueshirts in 1930s China*. Aldershot: Ashgate.

Clarke, D. 1995. The execution of civil judgements in China. *China Quarterly* 141 (March): 65–81.

———. 1996. Power and politics in the Chinese court system: The enforcement of civil judgments. *Columbia Journal of Asian Law* 10 (1): 1–92.

———. 1998–1999. Alternative approaches to Chinese law: Beyond the "rule of law" paradigm. *Waseda Proceedings of Comparative Law* 2: 49–62.

Clarke, D., and Andrew Godwin. 1997. Allocated or granted land? New rules blur the boundaries. *China Joint Venturer*, February, 11.

Clarke, P. 2008. *The Chinese Cultural Revolution: A history*. Cambridge: Cambridge University Press.

Clayton, C. W. 1992. *The politics of justice: The Attorney General and the making of legal policy*. Armonk, NY: M. E. Sharpe.

Cleare, J. 1998. *Distant mountains*. New York: Crown Publishing Group.

Clunas, C. 1991. *Superfluous things: Material culture and social status in early modern China*. Cambridge, U.K.: Polity Press.

———. 1996. *Fruitful sites: Garden culture in Ming dynasty China.* Durham, NC: Duke University Press.

———. 2005. *Pictures and visuality in early modern China.* Chicago: University of Chicago Press.

Coble, P. M. 1980. *The Shanghai capitalists and the nationalist government: 1927–1937.* Cambridge, MA: Harvard University Press.

———. 1991. *Facing Japan: Chinese politics and Japanese imperialism 1931–1937.* Cambridge, MA: Harvard University Press.

Cohen, J. A. 1968. *The criminal process in the People's Republic of China, 1949–1963: An introduction.* Cambridge, MA: Harvard University Press.

———. 1978. China's changing Constitution. *China Quarterly* 76 (December): 794–841. Cohen, P. A. 1997. *History in three keys: The boxers as event, experience, and myth.* New York: Columbia University Press.

———. 2003. *China unbound: Evolving perspectives on the Chinese past.* London: Routledge Curzon.

Cohen, P. A., and J. E. Schrecker, eds. 1976. *Reform in nineteenth century China.* Cambridge, MA: Harvard University Press.

The collection of laws and orders of the People's Central Government. 1958. Beijing: Law Press.

Compton, B., trans. 1952. *Mao's China: Party reform documents, 1942–44.* Seattle: University of Washington Press.

Conquest, R. 1990. *The great terror: A reassessment.* New York: Oxford University Press.

The Constitution of the People's Republic of China. 1978. Beijing: Foreign Languages Press.

Constitution of the People's Republic of China. 1982. *Beijing Review* 25 (December): 10–29.

Corne, P. H. 1996. *Foreign investment in China: The administrative legal system.* Hong Kong: Hong Kong University Press.

Crawford, R. B. 1961. Eunuch power in the Ming dynasty. *Tong Pao* 5.49: III: 115–148.

Creel, H. G. 1954. *The birth of China.* New York: Frederick Ungar Publishers.

———. 1970. *The origins of statecraft in China.* Chicago: University of Chicago Press.

Crossley, P. K. 1990. *Orphan warriors: Three Manchu generations and the end of the Qing world.* Princeton, NJ: Princeton University Press.

———. 1997. *The Manchus.* Cambridge, MA: Blackwell Publishers.

———. 1999. *A translucent mirror: History and identity in Qing imperial ideology.* Berkeley: University of California Press.

Crowell, W. G. 1983. Social unrest and rebellion in Jiangnan during the six dynasties. *Modern China* 9.3:319–354.

Crozier, B. 1976. *The man who lost China.* New York: Scribner.

Cua, A. 1978. *Dimensions in moral creativity.* University Park: Pennsylvania State University Press.

———. 1989. The concept of Li in Confucian moral theory. In *Understanding the Chinese mind: The philosophical roots*, ed. R. Allison, 209–235. Hong Kong: Oxford University Press.

Cui, Xiaozhong. 2003. *Qingnian Jiang Jieshi* [The young Chiang Kai-shek]. Beijing: Huawen Chubanshe.

Da Ming lü [The Great Ming Code]. 1988. In *Huang Ming zhishu*, volume 4, ed. Zhang Lu, 1605–2205. Taipei: Zhonghua Shuju.

Qin ding da Qing hui dian. (Da Qing hui dian) [Collected statutes of the great Ch'ing dynasty] 100 juan. Taibei: Qi wen Chubanshe.

Da Qing Lichao Shilu [Veritable records of successive reigns of the Qing dynasty] 1985–1987. 60 vols. Beijing: Zhonghua shu ju.

Dai, Li. 1978. *Zhengzhi zhentan* [Political spies]. Washington, DC: Center for Chinese Research Materials, Association of Research Libraries.

Dai, Qing. 1989. *Xiandai Zhongguo Zhishifenzi Qun: Liang Shuming, Wang Shiwei, Chu Anping* [Contemporary Chinese intellectuals: Liang Shuming, Wang Shiwei, and Chu Anping]. Nanjing: Jiangsu Wenyi Chubanshe.

———. 1991. *Mao Zedong, Dangtianxia, Ye Baihehua.* Xindian: Xinfeng Chubanshe.

———. 1994. *Wang Shiwei and "Wild Lilies": Rectification and purges in the Chinese Communist Party, 1942–1944.* Trans. N. Liu and L. Sullivan. Armonk, NY: M. E. Sharpe.

———. 2005. *Tiananmen follies: Prison memoirs and other writings.* Trans. and ed. N. Liu, P. Rand, and L. Sullivan. Norwalk, CT: EastBridge.

Dai Yunong. 1966. *Xiansheng nianpu* [Chronological biography of Dai Yunong]. Taibei: Guofangbu Qingbaoju.

Dang dai Zhongguo, ed. 1994. *Nie Rongzhen Zhuan* [A biography of Nie Rongzhen]. Beijing: Dangdai Zhongguo Chubanshe.

Dang de Jianshe [Construction of the party]. An official magazine of the CCP. Specific edition, 1986.

Dardess, J. W. 1973. *Conquerors and Confucians: Aspects of political change in late Yüan China.* New York: Columbia University Press.

———. 1983. *Confucianism and autocracy: Professional elites in the founding of the Ming dynasty.* Berkeley: University of California Press.

———. 1997. *A Ming society: T'ai-ho County, Kiangsi, in the fourteenth to seventeenth centuries.* Berkeley: University of California Press.

———. 2002. *Blood and history in China: The Donglin faction and its repression.* Honolulu: University of Hawaii Press.

Darling, A. B. 1990. *The Central Intelligence Agency: An instrument of government, to 1950.* University Park: Pennsylvania State University Press.

Daube, D. 1969. *Studies in biblical law.* New York: Ktav Publishing House.

Daubier, J. 1974. *A history of the Chinese Cultural Revolution.* Trans. R. Seaver. New York: Vintage Books.

Davies, G., ed. 2001. *Voicing concerns: Contemporary Chinese critical inquiry.* Lanham, MD: Rowman & Littlefield.

Davis, Fei-Ling. 1977. *Primitive revolutionaries of China: A study of secret societies in the late nineteenth century.* London: Routledge & Kegan Paul.

Davis, R. L. 1986. *Court and family in Sung China, 960–1279: Bureaucratic success and kingship fortunes for the Shih of Ming-chou.* Durham, NC: Duke University Press.

de Bono, E. 1972. *Po: Beyond yes and no.* Harmondsworth, U.K.: Penguin.

de Crespigny, Rafe, trans. 1989. *Emperor Huan and Emperor Ling: Being the chronicle of later Han for the years 157 to 189 A.D. as recorded in chapters 54–59 of the Zizhi Tongjian of Sima Guang.* Canberra: Faculty of Asian Studies, Australian National University.

DeBary, W. T. 1970. *Self and society in Ming thought.* New York: Columbia University Press.

———. 1975. *The unfolding of neo-Confucianism.* New York: Columbia University Press.

———. 1993. *Waiting for the dawn.* New York: Columbia University Press.

———. 1998. *Asian values and human rights: A Confucian communitarian perspective.* Cambridge, MA: Harvard University Press.

DeBary, W. T., and R. J. Lufrano, eds. 1999–2000. *Sources of Chinese tradition: From 1600 through the twentieth century*. New York: Columbia University Press.

Deng, Baoguang. 1986. Wosuo Zhidao de Dai Li he Juntong [The Dai Li and Military Statistics Bureau that I knew]. *Shanghai Wenshi Ziliao Xuanji* 55:150–163.

Deng, Rong (Maomao). 1995. *My father Deng Xiaoping*. New York: Basic Books.

——. 2005. *Wo de fu qin Deng Xiaoping: Wen ge sui yue* [Deng Xiaoping and the Cultural Revolution: A daughter recalls the critical years]. Trans. S. Shapiro. New York: C. Bertelsmann.

Deng, Tu. 1986. *Deng Tuo Wenji* [Collected works of Deng Tuo]. Beijing: Beijing Chubanshe.

Deng, Xiaoping. 1956. *The constitution of the Communist Party of China, Report on the revision of the constitution of the Communist Party of China*. Ed. CCP. Beijing: Foreign Languages Press.

——. 1983. *Deng Xiaoping Wenxuan* [Selected works of Deng Xiaoping, 1975–1982]. Beijing: Renmin Chubanshe.

——. 1984. *Selected works of Deng Xiaoping, 1975–1982*. Beijing: Foreign Languages Press.

——. 1987. *Jianshe you Zhongguo Tese de Shehuizhuyi* [Build socialism with Chinese characteristics]. Hong Kong: Joint Publishing Company.

——. 1994. *Selected Works of Deng Xiaoping*. Vol. 3. *1982–1992*. Beijing: Foreign Language Press.

Deng, Yuanzhong. 1984. *Sanminzhuyi Lixingshe shi* [A history of Lixing society]. Taibei: Shixian Chubanshe.

Dennerline, J. 1981. *The Chia-Ting loyalists: Confucian leadership and social change in seventeenth-century China*. New Haven, CT: Yale University Press.

Des Forges, R. V. 2003. *Cultural centrality and political change in Chinese history: Northeast Henan in the fall of the Ming.* Stanford, CA: Stanford University Press.

Deutscher, G., and N. J. C. Kouwenberg. 2006. *The Akkadian language in its semitic context: Studies in the Akkadian of the third and second millennium BC.* Leiden: Nederlands Instituut voor het Nabije Oosten.

DeWoskin, K. J., trans. 1983. *Doctors, diviners, and magicians of ancient China.* New York: Columbia University Press.

Di, Yongjun. 2002. *Qing dai Han lin yuan zhi du* [Hanlin Academy in Qing dynasty]. Beijing, She hui ke xue wen xian chu ban she.

Dicks, A. 1989. The Chinese legal system: Reforms in the balance. *China Quarterly* 119 (September): 540–576.

——.1995. Compartmentalized law and judicial restraint: An inductive view of some judicial barriers to reform. *China Quarterly* 141 (March): 82–109.

Dickson, B. J. 1997. *Democratization in China and Taiwan.* Oxford, U.K.: Clarendon Press.

——. 2003. *Red capitalists in China: The party, private entrepreneurs, and prospects for political change.* Cambridge: Cambridge University Press.

Dien, A. E., ed. 1991. *State and society in early medieval China.* Stanford, CA: Stanford University Press.

Di Palma, Guiseppe. 1990. *To craft democracies: An essay on democratic transitions.* Berkeley: University of California Press.

Ding, Huayong. 1989. *Cuncao Chunhui* [Short glasses and spring shine]. Taibci: Nanyang Wenxianshe.

Ding, Longjia, and Ting Yu. 1999. *Kang Sheng yu "Zhao Jianmin Yuan An"* [Kang Sheng and the unjust case of Zhao Jianmin]. Beijing: Renmin Chubanshe.

Ding, Wang, ed. 1969. *Peng Dehuai Wenti Zhuanji* [The case of Peng Dehuai]. Xiang Gang : Ming bao yue kan she.

——. 1976. *Hua Guofeng Zhuan* [A biography of Hua Guofeng]. Hong Kong: Xiandai Yanjiu Chubanshe.

——. 1977. *Wang Hongwen Zhang Chunqiao Pingzhuan* [A critical biography of Wang Hongwen and Zhang Chunqiao]. Hong Kong: Mingbao Yuekanshe.

——. 1979. *Yao Wenyuan Mao Yunxin Pingzhuan* [A critical biography of Yao Wenyuan and Mao Yunxin]. Hong Kong: Mingbao Yuekan.

Ding, Wenjiang, ed. 1958. *Liang Rengong Xiansheng Nianpu Changbian Chugao* [A draft of a chronology of Liang Qichao]. 3 vols. Taipei: Shijie.

Ding, Wenjiang, and Zhao Fengtian, eds. 1983. *Liang Qichao Nianpu Changbian* [Chronology of Liang Qichao]. Shanghai: Shanghai People's Press.

Ding, Xiaohe. 2006a. *Kuang Biao: Hongweibing Kuangxiangqu.* Beijing Shi: Zhonggong Dangshi Chubanshe.

——. 2006b. *Niepan: Laosanjie Suixiangqu.* Beijing: Zhonggong Dangshi Chubanshe.

Ding, Xueliang. 1994a. *The decline of communism in China: Legitimacy crisis, 1977–1989.* New York: Cambridge University Press.

——. 1994b. Institutional amphibiousness and the transition from communism: The case of China. *British Journal of Politics* 24:293–318.

Ding, Yi. 1983. *Mingdai Tewu Zhengzhi* [Politics of secret agents in the Ming dynasty]. Beijing: Zhonghua Shuju.

Dirlik, A. 1989. *The origins of Chinese communism.* New York: Oxford University Press.

——. 1991. *Anarchism in the Chinese revolution.* Berkeley: University of California Press.

Dirlik, A., and M. Meisner, eds. 1989. *Marxism and the Chinese experience*. Armonk, NY: M. E. Sharpe.

Ditmanson, P. B. 1999. Contesting authority: Intellectual lineages and the Chinese imperial court from the twelfth to the fifteenth centuries. PhD diss., Harvard University.

Dittmer, L. 1977. "Line struggle" in theory and practice. *China Quarterly* 72 (December): 675–712.

——. 1978. Base of power in Chinese politics: A theory and analysis of the fall of the "Gang of Four." *World Politics* 31 (October): 26–60.

——. 1981. Death and transfiguration: Liu Shaoqi's rehabilitation and contemporary Chinese politics. *Journal of Asian Studies*, 40(3): 455–480.

——. 1987. *China's continuous revolution*. Berkeley, University of California Press.

——. 1998. *Liu Shaoqi and the Chinese Cultural Revolution*. Armonk, NY: M. E. Sharpe.

Dittmer, Lowell, and Jo-hsi Ch'en. 1981. *Ethics and rhetoric of the Chinese Cultural Revolution*. Studies in Chinese terminology, no. 19. Berkeley, CA: Center for Chinese Studies, Institute of East Asian Studies, University of California.

Diyi, Tushuguan, ed. 1924. *Cao Kun Wu Peifu Hezhuan* [Biography of Cao Kun and Fu Peifu]. Shanghai: Diyi Tushuguan.

Domes, J. 1973. *The internal politics of China, 1949–1972*. New York: Praeger.

——. 1977a. *China after the Cultural Revolution: Politics between two party Congresses*. Berkeley: University of California Press.

——. 1977b. The "Gang of Four" and Hua Guo-feng: Analysis of political events in 1975–76. *China Quarterly* 71 (September): 477–478.

——. 1980. *Socialism in the Chinese countryside: Rural societal policies in the People's Republic of China, 1949–1979*. Montreal: McGill University Press.

——. 1985a. *The government and politics of the PRC: A time of transition*. Boulder, CO: Westview Press.

——. 1985b. *P'eng Te-huai: The man and the image*. Stanford, CA: Stanford University Press.

Dong, Baocun. 1992. *Tan Zhenlin Waizhuan* [An unofficial biography of Tan Zhenlin]. Beijing: Zuojia Chubanshe.

Dong, Yao. 1995. *Beiyang Junshi: Tianxiao Xu Shuzheng* [Beiyang general: Divine hero Xu Shuzheng]. Beijing: Tuanjie Chubanshe.

Doolin, D. 1964. *Chinese communism: The politics of student opposition*. Stanford, CA: Stanford University Press.

Dorff, E. N., and A. Rosett. 1988. *A living tree: The roots and growth of Jewish law*. Albany: State University of New York Press.

Dreyer, E. L. 1982. *Early Ming China: A political history, 1355–1435*. Stanford, CA: Stanford University Press.

Dreyer, J. T. 1993. *China's political system: Modernization and tradition*. New York: Paragon House.

Driver, G. R. 1957. *Aramaic documents of the fifth century BC*. Oxford, U.K.: Oxford University Press.

Du, You (Tang). 1988. *Tong Dian*. 5 vols. Beijing: Zhonghua Shuju.

Duan, Yusheng. 1989. *Ye Ting Jiangjun Zhuan* [Biography of General Ye Ting]. Beijing: Jiefangjun Chubanshe.

Duara, P. 1988. *Culture power and the state: Rural north China, 1900–1942*. Stanford, CA: Stanford University Press.

Duiker, W. J. 1978. *Cultures in collision: The Boxer Rebellion*. San Rafael, CA: Presidio Press.

Dull, J. L. 1990. The evolution of government in China. In *Heritage of China: Contemporary perspectives on Chinese civilization*, ed. P. S. Ropp, 55–85. Berkeley: University of California Press.

Dunch, R. 2001. *Fuzhou Protestant and the making of modern China, 1857–1927*. New Haven, CT: Yale University Press.

Dutton, M. 2004. *Policing Chinese politics: A history*. Durham, NC: Duke University Press.

Duyvendak, J. J. L. 1974. *The book of Lord Shang*. San Francisco: Chinese Materials Centre.

Dworkin, R. 1986. *Law's Empire*. Cambridge, MA: Harvard University Press.

Eastman, L. E. 1984. *Seeds of destruction: Nationalist China in war and revolution, 1937–1949*. Stanford, CA: Stanford University Press.

——. 1986. Nationalist China during the Sino-Japanese War. In *The Cambridge history of China, XIII*, ed. J. K. Fairbank and D. C. Twitchett, 116–167. Cambridge: Cambridge University Press.

——. 1990. *The abortive revolution: China under nationalist rule: 1927-1937*. Cambridge, MA: Harvard University Press.

——. 1991. *The nationalist era in China, 1927–1949*. New York: Cambridge University Press.

Eberhard, W. 1950. *A history of China*. Berkeley: University of California Press.

Edley, C. F., Jr. 1990. *Administrative law: Rethinking judicial control of bureaucracy*. New Haven, CT: Yale University Press.

Edmunds, C. 1987. The politics of historiography: Jian Bozan's historicism. In *Chinese intellectuals and the state: In search of new relationship*, ed. M. Goldman, T. Cheek, and C. L. Hamrin, 65–106. Cambridge, MA: Harvard University Press.

Eiichi, K. 1944. *Hōka shisō no kenkyū*. Tokyo: Kobundo.

Elbogen, I. 1993. *Jewish liturgy: A comprehensive history*. Trans. R. P. Scheidlin. New York: Jewish Publication Society.

Elleman, B. 2001. *Modern Chinese warfare, 1795–1989*. London: Routledge.

Elliot, M. C. 1993. Resident aliens: The Manchu experience in China, 1644–1760. PhD Diss., University of California.

———. 2001. *The Manchu way: The eight banners and ethnic identity in late imperial China*. Stanford, CA: Stanford University Press.

Elman, B. A. 1984. *From philosophy to philology: Intellectual and social aspects of change in late imperial China*. Cambridge, MA: Harvard University Press.

———. 1986. Scholarship and politics: Chuang Tsun-yu and the rise of the Ch'ang-chou new text school in late imperial China. *Late Imperial China* 7:63–86.

———. 1990. *Classicism, politics, and kinship: The Ch'ang-chou School of New Text Confucianism in late imperial China*. Berkeley: University of California Press.

———. 2000. *A cultural history of civil examinations in late imperial China*. Berkeley: University of California Press.

Elon, M. 1994. *Jewish law: History, sources, principles*. Philadelphia: Jewish Publication Society.

Elon, M., B. Auerbach, D. Chazin, and M. Sykes. 1999. *Jewish law (Mishpat Ivri): Cases and materials*. New York: Matthew Bender.

Elvin, M. 1973. *The pattern of the Chinese past*. London: Eyre Methuen.

Enatsu, Yoshiki. 2001. *Banner legacy: The rise of the Fengtian local elite at the end of the Qing*. Ann Arbor: University of Michigan Press.

Epstein, M. 2001. *Competing discourses: Orthodoxy, authenticity and engendered meanings in late imperial Chinese fiction*. Cambridge, MA: Harvard University Press.

Esherick, J. W. 1976. *Reform and revolution in China: The 1911 Revolution in Hunan and Hubei*. Berkeley: University of California Press.

———. 1987. *The origins of the Boxer uprising*. Berkeley: University of California Press.

———. 1995. Ten theses on the Chinese revolution. *Modern China* 21/1:45–76.

———. 2000. *Remaking the Chinese city: Modernity and national identity, 1900–1950*. Honolulu: University of Hawaii Press.

Esherick, J. W., and M. B. Rankin, eds. 1990. *Chinese local elites and patterns of dominance*. Berkeley: University of California Press.

Esmein, J. 1973. *The Chinese Cultural Revolution*. Trans. W. J. F. Jenner. New York: Anchor.

Eto, S., and H. Z. Schiffrin, eds. 1994. *China's republican revolution*. Tokyo: University of Tokyo Press.

Evasdottir, E. E. S. 2005. *Obedient autonomy: Chinese intellectuals and the achievement of orderly life*. Honolulu: University of Hawaii Press.

Fairbank, J. K., ed. 1978. *The Cambridge history of China, vol 10, Late Qing, 1800–1911, Part 1*. Cambridge, U.K. Cambridge University Press.

———.1982. *Chinabound: A fifty year memoir*. New York: Harper & Row.

———. 1992. *China: A new history*. Cambridge, MA: Harvard University Press.

Fairbank, J. K., and Kwang-Ching Liu, eds. 1980. *The Cambridge history of China, vol. 11, Late Qing, 1800–1911, Part 2*. Cambridge: Cambridge University Press.

Falaschi, N. 1988. *Palaeography shows a linguistic continuity from the Pelasgians, Thracians, Illyrians, Etruscans to the Albanians*. Roma: Tipografia Albedo.

Faligot, R., and R. Kauffer. 1989. *The Chinese secret service*. Trans. C. Donougher. New York: Morrow.

Falk, Z. 1964. *Hebrew law in biblical times*. Jerusalem: Wahrmann Books.

Falkenheim, V. C., ed. 1987. *Citizens and groups in contemporary China*. Ann Arbor: University of Michigan Press.

——, ed. 1989. *Chinese politics from Mao to Deng*. New York: Paragon.

Fan, Fangzhen. 2002. *Sun Zhongshan Chuanqi* [A biography of Sun Yatsen]. Nanjing: Jiangsu Guji Chubanshe.

Fan, K., ed. 1972. *Mao Tse-tung and Lin Piao: Post-revolutionary writing*. New York: Doubleday.

Fang, Ke. 2003. *Yuan Shikai*. Beijing: Minzu Chubanshe.

Fang, Hao. 1954. *Song Shi* [History of the Song dynasty]. 2 vols. Taipei: Ershiwu Shi Biankan Guan.

Fan, Shuo, and Gao Yi. 1995. Gandan Xiangzhao, Gongjie Guonan [Cooperation with utmost devotion in the solution of the national crises]. *Dang de wenxian* 1:78–88.

Fang, Yonggang. 2007. *Jiang Jieshi: Cong Xikou Dao Cihu* [Chiang Kaishek, from Xikou to Cihu]. Beijing: Huawen Chubanshe.

Fang, Zhu. 1995. Political work in the military from the viewpoint of the Beijing Garrison Command. In *Decision-making in Deng's China*, ed. C. L. Hamrin and S. Zhao, 118–132. Armonk, NY: M. E. Sharpe.

Farmer, E. L. 1976. *Early Ming government: The evolution of dual capitals.* Cambridge, MA: Harvard University Press.

——. 1989. The prescriptive state: Social legislation in the early Ming dynasty. In *Proceedings of the second international conference on sinology,* 161–187. Taipei: Academia Sinica.

——. 1990. Social regulations of the first Ming Emperor: Orthodoxy as a function of authority. In *Orthodoxy in late imperial China,* ed. Kwang-ching Liu, 103–125. Berkeley: University of California Press.

——. 1993. The great Ming commandment (Da Ming ling): An inquiry into early Ming social legislation. *Asia Major* 3rd Ser., 6.1:181–199.

——. 1995. *Zhu Yuanzhang and early Ming legislation: The reordering of Chinese society following the era of Mongol rule.* New York: E. J. Brill.

Farmer, E. L., R. Taylor, and A. Waltner. 1994. *Ming history: An introductory guide to research.* Minneapolis: University of Minnesota.

Fassberg, S. E., and A. Hurvitz, eds. 2006. *Biblical Hebrew in its northwest semitic setting: Typological and historical perspectives.* Jerusalem: Hebrew University Magnes Press; Winona Lake, Eisenbrauns.

Faure, D. 1979. Secret societies, heretic sects, and peasant rebellions in nineteenth century China. *Journal of the Chinese University of Hong Kong* I:189–206.

Fei, Yunwen. 1985. *Dai Li Xinzhuan* [A new biography of Dai Li]. Taibei: Shengwen Shuju.

Feifel, E. 1961. *Po Chu-I as a censor.* The Hague: Kluwer Law.

Feigenbaum, E. 2003. *China's techno-warriors: National security and strategic competition from the nuclear to the information age.* Stanford, CA: Stanford University Press.

Feigon, Lee. 1983. *Chen Duxiu: Founder of the Chinese Communist Party.* Princeton, NJ: Princeton University Press.

Fenby, J. 2003. *Generalissimo: Chiang Kai-Shek and the China he lost.* New York: The Free Press.

Feng, Chi-tsai. 1996. *Ten years of madness: Oral histories of China's Cultural Revolution.* San Francisco: China Books.

Feng, Meng-lung, Shuhui Yang, and Yunqin Yang. 2000. *Stories old and new: A Ming dynasty collection.* Seattle: University of Washington Press.

Feng, Yulan. 1952–1953. *A history of Chinese philosophy.* Trans. D. Bodde. 2 vols. Princeton, NJ: Princeton University Press.

Feng, Yuxiang. 1930. *Feng Yuxiang Riji* [The diary of Feng Yuxiang]. 2 vols. Beiping: N.p.

——. 1947. Why I broke with Chiang. *The Nation* 522 (November 15): 25.

——. 1949. *Wo de Shenghuo* [My life] 3 vols. Shanghai: Jiaoyu.

——. 2004. *Woso Renshih de Jiang Jieshi* [The Chiang Kai-shek that I knew]. Beijing: Wenshi Chubanshe.

Feng, Zhengqin, and Chengsheng Yang. 1993. *Zhongguo Gongchan-dang Tongyi Zhanxian Lilun Fazhan Shigao* [A draft history of the development of the CCP's united front theory]. Shanghai: Shanghai Shehui Kexue Yuan Chubanshe.

Fessler, L. 1967. The Long March of Lin Piao. *New York Times Magazine* (September 10): 61–65.

Fewsmith, J. 1985. *Party, state and local elites in Republican China: Merchant organisations and politics in Shanghai 1890–1930.* Honolulu: University of Hawaii Press.

——. 1994. *Dilemmas of reform in China: Political conflict and economic debate.* Armonk, NY: M. E. Sharpe.

——. 2001. *China since Tiananmen: The politics of transition.* Cambridge: Cambridge University Press.

Finder, S. 1989. Like throwing an egg against a stone? Administrative litigation in the People's Republic of China. *Journal of Chinese Law* 3:1.

———. 1993. The Supreme People's Court of the People's Republic of China. *Journal of Chinese Law* 7:145.

Finder, S., and Fu Hualing. 1997. Tightening up Chinese courts' "bags"—The amended PRC, Criminal Law. *China Law and Practice* 11:35.

Fingarette, H. 1972. *Confucius: The secular is sacred.* New York: Harper & Row.

Finnane, A. 2004. *Speaking of Yangzhou: a Chinese city, 1550–1850.* Cambridge, MA: Harvard University Press.

Fisher, C. T. 1990. *The chosen one: Succession and adoption in the court of Ming Shizong.* Boston: Allen & Unwin.

Fisher, T. 1980. Wu Han, the Cultural Revolution, and the biography of Zhu Yuanzhang: An introduction. *Ming Studies* 11:33–43.

———. 1986. Wu Han: The "upright official" as a model in the humanities. In *China's establishment intellectuals*, ed. C. L. Hamrin and T. Cheek, 155–184. Armonk, NY: M. E. Sharpe.

———. 1993. The play's the thing: Wu Han and Hai Rui revisited. In *Using the past to serve the present: Historiography and politics in contemporary China*, ed. Jonathan Unger, 9–37. Armonk, NY: M. E. Sharpe.

Fitzgerald, J., ed. 1989. *The nationalists and Chinese society 1923–1937: A Symposium.* Melbourne: University of Melbourne.

Fitzmyer, J. A. 1979. *A wandering Aramaean: Collected Aramaic essays.* Missoula, MT: Fortress.

Foccardi, G. 1986. *The Chinese travelers of the Ming period.* Wiesbaden: O. Harrassowitz.

Fogel, J., ed. 2000. *The Nanjing massacre in history and historiography.* Berkeley: University of California Press.

Forster, K. 1990. *Rebellion and factionalism in a Chinese province: Zhejiang, 1966–1976.* Armonk, NY: M. E. Sharpe.

Fox, W. F. 1997. *Understanding administrative law.* Albany, NY: Matthew Bender.

Franke, H. 2003. *Krieg und Krieger im chinesischen Mittelalter.* Stuttgart: Steiner.

Franke, W. 1985. *Preliminary notes on the important Chinese literary sources for the history of the Ming dynasty.* Philadelphia: Porcupine Press.

——. 1989. *Sino-Malaysiana: Selected papers on Ming and Qing history and on the overseas Chinese in Southeast Asia, 1942–1988.* Singapore: South Seas Society.

Franz, U. 1988. *Deng Xiaoping.* Boston: Harcourt Brace Jovanovich.

Fraser, J. 1980. *The Chinese: Portrait of a people.* New York: Summit Books.

Freedman, D. N., A. D. Forbes, and F. I. Andersen, eds. 1992. *Studies in Hebrew and Aramaic orthography.* Winona Lake, IN: Eisenbrauns.

Friedman, E. 1974. *Backward toward revolution: The Chinese Revolutionary Party.* Berkeley: University of California Press.

——.1982. Maoism, Titoism, Stalinism: Some origins and consequences of the Maoist theory of the socialist transition. In *The transition to socialism in China,* 159–214. ed. Selden and Lippitt. Armonk, NY: M. E. Sharpe.

——. 1987. The flaws and failures of Mao Zedong's communist fundamentalism. *Australian Journal of Chinese Affairs* 18 (July): 147–154.

——. 1994. *The politics of democratization: Generalizing East Asian experiences.* Boulder, CO: Westview Press.

——. 1995. *National identity and democratic prospects in socialist China.* Armonk, NY: M. E. Sharpe.

Friedrich, C. J. 1958. *The philosophy of law in historical perspective.* Chicago: University of Chicago Press.

Fu, Chunyang. 2007. *Minguo shi qi zheng ti yan jiu* [Research on the political system of republic], *1925–1947.* Beijing: Law Press.

Fu, H. 2002. The shifting landscape of dispute resolution in rural China. In *Implementation of law in the People's Republic of China,* ed. Chen Jianfu, Li Yuwen, and Jan Michiel Otto, 179–196. The Hague: Kluwer Law International.

Fu, P. 1993. *Passivity, resistance and collaboration: Intellectual choices in occupied Shanghai, 1937–1945.* Stanford, CA: Stanford University Press.

Fu, Weilin, ed. 1965–1970. *Ming shu,* 171 juan. Taibei: Yiwen Yinshuguan.

Fu, Zhengyuan. 1994. *Autocratic tradition and Chinese politics.* Cambridge: Cambridge University Press.

Fung, E. S. K. 1991. The alternative of loyal opposition: The Chinese Youth Party and Chinese democracy, 1937–1949. *Modern China* 17/2:260–289.

———. 1994. Recent scholarship on the minor parties and groups in Republican China. *Modern China* 20/2:478–508.

———. 2000. *In search of Chinese democracy: Civil opposition in nationalist China 1929–1949.* Cambridge: Cambridge University Press.

Furuno, Naoya. 1999. *Chō-ke sandai no kˉobō: Kˉobun, Sakurin,Gakuryō no "mihatenu yume"* [Rise and fall of Zhang in three generations]. Tōkyō : Fuyō Shobō.

Furuya, Keiji. 1981. *Chiang Kai-shek: His life and times.* New York: St John's University.

Galambos, I. 2006. *Orthography of early Chinese writing.* Budapest: Eotvos University Press.

Gan, Guoxun. 1984. *Lanyishe, Fuxingshe, Lixingshe* [The Blue Shirt Society, Fuxing Society, and Lixing Society]. Taibei: Zhuanji Wenxue Chubanshe.

Gao, H. 1980. Qinlu zhongde yaoshu wenti [Yaoshu wenti in Qin statutes]. *Kaogu* 6:530–535.

Gao, Qicai. 2005. Zhongguo Falü Zhidu Gaiyao [A summary of Chinese legal system]. Beijing: Qinghua University Press.

Gao, Wenqian, P. Rand, and L. R. Sullivan. 2007. *Zhou Enlai: The Last Perfect Revolutionary—A Biography*. New York: PublicAffairs.

Gao, Xin. 1995. *Zhong gong ju tou Qiao Shi* [Power head: Qiao Shi]. Taibei: Shijie Shuju.

Gao, Yuan. 1987. *Born red: A chronicle of the Cultural Revolution*. Stanford, CA: Stanford University Press.

Gao, Zhi, and Zhang Ni'er. 1993. *Jiyao Mishu de Sinian* [The memories of a secretary]. Beijing: Zhonggong Zhongyang Dangxiao Chubanshe.

Garver, J. W. 1988. The origins of the Second United Front: The Comintern and the Chinese Communist Party. *China Quarterly* 113:43–46.

Geisert, B. K. 2001. *Radicalism and its demise: The Chinese Nationalist Party, factionalism, and local elites in Jiangsu Province, 1924–1931*. Ann Arbor, MI: Center for Chinese Studies Publications.

Ghūl, Mahmūd Alī. 1993. *Early southern Arabian languages and classical Arabic sources: A critical examination of literary and lexicographical sources by comparison with the inscriptions*. Ed. Omar Al-Ghul. Irbid, Jordan: Yarmouk University.

Gillin, D. G. 1967. *Warlord: Yen Hsi-Shan in Shansi Province, 1911–1949*. Princeton, NJ: Princeton University Press.

Ginneken, Jaap van. 1972. *The rise and fall of Lin Piao*. Trans. Danielle Adkinson. New York: Avon.

Gittings, J. 1967. *The role of the Chinese Army.* Oxford, U.K.: Oxford University Press.

——. 2005. *The changing face of China: From Mao to market.* Oxford, U.K.: Oxford University Press.

Gold, T. B. 1985. After comradeship: Personal relations in China since the Cultural Revolution. *China Quarterly* 104:657–675.

Gold, T. B., D. Guthrie, and D. L. Wank, eds. 2002. *Social connections in China: Institutions, culture, and the changing nature of Guanxi.* Cambridge: Cambridge University Press.

Goldman, M. 1967a. The fall of Chou Yang. *China Quarterly* 27:132–148.

——. 1967b. *Literary dissent in Communist China.* Cambridge, MA: Harvard University Press.

——. 1969. The unique "blooming and contending" of 1961–67. *China Quarterly* 37 (January–March): 54–83.

——. 1975. China's anti-Confucian campaign, 1973–74. *China Quarterly* 63 (September): 435–489.

——. 1978a. The party and the intellectuals I. In *The Cambridge history of China*, ed. D. C. Twitchett and J. K. Fairbank, 218–254. Cambridge: Cambridge University Press.

——. 1978b. The party and the intellectuals II. In *The Cambridge history of China*. ed. D. C. Twitchett and J. K. Fairbank, 432–477. Cambridge: Cambridge University Press.

——. 1981. *China's Intellectuals: Advise and Dissent.* Cambridge, MA: Harvard University Press.

——. 1994. *Sowing the seeds of democracy in China: Political reform in the Deng Xiaoping era.* Cambridge, MA: Harvard University Press.

——. 2005. *From comrade to citizen: The struggle for political rights in China.* Cambridge, MA: Harvard University Press.

Goldman, M., T. Cheek, and C. L. Hamrin, eds. 1987. *Intellectuals and the state: In search of a new relationship*. Cambridge, MA: Harvard Council on East Asian Studies.

Goldman, M. T., and E. X. Gu, eds. 2004. *Chinese intellectuals between state and market*. New York: Routledge.

Goldman, M. T., and Leo Ou-Fan Lee, eds. 2002. *An intellectual history of modern China*. New York: Cambridge University Press.

Goldstein, A. 1991. *From bandwagon to balance-of-power politics: Structural constraints and politics in China, 1949–1978*. Stanford, CA: Stanford University Press.

Gong, Pengcheng. 2007. *Jindai Sichao yu Renwu* [Modern waves of ideas and characters]. Beijing: Zhonghua Shuju.

Gong, Xiaoxia. 1995. Repressive movements and the politics of victimization: Patronage and persecution during the Cultural Revolution. PhD diss., Harvard University.

Goodman, D. S. G. 1981. *Beijing street voices: The poetry and politics of China's democracy movement*. London: Marion Boyars.

———, ed. 1984. *Groups and politics in the People's Republic of China*. Armonk, NY: M. E. Sharpe.

Goodrich, L., L. Carrington, and Chaoying Fang, eds. 1976. *Dictionary of Ming biography, 1364–1644*. New York: Columbia University Press.

Graff, D. A. 2002. *Medieval Chinese warfare*. London: Routledge.

Graham, A. C. 1986. *Yin-Yang and the nature of correlative thinking*. Singapore: Institute of East Asian Philosophies.

Gray, J., ed. 1969. *Modern China's search for a political form*. Oxford, U.K.: Oxford University Press.

———. 1990. *Rebellions and revolutions: China from the 1800s to 1980s*. Oxford, U.K.: Oxford University Press.

Gray, J., and P. Cavendish. 1968. *Chinese communism in crisis: Maoism and the Cultural Revolution*. London: Pall Mall Press.

Gray, J., and G. White, eds. 1982. *China's new development strategy*. New York: Academic Press.

A great trial in Chinese history. 1981. Beijing: New World Press.

Greiff, T. E. 1985. The principle of human rights in nationalist China: John C. H. Wu and the ideological origins of the 1946 Constitution. *China Quarterly* 103:441–461.

Grieder, J. B. 1970. *Hu Shih and the Chinese renaissance: Liberalism in the Chinese revolution, 1917–1937*. Cambridge, MA: Harvard University Press.

———. 1981. *Intellectuals and the state in modern China: A narrative history*. London: The Free Press.

Griffin, K., ed. 1984. *Institutional reform and economic development in the Chinese countryside*. Armonk, NY: M. E. Sharpe.

Groot, G. 1997. Managing transitions: The Chinese Communist Party's united front work, minor parties and groups, hegemony and corporatism. PhD diss., University of Adelaide, Australia.

———. 2004. *Managing transitions: The Chinese Communist Party, united front work, corporatism, and hegemony*. London: Routledge.

Grove, L., and C. Christian. 1984. *State and society in China: Japanese perspectives on Ming-Qing social and economic history*. Tokyo: University of Tokyo Press.

Gruendler, B. 1993. *The development of the Arabic scripts*. Atlanta, GA: Scholars Press.

Gu, Mingdong. 2005. *Chinese theories of reading and writing*. Albany: State University of New York Press.

Gu, Sharron. 2006. *The boundaries of meaning and the formation of law. Legal concepts and reasoning in the English, Arabic and Chinese traditions*. Montreal: McGill-Queens University Press.

Gu, Yanwu. Ca. 1956. *Rizhilu* [A record of daily learning]. Taibei: Shangwu.

Gu, Yingtai. 1919. Mingshi jishi benmo [Narratives of Ming historical events]. In *Sibu congkan*. Shanghai: Shangwu.

Gu, Yongzhong. 2007. *He Long yu Gongheguo Yuanshuai* [He Long and Chinese Marshals]. Beijing: Renmin Chubanshe.

Gu, Yue. 2005. *Deng Xiaoping Bingfa yu Taolüe* [Deng Xiaping's military and political strategies]. Guangzhou: Guangdong Renmin Chubanshe.

Gugung-Bowuyuan-Ming-Qing-Danganbu [Department of Ming and Qing dynasties of Musuem of Imperial Palace], ed. 1995. *Qingmo Choubei Lixian Dangan Shiliao* [Historic material from the archives of constitutional reform of the later Qing]. 2 vols. Beijing: Gugong Bowuyuan Press.

Guillermaz, J. 1972. *A history of the Chinese Communist Party, 1921–1949*. New York: Random House.

———. 1976. *The Chinese Communist Party in power*. Boulder, CO: Westview Press.

Guisso, R. W. L. 1978. *Wu Tse-T'ien and the politics of legitimation in T'ang China*. Bellingham: Western Washington University.

Guo, Daohui. 1988. *Zhongguo Lifa Zhidu* [China's legislative system]. Beijing: Renmin Chubanshe.

———. 1996a. Shixian Fazhi de Siyao [On the four requirements for the realization of the rule of law]. In *Zhongguo Fazhi Shixian Fanglue (Bitanhui)* [Strategy for the realization of the rule of law (Written exchange of ideas)]. *FalüKexue* 3:3.

———. 1996b. Enlightenment on law and rule of law in China: Comments on certain recent theoretical views in the study of jurisprudence in China. *Journal of Chinese and Comparative Law* 2:1.

———. 1999. Shixing Sifa Duli yu Xiezhi Sifa Fubai [Implement judicial independence and eliminate judicial corruption]. In *Yifa Zhiguo yu Sifa*

Gaige [Ruling the country according to law and judicial reform], ed. Xin Chunying and Li Lin, 66–83. Beijing: Zhongguo Fazhi Chubanshe.

Guo, Hongjun. 2006. *Juxing Shanyao: Mao Zedong, Zhou Enlai, Zhu De zai Yiqi de Rizi* [Shining of giant stars: The days when Mao Zedong, Zhou Enlai and Zhu De were together]. Beijing: Zhongyang Wenxian Chubanshe.

Guo, Jianlin. 1997. *Beiyang Linghun: Xu Shichang*. Lanzhou: University of Lanzhou Press.

———. 2006. *Wu Peifu zhuan* [Biography of Wu Peifu]. Beijing: Beijing Tushuguan Chubanshe.

Guo, Jinrong. 1993. *Mao Zedong de Wannian Shenghuo* [Mao Zedong's later life]. Beijing: Jiaoyu Kexue Chubanshe.

Guo, Songjie. 1996. Lun Xingzheng Heli Linian yu Sifa Shencha de Fanwei [Discussion of the concept of administrative reasonableness and the scope of judicial review]. *Xingzheng Fazhi* 4:38.

Guo, Taifeng. 2004. *Fengyun Tu bian* [The world certainly changed]. Shanghai: Xuelin Chubanshe.

Guthrie, D. 1997. Between markets and politics: Organizational responses to reform in China. *American Journal of Sociology* 102:1258–1304.

———. 1998. The declining significance of Guanxi in China's economic transition. *China Quarterly* 154:255.

———. 1999. *Dragon in a three-piece suite*. Princeton, NJ: Princeton University Press.

Haar, B. J. 2006. *Telling stories: Witchcraft and scapegoating in Chinese history*. Leiden: E. J. Brill.

Hah, Chong-Do. 1972. The dynamics of the Chinese Cultural Revolution: An interpretation based on an analytical framework of political coalition. *World Politics* 24 (2): 182–220.

Hail, W. J. 1927. *Tseng Kuo-fan and the Taiping Rebellion*. New Haven, CT: Yale University Press.

Hall, D., and R. Ames. 1987. *Thinking through Confucius*. Albany: State University of New York Press.

———. 1999. *Democracy of the dead: Dewey, Confucius and the hope for democracy in China*. Chicago: Open Court.

Hamberg, T. 1935. *The visions of Hung-siu-tshuen, and origin of the Kwangi-si insurrection*. Beiping: Yenching University Library.

Hamrin, C. L. 1990. *China and the challenge of the future: Changing political patterns*. Boulder, CO: Westview Press.

Hamrin, C. L., and T. Cheek, eds. 1986. *China's establishment intellectuals*. White Plains, NY: M. E. Sharpe.

Han, Dongping. 2000. *The unknown Cultural Revolution: Educational reforms and their impact on China's rural development*. New York: Garland Publishing.

Han, M., ed. 1990. *Cries for democracy: Writings and speeches from the 1989 Chinese democracy movement*. Princeton, NJ: Princeton University Press.

Han Shu [Book of Han]. 1995. 100 juan by Ban Gu. *Qian Han shu buzhu*. Ed. Wang Xianqian. 3 vols. Shanghai: Guji Chubanshe.

Han, Suyin. 1994. *Eldest son: Zhou Enlai and the making of modern China, 1898–1976*. New York: Hill & Wang.

Han, Xiaorong. 2005. *Chinese discourses on the peasant, 1900–1949*. Albany: State University of New York Press.

Handlin, J. F. 1983. *Action in late Ming thought: The reorientation of Lu K'un and other scholar officials*. Berkeley: University of California Press.

Hansen, C. 1992. *A Daoist theory of thought*. New York: Oxford University Press.

Hansen, V. 1990. *Changing gods in medieval China, 1127–1276.* Princeton, NJ: Princeton University Press.

Hao, Bingrang. 2001. *Feng xi jun shi* [A military history of Feng army]. Shenyang: Liaohai Chubanshe.

Hao, Jiansheng. 2004. *Xi'an Shibian Qianhou de Zhou Enlai* [Zhou Enlai after Xi'an revolt. Beijing: Zhongyang Wenxian Chubanshe.

Hao, Yufan, and M. Johnson. 1995. Reform at the crossroads: An analysis of Chinese corruption. *Asian Perspectives* 19:117.

Hao, Zhidong. 2003. *Intellectuals at a crossroads: The changing politics of China's knowledge workers.* Albany: State University of New York Press.

Harding, H. 1972. China: The fragmentation of power. *Asian Survey*, XII (1): 1–15.

———. 1981. *Organizing China: The problem of bureaucracy 1949–1976.* Stanford, CA: Stanford University Press.

———. 1989. *China's second revolution: Reform after Mao.* Sydney: Allen and Unwin.

Harding, H., and Suisheng Zhao, eds. 1995. *Decision-making in Deng's China.* Armonk, NY: M. E. Sharpe.

Harrison, H. 2000. *The making of the republican citizen: Political ceremonies and symbols in China: 1911–1929.* Oxford, U.K.: Oxford University Press.

Harrison, J. P. 1969. *The communists and Chinese peasant rebellions.* New York: Atheneum.

———. 1972. *The long march to power: A history of the Chinese Communist Party, 1921–72.* New York: Praeger.

Hartford, K. 1981. Step by step: Resistance, reform and revolution in Jin-Cha-Ji. PhD diss., Stanford University.

Hartford, K., and S. M. Goldstein. 1989. *Single sparks: China's rural revolutions.* Armonk, NY: M. E. Sharpe.

Hatano, Yoshihiro. 1994. *Chūgoku kindai gunbatsu nuo kenkyū (Japanese)/Zhongguo jin dai jun fa zhi yan jiu (Chinese)* [Research in Chinese modern warlords]. Trans. Lin Mingde. Taibei: Jinhe Chubanshe.

Hayes, J. 2002. *South China village culture*. New York: Oxford University Press.

Hayford, C. W. 1990. *To the people: James Yen and village China*. New York: Columbia University Press.

He, Baogang. 1994. Dual roles of semi-civil society in Chinese democratisation. *Australian Journal of Political Science* 29/1:154–171.

He, Husheng. 2006. *Hongliu Dashi: Guogong Shengsi Bodou Dajishi* [A history of the red current: The history of life and death struggle between CCP and GMD] Beijing: Zhonggong Dangshi Chubanshe.

He, Qinhua, ed. 2004. *Lu Xue Kao* [A study of Lu Xue]. Beijing: Shangwu.

He, Xiya. 1925. *Zhongguo daofei wenti zhi yanjiu* [Study of the problem of banditry in China]. Shanghai: Taidong Tushuju.

He, Yuhuai. 1992. *Cycles of repression and relaxation: Politico-literary events in China, 1976–1989*. Bochum: N. Brockmeyer.

Hecht, N. S., B. S. Jackson, S. M. Passamaneck, D. Piattelli, and A. M. Rabello, eds. 1996. *An introduction to the history and sources of Jewish law*. Oxford, U.K.: Oxford University Press.

Hegel, R. E., and K. Carlitz, eds. 2007. *Writing and law in late imperial China: Crime, conflict, and judgment*. Seattle: University of Washington Press.

Heilmann, S. 2000. *The Chinese nomenklatura in transition: A study based on internal cadre statistics of the Central Organization Department of the Chinese Communist Party*. Trier, Germany: The Center for East Asian and Pacific Studies, Trier University.

Henderson, J. B. 1984. *Development and decline of Chinese cosmology*. New York: Columbia University Press.

———. 1991. *Scripture, canon, and commentary: A comparison of Confucian and Western exegesis.* Princeton, NJ: Princeton University Press.

Hetzron, R. 1997. *The semitic languages.* London: Routledge.

Hill, D. 1967. *Greek words with Hebrew meanings.* Cambridge: Cambridge University Press.

Hiniker, P. 1969. Chinese reactions to forced compliance: Dissonance reduction and national character. *Journal of Social Psychology* 77:157–176.

———. 1977. *Revolutionary ideology and Chinese reality.* Beverly Hills, CA: Sage Publications.

Hiniker, P., and J. Perlstein. 1978. Alternation of charismatic and bureaucratic styles of leadership in postrevolutionary China. *Comparative Political Studies* 10 (4): 529–554.

Hinton, W. 1972. *The hundred days' war: The Cultural Revolution in Tsinghua University.* New York: Monthly Review.

———. 1997. *Fanshen: A documentary of revolution in a China village.* Berkeley: University of California Press.

Hirayama, Shū. 1912. *Zhongguo Bimi Shehuishi* [History of China's secret societies]. Shanghai: Shangwu.

Ho, Pingti. 1959. *Studies on the population of China, 1368–1953.* Cambridge, MA: Harvard University Press.

———. 1962. *The ladder of success in imperial China: Aspects of social mobility, 1368–1911.* New York: Columbia University Press.

Ho, Pingti, and Tang Tsou, eds. 1968. *China in crisis: China's heritage and the communist political system.* Chicago: University of Chicago Press.

Ho, V. 2006. *Understanding Canton: Rethinking popular culture in the republican period.* New York: Oxford University Press.

Hobson, R. L. 1978. *The wares of the Ming dynasty.* Mineola, NY: Dover Publications.

Hodge, Bob, and L. Kam. 1998. *The politics of Chinese language and culture: The art of reading Dragons.* New York: Routledge.

Hochstrasser, T. J. 2000. *Natural law theories in the early Enlightenment.* Cambridge: Cambridge University Press.

Hoffman, J. M. 2004. *In the beginning: A short history of the Hebrew language.* New York: New York University Press.

Hofheinz, R. 1977. *The broken wave: The Chinese communist peasant movement, 1922–1928.* Cambridge, MA: Harvard University Press.

Holdsworth, M. 2002. *Adorning the empress.* Hong Kong: FormAsia.

Holm, D. 1991. *Art and ideology in revolutionary China.* New York: Oxford University Press.

——. 1992. The strange case of Liu Zhidan. *Australian Journal of Chinese Affairs* 27 (January): 77–96.

Holsti, K. J. 1996. *The state, war and the state of war.* Cambridge: Cambridge University Press.

Holzman, M. 2005. *Wei Jingsheng, un Chinois inflexible.* Paris: Bleu de Chine.

Hongjun Changzheng Shi, ed. 2006. *Zhonggong Zhongyang Dangshi.* Beijing: Zhonggong Dangshi Chubanshe.

Hongqi [Red flag]. An official magazine of the Central Committee of the CCP, which was relaunched and renamed as *Qiu Shi* [Seeking truth] in 1988. Various editions, 1983, 1985–1986.

Hook, B. B. 1996. *The individual and the state in China.* Oxford, U.K.: Oxford University Press.

Hornbeck , S. K. 1916. *Contemporary politics in the Far East.* New York: Appleton.

Hou Han shu, Hou Han shu jijie. 1988. 120 juan ed. Fan Ye. Taibei: Shijie shuju.

Hou Han shu, Hou Han shu jijie 1923. 120 juan. Fan Ye edition of Wang xianqian. Changsha.

Hou, Yijie. 1994. *Yuan Shikai Quanzhuan* [A complete biography of Yuan Shikai]. Beijing: Dangdai Zhongguo Chubanshe.

———. 2001. *Bai nian jia zu: Yuan Shikai* [A family of a century: Yuan Shikai]. Taibei: Lixu Wenhua.

———. 2003. *Yuan Shikai zhuan* [A biography of Yuan Shikai]. Tianjin: Baihua Wenyi Chubanshe.

Houston, S. D. 2004. *The first writing: Script inventions as history and process.* Cambridge: Cambridge University Press.

Howard, P. 1988. *Breaking the iron rice bowl.* Armonk, NY: M. E. Sharpe.

Hsia Chang, M. 1979. "Fascism" and modern China. *China Quarterly* 79:553–567.

———. 1985. *The Chinese Blue Shirt Society: Fascism, and developmental nationalism.* Berkeley: University of California Press.

Hsia, T. A. 1961. *Metaphor, myth, ritual and the people's commune.* Berkeley: University of California Press.

Hsia, Tao-tai, and C. A. Johnson. 1986. *Law making in the People's Republic of China: Terms, procedures, hierarchy, and interpretation.* Washington, DC: Law Library, Library of Congress.

Hsiao, Ching-chang, and T. Cheek. 1995. Open and closed media: External and internal newspapers in the propaganda system. In *Decision-making in Deng's China*, ed. C. L. Hamrin and S. Zhao, 76–87. Armonk, N.Y.: M.E. Sharpe.

Hsiao, Gungchuan, and Yang Youjiong. 1989. *Zhongguo Zhengzhi Sixiang shi* [A history of Chinese political thought]. 2 vols. Shanghai: Shanghai Shudian.

———. 1960. *Rural China: Imperial control in the nineteenth century.* Seattle: University of Washington Press.

———. 1964. Legalism and autocracy in traditional China. *Qinghua Xuebao* 2:108–121.

———. 1975. *A modern China and a new world: K'ang Youwei, reformer and utopian, 1855–1927.* Nanjing: Jiangsu Renmin Chubanshe.

———. 1979. *A History of Chinese Political Thought vol. 1 From the Beginnings tot he Sixth Century A.D.* Trans. F. W. Mote. Princeton, NJ: Princeton University Press.

Hsiao, Tso-liang. 1961. *Power relations within the Chinese communist movement, 1930–1934.* Seattle: University of Washington Press.

Hsieh, Pao Chao. 1925. *The government of China (1644–1911).* New York: Octagon Books.

Hsiung, J. C., and S. I. Levine, eds. 1992. *China's bitter victory: The war with Japan, 1937–1945.* Armonk, NY: M. E. Sharpe.

Hsu, C. Y. 1965. *Ancient China in transition.* Stanford, CA: Stanford University Press.

———. 1983. *The rise of modern China.* New York: Oxford University Press.

Hsu, Sung-Peng. 1979. *A Buddhist leader in Ming China: The life and thought of Han-shan Te-ch'ing, 1546–1623.* University Park: Pennsylvania State University Press.

Hu, Changming. 2005. *Mao Zedong yu Zhou Enlai* [Mao Zedong and Zhou Enlai]. Beijing: Zhonggong Dangshi Chubanshe.

Hu, Hanmin. 1969. *Hu Hanmin Zizhuan* [Autobiography of Hu Hanmin]. Taibei: Zhuanji Wenxue Chubanshe.

Hu, Houxuan. 2000. *Zhanhou NingHu Xinhuo Jiagu Ji* [A collection of oracle bone inscriptions discovered in Shanghai and Nanjing after World War II. Beijing: Beijing Library Press.

——. 2001a. *Jiaguwen Liulun* [Six essays on oracle bone inscription]. Beijing: Beijing Library Press.

——. 2001b. *Wushinian Jiaguwen Faxian Zongjie* [A summary of the discovery of oracle bone inscription in fifteen years]. Chengdu: Sichuan University Press.

——. 2003. *Yin Shang Shi* [A history of Yin and Shang]. Shanghai: Renmin.

Hu, Ping. 1988a. *Luanshi Liren* [A biography of Lin Biao]. Nanjing: Jiangsu Wenyi.

——. 1988b. *Zhongguo min yun fan si* [A reflection of the people's movement in China]. Hong Kong: Oxford University Press.

Hu, Qiaomu. 1994. *Hu Qiaomu huiyi Mao Zedong* [Hu Qiaomu's memory of Mao Zedong]. Beijing: Renmin Chubanshe.

Hu, Sheng, ed. 1994. *A concise history of the Communist Party of China*. Beijing: Foreign Languages Press.

Hu, Shi. 1924. Shuyuan zhi shilüe. *Tung-fang zazhi* xxi. 3:142.

——. 1953. The natural law in the Chinese tradition. *University of Notre Dame Natural Law Institute Proceedings* 5:119–153.

——. 1961. *Zhongguo Gudai Zhexueshi*. Taibei: Shang Wu.

Hu, Shikai. 1993. Representation without democratization: The signature incident and China's National People's Congress. *The Journal of Contemporary China*, 2 (1)(Winter–Spring): 3–34.

Hu, Sisheng. 1982. The last days of great General Peng. *Xin Guancha*, 7.

Hu, Yuhai. 2001. *Fengxi Zongheng* [History and spectrum of Feng warlord]. Shenyang: Liaohai Chubanshe.

——. 2005. *Fengxi Junfa Dashiji*. Shenyang: Liaoning Minzu Chubanshi.

Hua, Hsien-chin. 1944. The Chinese concept of face. *American Anthropologist* 46:45–64.

Hua, Shiping. 1994. One servant, two masters: The dilemma of Chinese establishment intellectuals. *Modern China* 26 (1): 92–114.

Huai, Xiaofeng. 1985. Mingdai zhongye de huanguan yu sifa [Eunuchs and legal administration in the mid-Ming]. *Zhongguo shehui kexue* 6:193–206.

Huang, Chang-chien, ed. 1955. *Da Ming Taizu Gao Huangdi shilu* [Veritable record of the great Ming founding emperor] 8 vols. Taipei: Academia Sinica.

——. 1977a. Da Ming Lügao Kao. [An investigation on the Great Ming Code with pronouncements]. *Ming Qing Shi Yanjiu Conggao* 2:155–207. Taipei: Shangwu.

——. 1977b. Ming Hongwu Yonglechao de Banwen Junling. [The placards and harsh regulations in the Ming Hongwu and Yongle reigns]. *Ming Qing shiyanjiu conggao* 2:237–286. Taipei: Shangwu.

——. 1979. *Ming Lüli Huibian* [A collection of the Code and regulations in the Ming dynasty]. 2 vols. Taipei: Academia Sinica.

Huang, Chang-chien, and Erik Zurcher, eds. 1993. *Norms and the state in China.* Leiden: E. J. Brill.

Huang, Jianrong. 2004. *The dynamics of China's rejuvenation.* New York: Palgrave.

Huang, Kecheng. 1994. *A memoir.* Beijing: Remin Chubanshe.

Huang, L. [1694] 1984. *A complete book concerning happiness and benevolence.* Tucson: University of Arizona Press.

Huang, Li. 1999. *Zhonggong Fengyunlu, 1921–1949* [Turbulent history of Chinese communists]. Beijing: Zuojia Chubanshe.

Huang, Lin. 2007. *Nanchang Qiyi Qinli Ji* [Eyewitness of Nanchang uprising]. Nanchang: Jiangxi Renmin Chubanshe.

Huang, P. C. 1972. *Liang Chi-chao and modern Chinese liberalism.* Seattle: University of Washington Press.

——. 1978. *Chinese communists and rural society, 1927–1934.* Berkeley: University of California Press.

——. 1990. *The peasant family and rural development in the Yangzi Delta, 1350–1988.* Stanford, CA: Stanford University Press.

——. 1993a. Between informal mediation and formal adjudication: The third realm of Qing justice. *Modern China* 19 (3): 251–298.

——. 1993b. Public sphere/civil society in China?: The third realm between state and society. *Modern China* 19 (2): 216–240.

——. 1996. *Civil justice in China: Representation and practice in the Qing.* Stanford, CA: Stanford University Press.

——. 2001. *Code, custom, and legal practice in China: The Qing and the Republic compared.* Stanford, CA: Stanford University Press.

Huang, P. C., and K. Bernhardt, eds. 1994. *Civil law in Qing and Republican China.* Stanford, CA: Stanford University Press.

Huang, Pei. 1974. *Autocracy at work: A study of the Yung-cheng period, 1723–1735.* Bloomington: Indiana University Press.

——. 1985. The Grand Council of the Ch'ing dynasty: A historiographical study. *London School of Oriental and African Studies Bulletin* 48.3: 502–515.

Huang, R. 1969. Fiscal administration during the Ming dynasty. In *Chinese government in Ming time: Seven studies,* ed. C. O. Hucker, 73–128. New York: Columbia University Press.

——. 1974. *Taxation and government finance in sixteenth-century Ming China.* Cambridge: Cambridge University Press.

——. 1981. *1587, a year of no significance.* New Haven, CT: Yale University Press.

Huang, Shaorong. 1996. *To rebel is justified: A rhetorical study of China's Cultural Revolution movement 1966–1969.* Lanham, MD: University Press of America.

Huang, Tsung-his. 1987. *The record of Ming scholars.* Ed. J. Ching. Honolulu: University of Hawaii Press.

Huang, Xiurong. 1992. *Guomin Geming Shi* [The history of nationalist revolution]. Chongqing: Chongqing Chubanshe.

Huang, Yao. 1996. *Luo Ronghuan.* Hangzhou: Zhejiang Renmin Chubanshe.

Huang, Zheng, ed. 1995. *Liu Shaoqi Yisheng* [A life of Liu Shaoqi]. Beijing: Zhongyang Dangan Chubanshe.

Hucker, C. O. 1951. The traditional Chinese censorate and the new Peking regime. *American Political Science Review* 45.1:1041–1057.

———. 1957. The Tung-lin movement of the late Ming period. In *Chinese thought and institutions,* ed. J. K. Fairbank, 132–162. Chicago: University of Chicago Press.

———. 1958. Governmental organization of the Ming dynasty. *Harvard Journal of Asiatic Studies* xxi:63–64.

———. 1961. *The Traditional Chinese state in Ming times 1368–1644.* Tucson: University of Arizona Press.

———. 1966. *The censorial system of Ming China.* Stanford, CA: Stanford University Press.

———, ed. 1969. *Chinese government in Ming times, Seven studies.* Stanford, CA: Stanford University Press.

———. 1971. *Two studies on Ming history.* Ann Arbor, MI: Center for Chinese Studies.

———. 1978. *The Ming dynasty: Its origins and evolving institutions.* Ann Arbor, MI: Center for Chinese Studies.

———. 1985. *A dictionary of official titles in imperial China.* Stanford, CA: Stanford University Press.

Hulsewe, A. F. P. 1955. *Remnants of Han law.* Leiden: E. J. Brill.

———. 1978. The Ch'in documents discovered in Hu-pe in 1975. *Tong Bao*. 64:175–217.

———. 1981. The legalists and the laws of Ch'in. *Leiden Studies in Sinology*: Papers presented at the conference held in celebration of the fiftieth anniversary of the Sinological Institute of Leyden University, December 8–12, 1980. 1–22.

———. 1985. *Remnants of Ch'in law*. Leiden: E. J. Brill.

Hung, Chang-tai. 1994. *War and popular culture: Resistance in modern China, 1937–1945.* Berkeley: University of California Press.

Hung, E. 1997. *Paradoxes of traditional Chinese literature: An analysis of literary works from the Tang dynasty to the late Qing.* Hong Kong: Chinese University Press.

Hung, W. 1952. *Tu Fu, China's greatest poet.* Cambridge, MA: Harvard University Press.

Hunt, C. F. 1988. *From the claws of the dragon.* Grand Rapids, MI: F. Asbury Press.

Hymes, R. P. 1986. *Statesmen and gentlemen: The elite of Fu-chou, Chiang-hsi, in northern and southern Sung.* New York: Cambridge University Press.

Hymes, R. P., and C. Shirokauer. 1993. *Ordering the world: Approaches to state and society in Sung dynasty China.* Berkeley: University of California Press.

Iechika, Ryōko. 2005. *Shō Kaiseki to Nankin kokumin seifu* (Japanese)/ *Jiang Jieshi yu Nanjing Guomin Zhengfu* (Chinese). [Jiang Jieshi and Nanjing nationalist government]. Trans. Wang Shihua. Beijing: Shehui Kexue Wenxian Chubanshe.

Ikeda, Tomohisa. 2005. *Hanmu Boshu Wuxing Yanjiu* [A study of the Wuxing texts from Hanmu Boshu]. Trans. Wang Qifa. Ed. Zhu Zhijiu. Beijing: Zhongguo Shehui Kexue Chubanshe.

Ishikawa, Yoshihiro. 2006. *Chūgoku kyōsantō seiritsushi* [Zhong-guo gong chan dang cheng li shi/A history of the establishment of the Chinese Communist Party]. Beijing: Zhongguo Shehui Kexue Chubanshe.

Issacs, H. R. 1938. *The tragedy of the Chinese revolution*. London: Secker and Warburg.

Iwamoto, Keiichi. 1995. Flower vases of the Chinese Communist Party: A study of the Chinese democratic parties. MA thesis, Harvard University.

Jacobini, H. B. 1991. *An introduction to comparative administrative law*. New York: Oceana Publications.

Jacobs, D. 1981. *Borodin: Stalin's man in China*. Cambridge, MA: Harvard University Press.

Jakobson, L. 2000. *A million truths: A decade in China*. New York: M. Evans & Company.

Jackson, B. S. 1989. Ideas of law and legal administration: A semi-otic approach. In *The world of ancient Israel: Sociological, anthro-pological and political perspectives*, ed. R. E. Clements, 185–202. Cambridge: Cambridge University Press.

Jami, C., P. M. Engelfriet, and G. Blue. 2001. *Statecraft and intellec-tual renewal in late Ming China: The cross-cultural synthesis of Xu Guangxi [i.e.Guangqi], 1562–1633*. Boston: E. J. Brill.

Jan, Yun-hua. 1983. Political philosophy of the Shih Liu Ching attrib-uted to the Yellow Emperor Daoism. *Journal of Chinese Philosophy* 10:205–228.

Jeans, R. B, ed. 1992. *Roads not taken: The struggle of opposition parties in twentieth century China*. Boulder, CO: Westview Press.

Jen, Yu-wen. 1973. *The Taiping revolutionary movement*. New Haven, CT: Yale University Press.

———. 1993. Jiang declares war on corruption. *Beijing Review* 36:5–6.

Jenner, W. J. F. 1992. *The tyranny of history: The roots of China's crisis.* London: Allan Lane.

Jensen, L. M. 1997. *Manufacturing Confucianism: Chinese traditions and universal civilization.* Durham, NC: Duke University Press.

Ji, F. 2004. *Linguistic engineering: Language and politics in Mao's China.* Honolulu: University of Hawaii Press.

Ji, Haijie. 1994. *Xiongba Tianxia: Kangzhan Hou Guogong Liangdang Dajiaofeng Jishi* [Rival for control: The history of the post-war battle between the Nationalist and Communist Parties]. Beijing: Zhongyang Bianyi Chubanshe.

Ji, Xue, and Zeng Fanhua. 2000. *Xiongguan Man dao: Peng Dehuai juan* [A biography of Peng Dehuai]. Beijing: Jiefangjun Chubanshe.

Jia, W. 2001. *The remaking of the Chinese character and identity in the 21st century: The Chinese face practices (civic discourse for the third millennium).* Westport, CT: Greenwood Press.

Jiang, Kefu. 1987. *Beiyang Junfa he Guomin Gemingjun* [Beiyang warlords National Revolutionary Army]. Beijing: Zhonghua Shuju.

——. 1992. *Minguo Junshishi Luegao* [A draft military history of the Republic]. Beijing: Zhonghua Shuju.

Jiang, Mingwu. 2004. *Zhou Enlai Shengping Quan Jilu* [The complete biography of record Zhou Enlai]. Beijing: Zhongyang Wenxian Chubanshe.

Jiang, Pei. 1994. Hongwei bing Kuangbiao [Red Guard, the hurricane]. Zhengzhou: Henan Renmin Chubanshe.

Jiang, Ping. 1999. *Aiguo Junzi, Minzhu Jiaoshou: Wang Zaoshi* [Patriot gentlemen and democratic Professor Wang Zaoshi]. Nanchang: Jiangxi Jiaoyu Chupanshe.

Jiang, Ping, and Luo Kexiang. 1993. *Li Jishen Zhuan* [A biography of Li Jishen]. Beijing: Dangan Chubanshe.

Jiang, Shaozhen. 1994. *Dai Li he Juntong* [Dai Li and Juntong]. Zheng-zhou: Henan Renmin Chubanshe.

Jiang, Tao. 2005. *Kangzhan Shiqi de Jiang Jieshi* [Chiang Kaishek during the war against Japan]. Beijing: Huawen Chubanshe.

Jiang, Weiguo. 1978. *Guomin Geming Zhanshi* [A history of war in Republic revolution]. Taipei: Liming Wenhua.

Jiang Yonglin, trans. 2004. *The Great Ming Code* [*Da Ming lu*]. Seattle: University of Washington Press.

Jin, Chongji, ed. 1988. *Zhou Enlai zhuan* [A biography of Zhou Enlai]. Beijing: People's Press.

——, ed. 1996. *Mao Zedong zhuan 1893–1949* [A biography of Mao Zedong, 1893–1949]. Beijing: Central Document Press.

——, ed. 2000. *Zhu De zhuan* [A biography of Zhu De]. Beijing: Central Document Press.

Jin, Feng. 1993. *Deng Yingchao*. Beijing: Remin Chubanshe.

Jin, Liangnian. 1991. *Kuxing yu Zhongguo Shehui* [Cruel punishment and Chinese society]. Hangzhou: Zhejiang Renmin Chubanshe.

Jin, Qiu. 1999. *The culture of power: The Lin Biao incident in the Cultural Revolution.* Stanford, CA: Stanford University Press.

Jing, Jun. 1996. *The temple of memories: History, power, and morality in a Chinese village.* Stanford, CA: Stanford University Press.

——, ed. 2000. *Feeding China's little emperors: Food, children and social change.* Stanford, CA: Stanford University Press.

Jing, Shenghong. 1989. Minguo Ansha Yao'an [Important assassination cases during the Republic]. Yangzhou: Jiangsu Guji Chubanshe.

Jingpan, Chen. 2001. *Confucius as a teacher: Philosophy of Confucius with special reference to its educational implications.* Collingdale, PA: Diane Publishing.

Jocelyn, E., and A. McEwen. 2006. *The Long March: The true story behind the legendary journey that made Mao's China.* London: Constable.

Joffe, E. 1971. *Party and army professionalism and political control in the Chinese officer corps, 1949–1964.* Cambridge, MA: Harvard University Press.

——. 1975. *Between two plenums: China's intraleadership conflict, 1959–1962.* Ann Arbor: Center for Chinese Studies.

——. 1987. *Chinese military after Mao.* Cambridge, MA: Harvard University Press.

Johnson, C. 1962. *Peasant nationalism and communist power: The emergence of revolutionary China, 1937–45.* Stanford, CA: Stanford University Press.

Johnson, C. A. 1990. *Chinese law: A bibliography of selected English language materials.* Washington, DC: Law Library of Congress, Far Eastern Law Division.

Johnston, A. I. 1995. *Cultural realism: Strategic culture and grand strategy in Ming China.* Princeton, NJ: Princeton University Press.

Johnston, R. F. 1987. *Lion and dragon in northern China.* New York: Oxford University Press.

Jones, W. C., trans. 1994. *The Great Qing Code: A new translation with introduction.* New York: Oxford University Press.

Jordan, D. 1976. *The Northern Expedition: China's revolution of 1926–1928.* Honolulu: University of Hawaii Press.

——. 2001. *China's trial by fire: The Shanghai War of 1932.* Ann Arbor: University of Michigan Press.

Joseph, W. A., C. P. W. Wong, and D. Zweig, eds. 1991. *New perspectives on the Cultural Revolution.* Cambridge, MA: Harvard University Press.

Junshi Yanjusuo [Military Research Institute]. 2005. *Zhonghua Renmin Gongheguo Junshi Shiyao* [The outline of military history of the People's Republic of China]. Beijing: Military Science Press.

Kang, Youwei. 1967. *K'ang Yu-wei: A biography and a symposium.* Ed. Lo Jung-pang. Monographs and papers (Association for Asian Studies), no. 23. Tucson: Published for the Association for Asian Studies by University of Arizona Press.

Kau, M. Y. M. 1972–1973. The case against Lin Piao. *Chinese Law and Government* (Fall–Winter): 3–30.

———, ed. 1975. *The Lin Piao affair: Power politics and military coup.* White Plains, NY: International Arts and Sciences Press.

Kau, Michael M. Y. M., and P. M. Perrolle. 1974. The politics of Lin Piao's abortive ,military coup. *Asian Survey* 14 (June): 558–577.

Kau, Ying-mao. 1971. *The political work system of the Chinese Communist Party: Analysis and documents.* Providence, RI: Brown University.

Keating, P. B. 1997. *Two revolutions: Village reconstruction and the cooperative movement in northern Shaanxi, 1934–1945.* Stanford, CA: Stanford University Press.

Keister, L. A. 2004. Guanxi in business groups: Social ties and the formation of economic relations. In *Social connections in China: Institutions, culture, and the changing nature of Guanxt*, ed. T. Gold, D. Guthrie, and D. Wank, 77–96. Cambridge: Cambridge University Press.

Keith, R. C. 1994. *China's struggle for the rule of law.* Basingstoke, NY: Palgrave.

Kelber, W. H. 1997. *The oral and the written Gospel. The hermeneutics of speaking and writing in the synoptic tradition, Mark and Paul.* Bloomington: Indiana University Press.

Kelley, D. 1986. Sect and society: The evolution of the Luo sect among Qing dynasty grain tribute boatmen, 1700–1850. PhD diss., Harvard University.

Kelliher, D. 1992. *Peasant power in China: The era of rural reform, 1979–1989.* New Haven, CT: Yale University Press.

Kent, A. E. 1968. *Indictment without trial: The case of Liu Shao-ch'i.* Canberra: Australian National University, Department of International Relations, Working Paper No. 11.

Kern, M. 2008. *Text and ritual in early China.* Seattle: University of Washington Press.

Kessen, W., ed. 1975. *Childhood in China.* New Haven, CT: Yale University Press.

Khrushchev, 1974. *Khrushchev remembers: The Last Testament.* Trans. and ed. S. Talbott. Boston: Little, Brown and Company.

Kim, I. J. 1973. *The politics of Chinese communism: Kiangsi under the Soviets.* Berkeley: University of California Press.

Kirby, W. C. 2004. *Realms of freedom in modern China.* Stanford, CA: Stanford University Press.

Ke, Shaomin, ed. 1988. *Xin Yuan Shi,* 257 juan. Beijing: Zhongguo Shudian.

Kracke, Edward A. 1953. *Civil service in early Sung China, 960–1067.* Cambridge, MA: Harvard University Press.

Kuhn, P. A. 1970. *Rebellion and its enemies in late imperial China.* Cambridge, MA: Harvard University Press.

——. 1990. *Soulstealers: The Chinese sorcery scare of 1768.* Cambridge, MA: Harvard University Press.

——. 2002. *Origins of the modern Chinese state.* Stanford, CA: Stanford University Press.

Kuhn, P. A., and T. Brook. 1989. *National polity and local power. The transformation of late imperial China.* Cambridge, MA: Harvard University Press.

K'ung, Te-liang. 1972. The impact of the Lin Piao incident on the Chinese Communist Party and government. *Issues and Studies* 8 (June): 23–29.

Kutcher, N. 1999. *Mourning in late imperial China: Filial piety and the state.* Cambridge: Cambridge University Press.

Kutscher, E. Y. 1982. *A history of the Hebrew language.* Leiden: E. J. Brill.

Kwan, Man Bun. 2001. *The salt merchants of Tianjin: State making and civil society in late imperial China.* Honolulu: University of Hawaii Press.

Kwong, J. 1988. *Cultural Revolution in China's schools: May 1966– April 1969.* Stanford, CA: Stanford University Press.

Kwong, L. S. K. 1984. *A mosaic of the hundred days: Personalities, politics, and ideas of 1898.* Cambridge, MA: Harvard University Press.

La Fargue, T. E. 1937. *China and the World War.* Stanford, CA: Stanford University Press.

Lai, Fushun. 1984. *Qianlong Zhongyao Zhanzheng zhi Junxu Yanjiu* [A study of the military requirements of Qianlong's important military battles]. Taipei: National Palace Museum.

Lai, Xinxia. 2000. *Bei yang jun fa shi* [A history of Beiyang warlords]. 2 vols. Tianjin: Nan kai University Press.

Lam, J. S. 1998. *State sacrifices and music in Ming China: Orthodoxy, creativity, and expressiveness.* Albany: State University of New York Press.

Lam, Willy Wo-lap. 1995. *China after Deng Xiaoping: The power struggle in Beijing since Tiananmen.* Hong Kong: P.A. Professional Consultants, Ltd.

Langlois, J. D. 1981. *China under Mongol rule.* Princeton, NJ: Princeton University Press.

———. 1982. Law, statecraft, and the spring and autumn annals in Yuan political thought. In *Yuan thought: Chinese thought and religion under the Mongols*, ed. H.-L. Chan and W. T. De Bary, 89–152. New York: Columbia University Press.

———. 1988. The Hung-wu reign, 1368–1398. In *Cambridge history of China, Vol. 7: The Ming dynasty, 1368–1644, Part 1*, ed. F. W. Mote, D. C. Twitchett, and J. K. Fairbank, 107–181. Cambridge: Cambridge University Press.

———. 1993. The code and ad hoc legislation in Ming Law. *Asia Major* 3rd. Ser. 6 (2): 85–112.

———. 1998. Ming law. In *The Cambridge history of China, Vol. 8: The Ming dynasty, 1368–1644, Part 2*, ed. F. W. Mote and D. C. Twitchett, 172–220. Cambridge: Cambridge University Press.

Langlois, J. D., and Sun K'o-k'uan. 1983. Three teachings syncretism and the thought of Ming T'ai-tsu. *Harvard Journal of Asiatic Studies* 43 (1): 97–139.

Lary, D. 1974. *Region and nation: The Kwangsi clique in Chinese politics, 1925–1937.* New York: Cambridge University Press.

———. 2007. *China's republic.* Cambridge: Cambridge University Press.

Law, Kam-yee, ed. 2003. *The Chinese Cultural Revolution reconsidered: Beyond purge and holocaust* New York: Palgrave.

Lawrance, A. 1991. *Mao Zedong: A bibliography.* New York: Greenwood Press.

Lee, Hong Yung. 1978. *The politics of Chinese Cultural Revolution.* Berkeley: University of California Press.

Lee, T. 1985. *Government education and examinations in Sung China.* Hong Kong: Chinese University Press.

———. 2000. *Education in traditional China: A history.* Leiden: E. J. Brill.

Lei, Haizong. 1989. *Zhongguo de Wenhua yu Zhongguo de Bing* [Chinese culture and the Chinese military]. Changsha: Yuelu Chubanshe.

Lei, Tsung-hai. 1936. The rise of the emperor system in ancient China. *Chinese Social and Political Science Review* 20:251–265.

Leng, Shaochuan, and N. D. Palmer. 1960. *Sun Yatsen and communism.* Westport, CT: Greenwood Press.

———. 1967. *Justice in Communist China.* Dobbs Ferry, NY: Oceana Publications.

Leng, Shao-Chuan, and Hungdah Chiu. 1985. *Criminal justice in post-Mao China.* Albany: State University of New York Press.

Leung, Conita S. C. 1998. Chinese law-making: A case of legislative disorder. *China Legal News* 27 (February): 1.

Leutner, M. 2002. *The Chinese revolution in the 1920s: Between triumph and disaster.* London: Routledge Curzon.

Levenson, J. R. 1965. *Confucian China and its modern fate: A trilogy.* Berkeley: University of California Press.

Levine, R. 1999. Law, finance and economic growth. *Journal of Financial Intermediation* 8:8.

Lewis, C. M. 1976. *Prologue to the Chinese revolution: The transformation of ideas and institutions in Hunan Province, 1891–1907.* Cambridge, MA: Harvard University Press.

Lewis, J. W. 1963. *Leadership in Communist China.* Ithaca, NY: Cornell University Press.

———. 1970. *Party leadership and revolutionary power in China.* London: Cambridge University Press.

Lewis, M. E. 1990. Sanctioned violence in early China. Albany: State University of New York Press.

———. 2005. *The construction of space in early China.* Albany: State University of New York Press.

———. 2007. *The early Chinese empires: Qin and Han.* Cambridge, MA: Belknap Press of Harvard University Press.

Leys, Simon. 1977a. *The chairman's new clothes: Mao and the Cultural Revolution.* Trans. C. Appleyard and P. Goode. New York: St. Martin's Press.

———. 1977b. *Chinese shadows.* New York: Viking Press.

———. 1986. *The burning forest: Essays on Chinese culture and politics.* New York: Holt, Rinehart and Winston.

Li, Buyun. 1998. *Zouxiang fazhi* [Toward the rule of law]. Changsha: Hunan Renmin Chubanshe.

Li, Chien-nung. 1956. *The political history of China, 1840–1928.* Trans. Teng Ssu-yu and Jeremy Ingalls. Princeton, NJ: D. Van Nostrand.

Li, Guojun. 1986. *Liang Qichao zhushu xinian* [The chronology of Liang Qichao's writings]. Shanghai: Fudan University Press.

Li, Guowen. 2004. *Zhongguo Wenren de Huofa* [The way that Chinese intellectual survive]. Beijing: Renmin Wenxue Chubanshe.

Li, Haiwen. 2003. *Peng Zhen Shizhang* [Mayor Peng Zhen]. Beijing: Zhonggong Dangshi Chubanshe.

Li, Hsiucheng. 1977. *Taiping rebel: The deposition of Li Hsiu-ch'eng.* Trans. and ed. C. A. Curwen. Cambridge: Cambridge University Press.

Li, Ke, and Hao Shengzhang. 1988. *Wenhau dageming zhong de zhongguo renmin jiefangjun* [The People's Liberation Army in the Cultural Revolution]. Beijing: Zhongyang Wenxian Chubanshe.

Li, Kuo. 2001. *Wang Jingwei quan zhuan* [A complete biography of Wang Jingwei]. Beijing: Zhongguo Wenshi Chubanshe.

Li, L. 1994. *Student nationalism in China, 1924–1949*. Albany, State University of New York Press.

Li, Lie, ed. 1996. *He Long nian pu* [Chronology of He Long]. Beijing: Renmin Chubanshe.

Li, Liejun. 1996. *Liejun selected works*. Ed. Zhou Yuangao, Meng Pengxing, and Shu Yingyun. Beijing: Zhonghua Shuju.

Li, Maosheng. 1992. The realisation of the CCP's leadership in the War of Resistance against Japan. *Zhonggong dang shi yanjiu* 1:59–62.

Li, Ming-fu, ed. 1935. *Chunqiu jiyi. Sibu Quanshu.* Shanghai: Commercial Press.

Li, Ping. 2001. *Kaiguo Zongli Zhou Enlai: Zhou Enlai yi sheng* [A biography of Zhou Enlai: The first prime minister]. Beijing: Zhongyang Wenxian Chubanshe.

———. 2006. *Zhongguo Gongnong Hongjun Changzheng Jianshi* [A short history of the Long March of the Chinese Red Army of workers and peasants]. Beijing: Zhonggong Dangshi Chubanshe.

Li, Pu. 1997. *Yidai Junshi Qicai: Liu Bocheng Yuanshuai Zhuan* [The military genius of the generation: A biography of Marshal Liu Bocheng]. Shanghai: Wenyi Chubanshe.

Li, Rui. 1989. *Lushan huiyi shilu.* Beijing: Chunqiu Chubanshe.

———. 1992. *Mao Zedong de Zaonian yu Wannian* [Mao Zedong in his early and late years]. Guiyang: Guizhou Renmin Chubanshe.

Li, Shijie. 1988. *Diaochaju Yanjiu* [A study of the Bureau of Investigation]. Taibei: Li Shijie.

Li, Sishen. 2005. *Li Lisan zhi Mi: Yige Zhongcheng Gemingzhe de Quzhe Rensheng* [The mystery of Li Lisan: The turbulent life of a royal revolutionary]. Beijing: Renmin Chubanshe.

Li, Tianmin. 1971. Lin Piao's situation. *Issues and Studies* 8 (November): 66–74.

———. 1973. The Mao-Lin relationship as viewed from the article "A single spark can start a prairie fire." *Issues and Studies* 9 (January): 78–85.

———. 1975. *Zhou Enlai Pingzhuan* [A critical biography of Zhou Enlai]. Hong Kong: Youlian Yanjiusuo.

———. 1978. *Lin Biao Pingzhuan* [A critical biography of Lin Biao]. Hong Kong: Mingbao Yuekan.

———. 1982. *Hua Guofeng yu Hua Guofeng Zhengquan* [Hua Guofeng and his government]. Taibei: Youshi Wenhua Shiye.

Li, V. H. 1971. Law and social order in the People's Republic of China. S.J.D. thesis, Harvard University.

———. 1978. *Law without lawyers: A comparative view of law in China and the United States*. Boulder, CO: Westview Press.

Li, Wenhai. 2003. *Peng Zhen Shizhang*. Beijing: Zhongyang Wenxian.

Li, Wenzhi. 1948. *Wanming minbian* [Popular revolts in the late Ming]. Shanghai: Zhonghua Shuju.

———. 1952. Wanming guanliao yibi tanwuzhang [Accounts of corruption of late Ming bureaucrats]. *Lishi jiaoxue* 19:18.

———.1983. Lun Ming Qing shidai de zongzuzhi [On the clan system during the Ming and Qing dynasties]. *Zhongguo Shehuikexueyuan, Lishi Jingji Yanjiusuo jikan* 4:278–338.

Li, Xin, and Zhu Hongshao, eds. 2005. *Bogu, 39 Sui de Huihuang yu Beizhuang* [A biography of Bogu]. Shanghai: Xuelin Chubanshe.

Li, Xinda. 1995. *Zhongguo Keju Zhidu Shi* [A history of imperial examination in Chinese]. Taibei: Wenjin Chubanshe.

Li, Yen. 1957. *Donglindang jikao*. Beijing: Zhonghua Shuju.

Li, Yibin. 1998. *Zhen jing shi jie di yi mu: Zhang Xueliang yu Xi'an shi bian* [An episode that shook the world: Zhang Xueliang and Xian incident]. Shanghai: Renmin Chubanshe.

Li, Yong, and Zhang Zhongtian, eds. 1995. *Jiang Jieshi Nianbiao* [The chronology of Chiang Kaishek]. Beijing: Dangshi Chubanshe.

Li, Zhisui. 1994. *The private life of Chairman Mao.* New York: Random House.

Li, Zhiying. 1994. *Bogu Zhuan* [A biography of Bogu]. Beijing: Dangdai Zhongguo.

Li, Zhongsheng. 1984. *Zhongguo Jianyu Fazhishi* [A history of Chinese legal system and its prisons]. Taipei: Shangwu.

———. 1985. *Zhonghua Faxi* [Legal systems of China]. 2 vols. Taipei: Huaxin Wenhua Shijie Zhongxin.

Li, Zongren (Li Tsung-jen). 1979. *The memoirs of Li Tsung-jen.* Ed. Te-kong Tong and Li Tsung-jen. Boulder, CO: Westview Press.

Lian, Song, ed. 1987. *Yuan shi.* [A history of Yuan dynasty]. 4 vols. Shanghai: Shanghai Guji Chubanshe.

Liang, Fangzhong. 1981. *Zhongguo Lishi Hukou, Tiandi, Tianfu Tongji.* Shanghai: Renmin Chubanshi.

Liang, Heng, and J. Shapiro. 1983. *Son of the revolution.* New York: Alfred A. Knopt.

Liang, Huakui. 2005. *Wenhua Weiren Qu Qiubai* [Qu Qiubai: Great man of culture]. Beijing: Zhongyang Wenxian Chubanshe.

Liang, Qichao. 1936a. *Yinbingshi heji-wenji* [Collected writings from the ice-drinker's studio: Collected essays]. 24 vols. Shanghai: China Books.

———. 1936b. Yuan Shikai zhi jiepao. *Yinbingshi heji* 34 (4): 15–21.

———. 1959. *Intellectual trends of the Ch'ing period.* Trans. I. C. Y. Hsu. Cambridge, MA: Harvard University Press.

——. 2000. *History of Chinese political thought during the early Tsin period*. Trans. L. T. Zhen. London: Routledge.

Liao, Gailong, ed. 1989. *1949–1989: Xin Zhongguo Biannian Shi* [1949–1989: A chronology of the new China]. Beijing: Remin Chubanshe.

Liao, Kuangsheng. 1976. Linkage politics in China: Internal mobilization and articulated external hostility in the Cultural Revolution. *World Politics* 28 (4): 590–610.

Liao, Yizhong. 1997. *Yi dai xiao xiong Yuan Shikai* [A hero of his generation: Yuan Shi Kai]. Beijing: Beijing Library Press.

Lidai guanzhi biao [A list of official titles of dynasties]. 1937. Shanghai: Shangwu.

Lieberman, S. J. 1977. *The Sumerian loanwords in old Babylonian Akkadian*. Missoula, MT: Scholars Press for Harvard Semitic Museum.

Lieberthal, K. 1978. *Chinese Politics in 1978: Modernization and the Ghost of Mao*. New York, China Council of the Asia Society.

——. 1987. The Great Leap Forward and the split in the Yenan leadership. *Cambridge History of China*. 14 (1): 293–359.

——. 1992. *Bureaucracy, politics, and decision making in post Mao China*. Berkeley: University of California Press.

——. 1995. *Governing China: From revolution through reform*. New York: W. W. Norton.

Lieberthal, K., and J. D. Bruce. 1989. *A research guide to central party and government meetings in China, 1949–1986*. Armonk, NY: M. E. Sharpe.

Lieberthal, K., and M. Oksenberg. 1988. *Policy making in China: Leaders, structures, and processes*. Princeton, NJ: Princeton University Press.

Liew, K. S. 1971. *Struggle for democracy: Sung Chiao-Jen and the 1911 Chinese revolution*. Berkeley: University of California Press.

Lifton, R. J. 1961. *Thought reform and the psychology of totalism: A study of "brainwashing" in China.* New York: W. W. Norton & Company.

Limbaugh, D. 2001. *Absolute power: The legacy of corruption in the Clinton-Reno Justice Department.* New York: DC Comics.

Lin, Biao. 1967. Nian 8 yue 9 ri tong Zeng Siyu he Liu Feng tongzhi de tanhua [Comrade Lin Biao's speech to comrades Zeng Siyu and Liu Feng, August 9, 1967]. In *Lin Biao jianghua* [Lin Biao's speeches]. N.p.: Library of the John Fairbank Center at Harvard University.

Lin Biao zai jundui ganbu dahui shang de jianghua [Lin Biao's speech at the meeting of military cadres, March 24, 1968]. 1988. In *"Wenhua Dageming" yanjiu ziliao* [Research materials on the Cultural Revolution], ed. Guofang Daxue, 2:87–94. Beijing: Guofang daxue dangshi jiaoyanshi.

Lin, Difei. 1999. *Zhang Naiqi.* Shijiazhuang: Huashan Wenyi Chubanshe.

Lin, Jing. 1991. *The Red Guards' path to violence: Political, educational, and psychological factors.* New York: Praeger.

Lin, Kuo. 2001a. *Dai Li Quanzhuan* [A complete biography of Dai Li]. Beijing: Zhongguo Wenshi Chubanshe.

——. 2001b. *Wang Jingwei Quanzhuan* [A complete bibliography of Wang Jingwei]. Beijing: Zhongguo Wenshi Chubanshe.

Lin, Qing. 1991. *Zhou Enlai de Zaixiang Shengya* [Zhou Enlai as minister]. N.p.: Changcheng Wenhua Chubanshe.

Lin, Qingshan. 1985. *Kang Sheng Waizhuan* [An unofficial biography of Kang Sheng]. Hong Kong: Chenxiang.

——. 1988. *Lin Biao Zhuan* [A biography of Lin Biao]. 2 vols. Beijing: Zhishi Chubanshe.

Lin, Wanjing. 1985. *Three translations of the "The true story of Ah Q": Some comparisons*. Singapore: Department of Chinese Studies, National University of Singapore.

Lin, Yi. 1987. *Minguo Cai Songpo xian sheng E nian pu* [Chronology of Mr. Cai Songpo]. Taibei: Shangwu.

Lin, Yitang, ed. 1980. *What they say: A collection of current Chinese underground publications.* Taipei: Institute of Current China Studies.

Lin, Zexu, ed. 1928. *Qingshi Liezhuan* [Qing Biographies]. Beijing: Zhonghua Shuju.

———. 1985. *Lin Zexu Ji Zougao* [Collected works: Memorials]. 3 vols. Beijing: Zhonghua Shuju.

Linebarger, P. 1927. *Sun Yat-sen and the Chinese Republic*. Shanghai: Sanmin.

———. 1938. *Government in Republican China*. New York: McGraw-Hill.

———. 1941. *The China of Chiang K'ai-shek: A political study*. Westport, CT: Greenwood Press.

Ling, Bing. 1988. *Aixinjueluo, Zaifeng: Qing mo jian guo she zheng wang* [Aixinjueluo Zeifeng: Last regent of Qing]. Beijing: Wenhua Yishu Chubanshe.

Lindsay, M. 1950. *Notes on educational policy in Communist China.* New York: IPR.

———, ed. 1976. *The new Constitution of Communist China*. Taipei: Institute of International Relations.

Lipinski, E. 1997. *Semitic languages: Outline of a comparative grammar*. Leuven: Peeters.

Lishi de Shenpan Bianjizu, ed. 1981. *Lishi de Shenpan* [A trial of history]. Beijing: Qunzhong Chubanshe.

Liu, A. L. 1976. *Political culture and group conflict in Communist China*. Santa Barbara, CA: Clio Books.

Liu, Bingrong. 1999. *He Long Dazhuan* [A long biography of He Long]. Beijing: Tong xin Chubanshe.

Liu, Binyan. 1990. *A higher kind of loyalty*. New York: Alfred A. Knopf.

Liu, Chang. 2007. *Peasants and revolution in rural China*. London: Routledge.

Liu, Ch'ang. 1969a. *Chunqiu Yilin*. Taipei: Datong shuju.

———. 1969b. *Chunqiu Zhuan*. Taipei: Datong shuju.

Liu, Chengyu, and Zhang boju. 1983. *Hongxian Jishishi Sanzhong*. Shanghai: Guji.

Liu, F. Fu. 1956. *A military history of modern China, 1926–1956*. Princeton, NJ: Princeton University Press.

Liu, Gong. 1962. Wo suo Zhidao de Zhongtong [The Central Committee Statistics Bureau that I knew]. *Wenshi Ziliao Xuanji* 36, 59–117.

Liu, Guokai, and A. Chan. 1987. *A brief analysis of the Cultural Revolution*. Armonk, NY: M. E. Sharpe.

Liu, Hong. 2001. *Jiang Jieshi da zhuan* [Jiang Jieshi, a complete biography]. Beijing: Tuanjie Chubanshe.

Liu, Huinian, Zhao Qi, Xu Xinhua, Zhou Cilin, and Yang Jinzhou. 1980. *Lin Biao fangeming zhenbian pochan ji* [The failure of Lin Biao's counter-revolutionary coup]. *People's Daily*, November 24.

Liu, J. 1959. *Reform in Sung China: Wang An-shih (1021–1086) and his new policies*. Cambridge, MA: Harvard University Press.

———. 1962. An administrative cycle in Chinese history: The case of northern Sung emperors. *Journal of Asiatic Studies* 21:137–152.

Liu, Jingwei et al., eds. 2004. *Woguo Minshi Lifa de Huigu yu Zhanwang* [History and perspective of China civil law]. Beijing: Renmin Fayuan Chubanshe.

Liu Junwen, ed. 1983. *Tang Lü shuyi* [The Tang Code with commentary]. Beijing: Zhonghua Shuju.

Liu, Kwang-ching. 1970. The Confucian as patriot and pragmatist: Li Hung-Chang's formative years, 1823–1866. *Harvard Journal of Asiatic Studies* 30:5–45.

Liu, Quan. 2004. *Deng Xiaoping Junshi Shengya* [Military career of Deng Xiaoping]. Beijing: Zhongyang Wenxian.

Liu, Shaoqi. 1964. How to be a good communist. In *Mao's China: Party reform documents, 1942–44*, trans. Boyd Compton, 108–155. Peking: Foreign Languages Press.

——. 1966. "Training the Communist Party member," August 1939. In *Mao's China: Party reform documents, 1942–44*, trans. Boyd Compton, 108–155. Seattle: University of Washington Press.

——. 1967. Report on the revision of the Party Constitution. In *Liu Shaoqi xuanji* [Selected writings of Liu Shaoqi], 135–223. Tokyo: Zhongguo Wenhua Fuwushe 135–223.

——. 1969. *Collected works of Liu Shaoch'i, 1945–1957*. Hong Kong: Union Research Institute.

——. 1981–1985. *Liu Shaoqi Xuanji* [Selected works of Liu Shaoqi]. 2 vols. Beijing: Remin Chubanshe.

——. 1984. *Selected works of Liu Shaoqi.* Beijing: Foreign Languages Press.

——. 1991. *Liu Shaoqi Lundang de Jianshe* [Liu Shaoqi on party construction]. Beijing: Central Document Press.

——. 2003. Liu Shaoqi Zishu [The memoir of Liu Shaoqi]. Ed. Research Institute of Central Committee of CCP. Beijing: Jiefangjun Wenyi Chubanshe.

———. 2005. *Jian guo yi lai Liu Shaoqi wen gao* [Works and manuscripts of Liu Shaoqi since the establishment of the Republic]. Ed. Research Institute of Literary Works of Central Committee. Beijing: Zhongyang Wenxian Chubanshe.

Liu, Shengrong, and Dan Wei. 2001. *Fubai Qizui Xingfa Jingyao* [A summary of the law and punishment for seven crimes of corruption]. Beijing: Fang Zheng Chubanshe.

Liu, Songmao. 1998. *Peng Dehuai yu Mao Zedong* [Peng Dehuai and Mao Zedong]. Changsha: Hunan Renmin Chubanshe.

Liu, Wangling. 1975. *Xinhai Geming Hou Dizhi Fubi he Fan Fubi Douzheng* [The struggle against imperial restoration after the Revolution of 1911]. Beijing: Renmin Chubanshe.

Liu, Wusheng, ed. 2000. *Zhou Enlai Junshi Huodong Jishi: 1918–1975* [Military activities of Zhou Enlai: 1918–1975]. Beijing: Zhongyang Wenxian Chubanshe.

Li, Xuezhi. 2004. *Minguo Chunian de Fazhi Sichao yu Fazhi Jianshe: Yi Guo Hui Lifa Huodong wei Zhongxin de Yanjiu* [Legal ideas and establishment in early Chinese Republic: A study on congressional legislation]. Beijing: Zhongguo Shehui Kexue Chubanshe.

Liu, Yongmou, and Wang Xingbin. 2005. *Jingxing Zhongguoren: Zoujin Chen Duxiu* [Waking up the Chinese: Approach to Chen Duxiu]. Beijing: Zhongguo Shehui Chubanshe.

Liu, Yongping. 1998. *Origins of Chinese law*. Hong Kong: Oxford University Press.

Liu, Yuen-sun. 1967. *The current and the past of Lin Piao*. Trans. R. Liang. Santa Monica, CA: Rand.

Liu, Zhi. 1972. *Huangpu Junxiao yu Guomindang Jun*. Taipei: Wenhai Press.

Lo, C. W. 1995. *China's legal awakening, legal theory and criminal justice in Deng's era*. Hong Kong: Hong Kong University Press.

Lo, Ergang. 1944. *Hong Xiuquan* [Hong Xiuquan]. Chongqing: Shengli Chubanshe.

——. 1979. *Taiping Tianguo Shishi Kao* [Research of the history of Taiping revolt]. Beijing: Sanlian Chubanshe.

——. 1984. Xiangjun Xinzhi [New gazetteer of the Hunan army]. Shanghai: Zhong Hua Shuju.

——. 1995. *Li Xiucheng Zishu Yuangao Zhu* [Notes on Li Xiucheng's biography]. Beijing: Zhongguo Shehui Kexue Chubanshe.

——. 1997. Wan Qing Mingzhi [Gazetteer of late Qing army]. 2 vols. Beijing: Zhonghua Shuju.

Lo, W. W. 1987. *An introduction to the civil service of Sung China: With emphasis on its personnel administration.* Honolulu: University of Hawaii Press.

——. 1997. The self-image of the Chinese military in historical perspective. *Journal of Asian History* 31 (1): 1–23.

Loh, P. P. Y. 1971. *The early Chiang Kaishek: A study of his personality and politics, 1887–1924.* New York: Columbia University Press.

Lorge, P. 2005. *War, politics and society in early modern China, 900–1795: Empire without nation.* London: Routledge.

Lotta, R., ed. 1978. *And Mao makes 5: Mao Tse-tung's last great battle.* Chicago: Banner Press.

Lötveit, T. 1978. *Chinese communism 1931–1934: Experience in civil government.* London: Curzon Press.

Lou, Dong, and Fu Huanguang. 1924. *Jiangsu Bingzai Diaochaji shi* [A investigation on military disaster in Jiangsu]. Shanghai: Relief Congress of War by Jiangsu Counties.

Lowe, M. 1986. The former Han dynasty. In *Cambridge history of China, Vol. 1: The Ch'in and Han Empires, 221 B.C.–A.D. 220*, ed. Twitchett and Fairbank, 102–222. Cambridge: Cambridge University Press.

Lowry, K. A. 2005. *The tapestry of popular songs in 16th- and 17th-century China: Reading, imitation, and desire.* Leiden: E. J. Brill.

Lu, Haijing. 2003. *Zhang Guotao Zhuanji he Nianpu* [A biography and chronology of Zhang Guotao]. Beijing: Dangshi Chubanshe.

Lu, Juntian. 1987. *Lu Rongting zhuan* [Biography of Lu Rongtian]. Nanning: Guangxi Minzu Chubanshe.

Lu, Weijun, and Wang Degang. 1996. *Sun Chuanfang.* Jinan: Shandong University Press.

Lü, Xiaobo. 2000. *Cadres and corruption: The organizational involution of the Chinese Communist Party.* Stanford, CA: Stanford University Press.

Lu, Xing. 2004. *Rhetoric of the Chinese Cultural Revolution: The impact on Chinese thought, culture, and communication.* Columbia: University of South Carolina Press.

Lu, Xun. 2006. *Gu ji xu ba ji* [A collection of prologues for classical texts]. Beijing: Renmin Wenxue Chubanshe.

Lu, Yongyan. 2006. *Puyi Zhuan: Cha tu ben* [Biography of Po-yi]. Beijing: Renmin Wenxue Chubanshe.

Lubman, S. B. 1982. "Emerging functions of legal institutions in China's modernization," in U.S. Congress Joint Economic Committee. In *The Chinese Economy Post-Mao*, pt. 2, 764–788. Washington, DC: U.S. Government Printing Office.

———. 1995. Introduction: The future of Chinese law. *China Quarterly* 141 (March): 1–21.

———. 1999. *Bird in a cage: Legal reforms in China after Mao.* Stanford: Stanford University Press.

Lubman, S. B., N. J. Diament, and K. J. O'Brien, eds. 2005. *Engaging the law in China: State, society, and possibilities for justice.* Stanford, CA: Stanford University Press.

Lujun, Bu. 1971. *Lujun Xingzheng Jiyao* [An account of important aspects of army administration]. Taibei: Wenhai Chubanshe.

Luk, M. 1990. *The origins of Chinese bolshevism: An ideology in the making.* Hong Kong: Oxford University Press.

Luo, Chunpu. 2004. *Yan Xishan zhuan* [A biography of Yan Xishan]. Taiyuan: Shanxi Renmin Chubanshe.

Luo, Erkang. 1937. Qingji Bing Wei Jiang You de Qiyuan [The origins of private armies in the Qing]. *Zhongguo Shehui Jingji Shi Jikan* 2:235–250.

Luo Guangbin, and Yang Yiyan. 1977. *Hong Yan* [Red Crag]. Hong Kong: Sanlian shudian.

Luo, Guanzhong. 1973. *Sanguo Yanyi.* 2 vols. Beijing: Renmin Wenxue Chubanshe.

———. 1995. *Three kingdoms.* Trans. Moss Reberts. 4 vols. Beijing: Foreign Languages Press.

Luo, Haocai, ed. 1997. *Xiandai Xingzhengfa de Pingheng Lun* [The balance theory of modern administrative law]. Beijing: Beijing University Press.

Luo, Laiyong, and Zhou Junlun. 2001. *Da mo chang kong. Nie Rongzhen juan* [A biography of Nie Rongzhen]. Beijing: Jiefangjun Chubanshe.

Luo, Yingcai. 1996. *Chen Yi.* Hangzhou: Zhejiang Renmin Chubanshe.

Ma, Chi. 2007. *Dai Li Quanzhuan: Zhongguo zui diao la de jun tong mo tou* [A complete biography of Dai Li]. Beijing: Zhongguo Wenshi Chubanshe.

Ma, L. E. A. 1990. *Revolutionaries, monarchists, and Chinatowns: Chinese politics in the Americas and the 1911 Revolution.* Honolulu: University of Hawaii Press.

Ma, Lie. 2007. *Jiang jia fu zi yu San qing tuan* [Jiang Jieshi, his son and Sanqing Tuan]. Beijing: Zhongguo Wenshi Chubanshe.

Ma, Weian. 1999. *Quanli Dianfeng de Mijin: Gao Gang, Rao Shushi Shijian Shimo* [Illusion at the top of authority: The beginning and the end of Gao Gang, Rao Shushi incidence]. Beijing: Dang dai Zhongguo chu ban she.

Ma, Xiaohong. 2004a. *Li yu Fa: Fa de Lishi Lianjie, Goujian yu Jiexi Zhongguo Chuan-tong Fa* [Li and Fa: Historic connection, structure, and critic to Chinese traditional law]. Beijing: Beijing University Press.

———. 2004b. *Zhongguo Gudai Falü Sixiang Shi* [A history of jurisprudence in ancient China]. Beijing: Falü Chubanshe.

Ma, Zhongyang. 1997. *Zou Taofen zhuan ji* [A biography of Zou Taofen]. Chongqing: Chongqing Chubanshe.

Macauley, M. 1998. *Social power and legal culture: Litigation masters in late imperial China.* Stanford, CA: Stanford University Press.

MacFarquhar, R. 1960. *The hundred flowers campaign and the Chinese intellectuals.* New York: Praeger.

———. 1974. *The origins of the Cultural Revolution, I: Contradictions among the people, 1956–1957.* New York: Columbia University Press.

———. 1983a. *The Great Leap Forward, 1958–1960.* New York: Columbia University Press.

———. 1983b. *The origins of the Cultural Revolution, II: The Great Leap Forward 1958–1960.* New York: Columbia University Press.

———, ed. 1993. *The politics of China: 1949–1989.* Cambridge: Cambridge University Press.

———. 1997a. *The coming of the cataclysm, 1961–1966.* New York: Oxford University.

———. 1997b. *The origins of the Cultural Revolution, III: The coming of the cataclysm.* Oxford, U.K.: Oxford University Press.

———. 1999. *The paradox of China's post-Mao reforms*. Cambridge, MA: Harvard University Press.

MacFarquhar, R., T. Cheek, and E. Wu, eds. 1989. *The secret speeches of Chairman Mao: From the hundred flowers to the Great Leap Forward*. Cambridge, MA: Harvard University Press.

MacFarquhar, R., and M. Schoenhales. 2006. *Mao's last revolution*. Cambridge, MA: Harvard University Press.

MacFarquhar, R., and A. Saich. 2003. *Mao re-evaluated: A conference to mark the 110th anniversary of the birth of Mao Zedong and honor Stuart Schram for his signal contribution to Mao studies*. Cambridge, MA: Harvard University.

MacKinnon, S. 1980. *Power and politics in late imperial China: Yuan Shikai in Beijing and Tianjin, (1901–1908)*. Berkeley: University of California Press.

MacNair, H. F. 1931. *China in revolution: An analysis of politics and militarism under the Republic*. Chicago: University of Chicago Press.

Madsen, R. 1986. *Morality and power in a Chinese village*. Berkeley: University of California Press.

Mair, V. H. 1985. Language and indeology in the written popularizations of the sacred edict. In *Popular culture in late imperial China*, ed. D. Johnson et al., 325–359. Berkeley: University of California Press.

Malraux, A. 1934. *Man's fate*. New York: Vitage.

Mammitzsch, U. H. 1968. Wei Chung-hsien (1568–1628): A reappraisal of the eunuch and the factional strife at the late Ming court. PhD diss., University of Hawaii.

Man-Cheong, Iona. 2004. *The class of 1761*. Stanford, CA: Stanford University Press.

Manela, E. 2007. *The Wilsonian moment: Self-determination and the international origins of anticolonial nationalism.* New York: Oxford University Press.

Mann, S. 1987. *Local merchants and the Chinese bureaucracy.* Stanford, CA: Stanford University Press.

Mao, Zedong. 1974. *Mao Zedong sixiang wansui* [Long live Mao Zedong thought]. 2 vols. Taipei: Zhongguo Guoji Guanxi Yuanjiusou.

——. 1969–1971. *Mao Zhuxi Shizi.* 4 vols. Hong Kong: Kunlun Chubanshe.

——. 1970. *Mao Papers: Anthology and bibliography.* Ed. J. Ch'en. London: Oxford University Press.

——. 1970–1972. *Collected works of Mao Tse-tung.* Ed. Takeuchi Minoru et al. 10 vols. Tokyo: Hokubosha.

——. 1974. *Mao Tse-tung unrehearsed, talks and letters: 1956–71.* Ed. S. Schram. Harmondsworth: Penguin Books.

——. 1981. *Selected works of Mao Zedong.* 5 vols. Beijing: Foreign Language Press.

——. 1987–1998. *Jiangguo yilai Mao Zedong Wengao.* 13 vols. Beijing: CCP Central Document Press.

——. 1991. *Mao Zedong Xuanji.* Beijing: Renmin Chubanshe.

Martin, B. 1996. *The Shanghai green gang: Politics and organised crime, 1919–1937.* Berkeley: University of California Press.

Martin, H. 1982. *Cult and canon: The origins and development of state Maoism.* Armonk, NY: M. E. Sharpe.

Matti, M. 2000. *History of Syriac literature and science.* Pueblo, CO: Passeggiata Press.

Mawangdui Hanmu Boshu. [Texts from Han tomb in Mawangdui]. 1980. Beijing: Wenwu.

Mazur, M. 1990. Studying Wu Han: The political academic. *Republican China* 15 (2):17–39.

——. 1994. Wu Han: A man of his times. PhD diss., University of Chicago.

——. 1997. The united front redefined for the party-state. In *New perspectives on state socialism in China*, ed. T. Cheek and T. Saich, 51–75. Armonk, NY: M. E. Sharpe.

McCord, E. A. 1993. *The power of the gun: The emergence of modern Chinese warlordism.* Berkeley: University of California Press.

——. 1996. Warlords against warlordism: The politics of anti-militarism in early twentieth-century China. *Modern Asian Studies* 30 (4): 795–821.

McCormick, B. L. 1990. *Political reform in post-Mao China, democracy and bureaucracy in a Leninist state.* Berkeley: University of California Press.

McCormick, B. L., and J. Unger, eds. 1996. *China after socialism: In the footsteps of Eastern Europe or East Asia?* Armonk, NY: M. E. Sharpe.

McCormack, G. 1977. *Chang Tso-Lin in northeast China, 1911–1928: China, Japan, and the Manchurian idea.* Stanford, CA: Stanford University Press.

McCormack, Geoffry. 1996. *The spirit of traditional Chinese law.* Athens: University of Georgia Press.

McDermott, J. P. 1999. *State and court ritual in China.* New York: Cambridge University Press.

McDonald, A. W. 1978. *The urban origins of rural revolution: Elites and the masses in Hunan Province, China, 1911–1927.* Berkeley: University of California Press.

McKerras, C. 1982. *Modern China: A chronology from 1842 to the present day.* London: Thames and Hudson.

——. 1992. *Law and order in Sung China.* Cambridge: Cambridge University Press.

McKnight, B., James Liu, trans. 1999. *The enlightened judgments: Ch'ing Ming Chi*. Albany: State University of New York Press.

McLaren, A. E. 1998. *Chinese popular culture and Ming chantefables*. Boston: E. J. Brill.

McMahon, K. 2002. *The fall of the god of money: Opium smoking in nineteenth-century China*. Lanham, MD: Rowman & Littlefield.

McMorran, I. 1975. Wang Fu-chih and the neo-Confucian traditions. In *The unfolding of neo-Confucianism*, ed. W. T. De Bary, 413–467. New York: Columbia University Press.

——. 1979. The patriot and the partisans. In *From Ming to Ch'ing: Conquest, region*, ed. J. D. Spence and J. E.Wills Jr., 133–166. New Haven, CT: Yale University Press.

McMullen, D. 1988. *State and scholars in T'ang China*. Cambridge: Cambridge University Press.

Mei, Jian, ed. 1997. *Guogong Mishi: Guogong Fenhe Sanbuqu* [The sectret history of cooperation of communists and nationalists: Three periods]. Beijing: Zhongguo Wenshi Chubanshe.

Meisner, M. 1982. *Marxism, Maoism and utopianism: Eight essays*. Madison: University of Wisconsin Press.

Meng, Qingshu. 2006. *Wuzhengfu Zhuyi yu Wusixin Wenhua: Weirao "Xin qing nian" Tongren Suozuo de Kaocha* [Anarchism and the new culture of May Fourth: Around people with new youth. Kaifeng: Henan University Press.

Meskill, J. 1969. Academies and politics in the Ming dynasty. In *Chinese government in Ming times*, ed. Hucker, 149–174. New York: Columbia University Press.

——. 1982. *Academies in Ming China: A historical essay*. Ann Arbor: University of Michigan Press.

Metzger, T. A. 1973. *The internal organization of Ch'ing bureaucracy: Legal, normative, and communication aspects.* Cambridge, MA: Harvard University Press.

——. 1977. *Escape from predicament: Neo-Confucianism and China's evolving political culture.* New York: Columbia University Press.

Mi, Hedu. 2005. *Jujiao Hongweibing* [Focus on Red Guard]. Hong Kong: Sanlian Shudian.

Michael, F. 1942. *The origin of Manchu rule in China: Frontier and bureaucracy as interacting forces in the Chinese Empire.* Ed. S. Spector. Baltimore: Johns Hopkins University Press.

——. 1964. Introduction: Regionalism in nineteenth-century China. In *Li Hung-chang and the Huai army: A study in nineteenth-century Chinese regionalism,* ed Stanley Spector, xxi–xliii. Seattle: University of Washington Press.

——. 1971. *The Taiping Rebellion history and documents.* Seattle: University of Washington Press.

Michel, E. 2000. *An orchestra of voices: Making the argument for greater speech and press freedom in the People's Republic of China.* Westport, CT: Greenwood Press.

Millward, J. 1998. *Beyond the pass: Economy, ethnicity, and empire in Qing Central Asia, 1759–1864.* Stanford, CA: Stanford University Press.

——. 2004. *New Qing imperial history: The making of inner Asian Empire at Qing Chengde.* New York: Routledge/Curzon.

Min, Tu-gi, P. A. Kuhn, and T. Brook, eds. 1989. *National polity and local power: The transformation of late imperial China.* Cambridge, MA: Harvard University Press.

Ming shi gao 1723. eds. Wang Hongxu et al. Blockprint edition.

Ming shu [The Books of Ming]. 1937. Ed. Fu Weilin ed. Guoxue jiben zongshu edition. Shanghai: Zhonghua Shuju.

Mitamura, T. 1970. *Chinese eunuchs: The structure of intimate politics.* Rutland, VT: Charles E. Tuttle.

Mo, Jianlai. 2004. *Wan xi jun fa tong zhi shi gao* [A history of government of Wan warlord]. Tianjin: Guji Chubanshe.

Moody, P. R. 1977. *Opposition and dissent in contemporary China.* Stanford, CA: Stanford University Press.

——. 1989. The Communist Party of China as a political institution. In *Chinese politics from Mao to Deng*, ed. V. C. Falkenheim, 165–202. New York: Professors World Peace Academy.

——. 1995. *Tradition and modernization in China and Japan.* Belmond: Wadsworth.

Mote, F. W. 2000. *Imperial China, 900–1800.* Cambridge, MA: Harvard University Press.

Mowry, R. D., J. Cuno, E. Farrell, and N. C. Rousmaniere. 1997. *Hare's fur, tortoiseshell and partridge feathers: Chinese brown- and black-glazed ceramics, 400–1400.* Cambridge, MA: Harvard University Art Museums.

Mulvenon, J. C. 1997. *Professionalization of the Senior Chinese Officer Corps: Trends and implications.* Santa Monica, CA: Rand.

——. 2004. Party-army relations since the 16th Party Congress. In *Civil-military change in China: Elites, institutes, and ideas after the 16th Party Congress*, ed. Scobell and W. Carlisle, 11–48. Barracks, PA: Strategic Studies Institute.

Mungello, D. E. 1989. *Curious land: Jesuit accommodation and the origins of sinology.* Honolulu: University of Hawaii Press.

——. 2005. *The great encounter of China and the West, 1500–1800.* Lanham, MD: Rowman & Littlefield.

Munro, D. J. 1985. *Individualism and holism: Studies in Confucian and Taoist values.* Ann Arbor, University of Michigan Press.

——. 1988. *The image of human nature: A Sung portrait.* Princeton, NJ: Princeton University Press.

——. 1996. *The imperial style of inquiry in twentieth-century China: The emergence of new approaches.* Ann Arbor: University of Michigan Press.

——. 2001. *The concept of man in early China.* Ann Arbor, The University of Michigan Press.

Murray, Williamson, MacGregor Knox, and Alvin H. Bernstein. 1994. *The making of strategy: Rulers, states, and war.* Cambridge, U.K.: Cambridge University Press.

Nakata, S. 2005. *Manshūkoku kōtei no hiroku: rasuto enperā to "Genpi kaikenroku" no nazo* [Secret record of Qing emperor]. Tōkyō: Genki Shobō.

Naquin, Susan. 1976. *Millenarian rebellion in China: The eight trigrams uprising of 1813.* New Haven, CT: Yale University Press.

——. 1981. *Shantung Rebellion: The Wang Lun uprising of 1774.* New Haven, CT: Yale University Press.

Nathan, A. 1973. A Factionalism model of CCP politics. *China Quarterly* 53 (January–March): 34–66.

——. 1976. *Peking politics.* Berkeley: University of California Press.

——. 1986a. *Chinese democracy.* New York: Knopf.

——. 1986b. Sources of Chinese rights thinking. In *Human rights in contemporary China*, ed. R. R. Edwards, L. Henkin, and A. Nathan. New York: Columbia University Press.

——. 1990. *China's crises, dilemmas of reform and prospects for democracy.* New York: Columbia University Press.

——. 1993. *Norms and the state in China.* Ed. Chun-Chieh Huang. Leiden: E. J. Brill.

———. 1997. *China's transition*. New York: Columbia University Press.

Nathan, A., R. R. Edwards, and L. Henkin, eds. 1986. *Human rights in contemporary China*. New York: Columbia University Press.

Nathan, A., and Tianjian Shi. 1993. Cultural requisites for democracy in China: Findings from a survey. *Daedalus* 122:2.

Needham, J. 1956. *Science and civilisation in China*. Vol. 2. Cambridge: Cambridge University Press.

Nelson, D., and W. Stephen, eds. 1982. *Communist legislatures in comparative perspective*. Albany: State University of New York Press.

Neville, R. 2000. *Boston Confucianism*. Albany: State University of New York Press.

Neville-Brown, L., and J. Bell. 1993. *French administrative law*. New York: Oxford University Press.

Nichols, P. 1997. The viability of transplanted law: Kazakhstani reception of a transplanted foreign investment code. *University of Pennsylvania Journal of International Economic Law* 18:1235.

Nie, Leng. 1994. *Bian zi da shuai Zhang Xun* [Great general with a bride: Zhang Xun]. Beijing: Zhongguo Qingnian Chubanshe.

Nie, Rongzhen. 1983. *Nie Rongzhen Huiyilu* [Memoirs of Nie Rongzhen]. Beijing: Zhanshi Chubanshe.

Niming. 1979. *Qishi Niandai* [The seventies]. A monthly magazine.

Niu, Niu. 2001. *No tears for Mao: Growing up in the Cultural Revolution*. Chicago: Academy Chicago Publishers.

Nivison, D. 1956. Communist ethics and Chinese tradition. *Journal of Asian Studies* 16 (1) November: 51–74.

Nolan, P., and Wang Xiaogang. 1999. Beyond privatization: Institutional innovation and growth in China's large state-owned enterprises. *World Development* 27:169.

North, R. C. 1952. *Kuomintang and Chinese communist elites.* Stanford, CA: Stanford University Press.

O'Brien, K. 1987. The National People's Congress: Continuity and change in Chinese legislative politics. PhD diss., Yale University.

———.1989. Legislative development and Chinese political change. *Studies in Comparative Communism,* XXII (1) Spring: 57–75.

———. 1990a. Is China's National People's Congress a conservative legislature? *Asian Survey,* Vol. XXX. 8 (August): 782–794.

———. 1990b. *Reform without liberalization.* New York: Cambridge University Press.

———. 1994a. Agents and remonstrators: Role accumulation by Chinese People's Congress deputies. *China Quarterly* 138 (June): 359–380.

———. 1994b. Chinese People's Congresses and legislative embeddedness: Understanding early organizational development. *Comparative Political Studies* 27:80.

———. 1994c. Implementing political reform in China's villages. *Australian Journal of Chinese Affairs* 32:33.

———. 1999a. Hunting for political change. *The China Journal* 41:159.

———. 1999b. The two-ballot system in Shanxi. *The China Journal* 42:103.

O'Brien, K., and Lianjiang Li. 2000. Accommodating "democracy" in a one-party state: Introducing village elections in China. *China Quarterly* 162:465.

———. 1999. Selective policy implementation in rural China. *Comparative Politics* 31:167.

Ocko, J. 1988. I'll take it all the way to Beijing: Capital appeals in the Qing. *Journal of Asian Studies* 47:291.

———. 1997. A review of Geoffrey MacCormack, the spirit of traditional Chinese law. *McGill Law Journal* 42:733.

——. 2000. Using the past to make a case for the present. In *The limits of the rule of law in China*, ed. Karen Turner-Gottschang, James V. Feinerman, and R. Kent Guy, 65–87. Seattle: University of Washington Press.

Oda, Yurozo. 1905–1911. *Qingkuo Xingzheng Fa* [Administrative laws of the Ch'ing state]. Trans. Shinkoku gyoseiho. Shanghai: Guangzhi Shuju.

Ogden, S. 1992. *China's unresolved issues: Politics, development, and culture*. London: Prentice Hall.

Oi, J. 1989. *State and peasant in contemporary China: The political economy of village government*. Berkeley: University of California Press.

——. 1999. *Rural China takes off.* Berkeley: University of California Press.

Oi, J., and S. Rozelle. 2000. Elections and power: The locus of decision-making in Chinese villages. *China Quarterly* 162:513.

Oi, J., and A. Walder, eds. 1999. *Property rights and economic reform in China.* Stanford, CA: Stanford University Press.

Oksenberg, M. 1968. The institutionalization of the Communist Revolution. *China Quarterly* 36 (October–December): 61–92.

——. 1970. Getting ahead and along in Communist China: The ladder of success on the eve of the Cultural Revolution. In *Party, leadership, and revolutionary power in China*, ed. J. W. Lewis, 304–350. Cambridge: Cambridge University Press.

——. 1971. Policy making under Mao, 1949–68: An overview. In *China: Management of a Revolutionary Society*, ed. J. M. H. Lindbeck, 3–21. Seattle: University of Washington Press.

——. 1974. Methods of communication within the Chinese bureaucracy. *China Quarterly* 57 (January–March): 1–39.

——. 1976. The exit pattern from Chinese politics and its implications. *China Quarterly* 67:501–518.

——. 1977. The political leader. In *Mao Tse-tung in the scale of history*, ed. De. Wilson, 384–394. Cambridge: Cambridge University Press.

——. 2001. China's political system: Challenges of the twenty-first century. *The China Journal* 45:21.

Oksenberg, M., and S. Goldstein 1974. The Chinese political spectrum. *Problems of Communism* 23 (2): 2–9.

Oksenberg, M., and Sai-Cheung Yeung. 1977. Hua Kuo-feng's pre-Cultural Revolution Hunan years, 1949–66: The making of a political generalist. *China Quarterly* 69 (March): 9–16.

Orts, E. 2001. The rule of law in China. *Vanderbilt Journal of Transnational Law* 34:43.

Otto, Jan Michiel et al., eds. 2000. *Law-making in the People's Republic of China.* The Hague: Kluwer Law International.

Ownby, D. 1996. *Brotherhoods and secret societies in early and mid-Qing China: The formation of a tradition.* Stanford, CA: Stanford University Press.

Oxnam, R. B. 1975. *Ruling from horseback: Manchu politics in the Oboi regency, 1661–1669.* Chicago: University of Chicago Press.

Palmer, L. 1996. Party and law in China. In *State and law in eastern Asia*, ed. L. Palmer, 9–22. Aldershot: Dartmouth Publishing.

Pan, Ku. 1969. *The history of the former Han dynasty.* 3 vols. Trans. H. H. Dubs. Baltimore: Waverly Press.

Pan, Rong. 2000. *Feng Guozhang jia zu* [The family of Feng Quozhang]. Beijing: Jin-cheng Chubanshe.

Pang, Xianzhi, ed. 2002. *Mao Zedong nian pu.* [A yearbook of Mao Zedong]. Beijing: Zhongyang Wenxian Chubanshe.

Pantsov, A. 2000. *The Bolsheviks and the Chinese revolution, 1919–1927*. Richmond, U.K.: Curzon.

Parker, G. 1996. *The military revolution: Military innovation and the rise of the West, 1500–1800*. Cambridge: Cambridge University Press.

Parrish, W. L. 1973. Factions in Chinese military politics. *China Quarterly* 56:667–679.

Parsons, J. B. 1957. The culmination of a Chinese peasant rebellion: Chang Hsien-chung in Szechwan, 1644–46. *Journal of Asian Studies* 16 (3): 387–400.

———.1970. *The peasant rebellions of the late Ming dynasty*. Tucson: University of Arizona Press.

Patrick, D. 1985. *Old Testament law*. London: SCM Press.

Paul, S. 1970. *Studies in the book of the covenant in the light of cuneiform and biblical law*. Leiden: E. J. Brill.

Pearson, M. 1997. *China's new business elite: The political consequences of economic reform*. Berkeley: University of California Press.

Peck, G. 1967. *Two kinds of time*. Boston: Houghton Mifflin.

Peerenboom, R. P. 1988. Han dynasty cosmology: The emergence of naturalism. *Asian Culture Quarterly* 16:13–40.

———. 1990a. Confucian jurisprudence: Beyond natural law. *Asian Culture Quarterly* 36:12.

———. 1990b. Natural law in the Huang Lao Boshu. *Philosophy East and West* 40:309–329.

———. 1993a. *Law and morality in ancient China: The silk manuscripts of Huang-Lao*. Albany: State University of New York Press.

———. 1993b. The victim in Chinese criminal theory and practice: A preliminary study. *Journal of Chinese Law* 7:63.

———. 1995. Rights, interests and the interest in rights in China. *Stanford Journal of International Law* 31:359.

——. 2000a. Beyond apologia: Respecting legitimate differences of opinion while not toadying to dictators. *Philosophy East and West* 50:92.

——. 2000b. The evolving regulatory framework for the enforcement of arbitral awards in the PRC. *Asian Pacific Law and Policy Journal* 1:13.

——. 2000c. Human rights and Asian values: The limits of universalism. *China Review International* 7:295.

——. 2000d. The limits of irony: Rorty and the China challenge. *Philosophy East and West* 50:56.

——. 2000e. Review of bird in a cage: Legal reform in China after Mao, by Stanley Lubman. *China Review International* 7:135.

——. 2001a. Globalization, path dependency and the limits of law: Administrative law reform and the rule of law in the People's Republic of China. *Berkeley Journal of International Law* 19:161.

——. 2001b. Seek truth from facts: An empirical study of enforcement of arbitral awards in the PRC. *American Journal of Comparative Law* 49: 249–328.

——. 2002a. *China's long march toward rule of law*. New York: Cambridge University Press.

——. 2002b. Law and religion in early China. In *Religion, law, and tradition*, ed. A. Huxley, 84–107. London: Taylor and Francis.

——. 2002c. Law enforcement and the legal profession in China. In *Implementation of law in the People's Republic of China*, ed. Chen Jianfu, Li Yuwen, and Jan Michiel Otto, 125–148. The Hague: Kluwer Law International.

Peers, C. 1998. *Warlords of China, 700 B.C. to A.D. 1662*. London: Arms & Armour.

Pei, M. 1995. Creeping democratization in China. *Journal of Democracy* 6:65.

——. 1997a. Citizens v. Mandarins: Administrative litigation in China. *China Quarterly* 152:832.

——. 1997b. Racing against time: Institutional decay and renewal in China. In *China Briefing: The contradictions of Change*, ed. W. A. Joseph, 11–50. Armonk, NY: M. E. Sharpe.

——. 1998a. Chinese civic associations. *Modern China* 24:285.

——. 1998b. Constructing the political foundations of an economic miracle. In *Behind East Asian growth*, ed. H. S. Rowen, 39–60. New York: Routledge.

——. 2000. Rights and resistance: The changing contexts of the dissident movement. In *Chinese society: Change, conflict and resistance*, ed. E. Perry and M. Selden, 23–46. London: Routledge.

Peing, Changlu. 2001. *Wu Peifu shang jiang jun nian pu* [Chronology of General Wu Peifu]. Beijing: National Library.

Peng, Dehuai. 1981. *Peng Dehuai zishu* [Autobiographical account of Peng Dehuai]. Shanghai: Renmin Chubanshe.

——. 1984. *Memoirs of a Chinese marshal: The autobiographical notes of Peng Dehuai (1898–1974)*. Trans. Zheng Longpu, ed. S. Grimes. Beijing: Foreign Languages Press.

——. 1990. Wo weishenme yao xiexin gei Mao zhuxi [Why I wanted to write to Chairman Mao]. *Xinhua Wenzhai* 21:140–142.

——. 2002. *Peng Dehuai Zizhuan* [An autobiography of Peng Dehuai]. Beijing: Jiefangjun Wenyi Chubanshe.

Peng, Guicai. 1999. Guanyu Xingzheng Susong Kunjing de Falü Sikao [Legal reflections on the difficult areas of administrative litigation]. *Fazhi Yu Shehui Fazhan* 3:14.

Peng, Yuxin. 1958. Qingmo zhongyang yu gesheng caizhong guanxi. *Zhongguo jindaishi luncong* ed. Li Dingyi, 2 (5): 8–9.

Penner, T. 1987. *Ascent from nominalism*. Boston: D. Reidel.

Pepper, S. 1978. *Civil war in China: The political struggle, 1945–1949.* Berkeley: University of California Press.

——. 1984. *China's universities: Post-Mao enrollment policies and their impact on the structure of secondary education.* Ann Arbor, MI: Center for Chinese Studies.

——. 2000. *Radicalism and education reform in 20th-century China: The search for an ideal development model.* New York: Cambridge University Press.

Perdue, P. C. 1987. *Exhausting the earth: State and peasant in Hunan, 1500–1850.* Cambridge, MA: Harvard University Press.

——. 2005. *China marches west: The Qing conquest of Eurasia* Cambridge, MA: Harvard University Press.

Perry, E. J. 1980. *Rebels and revolutionaries in North China, 1845–1945.* Stanford, CA: Stanford University Press.

——. 2006. *Patrolling the revolution: Worker militias, citizenship, and the modern Chinese state.* Lanham, MD: Rowman & Littlefield.

——. 2007. *Grassroots political reform in contemporary China.* Ed. E. J. Perry and M. Goldman. Cambridge, MA: Harvard University Press.

Perry, E. J., and C. Wong, eds. 1958. *The political economy of reform in post-Mao China.* Cambridge, MA: Harvard University Press.

Peterson, G. 1998. *The power of words: Literacy and revolution in South China, 1949–1995.* Vancouver: University of British Columbia Press.

Pi, Chunxie, and Li Yuji. 1998. 1997 Nian Xingzheng Faxue Yanjiude Huigu yu Zhanwang [Retrospect of 1997 administrative law studies and future prospects]. *Faxuejia* 1:36–42.

Pistor, K, and P. A. Wellons. 1999. *The role of law and legal institutions in Asian economic development 1960–1995.* New York: Oxford University Press.

Platteau, Jean-Phillipe. 1994. Behind the market stage where real societies exist: Part I. *Journal of Development Studies* 30:553.

Po Yi, Aisin-Gioro. 1979. *From emperor to citizen*. Beijing: Foreign Languages Press.

Pokotilov, D. 1947–1949. *History of the eastern Mongols during the Ming dynasty from 1368 to 1634*. 2 vols. Trans. R. Lowenthal. Chendu: Chinese Cultural Studies Research Institute, West China Union University.

Pomeranz, K. 1993. *The making of a hinterland: State, society, and economy in inland North China, 1853–1937*. Berkeley: University of California Press.

Pomfret, John. 2000. China's poor fear cost of free trade. *Washington Post*, September 24.

———. 2001. A foe rattles Beijing from abroad. *Washington Post Foreign Service*, March 9.

Porten, B., and J. A. Lund, eds. 2002. *Aramaic documents from Egypt:A key-word-in-context concordance*. Winona Lake, IN: Eisenbrauns.

Potter, P. B. 1986. Peng Zhen: Evolving views on party organization and law. In *China's establishment intellectuals*, ed. C. L.Hamrin and T. Cheek, 21–50. Armonk, NY: M. E. Sharpe.

———, ed. 1994a. The administrative law of the PRC. In *Domestic reforms in post-Mao China*. Armonk, NY: M. E. Sharpe.

———. 1994b. *Domestic law reforms in post-Mao China*. Armonk, NY: M. E. Sharpe.

———. 1994c. Riding the tiger: Legitimacy and legal culture in post-Mao China. *China Quarterly* 138:325.

———. 1995a. *Foreign business law in China: Past progress and future challenges*. South San Francisco: 1990 Institute.

———. 1995b. Foreign investment law in the People's Republic of China: Dilemmas of state control. *China Quarterly* 141:155.

———. 1999. The Chinese legal system: Continuing commitment to the primacy of power. *China Quarterly* 159:673.

———. 2000. PRC contract law. *Doing business in China.* ed. Freshfields. Yonkers: Juris Publishing, Inc.

———. 2003. *From Leninist discipline to socialist legalism: Peng Zhen on law and political authority in the PRC.* Stanford, CA: Stanford University Press.

Potter, S., and J. M. Potter. 1990. *China's peasants.* New York: Cambridge University Press.

Price, F. W., trans. 1927. *San Min Chu I: The three principles of the people.* Taipei: China Publications.

Ptak, R. 2004. *China, the Portuguese, and the Nanyang: Oceans and routes, regions and trades (c. 1000–1600).* Aldershot: Ashgate.

Pu, Xingjue. 2005. *Deng Xiaoping zai Lishi Zhuanzhe Guantou* [Deng Xiaoping at the moment of historical transition] Beijing: Zhongguo Shehui Chubanshe.

Pu Yi. 1987. *Wode Qian Pansheng* [The last Manchu: The autobiography of Henry Pu Yi, last emperor of China]. Trans. Kuo Ying Paul Tsai. New York: Pocket Books.

———. 1996. *Puyi Riji* [Puyi diaries]. Tanjing: Renmin Chubanshe.

Pulleyblank, E. G. 1982. *The background of the rebellion of An Lu-shan.* Westport, CT: Greenwood Press.

Purcell, V. 1974. *The Boxer uprising.* Hamden: Archon Books.

Pye, L. W. 1971. *Warlord politics: Conflict and coalition in the modernisation of Republic China.* New York: Praeger.

———. 1976. *Mao Tse-Tung: The man in the leader.* New York: Basic Books.

———. 1981. *The dynamics of Chinese politics.* Cambridge, MA: Oelgeschlager, Gunn & Hain.

———. 1985. *Asian power and politics: The cultural dimensions of authority.* Cambridge, MA: Harvard University Press.

———. 1988. *The mandarin and the cadre: China's political cultures.* Ann Arbor: University of Michigan Center for Chinese Studies.

Qian, Maowei. 2004. *Guojia, Keju yu Shehui: yi Mingdai wei Zhongxin de Kaocha* [State, imperial examination, and society: A study with Ming focus]. Beijing: Tushuguan Chubanshe.

Qian, Mu. 1935. *XianQin Zhuzi Xiniankao* [Chronological studies of the pre-Qing philosophers]. 2 vols. Hong Kong: University of Hong Kong Press.

———. 1956. *Guoshi Dagang* [A general survey of Chinese history]. 2 vols. Taipei: Guoli Bianyi.

———. 1969. *Zhongguo lidai zhengzhi lishi* [History of Chinese political institutions].Taipei: Sanming.

———. 1982. *Traditional government in Imperial China: A critical analysis.* Trans. Chuntu Hsueh and G. O. Totte. New York: St. Martin's.

———. 1982. *Zhongguo Tongshi Cankao Ziliao.* Taipei: Dongshen.

Qian, Mu. 1969. *Zhongguo lidai zhengzhi deshi* [The gain and loss of Chinese politics during dynasties]. Taipei: Sanmin shuju.

Qin, Guojing. 1996. Cong Qinggong Dangan kan Yingshi Magareni fanghua lishi shishi. In *Zhongguo Tongshi Rebai Zhounian Xueshu Taolunhui Wenji*, ed. Zhang Zhilian, 235–238. Beijing: Zhongguo shehui kexueyuan chubanshe.

Qin, Zhihua. 1993. *Xinzhi yu Zhengzhi: Lun Zhongguo Dezhi Zhuyi Chuantong* [Rule by heart and politics: On the Chinese tradition of ruling by ethics]. Nanning: Guangxi Renmin Chubanshe.

Qinghua, Daxue Lishixi. 1998. *Wuxu Bianfa Wenxian Ziliao Xiri*. Shanghai: Shudian Chubanshe.

Quan Tang shi [A complete collection of Tang poetry]. 1960. Comp. Cao
Yin and ed. Pong Dingqiu and others. Beijing: Zhonghua Shuju.

Quan Tang wen [A complete collection of Tang prose writing]. 1965.
Comp. Dong Gao and others. Taipei: Huawen shuju.

Quan, Yanchi. 1989a. *Hongqiang Neiwai* [Inside and outside the Red
Walls]. Beijing: Kunlun Chubanshe.

———. 1989b. *Zouxia shentan de Mao Zedong* [Mao Zedong, man, not
God]. Beijing: Zhongwai wenhua Chuban Gongsi.

———. 1991. *Tho Zhu zai "wenhua dageming" zhong* [Tao Zhu in the
"Cultural Revolution"]. Beijing: Zhonggong Zhongyang Dangxiao
Chubanshe.

———. 1993. *Shenghuo zhong de lingxiumen* [Leaders in their lives].
Kunming: Yunnan renmin chubanshe.

Quanguo Zhengxie Wenshi Ziliao Weiyuanhui, ed. 2001. *Jizha Quan-
bian: Jiang Jieshi yu Gepaixi Junfa Zhengdou Neimu* [Deception and
changing strategies: Inside stories between Chiang Kaishek and various fractions of warlords]. Beijing: Zhongguo Wenshi Chubanshe.

Rabin, C. 1991. *Semitic languages. An introduction* [Hebrew]. Jerusalem: Mosad Beyaliq.

Rankin, M. B. 1986. *Elite activism and political transformation in
China: Zhejiang Province, 1865–1911*. Stanford, CA: Stanford
University Press.

Rapp, J. A., and A. M. Andrew. 2000. *Autocracy and China's rebel
founding emperors: Comparing Chairman Mao and Ming Taizu*.
Lanham, MD: Rowman & Littlefield.

Ratchnevsky, P. 1937–1985. *Un Code des Yuan*. 4 vols. Paris: E.
Leroux.

Rawski, E. S. 1998. *The last emperors: A social history of Qing imperial institutions.* Berkeley: University of California Press.

Reid, J. G. 1935. *The Manchu abdication and the powers, 1908–1912.* Berkeley: University of California Press.

Ren, Jianshu. 1989. *Chen Duxiu Zhuan* [A biography of Chen Duxiu]. Shanghai: Renmin Chubanshe.

Renmin Ribao [People's daily]. An official newspaper of the Chinese Communist Party and government; referred to in notes as *RMRB*. Various editions, 1966, 1982–1987, 1989.

———. 1966. The decision of the Central Committee of the Chinese Communist Party about proletarian cultural revolution. August 8.

Rhoads, E. J. M. 1975. *China's republican revolution: The case of Kwangtung, 1895–1913.* Cambridge, MA: Harvard University Press.

Rhoads, Q., and J. M. Edwards. 2000. *Manchus and Han: Ethnic relations and political power in late Qing and early Republican China, 1861–1928.* Seattle: University of Washinton Press.

Rice, E. E. 1972. *Mao's way.* Berkeley: University of California Press.

———. 1976. The second rise and fall of Teng Hsiao-p'ing. *China Quarterly.* 67 (September): 494–500.

Rindova, V. P., and W. H. Starbuck. 1997. Ancient Chinese theories of control. *Journal of Management Inquiry*, 6:144–159.

Robinson, D. M. 2001. *Bandits, eunuchs, and the son of Heaven: Rebellion and the economy of violence in mid-Ming China.* Honolulu: University of Hawaii Press.

———, ed. 2008. *Culture, courtiers, and competition: The Ming court (1368–1644)* Cambridge, MA: Harvard University Press.

Robinson, T. W., ed. 1971a. *The Cultural Revolution in China.* Berkeley: University of California Press.

———. 1971b. *A politico-military biography of Lin Piao.* Pt. 1, 1907–1949. Santa Monica, CA: Rand.

———. 1972. Lin Piao as an elite type. In *Elites in the People's Republic of China*, ed. R. A. Scalapino, and G. A. Bennett, 149–197. Seattle: University of Washington Press.

Roderick, T. Long, and Tibor R. Machan, eds. 2007. *Anarchism/minarchism: Is a government part of a free country?* Aldershot: Ashgate.

Rong, Hong. 1915. *Xixue Dongjian Ji* [Western learning crapes into the East]. Shanghai: Shangwu.

Rong, Zaozu. 1972. *Han Fei Zi kaozheng.* Taibei: Tailian Guofeng Publishing.

Rosen, S. 1982. *Red Guard factionalism and the Cultural Revolution in Guangzhou.* Boulder, CO: Westview Press.

Rosinger, L. K. 1944. *China's wartime politics, 1937–1944.* Princeton, NJ: Princeton University Press.

Rossabi, M. 1982. *The Jurchens in the Yuan and Ming.* Ithaca, NY: Cornell University Press.

Ruan, Ming. 1994. *The Empire of Dong.* Boulder, CO: Westview Press.

Rubin, K. 1984. Writers' discontent and Party response in Yan'an before "wild lily": The Manchurian writers and Zhou Yang. *Modern Chinese Literature*, 1 (I): 79–102.

Rue, J. E. 1966. *Mao Tse-tung in opposition, 1927–35.* Stanford, CA: Stanford University Press.

Sáenz-Badillos, A. 1993. *History of the Hebrew language.* Cambridge: Cambridge University Press.

Sah, Mongwu. 1957. The impact of Hanfeism on the earlier Han censorial system. *Chinese Culture* 1:75–111.

Saich, T. 1981. *China: Politics and government.* New York: St. Martin's Press.

———. 1989. Seven sources on Party history. *CCP Research Newsletter* 4 (Fall–winter): 1–12.

———, ed. 1991. *Origins of the first united front in China: The role of Sneevliet (alias Maring)*. 2 vols. Leiden: E. J. Brill.

———. 1995. *New perspectives on the Chinese Communist Revolution*. Armonk, NY: M. E. Sharpe.

———, ed. 1996. *The rise to power of the CCP*. Armonk, NY: M. E. Sharpe.

———. 2004. *Governance and politics of China*. New York: Palgrave.

Saich, T., and R. MacFarquhar, eds. 2003. *Mao re-evaluated: A conference to mark the 110th anniversary of the birth of Mao Zedong and honor Stuart Schram for his signal contribution to Mao studies*. Cambridge, MA: Harvard University.

Salisbury, H. E. 1985. *The Long March: The untold story*. New York: Harper & Row.

———. 1992. *The new empires: China in the era of Mao and Deng*. Boston: Little Brown.

Satō, Tetsujirō. 2005. *Yige Riben jizhe Bixia de Yuan Shikai* [Yuan Shikai in the eyes of Japanese reporter]. Trans. Kong Xiangji. Tianjin: Guji Chubanshe.

Scalapino, A. 1962. *Elites in the People's Republic of China*. Seattle: University of Washington Press.

Scalapino, A., and G. T. Yu, 1961. *The Chinese anarchist movement*. Westport, CT: Greenwood Press.

Schell, O. 1994. *Mandate of Heaven: A new generation of entrepreneurs, dissidents, bohemians, and technocrats lays claim to China's future*. New York: Simon & Schuster.

Schiffrin, H. Z. 1970. *Sun Yat-sen and the origins of the Chinese revolution*. Berkeley: University of California Press.

Schneider, L. A. 1971. *Ku Chieh-kang and China's new history: Nationalism and the quest for alternative tradition*. Berkeley: University of California Press.

Schoenhals, M. 1992. *Doing things with words in Chinese politics.* Berkeley: University of California Press.

———. 1996. *China's Cultural Revolution, 1966–1969: Not a dinner party.* Armonk, NY: M. E. Sharpe.

Schram, S. R. 1963. *The political thought of Mao Tse-tung.* New York: Praeger.

———. 1967. *Mao Tse-tung.* New York: Simon and Schuster.

———. 1969. *The political thought of Mao Tse-tung.* New York: Praeger.

———. 1971. Mao Tse-tung and the theory of permanent revolution. *China Quarterly* 46 (April): 223.

———, ed. 1973. *Authority, participation and cultural change in China.* Cambridge: Cambridge University Press.

———, ed. 1992. *Mao's road to power: Revolutionary writings 1912–1949.* 7 vols. Armonk, NY: M. E. Sharpe.

Schrecker, J. E. 2004. *The Chinese revolution in historical perspective.* Westport, CT: Praeger.

Schrift, M. 2001. *Biography of a Chairman Mao badge: The creation and mass consumption of a personality cult.* Piscataway, NJ: Rutgers University Press.

Schurmann, F. 1971. *Ideology and organization in Communist China.* Berkeley: University of California Press.

Schwartz, B. 1957. On attitudes toward law in China. In *Government under law and the individual*, ed. M. Katz, 27–39. Washington D.C.: American Council of Learned Societies.

———. 1964. *Chinese Communism and the rise of Mao.* Cambridge, MA: Harvard University Press.

———. 1970. *Self and society.* New York: Columbia University Press.

———. 1972. *Reflections on the May Fourth Movement: A symposium.* Cambridge, MA: Harvard University Press.

———. 1985. *The world of thought in ancient China.* Cambridge, MA: Harvard University Press.

———. 1991. *Administrative law.* Boston: Little, Brown.

Schweber, H. H. 2007. *The language of liberal constitutionalism.* Cambridge: Cambridge University Press.

Scobell, A., and L. Wortzel, eds. 2004. *Civil-military change in China: Elites, institutes, and ideas after the 16th Party Congress.* Carlisle, PA: Strategic Studies Institute.

Seagave, S. 1985. *The Soong dynasty.* New York: Harper & Row.

Secretariat of the National Working Conference on Collecting Materials of the History of CPP, ed. 1982. *Dangshi Huiyi Baogaoji* [Collection of speeches at the Party History Conference]. Beijing: Central Party School Press.

Selden, M. 1971. *The Yenan way in revolutionary China.* Cambridge, MA: Harvard University Press.

Seybolt, P. J. 1986. Terror and conformity, counterespionage campaigns, rectification, and mass movements, 1942–1943. *Modern China,* 12 (1): 39–73.

Seymour, J. D., ed. 1980. *The fifth modernization: China's human rights movement, 1978–79.* Stanfordville, NY: Coleman.

Sha, Jiansun, ed. 2006. *Zhongguo Gongchandang Shigao (1921–1949)* [A draft of the history of the Chinese Communist Party]. 5 vols. Beijing: Zhongyang Wenxian Chubanshe.

Shambaugh, D. 1984. *The making of a premier: Zhao Ziyang's provincial career.* Boulder, CO: Westview Press.

———. 2002. *Modernizing China's military: Progress, problems, prospects.* Berkeley: University of California Press.

——. 2008. *China's Communist Party: Atrophy and adaptation*. Berkeley: University of California Press.

Shao, Hua. 2003. *Lin Biao de Zheyisheng* [A biography of Lin Biao]. Wuhan: Hubei Renmin Chubanshe.

Shao, Yihai. 1988a. *"Lianhe Jiandui" de Fumie* [Destruction of a "Joint Fleet"]. Beijing: Chunqiu Chubanshe.

——. 1988b. Lin Biao Chutao Zhenxiang [The truth about Lin Biao's escape]. *Zhui Qiu* 6:78–105.

——. 1988c. *Lin Biao Wangchao Heimu* [Inside the Dark dynasty of Lin Biao]. Chengdu: Sichuan Wenyi Chubanshe.

Sharman, L. 1934. *Sun Yat-sen, his life and its meaning: A critical biography*. Hamden: Archon Books.

Shen, G. 2005. *Elite theatre in Ming China, 1368–1644*. London: Routledge.

Shen, Jiaben. 1913–1929. *Ming Dagao Junling Kao* [A study of Ming Dagao].

Shen, Meijuan. 1996. *Dai Li Xinzhuan* [A new biography of Dai Li]. Taibei: Guojicun Wenku Shudian.

Shen, Yuan. 1991. *Jiangshan Dai Li* [Jiangshan's Dai Li]. Beijing: Zhongguo Wenshi Chubanshe.

Shen, Yunlong. 1972. *Li Yuanhong Pingzhuan* [Biography of Li Yuanhong]. Taibei: Wenhai Chubanshe.

——. 1979. *Xu Shichang Pingzhuan* [Biography of Xu Shichang]. Taibei: Zhuanji Wenxue Chubanshe.

Shen, Zui. 1962. Jiang Jieshi Zhunbei Ansha Li Zongren de Yinmo [Chiang Kaishek's secret plot to assassinate Li Zongren]. *Wenshi ziliao xuanji* 32:118–121.

——. 1979. Yang Hucheng Jiangjun Beiqiujin he Bei Kansha de Jingguo [The process of General Yang Hucheng's imprisonment and murder]. In *Jiang Bang Tewu Zuixing Lu* [A record of the crimes of the Jiang Gang's Special Services]. 79–92. Beijing: Qunzhong chubanshe.

———. 1983. *Dalu Shenghui Sanshi Nian* [Thirty years on the mainland]. 2 vols. Hong Kong: Jingbao Wenhua Qiye Youxian Gongsi.

———. 1984. *Juntong Neimu* [The inside story of the Military Statistics (Bureau)]. Beijing: Wenshi Ziliao Chubanshe.

Shen, Zui, and Wen Qiang, eds. 1980. *Dai Li Qiren* [Dai Li the man]. Beijing: Wenshi Ziliao Chubanshe.

Sheng, Langxi. 1934. *Zhonguo Shuyuan Zhidu.* Shanghai: Zhonghua Shuju.

Sheridan, J. E. 1966. *Chinese warlord; the career of Feng Yu-Hsiang.* Stanford, CA: Stanford University Press.

———. 1975. *China in disintegration: The Republic era in Chinese history, 1912–1949.* New York: Free Press.

Shi, Bo. 1993. *Zhang Guotao de Fuchen* [The rise and fall of Zhang Guotao]. Beijing: Renmin Zhongguo.

Shi, Dongbing. 1994. *Gao Gang Hunduan Zhongnanhai* [The death of Gao Gang]. Hong Kong: Tiandi Tushu.

Shi, Haoming et al., eds. 2006. *Zhongguo Minshi Falü Zhidu Jicheng yu Chuang xin* [Reference and innovation of Chinese civil law]. Beijing: Renmin Fayuan Chubanshe.

Shi, Shiming. 2001. *Wei shou xian de yuan shuai Ye Ting* [Untitled General Ye Ting] Shanghai: Renmin Chubanshe.

Shi, Tianjian. 1997. *Political participation in Beijing.* Cambridge, MA: Harvard University Press.

Shi, Yuping. 1996. Shilun Xingzheng Lanyong Zhiquan ji qi Falü Zhiyue [Administrative abuse of power and its legal restraint]. *Fashang Yanjiu* 1:81.

Shi, Zhongquan, and Chen Dengcai, eds. 2006. *Mao Zedong de gu shi* [The story of Mao Zedong]. Beijing: Zhongyang Dangshi.

Shiga, Shuzo. 1974. Criminal procedure in the Ch'ing dynasty. *Memoirs of the Research Department of Tokyo Bunko* 32:1.

Shih, Chih-yu. 1999. *Collective democracy: Political and legal reform in China.* Hong Kong: The Chinese University Press.

Shih, V. Y. C. 1967. *The Taiping ideology: Its sources, interpretations, and influences.* Seattle: University of Washington Press.

Shirk, Susan. 1993. *The political logic of economic reform in China.* Berkeley: University of California Press.

1987. *Shiyijie Sanzhong Quanhui Yilai Zhongyao Wenxian Xuandu* [Selected readings of the important documents since the Third Plenum session of the eleventh congress of CPC]. Beijing: Renmin Chubanshe.

Shu, V. 1988. *The reach of the state: Sketches of the Chinese body politics.* Stanford, CA: Stanford University Press.

Shu, Yun. 2005. *Luo Ruiqing da jiang* [General? Luo Ruiqing] Beijing: Jiefangjun Wenyi Chubanshe.

———. 2006. *Lin Biao Shijian Wanzheng Diaocha* [A complete investigation of the incidence of Lin Biao]. Carle Place, NY: Mingjing Chubanshe.

Shum, Kui-kwong. 1988. *The Chinese Communists' road to power: The anti-Japanese national front, 1935–1945.* Hong Kong: Oxford University Press.

Sichuan Daxue Ma Lie Jiaoyanshi, ed. 1984. *Guomin Canzhenghui Ziliao* [The sources for the National People's Consultative Congress]. Chongqing: Sichuan Renmin Chubanshe.

Sih, P. K. T., ed. 1970. *The strenuous decade: China's nation-building efforts, 1927–1937.* Jamaica, NY: St. John's University Press.

Sima, Guang. 1936. *Ch'ien-hsu Ts'ung-shu jicheng* ed. vol. 697. Shanghai: Shangwu.

———. 1956. *Zizhi Tongjian* [Comprehensive mirror to aid in government]. Beijing: Guji Chubanshe.

Sima, Qian. 1959. *Shi ji.* Beijing: Zhonghua Shuju.

———. 1993. *Records of the Grand Historian.* Trans. B. Watson. 3 vols. New York: Columbia University Press.

Siren, Yao, ed. 1993. *Da Ming Lu fuli Zhujie* [The commentaries to the Ming Code and Regulations]. Beijing: Beijing University Press.

Smedley, A. 1956. *The great road: The life and times of Chu Teh.* New York: Monthly Review Press.

Smith, K., P. K. Bol, J. A. Adler, and D. J. Wyatt. 1990. *Sung dynasty uses of the I Ching.* Princeton, NJ: Princeton University Press.

Smith, P. J., and R. Von Glahn, eds. 2003. *The Song-Yuan-Ming transition in Chinese history.* Cambridge, MA: Harvard University Press.

Smith, R. J. 1994. *China's cultural heritage: The Qing dynasty, 1644–1912.* Boulder, CO: Westview Press.

Smith, S. 2000. *A road is made: Communism in Shanghai, 1920–1927.* Honolulu: University of Hawaii Press.

———. 2002. *Like cattle and horses: Nationalism and labor in Shanghai.* Durham, NC: Duke University Press.

Snow, E. 1942. *The battle for Asia.* Cleveland, OH: World Publishing.

———. 1961a. *The other side of the river: Red China today.* New York: Random House.

———. 1961b. *Red star over China.* New York: Grove.

———. 1971. *Random notes on red China, 1936–1945.* Cambridge, MΛ: Harvard University Press.

——. 1972a. *The Chinese Communists: Sketches and autobiographies of the old guard.* Westport, CT: Greenwood Press.

——. 1972b. *The long revolution.* New York: Random House.

Solinger, D. J. 1991. *China's transients and the state: A form of civil society?* Hong Kong: Chinese University of Hong Kong.

Solomon, R. 1969. Mao's effort to reintegrate the Chinese polity: Problems of authority and conflict in the Chinese social process. In *Chinese communist politics in action*, ed. A. Doak Barnett, 271–365. Seattle: University of Washington Press.

——. 1971. *Mao's revolution and Chinese political culture.* Berkeley: University of California Press.

Spector, Stanley. 1964. *Li Hung-chang and the Huai Army: A study in nineteenth-century Chinese regionalism.* Seattle: University of Washington Press.

Spence, J. D. 1974. *Emperor of China, self-portrait of K'ang-his.* New York: Knopt.

——. 1981. *The gate of heavenly peace: The Chinese and their revolution, 1895–1980.* New York: Viking Press.

——. 1988. *Ts'ao Yin and the K'ang-Hsi Emperor: Bondservant and master.* New Haven, CT: Yale University Press.

——. 1996. *God's Chinese son. The Taiping heavenly kingdom of Hong.* New York: W. W. Norton.

Spence, J. D., and J. E. Wills Jr. 1979. *From Ming to Ch'ing: Conquest, region and continuity in seventeenth century China.* New Haven, CT: Yale University Press.

Spies, M. 1997. *Arctic routes to fabled lands: Olivier Brunel and the passage to China and Cathay in the sixteenth century.* Amsterdam: Amsterdam University Press.

Spigelman, J. J. 2005. Judicial review and the integrity branch of government address. World Jurist Association Congress, Shanghai, September 8.

Stacey, J. 1983. *Patriarchy and socialist revolution in China.* Berkeley: University of California Press.

Starr, J. B. 1976. From the 10th Party Congress to the premiership of Hua Kuo-feng. *China Quarterly* 67 (September): 457–488.

Steinbauer, B. 1989. *Rechtsakt und Sprechakt: pragmalinguistische Untersuchungen zu deutschsprachigen Urkunden des 13. Jahrhunderts.* Innsbruck: Universität Innsbruck.

Stephens, T. 1992. *Order and discipline in China.* Seattle: University of Washington Press.

Stockman, N. 2000. *Understanding Chinese society.* Malden, MA: Polity Press.

Stranahan, P. 1990. *Molding the medium: The Chinese Communist Party and the "Liberation Daily."* Armonk, NY: M. E. Sharpe.

———. 1998. *Underground: The Shanghai Communist Party and the politics of survival, 1927–1937.* Lanham, MD: Rowman & Littlefield.

Strauss, J. C. 1998. *Strong institutions in weak politics: State building in Republican China.* Oxford, U.K.: Clarendon Press.

———. 2000. The evolution of republican government. In *Reappraising Republican China,* eds. F. Wakeman Jr. and R. L. Edmonds, 75–97. Oxford, U.K.: Oxford University Press.

Struve, L., trans. 1993. *Voices from the Ming-Qing cataclysm: China in tiger's jaw.* New Haven, CT: Yale University Press.

Struve, L. A. 1984. *The southern Ming, 1644–1662.* New Haven, CT: Yale University Press.

———. 1988. *The Ming-Qing conflict, 1619–1683: A historiography and source guide.* Ann Arbor, MI: Association for Asian Studies.

Su, Shuangbi. 1984. *Wu Han Zhuan* [A biography of Wu Han]. Beijing: Beijing Chubanshe.

Su, Tairen, ed. 2004. *Deng Xiaoping Sheng ping Quan Jilu: Yige Weiren he Tade Yige Shiji* [A complete chronology and biography of Deng Xiaoping]. Beijing: Zhongyang Wenxian Chubanshe.

Sulayman, Amir. 1991. *Al-Lughah al-Akkadiyah: Tarikhuha wa-Taewinuha wa-Qwaiduha* [Akkadian language]. al-Mawsil: Wizārat al-Ta'līm al-'Ālī wa-al-Ba'th al-'Ilmī, Jāmi'at al-Mawil, Dār al-Kutub.

——. 2002. *Namādhij min al-Kitābāt al-Mismārīyah* [Collection of Mismariyah writing]. Baghdād: Dā'irat al-Turāth al-'Arabī wa-al-Islāmī.

Suleski, R. 2002. *Civil government in warlord China: Tradition, modernization and Manchuria.* New York: Peter Lang.

Sun, Chenggu. 1983. *Lifa Quan yu Lifa Chengxu* [Legislative authority and legislative procedure]. Beijing: Renmin Chubanshe.

Sun, Jingyue, and Guo Janping, eds. 2000. *Fengxi Junfa Feng Yun Jishi* [Record of the history of Feng warlord]. Shenyang: Liaoning University Press.

Sun, Peiqing, and Li Guojun. 1995. *Zhongguo Jiaoyu Sixiang Shi* [A history of Chinese thought on education]. 3 vols. Shanghai: Huadong Shifan Daxue Chubanshe.

Sun, Yatsen. 1981–1985. *Sun Zhongshen Quanji* [Complete works of Sun Yatsen]. 3 vols. Beijing: Zhonghua Shuju.

——. 1981–1986. *Sun Zhongshen Xuanji* [Selected works of Sun Yatsen]. 5 vols. Beijing: Zhonghua Shuju.

——. 1990. *The three principles of the people.* Trans. Frank W. Price. Taipei: China Cultural Service.

——. 1994. *Prescriptions for saving China: Selected writings of Sun Yat-sen,* ed. J. L. Wei, R. H. Myers, and D. G. Gillin. Trans. J. L. Wei, E-su Zen, and L. Chao. Stanford, CA: Hoover Institution Press.

——. 2003. *Wode Huiyi* [My memoir]. Wuhan: Hubei Renmin Chubanshe.

Sun, Yeli. 1996. *Gongheguo Jingji Fengyun Zhongde Chen Yun* [Chen Yun in the economic movements to establish PRC]. Beijing: Zhongyang Wenxian Chubanshe.

Sun, Yixian. 2001. *Zai Damo Nabian: Qinli Lin Biao Zhuiji Shijian he Zhong Meng Guanxi Bozhe: Yige Qianzhu Meng Waijiaoguan de Huiyilu* [The other side of the desert: The incident of the crash of Lin Biao's air plane and the Sino-Mongolian relationship: A memoir of diplomat]. Beijing: Zhongguo Qingnian Chubanshe.

Sunstein, C. 1995. Problems with rules. *California Law Review* 83:953.

——. 1996. *Legal reasoning and political conflict*. New York: Oxford University Press.

Sutton, D. S. 1980. *Provincial militarism and the Chinese Republic: The Yunnan Army, 1905–25*. Ann Arbor: University of Michigan Press.

Swope, K. M., Jr. 2001. The three great campaigns of the Wanli Emperor, 1592–1600: Court, military, and society in late sixteenth-century China. PhD diss., University of Michigan.

——, ed. 2005. *Warfare in China since 1600*. Berlington: Ashgate.

Tan, C. C. 1955. *The Boxer catastrophe*. New York: Columbia University Press.

Tan, Yiqing. 2000. *Zhongguo Lidai Zhanlüe Sixiang Jiaocheng* [Textbook for military strategies of Chinese dynasties]. Beijing: Military Science Press.

Tanaka, Hitoshi. 2002. *1930-nendai Chūgoku seijishi kenkyū: Chūgoku Kyōsantō no kiki to saisei* [A study of the political history of China in 1930s]. Tōkyō: Keisō Shobō.

Tang, Fei. 2005. *Hu Yaobang Zhuan* [A biography of Hu Yaobang]. Beijing: Renmin Chubanshe.

Tang, Jun-I. 1973. *Yuan dao pian* [An original treatise of Dao]. Vol. 1. Zhongguo Zhexue Lun. Taipei: Xinya Shuyuan Yenjiuso.

Tang, Lan. 1975. Mawangdui Chutu Lao Zi Yiben Juanqian Guyishu de Yanjiu [Research on the lost ancient text preceding the Lao Zi B discovered at Mawangdui]. *Kaogu xuebao* 1:7–38.

Tang, Tsou. 1976. Prolegomenon to the study of informal groups in CCP politics. *China Quarterly* 65 (January): 98–114.

Tang, Xiaobing. 1996. *Global space and the nationalist discourse of modernity: The historical thinking of Liang Qichao.* Stanford, CA: Stanford University Press.

Tanigawa, M. 1985. *Medieval Chinese society and the local community.* Trans. and ed. J. A. Fogel. Berkeley: University of California Press.

Tanner, M. S. 1990. The organizational evolution of Communist Party control over lawmaking in China. In *Facing East/facing West: North America and the Asia/Pacific region in the 1990s,* 218–226. Kalamazoo: University of Michigan Press.

——. 1994a. The erosion of Central Party control over lawmaking. *China Quarterly* 138 (June): 381–403.

——. 1994b. Law in China: The terra incognita of political studies. *China Exchange News,* 22 (4 Winter): 20–24.

——. 1994c. Organizations and politics in China's post-Mao law-making system. In *Domestic law reforms in post-Mao China,* ed. Potter, 56–96. Armonk, NY: M. E. Sharpe.

——. 1995. How a bill becomes a law in China: Stages and processes in lawmaking. *China Quarterly* 141 (March): 39–64.

——. 1999. *The politics of lawmaking in post-Mao China: Institutions, processes, and democratic prospects.* Oxford, U.K.: Clarendon Press.

Taofen. 2000. *Taofen Zishu* [An autobiography of Taofen]. Beijing: Xuelin Chubanshe.

Tay, A. E. 1987. The struggle for law in China. *University of British Columbia Law Review* 21:562.

———. 1990. Communist visions, communist realities, and the role of law. *Journal of Law and Society* 17:155.

Taylor, R. L. 1990. *The religious dimensions of Confucianism.* Albany: State University of New York Press.

Teiwes, F. C. 1966. The purge of provincial leaders, 1957–1958. *China Quarterly* 27 (July–September): 14–32.

———. 1971. Rectification campaigns and purges in Communist China, 1950–61. PhD diss., Columbia University.

———. 1974b. *Provincial leadership in China: The Cultural Revolution and its aftermath.* Ithaca, NY: Cornell University Press.

———. 1976. The origins of rectification: Inner party purges and education before liberation. *China Quarterly* 65:15–53.

———. 1978. *Elite discipline in China: Coercive and persuasive approaches, 1950–1953.* Canberra: Australian National University Press.

———. 1984. *Leadership, legitimacy, and conflict in China.* Armonk, NY: M. E. Sharpe.

———.1979. *Politics and purges in China, rectification and the decline of party norms 1950–1965.* Armonk, NY: M. E. Sharpe.

———. 1988. Mao and his lieutenants. *The Australian Journal of Chinese Affairs* 19/20:1–80.

———. 1990. *Politics at Mao's court: Gao gang and party factionalism in the early 1950s.* Armonk, NY: M. E. Sharpe.

———. 1993. *Politics and purges in China.* Armonk, NY: M. E. Sharpe.

———. 2001. Normal politics with Chinese characteristics. *The China Journal* 45:255.

Teiwes, F. C., and W. Sun. 1995. From a Leninist to a charismatic party: The CCP's changing leadership, 1937–1945. In *New perspectives on the Chinese Communist Revolution*. ed. T. Saich and Hans J. Van de Ven, 339–406. Armonk, NY: M. E. Sharpe.

——. 1996. *The tragedy of Lin Biao: Riding the tiger during the Cultural Revolution, 1966–1971.* Honolulu: University of Hawaii Press.

——. 2007. *The end of the Maoist era: Chinese politics during the twilight of the Cultural Revolution, 1972–1976.* Armonk, NY: M.E. Sharpe.

Terrill, R. 1999. *Madame Mao: The White Boned Demon.* Stanford, CA: Stanford University Press.

Thaxton, R. 1997. *Salt of the earth: The political origins of peasant protest and Communist Revolution in China.* Berkeley: University of California Press.

Thireau, I., and L. Hua. 1997. Legal disputes and the debate about legitimate norms. In *China Review*, ed. KuanHs in-chi and M. Brosseau. Hong Kong: Chinese University Press.

Thompson, P. 1979. *The Shen Tzu fragments.* Oxford, U.K.: Oxford University Press.

Thompson, R. 1995. *China's local councils in the age of constitutional reform, 1898–1911.* Cambridge, MA: Harvard University Press.

Thornton, R. C. 1972. The structure of communist politics. *World Politics* 24 (4) July.

——. 1973. *China, the struggle for power, 1917–1922.* Bloomington: Indiana University Press.

Thurston, A. F. 1988. *Enemies of the people: The ordeal of intellectuals in China's Great Cultural Revolution.* Cambridge, MA: Harvard University Press.

Tian, Gang. 2005. *Lu Xun yu Zhongguo Shiren Chuantong* [Lu Xun and the tradition of Chinese intellectuals]. Beijing: Zhongguo Shehui Kexue Chubanshe.

Tian, Guoliang. 1989. *Hu Yaobang Zhuan* [A biography of Hu Yaobang]. Beijing: Zhonggong Dangshi Ziliao Chubanshe.

Tian, Jianrong. 2004. *Zhongguo Kaoshi Sixiang Shi* [A history of Chinese thought on examination]. Beijing: Shangwu.

Tian, Yuqing. 1991. *Dongjin Menfa Zhengzhi* [Politics of nobilities in eastern Jin]. Beijing: People's University Press.

———. 2004. *Qin, Han, Wei, Jin Shi Tiansuo* [Further studies on the history of Qin, Han, Wei, and Jin]. Beijing: Zhonghua Shuju.

Tiefer, C. 2004. *Veering right: How the Bush Administration subverts the law for conservative causes.* Berkeley: University of California Press.

Tillman, H. C. 1992. *Confucian discourse and Chu His's ascendancy.* Honolulu: University of Hawaii Press.

Tong Dian. 2005. 2 vols. ed. Du You (Tang). Beijing: Beijing Tushuguan Chubanshe.

Tong, H. K. 1952. *Jiang Zongtong Zhuan* [A biography of President Jiang]. Taipei: Zhonghua Wenhua Chubanshe.

Tong, J. 1991. *Disorder under heaven: Collective violence in the Ming dynasty.* Stanford, CA: Stanford University Press.

Tong, Te-kong, and Li Tsung-jen. 1979. *The memoirs of Li Tsung-jen.* Boulder, CO: Westview Press.

Toshihiko, Uchiyama. 1978. *Maōtai bosho Keihō, Jūdaikyō, Shō, Dōgen shoko* [A brief study of the silk manuscripts unearthed at Mawangdui— *Jing Fa, Shi Da Jing, Cheng, and Dao Yuan*]. *Tōhōgaku* 56:1–16.

Townsend, J. 1969. *Political participation in Communist China.* Berkeley: University of California Press.

Townsend, J. R., and B. Womack. 1986. *Politics in China.* 2 vols. Boston: Little, Brown.

Tsai, Shih-Shan H. 2001. *Perpetual happiness: The Ming Emperor Yongle.* Seattle: University of Washington Press.

Tsien, Tsuen-hsuin. 1996. *The eunuchs in the Ming dynasty.* New York: State University of New York Press.

——. 2004. *Written on bamboo and silk*. Chicago: University of Chicago Press.

Tsou, Tang. 1999. *The Cultural Revolution and post-Mao reforms: A historical perspective*. Chicago: University of Chicago Press.

Tu, Wei-ming. 1985. *Confucian thought: Selfhood as creative transformation*. Albany: State University of New York.

——. 1986. Toward a third epoch of Confucian humanism: A background understanding. In *Confucianism: The dynamics of tradition*, ed. I. Eber, 3–21. New York: Macmillan.

——. 1993. *Way, learning, and politics: Essays on the Confucian intellectual*. Albany: State University of New York.

Tumen and Xiao Sike. 2003. *Tebie Shenpan: Lin Biao, Jiang Qing-Fangeming Jituan Shoushen Shilu* [Special judgment: A record of court ruling against anti-party faction of Lin Biao and Jiang Qing]. Beijing: Zhongyang Wenxian Chubanshe.

Tung, Yueh. 2001. *The tower of myriad mirrors*. Trans. Shuen-fu Lin and L. J. Schulz. Ann Arbor, MI: Center for Chinese Studies.

Tuo, Tuo, ed. 1936. *Song Shi* [The history of Song]. Beijing, Zhonghua Shuju.

Turner, K. 1989. The theory of law in the *Ching-fa*. *Early China* 14:55.

——. 1990. Sage kings and laws in the Chinese and Greek traditions. In *Heritage of China: Contemporary perspectives on Chinese civilization*, ed. P. S. Ropp, ch.4. Berkeley: University of California Press.

Turner, K., J. V. Feinerman, and R. K. Guy, eds. 2000. *The limits of the rule of law in China*. Seattle: University of Washington Press.

Twitchett, D. C. 1996. How to be an emperor: T'ang T'ai-tsung's vision of his role. *Asia Major* 3rd Series volume 9, parts 1–2: 1–102.

Twitchett, D. C., and J. K. Fairbank, eds. 1978. *The Cambridge history of China: The Ming dynasty, 1368–1644*. New York: Cambridge University Press.

Twitchett, D. C., and J. K. Fairbank, eds. 1983. *The Cambridge history of China.* Vol. 12, *Republican China, 1912–1949, Part 1.* New York: Cambridge University Press.

——. 1986. *The Cambridge History of China.* Vol. 13, *Republican China, 1912–1949, Part 2.* New York, Cambridge University Press.

Übelhör, M. 1986. *Wang Gen (1483–1541) und seine Lehre: Eine kritische Position im späten Konfuzianismus.* Berlin: D. Reimer.

Uchida, T, ed. 2005. *Kanjo keishō shi.* [Bangu's criminal law]. Kyoto: Dōshishia University.

Uhalley, S. Jr. 1988. *A history of the Chinese Communist Party.* Stanford, CA: Stanford University Press.

Unger, J. 1993. *Using the past to serve the present: Historiography and politics in contemporary China.* Armonk, NY: M. E. Sharpe.

Vinacke, H. 1920. *Modern constitutional development in China.* Princeton, NJ: Princeton University Press.

Ven, H. van de. 1991. *From friend to comrade: The founding of the Chinese Communist Party, 1920–1927.* Berkeley: University of California Press.

——. 1996. Public finance and the rise of warlordism. *Modern Asian Studies* 30 (4): 829–868.

——. 1997. The military in the Republic. *China Quarterly* 150:52–74.

——. 2000. *Warfare in Chinese history.* Leiden: E. J. Brill.

——. 2003. *War and nationalism in China 1925–1945.* London: Routledge.

Van der Sprenkel, S. 1962. *Legal institutions in Manchu China.* London: University of London Press.

Van Slyke, L. P. 1967. *Enemies and friends: The united front in Chinese Communist history.* Stanford, CA: Stanford University Press.

——, ed. 1968. *The Chinese Communist Movement; A report of the United States War Department, July 1945.* ed. L. P. Van Slyke. Stanford, CA: Stanford University Press.

Vermeer, E. B., and I. d'Hooghe, eds. 2002. *China's legal reforms and their political limits.* Richmond, U.K.: Curzon.

Vinacke, H. M. 1922. *Modern constitutional development in China.* Princeton, NJ: Princeton University Press.

Vladimirov, P. P. 1975. *The Vladimirov diaries: Yenan, China, 1942–45.* Garden City, NY: Doubleday.

Vogel, E. 1969. *Canton under communism.* Cambridge, MA: Harvard University Press.

Vollmer, J. M. 2000. *Clothed to rule the universe: Ming to Qing textiles at the Art Institute of Chicago.* Seattle: University of Washington Press.

Von Glahn, R. 1996. *Fountain of fortune: Money and monetary policy in China, eleventh to seventeenth centuries, 1000–1700.* Berkeley: University of California Press.

Wagner, R. G. 1982. *Reenacting the Heavenly Vision: The Role of Religion in the Taiping Rebellion.* Berkeley: University of California Press.

Wakeman, F. Jr. 1966. *Strangers at the gate: Social disorder in South China, 1839–1861.* Berkeley: University of California Press.

——. 1975. *The fall of imperial China.* New York: Free Press.

——, ed. 1981. *Ming and Qing historical studies in the People's Republic of China.* Berkeley: University of California Press.

——. 1985. *The Great Enterprise: The Manchu reconstruction of imperial order in seventeenth century China.* 2 vols. Berkeley: University of California Press.

——. 1995. *Policing Shanghai, 1927–1937.* Berkeley: University of California Press.

———. 2003. *Spymaster: Dai Li and the Chinese secret service*. Berkeley: University of California Press.

Wakeman, F. Jr., and C. Grant, eds. 1976. *Conflict and control in late imperial China*. Berkeley: University of California Press.

Wakeman, F. Jr., and R. L. Edmonds, eds. 2000. *Reappraising Republican China*. Oxford, U.K.: Oxford University Press.

Walder, A. G. 1978. *Chang Ch'un-ch'iao and Shanghai's January revolution*. Ann Arbor: University of Michigan Press.

Waldron, A. 1991. The warlord: Twentieth-century Chinese understandings of violence, militarism, and imperialism. *The American Historical Review* 96 (4): 1073–1100.

———. 1992. *The Great Wall of China: From history to myth*. New York: Cambridge University Press.

———. 1995. *From war to nationalism: China's turning point, 1924–1925*. New York: Cambridge University Press.

Wales, N. 1945. *The Chinese labor movement*. New York: John Day Company.

Waley, A. 1949. *The life and times of Po Chu-I*. London: G. Allen & Unwin.

Waley-Cohen, J. 1998. Religion, war, and empire-building in eighteenth-century China. *International History Review* 20 (2): 336–352.

———. 2000. Civil-military relations in imperial China: Introduction. *War and Society* 18 (2): 4–7.

Walker, A. R. 1998. *Creating heaven, creating earth: An epic myth of the Lahu people in Yunnan*. Seattle: University of Washington Press.

Walker, R. L. 1947–1948. The control system of the Chinese government. *The Far Eastern Quarterly* vii:2–21.

Walton, L. A. 1999. *Academies and society in Southern Sung China*. Honolulu: University of Hawaii Press.

Wan Renyuan and Fang Qingqiu, eds. 1994. *Jiang Jieshi Nianpu* [Chronological biography of Chiang Kaishek]. Beijing: Dangan Chubanshe.

Wang, B. 2005. *Illuminations from the past: Trauma, memory, and history in modern China.* Stanford, CA: Stanford University Press.

Wang, Bisheng. 1986. *Deng Tuo Pingzhuan* [Critical biography of Deng Tuo]. Beijing: Qunzhong.

Wang, Cheng. 1982. *The Kuomintang: A sociological study in demoralization.* New York: Garland Publishing.

Wang, Cheng-Chih. 2002. *Words kill: Calling for the destruction of "class enemies" in China, 1949–1953.* New York: Routledge.

Wang, Chengguang. 1996. *Peng Dehuai.* Hangzhou: Zhejiang Renmin Chubanshe.

Wang, Cheng-mien. 1999. *The life and career of Hung Ch'eng-Ch'ou, 1593–1665: Public service in a time of dynastic change.* Ann Arbor, MI: Association for Asian Studies.

Wang, D., and S. Wei, eds. 2005. *Dynastic crisis and cultural innovation: From the late Ming to the late Qing and beyond.* Cambridge, MA: Harvard University Press.

Wang, Dongxing. 1993. *Wang Dongxing Riji* [Wang Dongxing diaries]. Beijing: ShiHui Kexue Chubanshe.

———. 1994. Mao Zhuxi Zai Fensui Lin Biao Fangeming Zhengbian Yinmo de Rizili [Chairman Mao in the days of crushing Lin Biao's counter-revolutionary conspiracy of coup d'état. *Zhonggong Dangshi Ziliao* [Materials on the history of Chinese Communist Party] 49:56–82.

———. 1997. *Wang Dongxing Huiyi: Mao Zedong yu Lin Biao Fangeming Jituan de Douzheng* [Wang Dongxing's memoir: The struggle between Mao Zedong and Lin Biao's counter-revolutionary clique]. Beijing: Dangdai Zhongguo Chubanshe.

Wang, Fei-Ling. 2005. *Organizing through division and exclusion: China's Hukou system.* Stanford, CA: Stanford University Press.

Wang Gong'an and Mao Lei, eds. 1988. *Guo Gong Liang Dang Guanxi Shi* [A history of KMT CPP Relations]. Wuhan: Wuhan Chubanshe.

Wang, Gungwu. 1963. *The structure of power in North China and during the Five Dynasties.* Kuala Lumpur: University of Malaya Press.

Wang, Hongxu, ed. 1962. *Ming Shi Gao.* [A draft history of Ming]. Taibei: Wenhai Chubanshe.

Wang, Hsiao-po, and L. Chang. 1986 *Philosophical foundations of Han Fei's political theory.* Honolulu: University of Hawaii Press.

Wang, Jieping. 1982. *Zhongguo Falu yu Fashi Sixiang* [Chinese law and legal thought]. Taipei: Sanmin.

Wang, Jing. 1996. *High culture fever: Politics, aesthetics, and ideology in Deng's China.* Berkeley: University of California Press.

Wang, Ming. 1979. *Mao's betrayal.* Moscow: Progress Publishers.

Wang, Pi. 1979. *Commentary on the "Lao Tzu."* Trans. A. Rump in collaboration with W. Chan. Honolulu: University of Hawaii Press.

Wang, S. 1995. *Failure of charisma: The Cultural Revolution in Wuhan.* New York: Oxford University Press.

Wang, Shixiang. 1998. *Connoisseurship of Chinese furniture: Ming and early Qing dynasties.* London: Kegan Paul.

Wang, Shiyi. 1992. *Liu Shaoqi dang jian si xiang yan jiu* [A research on Liu Shaoqi's idea of party cultivation]. Nanjing: University of Nanjing Press.

Wang, Shounan, ed. 1999. *Zhongguo Lidai Sixiangjia: Zeng Guofan, Guo Songtao, Wang Tao, Xue Fucheng, Zheng guanying, Hu Liyuan.* Taibei: Taiwan Shangwu.

Wang, Tao. 1984a. Da qiang ruolun. *Jindai Zhongguo dui xifang ji lieqiang renshi ziliao huibian* 2 (2): 1144–1145.

——. 1984b. Lun bianfa. *Jindai Zhongguo dui xifang ji lieqiang renshi ziliao huibian* 3 (2): 858–860.

Wang, Wenzheng. 2006. *Gongheguo Dashen Pan: Shenpan Lin Biao, Jiang Qing Fange ming Jituan Qinliji* [A eyewitness account of the trial of Gang of Four of Lin Biao and Jiang Qing]. Beijing: Dangdai Zhongguo.

Wang, Xiang, ed. 1999. *Yan Xishan yu Jinxi* [Yan Xishan and Jinxi]. Nanjing: Jiangsu Guji Cubanshe.

Wang, Xiaohua. 2000. *Beiyang Xiaojiang Sun Chuanfang* [Brave general of Beiyang Sun Chuanfang]. Shanghai: Renmin Chubanshe.

Wang, Xilan. 1997. *Zhan shen Liu Bocheng* [God of war: Liu Bocheng]. Beijing: Zhongguo Dangan Chubanshe.

Wang, Xuewen. 1969. *Zhonggong Wenhua Dageming yu Hongweibing* [The Chinese Cultural Revolution and Red Guard]. Taipei: Guoji Guanxi Yanjiusuo.

Wang, Ya Ping. 2004. *Urban poverty, housing, and social change in China.* New York: Routledge.

Wang, Yanan. 1981. *Zhongguo Guanliao Zhengzhi Yanjiu.* Beijing: Zhongguo Shehui Kexue Chubanshe.

Wang, Yu-ch'uan. 1949. An outline of the central government of the former Han dynasty. *Harvard Journal of Asiatic Studies* 12:134–187.

Wang, Yungao. 2004. *Caomang Shangjiangjun: Lu Rongting Zhuanji* [The biography of Great General Lu Rongting]. Nanjing: Guangxi Renmin Chubanshe.

Wang Zhang Jiang Yao zhuanan zu, ed. 1976–1977. *Wang Hongwen, Zhang Chunqiao, Jiang Qing, Yao Wenyuan fan dang ji tuan zui zheng* [The evidence of the crimes of the anti party group of Wang Hongwen, Zhang Chunqiao, Jiang Qing and Yao Wenyuan]. 3 vols. Beijing: Zhonggong Zhongyang Bangongting.

Wang, Zhangling. 1967. *Zhonggong de Wenyi Zhengfeng* [Chinese Communist literary rectification]. Taipei: Guoji Guanxi Yanjiusuo.

Wang, Zhenghua. 1995. *Lin Biao Wangchao Xingshuai Shilu* [A true account of the rise and fall of Lin Biao's dynasty]. Hong Kong: Tai Ping Shan Publishing & Cultural Company.

Wank, D. L. 1994. The institutional culture of capitalism: Social relations and private enterprise in a Chinese city. Paper presented at the annual meeting of the Association for Asian Studies, Boston, March 23–27.

———. 1995. Bureaucratic patronage and private business: Changing networks of power in urban China. In *The waning of the communist state: The economic origins of political decline in China and Hungary*. ed. A. Walder, 153–183. Berkeley: University of California Press.

———. 1996. The institutional process of market clientelism: *Guanxi* and private business in a South China city. *China Quarterly* 144:820–838.

———. 1999. *Commodifying communism: Business, trust, and politics in a Chinese city*. New York: Cambridge University Press.

Wasserman, N., and W. Jefferey. 1991. *Student protests in twentieth-century China: The view from Shanghai*. Stanford, CA: Stanford University Press.

Wasserstein, B. 1999. *Secret war in Shanghai*. Boston: Houghton Mifflin.

Wasserstrom, J. 1991a. *Student protests in twentieth-century China: The view from Shanghai*. Stanford, CA: Stanford University Press.

———. 1991b. Tiananmen: More lessons for scholars. *CCP Research Newsletter* 8:66–79.

———. 1992. Towards a social history of the Chinese revolution: A review-Part I: The evolution of a field. *Social History* 17 (1): 1–21 and Part II: The state of the field 17 (2): 289–317.

Wasserstrom, J., and E. Perry Elizabeth. 1992. *Popular protest and political culture in China: Learning from 1989.* Boulder, CO: Westview Press.

Watson, B. 1958. *Ssu-ma Ch'ien, Grand Historian of China.* New York: Columbia University Press.

Watson, J. 1984. *Class and social stratification in post-revolution China.* New York: Cambridge University Press.

Watson, J. L., and P. B. Ebrey. 1986. *Kinship organization in late imperial China, 1000–1940.* Berkeley: University of California Press.

Watson, W. 2000. *Arts of China, 900–1700.* New Haven, CT: Yale University Press.

Watt, J. R. 1972. *The district magistrate in late imperial China.* New York: Columbia University Press.

Weakland, J. H. 1950. The organization of action in Chinese Culture. *Psychiatry* 13:361–370.

Wechsler, H. J. 1974. *Mirror to the son of heaven: Wei Cheng at the court of T'ang T'ai-tsung.* New Haven, CT: Yale University Press.

———. 1979. The founding of the T'ang dynasty: Kao-tsu (reign 618–626). In *The Cambridge history of China, vol. 3 Sui and T'and China, 589–906 AD, Part I*, ed. D. C. Twitchett, 150–187. Cambridge: Cambridge University Press.

———. 1985. *Offerings of jade and silk: Ritual and symbol in the legitimation of the Tang dynasty.* New Haven, CT: Yale University Press.

Wei, Jingsheng. 1997. *The courage to stand alone: Letters from prison and other writings.* Trans. and ed. K. M. Torgeson. New York: Viking.

———. 1980. Yao minzhu haishiyao xinde ducai. Reprinted in *Ming Bao*, January, 29–30.

Wei, W. 1985. *Counter-revolution in China: The nationalists in Jiangxi during the Soviet period.* Ann Arbor: University of Michigan Press.

Wei, Weijun. 1988. *Dangde Bajie Shizhong Quanhui* [The tenth plenum of the eighth PC] *Zhongguo Dangshi Zhuanti Jiangyi* [Teaching materials on specific issues in the CCP history]. Beijing: CCParty School Press.

Weisbard, P. H., and D. Schonberg. 1989. *Jewish law: Bibliography of sources and scholarship in English*. Littleton: Fred B. Rothman.

Weller, R. P. 1994. *Resistance, chaos, and control in China: Taiping rebels, Taiwanese ghosts, and Tiananmen*. Seattle: University of Washington Press.

Wen, Chihua. 1995. *The red mirror: Children of China's Cultural Revolution*. Ed. B. Jones. Boulder, CO: Westview Press.

Wen, Fang. 2004. *Bing Huo*. Beijing: Zhongguo Wenshi Chubanshe.

Wen, Fei, ed. 2004a. *Wo suo zhidao de "Beiyang Sanjie": Wang Shizhen, Duan Qirui, Feng Guozhang* [The three heroes of Beiyang, Wang Shizhen, Duan Qirei, and Fong Guozhang that I know]. Beijing: Zhongguo Wenshi Chubanshe.

——, ed. 2004b. *Wo suo zhidao de Wu Peifu* [The Wu Peifu that I know]. Beijing: Zhongguo Wenshi Chubanshe.

——, ed. 2004c. *Wo suo zhidao de Zhang Zuolin* [My personal knowledge of Zhang Zuolin]. Beijing: Zhongguo Wenshi Chubanshe.

——, ed. 2004d. *Wo suo zhidao de Yuan Shikai* [My personal knowledge of Yuan Shi kai]. Beijing: Zhongguo Wenshi Chubanshe.

——, ed. 2004e. *Wo suo zhidao de Zhang Zongchang* [The Zhang zongchang that I know]. Beijing: Zhongguo Wenshi Chubanshe.

——, ed. 2005. *Wo suo zhidao de Hanjian Wang Jingwei he Chen Bijun* [The Wang Jingwei and Chen Bijun that I know]. Beijing: Zhongguo Wenshi Chubanshe.

Wen, Gongzhi. 1930. *Zuijin Sanshihnien Zhongguo Junshishi* [A history of Chinese military affairs in the last thirty years]. 2 vols. Shanghai: Taipingyang Shudian.

Wen, Shaohua. 2007. Wang Jingwei Zhuan [A biography of Wen Jingwei]. Beijing: Tuanjie Chubanshe.

Wen, Si. 2003a. *Wosuo Zhidao de Bai Chongxi* [The Bai Chongxi that I know]. Beijing: Zhongguo Wenshi Chubanshe.

——, ed. 2003b. *Wosuo Zhidao de Jiang Jieshi* [The Jiang Jieshi the I know]. Beijing: Zhongguo Wenshi Chubanshe.

Wen, Wen, ed. 2006. *Jiu Zhongguo Junshi Yuanxiao Midang* [Secret archives of military academies in old China]. Beijing: Zhongguo Wenshi Chubanshe.

Weng, Yuan. 2003. *Wozai Jiang Jieshi Fuzi Shenbian Sishisan Nian* [Thirteen years beside Chiang Kaishek and his son]. Ed. Wang Feng. Beijing: Huawen Chubanshe.

Wenxian, Zhongyang, ed. 2005. *Deng Xiaoping Zishu*. Beijing: Jiefangjun Chubanshe.

Westad, O. A. 2002. *Decisive encounters: The Chinese civil war, 1945–1950*. Stanford, CA: Stanford University Press.

Westbrook, R. 1985. Biblical and cuneiform law codes. *Revue Biblique* 92:247–264.

——. 1988. *Studies in biblical and cuneiform law*. Paris: Gabalda.

White, G. 1976. *The politics of class and class origin: The case of the Cultural Revolution*. Canberra: Contemporary China Center, Australian National University.

White, L. 1989. *Policies of chaos: The organizational causes of violence in China's Cultural Revolution*. Princeton, NJ: Princeton University Press.

White, T. 1978. *In search of history*. New York: Harper & Row.

Whiting, S. 2001. *Power and wealth in rural China*. Cambridge: Cambridge University Press.

Whitson, W. W. 1972. *The military and political power in China in the 1970s*. New York: Praeger.

——. 1973. *Chinese military and political leaders and the distribution of power in China, 1956–71.* Santa Monica, CA: Rand Corporation.

Whitson, W. W., and Huang Chen-hsia. 1973. *The Chinese high command: A history of communist military politics, 1927–1971.* New York: Praeger.

Whyte, M. K. *Small groups and political rituals in China.* Berkeley: University of California Press.

Wilbur, C. M. 1984. *The nationalist revolution in China, 1923–1928.* Cambridge: Cambridge University Press.

Wilbur, C. M., and Julie Lien-ying How. 1989. *Missionaries of revolution: Soviet advisers and nationalist China, 1920–1927.* Cambridge, MA: Harvard University Press.

Williamsen, T. M. 1975. Political training and work at the Whampoa Military Academy prior to the Northern Expedition. PhD diss., Duke University.

Willmott, W. E. 1972. *Economic organization in Chinese society.* Stanford, CA: Stanford University Press.

Wilson, D. 1977a. *The Long March, 1935: The epic of Chinese communism's survival.* Harmondsworth: Penguin.

——, ed. 1977b. *Mao Tse-tung in the scales of history: A preliminary assessment.* Cambridge, MA: Harvard University Press.

——. 1984. *Zhou Enlai: A biography.* New York: Viking.

——. 1991. *China's revolutionary war.* London: Weidenfeld and Nicolson.

Wilson, T. A. 1995. *Genealogy of the way: The construction and uses of the Confucian tradition in late imperial China.* Stanford, CA: Stanford University Press.

——. 2002. *On sacred grounds: Culture, society, politics, and the formation of the cult of Confucius.* Cambridge, MA: Harvard University Press.

Witke, R. 1977. *Comrade Chiang Ch'ing*. Boston: Little, Brown.

Wong, John. 1973. *Land reform in the People's Republic of China: Institutional transformation of agriculture*. New York: Praeger.

Wong, Yuan. 2003. *Wozai Jiang Jieshi Fuzi Shenbian Sishisan Nian* [Forty three years next to Jiang Jieshi and Jiang Jingguo: An oral history]. Beijing: Huawen Chubanshe.

Wood, A. 1995. *Limits to autocracy: From Sung neo-Confucianism to a doctrine of political rights*. Honolulu: University of Hawaii Press.

Woodhead, H. G. W. 1925. *The truth about the Chinese Republic*. London: Hurst & Blackett Ltd.

——, ed. 1912–1939. *China year book*. 20 vols. Shanghai: North China Daily News & Herald.

Woody, P. R. Jr. 1989. Communist Party as political institution. In *Chinese politics from Mao to Deng*, ed. V. C. Falkenheim, 165–202. New York: Professors World Peace Academy.

World Journal. 1989. July 15, p. 31.

Worthing, P. M. 2007. *A military history of modern China*. New York: Praeger.

Worthy, E. H. 1975. The founding of Sung China, 950–1000: Integrative changes in military and political institutions. PhD diss., Princeton University.

Wou, O.Ying-Kwang. 1970. Militarism in modern China as exemplified in the career of Wu P'ei-fu. PhD diss., Columbia University.

Wright, M. C. 1957. *The last stand of Chinese conservatism: The T'ung Chih restoration, 1862–1874*. Stanford, CA: Stanford University Press.

——. 1968. *China in revolution*. New Haven, CT: Yale University Press.

Wu, Baopu, and Li Zhiying. 2007. *Qin Bangxian (Bogu) Zhuan* [A biography of Bogu]. Beijing: Dangshi Chubanshe.

Wu, Changyi. 1993. *Qiangu Gongchen Yang Hucheng* [Immortal General Yang Hucheng]. Beijing: Wenshi Chubanshe.

——, ed. 2001. *Hun Duan Zijincheng* [Lost ghost in forbidden city]. Beijing: Zhongguo Wenshi Chubanshe.

Wu, Daying et al. 1987. *Zhongguo Shehuizhuyi Falu Jiben Lilun* [Basic theory of China's socialist legal system]. Beijing: Falu Chubanshe.

Wu, De. 2004. *Wude Koushu: Shinian Fengyu Jishi* [The record of ten years of turbulence, narrated by Wu De]. Ed. Fang Tan. Beijing: Dangdai Zhongguo.

Wu, Haimin. 1990. *Gongheguo Fachu Zuihou Tongdie: A report on Wuwan Tanguan Zishou* [Republican last announcement: Fifty south and corrupted officials turned themselves in]. Beijing: Xueyuan Chubanshe.

Wu, Han. 1972. *Hai Rui dismissed from office*. Trans. C. C. Huang. Honolulu: University of Hawaii Press.

——. 1989. *Zhu Yuanzhang Zhuan* [A biography of Zhu Yuanzhang]. Shanghai: Shanghai Shudian.

Wu, Jianxiong, ed. 1986. *Zhonghua Minguo de Dizao yu Hanwei Zhe* [The founder and guardian of the Republic of China]. Taibei: Mingxong Press.

Wu, Jingping. 1992. *Song Ziwen Ping Zhuan* [Song Ziwen: A biography]. Fuzhou: Fujian Renmin Chubanshe.

——. 1998. *Song Ziwen Zhengzhi Shengya Biannian* [Song Ziwen political chronology]. Fuzhou: Fujian Renmin Chubanshe.

Wu, K. C. 1928. *Ancient Chinese political theories*. Shanghai: Commercial Press.

Wu, Runsheng. 2006. *Lin Biao yu Wenhua Dageming* [Lin Biao and the Cultural Revolution]. Carle Place, NY: Mingjing Chubanshe.

Wu, S. H. 1967. The memorial systems of the Qing dynasty. *Harvard Journal of Asiatic Studies*, 27:7–75.

———. 1970. *Communication and imperial control in China: Evolution of the palace memorial system, 1693–1735.* Cambridge, MA: Harvard University Press.

———. 1970a. Emperors at work: The daily schedules of the Kang-his and Yung-cheng emperors, 1661–1735. *Qinghua Journal of Chinese Studies* 8:1 and 2:210–217.

———. 1971. Qing Dai Qunjichu Jianzhi Tisai Jiantao [A reappraisal of the establishment of the Grand Council under the Qing]. *Ku Kong Wen Xian* 2 (4): 21–45.

Wu, S. H. L. 1970. *Communication and imperial control in China: Evolution of the palace memorial system, 1693–1735.* Cambridge, MA: Harvard University Press.

Wu, Shuchen. 2004. *Zhongguo Falü Sixiang Shi* [History of Chinese legal thoughts]. Beijing: Falu Chubanshe.

Wu, Silas H. L. 1970. *Communication and imperial control in China: Evolution of the palace memorial system, 1693–1735.* Cambridge, MA: Harvard University Press.

Wu, Tan. 1992. *Da Qing Lü Li Tongkao Jiaozhu* [A comprehensive investigation of the Great Qing Code and Regulations, collated and annotated]. Ed. Ma Janshi and Yang Yutang. Beijing: Zhongguo Zhengfa Daxue Chubanshe.

Wu, Tienwei. 1974. *Mao Tse-tung and the Tsunyi Conference.* Washington, DC: Center for Chinese Research Materials, Association of Research Libraries.

———. 1976. *The Sian incident: A pivotal point in modern Chinese history.* Ann Arbor: Center for Chinese Studies, University of Michigan.

———. 1983. *Lin Biao and the Gang of Four: Contra-Confucianism in historical and intellectual perspective.* Carbondale: Southern Illinois University Press.

Wu, Tingxie. 2007. *Duan Qirei Nianpu: Wu Peifu Zheng Zhuan*. Beijing: Zhonghua Shuju.

Wu, Xiuquan. 1986. *Wo de shengya: 1908–1949* [My career: 1908–1949]. Beijing: Renmin Chubanshe.

Wuchanjieji Wenhua Dageming Ziliao Huibian [Collected materials on the Great Proletarian Cultural Revolution]. 1967. Beijing: Hebei Beijing Shifan Xueyuan.

Wuji, Changsun. 1983. *Tang Lü shuyi* [Tang Code]. Ed. Liu Junwen. Beijing: Zhonghua Shu-ju.

Wylie, R. F. 1980. *The emergence of Maoism*. Stanford, CA: Stanford University Press.

Xia, Shuzhang, and Wang Shujun, eds. 2002. *Xingzheng Qicai: Zhou Enlai* [Brilliant administrator: Zhou Enlai]. Guangzhou: Zhongshan Daxue Chubanshe.

Xia, Xinhua. 2007. *Jindai Zhongguo Xianfa yu Xianzheng Yanjiu* [A research of Constitution and constitutional rule in modern China]. Beijing: Zhongguo Fazhi Chubanshe.

Xiao, Chaoran, and Xiao Wei. 2000 *Dangdai Zhongguo Zhengdang Zhidu Lungang* Harbin: Heilongjiang Renmin Chubanshe.

Xiao, Shengxi, ed. 1996. *Zhongguo Lüshifa Duben* [The PRC Lawyers Law Reader]. Beijing: Xinhua Press.

Xiao, Zuolin. 1960. Fuxingshe Shulüe [A brief account of the Fuxing society]. In *Wenshi Ziliao Xuanji* [Selections of historical materials], 11:21–71. Beijing: Zhonghua Shuju.

———. 1986. Xi'an Shibian de Fuxingshe Henan Fenshe de Huodong [The activities of the Henan branch of the Fuxingshe at the time of thc Xi'an incident]. In *Xi'an Shibian Qinliji* [Successive personal accounts of the Xi'an incident], ed. Wu Fuzhang, 286–291. Beijing: Zhongguo wenshi chubanshe.

Xiaotong, Fei. 1992. *From the soil: The foundations of Chinese society, a translation of Fei Xiaotong's Xiangtu Zhongguo.* Berkeley: University of California Press.

Xie, Guozhen. 1935. *Ming Qing Zhiji Dangshi Yuandong Kao.* Reprint, Shanghai: Zhonghua Shuju.

Xin, Chunying. 1999. *Zhongguo de Falü Zhidu Jiqi Gaige* [Chinese legal system and current legal reform]. Beijing: Falü Chubanshe.

Xing, Fan. 2001. *Communications and information in China: Regulatory issues, strategic implications.* Lanham, MD: University Press of America.

Xiu, Ouyang, et al., eds. 1975. *Xin Tang shu* [The new book of Tang]. Beijing: Zhonghua Shuju.

Xu, Chao-yang. 1973. *Zhong-guo su-song fa suo-yuan.* Taipei: Shang wu.

Xu, Che. 2004. *Zhang Zuolin Zhuan* [Biography of Zhang Zuolin]. Tianjin Shi: Baihua Wenyi Chubanshe.

Xu, Daolin. 1953. *Tang Lu Tonglun* [A general critic of Tang code]. Taipei: Zhongzheng Shuju.

Xu, Fuguan. 1963. *Zhongguo Renxing Lunshi* [A history of theories of human nature in China]. Taichong: Tonghai University Press.

Xu, Guoqi. 2005. *China and the great war: China's pursuit of a new national identity and internationalization.* New York: Cambridge University Press.

Xu, Kangsheng. 1979. Lueshuo Huang-Lao Xuepai de Chansheng he Yanbian [A brief comment on the origin and evolution of the school of thought of Huang Di and Lao Zi]. *Wen Shi Zhe* 3:71–76.

Xu, Wanmin. 2002. *Sun Zhongshan yu Xinhai Geming* [Sun Yatsen and Xinhai revolution]. Beijing: Beijing Library Press.

Xu, Xiaoqun. 1997. The fate of judicial independence in Republican China, 1912–37. *China Quarterly* 149 (March): 1–28.

———. 2000. *Chinese professionals and the republican state: The rise of professional associations in Shanghai, 1912–1937*. New York: Cambridge University Press.

———. 2001. *Chinese professional and the republican state*. Cambridge: Cambridge University Press.

Xu, Zi. 2000. *Yuan Dai Shuyuan Yanjiu* [Research on Yuan Academy]. Beijing: Shehui Kexue Wenxian Chubanshe.

Xu, Zifang. 1981. *Tao Zhu Shengming de Zuihou Sishisan Tian* [The last 43 days of Tao Zhu's life]. Chengdu: Sichuan Renmin Chubanshe.

Xue, Jundu. 1961. *Huang Hsing and the Chinese revolution*. Stanford, CA: Stanfrod University Press.

———. 1971. *Revolutionary leaders of modern China*. New York: Oxford University Press.

Xue, Ruizhao. 2004. *Jindai Keju* [Imperial examination in Jin dynasty] Beijing: Shehui Kexue Chubanshe.

Xue, Yunsheng [Qing]. 1990. *Tang Ming Lu Hebian* [A joint edition of the Tang and Ming codes]. Beijing: Zhonghua Shudian.

Xuexi yu Yanjiu [Study and research]. An official magazine of the CCP. Specific edition, 1986.

Xunzi. *Xunzi ji jie* [Collected commentaries on Xunzi]. 1988. Ed. Wang Xianqian. Beijing: Zhonghua Shuju.

———. 1928. *The works of Hsuntze*. Trans. H. H. Dubs. London: Probsthain.

Xuong, Guong-zhe. 1975. *Xunzi Jinzhu Jinyi* [Modern commentaries and interpretations on Xunzi]. Taipei: Shangwu.

Yamamoto, Masahiro. 2000. *Nanking: Anatomy of an atrocity*. London: Praeger.

Yan, Jiaqi. 1990. *History of the Chinese Cultural Revolution.* Honolulu: University of Hawaii Press.

———. 1991. "Imperial power" and "imperial position": Two characteristics of autocracy. In *Yan Jiaqi and China's struggle for democracy*, ed. Bachman and Yang, 9–15. Armonk, NY: M. E. Sharpe.

———. 1995. The nature of Chinese authoritarianism. In *Decision-makings in Deng's China*, ed. C. L. Hamrin and S. Zhao, 3–14. Armonk, NY: M. E. Sharpe.

Yan, Jiaqi, and Gao Cao. 1996. *Turbulent decade: A history of the Cultural Revolution.* Honolulu: University of Hawaii Press.

Yan, Shi. 1998. *Zhongguo Fanfu Ershi Nian* [A battle of twenty years against corruption in China]. Haerbin: Heilongjiang Renmin Chubanshe.

Yan, Xishan. 1997. *Yan Bochuan Xiansheng Gan Xiang Lu* [Yan Xishen diaries]. Taibei: Yan Bochuan Xiansheng Jinianhui.

Yan, Yun-Xiang. 1996. *The flow of gifts: Reciprocity and social networks in a Chinese village.* Stanford, CA: Stanford University Press.

Yan, Yunxiang. 2003. *Private life under socialism: Love, intimacy, and family change in a Chinese village, 1949–1999.* Stanford, CA: Stanford University Press.

Yang, Aizhen. 2004. *Dangdai Zhengguo Zhengdang Zhidu Yanjiushi* [A history of the research on modern Chinese political parties]. Shanghai: Xuelin.

Yang, B. 1986. The Zunyi conference as one step in Mao's rise to power: A survey of historical studies of the Chinese Communist Party. *China Quarterly* 106:235–271.

Yang, B. 1990. *From revolution to politics: Chinese Communists on the Long March.* Boulder, CO: Westview Press.

Yang, Bingzhang. 2004. *Deng Xiaoping Dazhuan: 1904–1997* [A complete biography of Deng Xiaoping]. Hong Kong: Shidai Guoji Chubanshe.

Yang, C. K. 1965. *Chinese Communist society: The family and the village.* Boston: MIT Press.

Yang, Guo. 1996. *Zhongguo han lin zhi du yan jiu* [A study of Chinese Hanlin Academy]. Wuchang: Wuhan da xue chu ban she.

Yang, Han. 2007. *Yang Hucheng da zhuan* [A comprehensive biography of Yang Hucheng]. Beijing: Tuanjie Chubanshe.

Yang, Huong-lie. 1933. Zhongguo Falu Fada Shi [A history of the development of Chinese law]. 2 vols. Shanghai: Shang wu.

Yang, Jing. 1999. *Song Ziwen Zhuan* [A biography of Song Ziwen]. Shijiazhuang: Hebei Renmin Chubanshe.

Yang, Jisheng. 1998. *Deng Xiaoping Shidai: Zhongguo Gaige Kaifang Sanshinien Jishi* [The age of Deng Xiaoping: The record of thirty years of Chinese reform and open door movement]. Beijing: Zhongyang Bianyi Chubanshe.

Yang, Kuisong. 1992. *Shiqu de Jihui: Zhanshi Guo Gong Tanpan Shilu* [Lost chance: true record of wartime KMT CCP negotiations]. Guilin: Guangxi Shifan Daxue Chubanshe.

Yang, Liguang. 1996. *Meiyou Jiayuan de Linghun: Wang Jianye* [A homeless soul: Wang Jianye]. Beijing: Jiuzhou Tushu Chubanshe.

Yang, M. 1994. *Gifts, favors, and banquets: The art of social relationships in China.* Ithaca, NY: Cornell University Press.

Yang, Mu, and Lye Liang Fook. 2007. *The Chinese Communist Party Propaganda Department: Struggling to balance control and progress.* Singapore: East Asian Institute, National University of Singapore.

Yang, P., and P. Chin-chih Lai. 1966. *Military campaigns in China, 1924–1950.* Trans. W. W. Whitson. Taipei: Military History Office.

Yang, Shangkun. 2001a. *Yang Shangkun Diaries*. Beijing: Zhongyang Wenxian.

———. 2001b. *Yang Shangkun Huiyilu* [A memoir of Yang Shangkun]. Beijing: Zhongyang Wenxian Chubanshe.

Yang, Tianshi. 2002. *Jiangshi Midang yu Jiang Jieshi Zhenxiang* [Secret archive and the reality of Chiang Kaishek]. Beijing: Shehui Kexue Wenxian Chubanshe.

Yang, Tianshi, and Xie Chutao, eds. 2005. *Deng Xiaoping xie zhen* [The real Deng Xiaoping]. Shanghai: Cishu Chubanshe.

Yang, Tingfu. 1982. *Tanglu Chutan* [A preliminary study of Tang statutes]. Tianjing: Renmin Chubanshe.

Yang, Xiguang. 1997. *Captive spirits: Prisoners of the Cultural Revolution*. New York: Oxford University Press.

Yang, Xuewei, Sun Peiqing et al., eds. 2004. *Zhongguo Kaoshi Tongshi* [A complete history of Chinese examination]. 5 vols. Beijing: Shoudu Shifan Daxue Chubanshe.

Yang, Yifan. 1988. *Ming Dagao Yanjiu* [A study of the grand pronouncements]. Nanjing: Jiangsu Renmin chubanshe.

———. 1992. *Hongwu Falü Dianji Kaozheng* [Textual research on legal documents of the Hongwu period]. Beijing: Falü Chubanshe.

———. Zhuan, Gaoren, Wang Zhiqiang et al. 2005. *Xinbian Zhongguo Fazhi Shi* [A new compilation of Chinese legal history]. Beijing: Shehui Kexue Wenxian Chubanshe.

Yang, Yonghua, ed. 2005. *Zhongguo Gongchandang Lianzheng Fazhi Shi Yanjiu* [A study in the history of communist ethics in China]. Beijing: Renmin Chubanshe.

Yang, Youjiong. 1984. *Zhongguo Zhengdang Shi* [A history of Chinese political parties]. Shanghai: Shanghai Shudian.

Yang, Zhesheng. 1993. *Tegongwang Dai Li* [Dai Li, king of special operations]. Shanghai: Renmin Chubanshe.

——. 2001. *Guomindang Jinrong Zhifu Song Ziwen* [The founding father of GMD's finance]. Shanghai: Renmin Chubanshe.

Yang, Zhongmei. 1988. *Hu Yaobang: A Chinese biography.* Armonk, NY: M. E. Sharpe.

Yang, Zulie. 1970. *Zhang Guotao Fujen Huiyiilu* [The memoir of Madame Zhang Guotao]. Hong Kong: Zuolien Chupenshe.

Yao, Ji-hen. 1963. *Shijing Tonglun* [A general study of Shijing]. Hong Kong: Zhonghua.

Yao, Jinguo, ed. 2006. *Gong Chan Guoji yu ZhuMao Hongjun, 1927–1934* [The Communist International and the Red Army of Zhu and Mao]. Beijing: Zhongyang Wenxian Chubanshe.

Yao, Siren. 1993. *Da Ming lu fuli zhujie* [Commentaries on Ming Code and its attached cases]. Beijing: Beijing da xue chu ban she.

Yaron, R. 1957. On divorce in Old Testament times. *Revue Internationale des Droits de l'antiquité* 3rd ser., 4:117–128.

——. 1962. Forms in the laws of Eshnunna. *Revue internationale des droits de l'Antiquité* 3rd ser., 9:137–153.

——. 1969. *The law of Eshunna.* Jerusalem: Magnes Press and University of Jerusalem Press.

——. 1988. The evolution of biblical law. In *La Formazione del diritto nel vicino oriente antico*, ed. A. Theodorides et al., 77–108. Rome: Edizioni Scientifiche Italiane.

Ye, Yang. 1999. *Vignettes from the late Ming: A Hsiao-P in anthology.* Seattle: University of Washington Press.

Ye, Yonglie. 1992. *Mingren Fengyun lu* [Famous men of the time]. Guilin: Lijiang Chubanshe.

———. 1993a. *Chen Boda Zhuan* [A biography of Chen Boda]. Beijing: Zuojia Chubanshe.

———. 1993b. *Jiang Qing Zhuan* [A biography of Jiang Qing]. Beijing: Zuojia Chubanshe.

———. 1993c. *Yao Wenyun Zhuan* [A biography of Yao Wenyuan]. Changchun: Shidai Wenyi.

———. 1993d. *Zhang Chunqiao Zhuan* [A biography of Zhang Chunqiao]. Changchun: Shidai Wenyi Chubanshe.

———. 1997. *Cong Hua Guofeng dao Deng Xiaoping: Zhonggong Shiyijie Sanzhong Quanhui Qianhou* [From Hua Guofeng to Deng Xiaoping: Before and after the Third Plenum of the Eleventh Party Congress]. Hong Kong: Tiandi Tushu.

———. 2002. *Mao Zedong yu Jiang Jieshi* [Mao Zedong and Chiang Kaishek]. 2 vols. Taibei: Fengyun Shidai.

Yeh, Wen-hsin. 1990. *The alienated academy: Culture and politics in Republican China, 1919–1937*. Cambridge, MA: Harvard University Press.

———. 1996. *Provincial passages: Culture, space, and the origins of Chinese communism*. Berkeley: University of California Press.

Yi, Yang. 2004. *Jiang Jieshi Guanchang Shu* [Chiang Kaishek's political strategy]. Beijing: Tuanjie Chubanshe.

Yin, Jiamin. 2004. *Jiang Jieshi yu Huangpu "San jie"* [Chiang Kaishek and three generals of Huangpu]. Nanchang: Baihuazhou Wenyi Chubanshe.

Yin, Yingzhang. 1985 *Qing jian*. 2 vols. Beijing: Zhongguo Shudian.

Ying, Quan. 1996. *Chen Yonggui Zhuan* [A biography of Chen Yonggui]. Wuhan: Changjiang Wenyi Chubanshe.

Young, A. N. 1971. *China's nation-building effort, 1927–1937: The financial and economic record*. Stanford, CA: Hoover Institute Press.

Young, E. 1977. *The presidency of Yuan Shih-Kai*. Ann Arbor: University of Michigan Press.

Young, M. B. 2004. Law and modern state-building in early Republican China: The Supreme Court of Peking (1911–1926). PhD diss., Harvard University.

Yu, Daiyun, and C. Wakeman. 1985. *To the storm: The odyssey of a revolutionary Chinese woman*. Berkeley: University of California Press.

Yu, G. T. 1966. *Party politics in Republican China: The Kuomintang, 1912–1924*. Berkeley: University of California Press.

Yu, Liang. 1955. *Kong Xiangxi*. Hong Kong: Kaiyuan Shudian.

Yu, Taishan. 2004. *A hypothesis on the origin of the Yu State*. Philadelphia: University of Pennsylvania.

Yu, Wei-chao, and M. Gao. 1978–1979. Zhoudai Youngding Zhidu Yanjiu [A study of the system of use of Ting-tripods ding in the Zhou dynasty]. *Peking University Journal* 1978/1: 84–98; 1978/2: 84–97; 1979/1 (1): 83–96.

———, eds. 1997. *A journey into China's antiquity: Yuan dynasty–Qing dynasty*. Beijing: Morning Glory Press.

Yu, Xiaoming. 1989. Quxiao hongdeng de zhenglun. In *Dixue de tongxin—Haizi xinzhong de wenge* [Bloodstained innocence—The Cultural Revolution in the hearts of the young], ed. Li Hui and Gao Lilin, 293–295. Beijing: Zhongguo shaonian ertong chubanshe.

Yu, Xingzhong. 1989. Legal pragmatism in the People's Republic of China. *Journal of Chinese Law* 3:29.

Yu, Yingshi. 1980. *Zhongguo Zhishi Jieceng Shilun* [A study of the history of Chinese intellectuals]. Taipei: Lianjing.

Yueh, Nan, Shi Yang, Tingquan Zhang, and B. Sneck. 1996. *The dead suffered too: The excavation of a Ming tomb*. Beijing: Chinese Literature Press.

Yunis, H. 1996. *Taming democracy: Models of political rhetoric in classical Athens*. Ithaca, NY: Cornell University Press.

Zang, Xiaowei. 2000. *Children of the Cultural Revolution: Family life and political behavior in Mao's China*. Boulder, CO: Westview Press.

Zelin, M. 1984. *The magistrate's Tael: Rationalizing fiscal reform in eighteenth-century Ch'ing China*. Berkeley: University of California Press.

Zeng, Xianlin. 1991. *Beifa Zhanzheng Shi* [A military history of Northern Expedition]. Chengdu: Sichuan Renmin Chubanshe.

Zeng, Yi. 1991. *Family dynamics in China: A life table analysis*. Madison: University of Wisconsin Press.

Zhan, Hengju. 1973. *Zhongguo Jindai Fazhishi* [Modern Chinese legal history]. Taibei: Shangwu.

Zhang, Bofeng, and Li Zongyi, eds. 1989. *Beiyang Junfa* [The northern warlords]. Wuhan: Wuhan Chubanshe.

Zhang, Bofeng et al., eds. 1987. *Beiyang Lujun Shiliao* [Historical materials for the Beiyang Army]. Tianjin: Tianjin Renmin Chubanshe.

Zhang, Cixi. 1999. *Wang Jingwei xian sheng zhu shu nian biao* [Chronology of works of Wang Jingwei]. Beijing: Beijing Tushuguan Chubanshe.

Zhang, Dexin, and Mao Peiqi, eds. 1995. *Hongwu Yuzhi Quanshu* [Complete imperial writings during the Hongwu reign]. Anhei: Huangshan shushe.

Zhang, Geng, ed. 1997. *Zhongguo Lüshi Zhidu de Lichengbei: "Zhonghua Renmin Gongheguo Lüshifa" Lifa Guocheng Huigu* [A milestone in the development of the PRC lawyers system: A look back at the legislative process of the PRC Lawyers Law]. Beijing: Falu Chubanshe.

Zhang, Geng, and Hu Kangsheng, eds. 1996. *Zhonghua Renmin Gong-heguo Lüshifa Quanshu* [Compendium of the PRC Lawyers Law]. Beijing: Blue Sky Press.

Zhang, Guangan. 1973. *Fubi Xiangji* [Detail record of restoration]. Taibei: Wenhai Chubanshe.

Zhang, Guohua, and Xin-xian Yao. 1984. *Zhongguo Falu Sixiang Shigang* [A outline of Chinese leal ideas]. Lanzhou: Gansu Remin Chubanshe.

Zhang, Guotao. (Chang Kuo-t'ao) 1972. *The rise of the Chinese Communist Party*. 2 vols. Lawrence: University of Kansas Press.

———. 1991. Wode Huiyi [My memoir]. 3 vols. Beijing: Dongfang Chubanshe.

Zhang, Hao. 2006. *Liang Qichao yu Zhongguo Sixiang de Guodu (1890–1907)* [Liang Qichao and intellectual transition in China 1890–1907]. Beijing: Xinxing Chubanshe.

Zhang, Jiansheng. 1998. Youguan Xingzheng Susong Shouan Fanwei de jige Lilun Wenti Tanxi [Examination of several theoretical problems relating to the scope of administrative litigation]. *Zhongguo Faxue* 2:45.

Zhang, Jianzhi. 2004. *Zhang Jingjiang Zhuan* [A biography of Zhang Jingjiang]. Wuhan: Hubei Renmin Chubanshe.

Zhang, Jinfan, ed. 1999. *Zhongguo Fazhi Tongshi* [A general history of Chinese legal system]. 10 vols. Beijing: Falü Chubanshe.

———. 2004. *Zhongguo Xianfa Shi* [A history of Chinese Constitution]. Chang Chun: Jilin Remin Chubanshe.

———. 2005. *Zhongguo Falü de Chuantong yu Jindai Zhuanxing* [The tradition and modern transition of Chinese law]. Beijing: Falu Chubanshe.

———. 2007. Zhongguo Jiancha Fazhi Shigao [A draft history of Chinese censorial law]. Beijing: Shangwu.

Zhang, Jinfan, Liu Guang'an, Zhuan gaoren Wang Liyan et al. 2004. *Zhongguo Sifa Zhidu Shi* [A history of Chinese administrative law]. Beijing: Falu Chubanshe.

Zhang, Jinfan, Zhang Xipo, and Zeng Xianyi, eds. 1981. *Zhongguo Fazhi Shi* [A history of Chinese legal system]. Beijing: Qun Zhong.

Zhang, Jingru et al., eds. 1993. *Guo min zheng fu tong zhi shi ji Zhongguo she hui zhi bian qian* [Social change in China during the rule of Guomindang]. Beijing: Renming University Press.

Zhang, Jungu. 1971. *Li Yuanhong Zhuan* [Biography of Li Yuanhong]. Taibei: Zhongwai Tushu.

Zhang, Lei. 2005. *Minzhu Geming de Xianxingzhe: Sun Zhongshan* [The pioneer of democratic revolution]. Guangzhou: Guangdong Renmin Chubanshe.

Zhang, Liangshan. 1998. *Jiang Jieshi xian sheng ping zhuan* [The rise and fall of Chiang Kai-shek. Taibei Shi: Yuegui Chubanshe.

Zhang, Ming. 1989. *Wufu Zhiguo Meng: Zhongguo Junfa Shili de Xingcheng Jiqi Shehui Zuoyong* [The dream of solders: The formation and social function of the force of Chinese warlords]. Beijing: National Press of Culture.

Zhang, Naigen. 1997. Intellectual property in China. *Annual Survey of International and Comparative Law* 4:4.

Zhang, Pufan. 1996. Wanshan Shehuifazhi de Diandi Sikao [Some accumulated reflections on the perfection of a socialist legal system] Zhongguo Fazhi Shixian Fanglue [Strategy for the realization of the rule of law]. *FalüKexue* 3: 6.

Zhang Qiyun, ed. 1960. *Guofu Quanshu* [Complete Writings of the Father of the Nation]. Taibei: Guofang Yanjiuyuan.

Zhang, Ruide. 1993. *Kang Zhan Shiqi de Guojun Renshi* [Personal politics in the Nationalist Army during the war against Japanese]. Taibei: Zhongyang Yanjiuyuan Jindaishi Yanjiusuo.

Zhang, Tinyu. 1736. Reprint 1974. *Ming Shi* [History of the Ming dynasty]. 28 vols. Beijing: Zhonghua shuju.

Zhang, W. 2002. *Chinese economic reforms and fertility behaviour: A study of a North China village.* London: China Library.

Zhang, Wanlu. 2006. *Mao Zedong de Daolu: (1921–1935)* [The road of Mao Zedong]. Beijing: Zhongyang Wenxian Chubanshe.

Zhang, Weihan. 1992. Dai Li yu pangda de Juntong ju zuzhi [Dai Li and the gigantic Military Statistics Bureau organization]. In *Xishuo Zhongtong Juntong* [Detailed accounts of central statistics and military statistics], ed. Xu Enzeng et al., 277–358. Taibei: Zhuanji Wenxue Chubanshe.

Zhang, Weihua. 1981. Xihan Chunian Huang-Lao Zhengzhi Sixiang [The political philosophy of the early western Han Huang-Lao school). *Zhongguo Shehui Kexue* 5:199–208.

———. 1982. Dai Li yu "Juntong ju" [Dai Li and the "Military Statistics Bureau"]. In *Zhejiang wenshi ziliao xuanji*, ed. Wenshi Ziliao Yanjiu Weiyuanhui, no. 23:79–151. Hangzhou: Zhejiang Renmin Chubanshe.

Zhang, Weiren. 1976. *Zhongguo fazhi shi shumu* [Bibliography on Chinese legal history]. 3 vols. Taipei: Zhongyang Yanjiuyuan Lishi Yuyan Yanjiusuo.

———. 1983. *Qingdai Fazhi Yanjiu* [Studies in the Qing legal system]. 3 vols. Taibei: Academia Sinica.

Zhang, Wenxian. 1996. *Lun Lifazhong de Falü Yizhi* [On the legal transplant of legislation]. *Faxue* 1:6.

Zhang, Wusheng, and Wu Zeyong. 2000. Sifa Duli yu Fayuan Zuzhi Jigou de Tiaozheng [On judicial independence and the adjustment of the organization and structure of the courts], pt. 1. *Zhongguo Faxue* 2:55.

Zhang, Xianwen, and Fang Qingqiu. 1996. *Jiang Jieshi Quanzhuan* [A complete biography of Chiang Kaishek]. Zhengzhou: Henan Renmin Chubanshe.

———. 2001. *Zhongguo Kang Ri Zhanzheng Shi* [History of China's War of Resistance against Japan]. Nanjing: Nanjing Daxue Chubanshe.

Zhang, Xiaolin, comp. 1993. *Lingxiu yizu: gongheguo xinshengdai jishi* [Descendants of the leaders: True accounts of the new generation of the People's Republic]. Beijing: Tuanjie Chubanshe.

Zhang, Xiaosheng. 1988. *Zhongguo Gudai Zhanzheng Tonglan* [Wars in ancient China]. Beijing: Xinhua Shudian.

———. 1993. *Zhongguo jin dai zhan ce ji yao* [Military strategy in early modern China]. Beijing: Junshi Kexue Chubanshe.

Zhang, Xibo, and Xian yi Zeng. 1982. *Zhongguo Falü Shi* [A history of Chinese law]. Beijing: Zhongguo Renmin Daxue chubanshe.

Zhang, Xibo, Xian yi Zeng, and Wang Zhigang. 1985. *Jian yu Ganggan: Zhongguo Gudai Falu Jianlun* [The sword and the lever: Short essays on ancient law in China]. Xi'an: Shaaxi Renmin Jiaoyu Chubanshe.

Zhang, Xin. 2000. *Social transformation in modern China: The state and local elites in Hunan, 1900–1937.* New York: Cambridge University Press.

Zhang, Xiuzhang. 2007. *Jiang Jieshi ri ji jie mi* [Chiang Kaishek's secret diaries]. Beijing: Tuanjie Chubanshe.

Zhang, Xueji. 1996. *Ba Gui Xiaojiang: Bai Chongxi* [General Bai Chong xi]. Lanzhou: Lanzhou University Press.

———. 2006. *Zhang Xueliang Quanzhuan* [A comprehensive biography of Zhang Xueliang]. Beijing: Jingjiribao Chubanshe.

Zhang, Yu-i. 1957. *Chung-kuo chin-tai nung-yeh shih tzu-liao* [Sources on the recent Chinese agricultural history]. 2 vols. Beijing: San Lian Shudian.

Zhang, Yuwen. 2000. *Siwang Lianmeng: Gao Rao Shijian Shimo* [Death alliance: The Gao Rao incidence]. Beijing: Beijing Chubanshe.

Zhang, Zhuhong. 1987. *Zhongguo Xiandai Gemingshi Shiliaoxue* [Historiography of China's modern revolutionary history]. Beijing: CCP

Party History Materials Press. English translation. *Chinese Studies in History*, 23 (4); 24 (3) and *Chinese Sociology and Anthropology* 22 (3–4).

Zhao, Erxun et al., eds. 1960. *Qing Shigao* [Draft history of the Qing dynasty]. 2 vols. Hong Kong: Wenxue Yanjiu.

Zhao, Jianguo. 2001. *Xin Sun Wu : Liu Bocheng juan* [A biography of Liu Bocheng]. Beijing: Jiefangjun Chubanshe.

Zhao, Jie. 2007. *Zhang Xueliang: Huiyu Youren* [A biography of Zhang Xueliang]. Beijing: Zhongguo Wenshi Chubanshe.

Zhao, Suisheng. 1996. *Power by design: Constitution-making in nationalist China*. Honolulu: University of Hawaii Press.

Zhao, Wei. 1989. *The biography of Zhao Ziyang*. Hong Kong: Educational and Cultural Press.

——. 2004. *Xihuating Suiyue: Wo zai Zhou Enlai Deng Yingchao Shenbian Sanshi qi Nian* [Years of Western Hall: Thirty-seven years beside Zhou Enlai and Deng Yingchao]. Beijing: Zhongyang Wenxian.

Zhao, Yi. 1977. *Naner Shi Zhaji* [Critical studies on the twenty-two standard histories]. 36 vols. Reprint. Shanghai: Shangwu yinshu guan, 1937; ed. Tu Weiyun. Taibei: Huashi chubanshe.

Zhao, Ziyang. 1987. Advance along the road of socialism with Chinese characteristics. *Foreign Broadcasting Information Service, China* 26 (October): 10–34.

Zheng, Bo. 2001. *Da jiang Huang Kecheng* [General Huang Kecheng]. Beijing: Jiefang jun Wenyi Chubanshe.

Zheng, Derong et al., eds. 1986. *Xinzhongguo jishi 1949–1984* [Chronicle of new China 1949–1984]. Changchun: Dongbei Shifan Daxue Chubanshe.

Zheng, Qi. 1998. *Mao Zedong yu Peng Dehuai* [Mao Zedong and Peng Dehuai]. Chang Chun: Jilin Renmin Chubanshe.

Zheng, Shiping. 1997. *Party vs. State in post-1949 China*. Cambridge: Cambridge University Press.

Zheng, Xiaofeng. 1992. *Tao Zhu Zhuan* [A biography of Tao Zhu]. Beijing: Zhongguo Qingnian Chubanshe.

Zheng, Xuan, ed. 1953. *Li Ji*. Taibei: Shi jie shu ju.

Zheng, Zhenman. 2001. *Family lineage organization and social change in Ming and Qing Fujian*. Honolulu: University of Hawaii Press.

Zhonggong Zhongyang Dangshi Ziliao Zhengji Weiyuanhui and Zhongyang Dang'an Guan, eds. 1985. *Zunyi Huiyi Wenxian* [Selected documents on Zunyi Conference]. Beijing: Renmin Chubanshe.

Zhonggong Zhongyang Shujichu Yanjiushi Zonghezu [The Research Department of the Secretariat of the Central Committee of the CCP], ed. 1987. *Dangde Shiyijie Sanzhong Quanhui Yilai Dashiji* [Major events since the third plenum of the eleventh CC]. Beijing: Hongji Press.

Zhonggong Zhongyang Wenxian Yanjiushi, ed. 1998. *Zhou Enlai Nianpu, 1898–1949* [Zhou Enlai Chronology]. Beijing: Zhongyang Wenxian Chubanshe.

Zhongguo Guomindang Dangshi Shiliao Bianzuan Weiyuanhui [The editorial committee for party history of GMD], ed. 1955. *Huangpu Jianjun Shi* [A history of the Huangpu Academy]. Taipei: Lujun Junguan Xuexiao.

Zhongguo Gongchandang Lichi Zhongyao Huiyi Ji [Collections of important meetings of the Chinese Communist Party]. 1983. Shanghai: Renmin Chubanshe.

Zhongguo Liang Han Sixiang Shi [A history of ideas during Western and Eastern Han dynasties]. 1976. 2 vols. Taipei: Xuesheng Shuju.

Zhongguo Nianjian [People's Republic of China yearbook]. 1983–1996. Beijing: Xinhua Chubanshe.

Zhonghua Renmin Gongheguo Fagui Huibian. [A collection of laws and regulations of the People's Republic of China]. 1956. Beijing: Falu Chubanshe.

Zhonghua Renmin Gongheguo Fagui Huibian, 1979–1984 [Collection of laws of the People's Republic of China, 1979–1984]. 1986. Beijing: Falu Chubanshe.

Zhonghua, Shuju. 1957. *The complete works of Zhuang-tzu*. Trans. B. Watson. New York: Columbia University Press.

Zhongshan Daxue "Ye Ting" Bianxiezu. 1979. *Ye Ting*. Shaoguan: Guangdong Renmin Chubanshe.

Zhonguuo Dier Lishi Danganguan, ed. 1994. *Guomindang Zhengfu Zhengzhi Zhidu Dang'an Shiliao Xuanbian* [Compilation of archival sources for the KMT government's political system]. Hefei: Anhui Jiaoyu Chubanshe.

Zhou, Daoji. 1964. *Han Tang Zaixiang zhidu* [The institution of the prime office in the Han and Tang dynasties]. Taipei: Jiaxin Shuini Gongsi Wenhua jijinhui.

Zhou, Enlai. 1981. *Selected works of Zhou Enlai*. Beijing: Foreign Languages Press.

Zhou, Guoquan. 1993. *Dongluan zhongde Chen Boda* [Chen Boda in turmoil]. Hefei: Anhui Renmin Chubanshe.

———. 2003. *Wang Ming zhuan* [A biography of Wang Ming]. Hefei: Anhui Renmin Chubanshe.

Zhou, Meihua, ed. 1996. *Guomin Zhengfu Junzheng Zuzhi Shiliao* [The historical sources for the organisation of military administration of the national government]. Taibei: Guoshiguan.

Zhou, Quan. 1995. *Huangpu Jiang Shuai. Tang Shengzhi* [Huang Pu General, Tang Shengzhi]. Beijing: Changzheng Chubanshe.

Zhou, Tiandu. 2002. *Li Gongpu Zhuan* [A biography of Li Gongpu]. Beijing: Qunyan Chubanshe.

——. 2006. *Shen Junru Zhuan* [A biography of Shen Junru]. Beijing: Renmin Chubanshe.

Zhou, Wangsheng. 1994. *Lifa Lun* [On legislation]. Beijing: Beijing Daxue Chubanshe.

Zhou, Xingliang. 2004. *Guomin Geming yu Tongyi Jianshe: 20 Shijichu Sun Zhongshan ji Guo Gong Renwu de Fendou* [National revolution and construction]. Tianjin: Tianjin Guji Chubanshe.

Zhou, Yu'e, and Chen Hongmin. 1994. *Hu Hanmin*. Guangdong: Guang Zhou Renmin Chubanshe.

Zhou, Yumin, and Shao Yong. 1993. *Zhongguo banghuishi* [The history of Chinese secret societies]. Shanghai: Renmin Chubanshe.

Zhu, De. 2003. *Zhu De zi shu* [Autobiography of Zhu De]. Beijing: Jiefangjun Wenyi Chubanshe.

Zhu, Guobin. 1995. Reform or reorganization: Constructing and implementing the new Chinese civil service. *International Review of Administrative Sciences* 61:91.

Zhu, Hanguo, ed. 1993. *Nanjing Guomin Zhengfu Jishi* [Chronology of the Nanjing national government]. Hefei: Anhui Renmin Chubanshe.

Zhu, Jianhua. 1994. *Jiang Jieshi he Yan Xishan* [Chiang Kaishek and Yan Xishan]. Changchun: Jilin Wenshi Chubanshe.

Zhu, Jiamu. 2000. *Chen Yun Nianpu* [Chronology of Chen Yun]. Beijing: Zhongyang Wenxian Chubanshe.

Zhu, Jingwen. 2000. Public participation in law-making in the PRC. In *Law-making in the People's Republic of China*, ed. J. M. Otto et al., 141–156. The Hague: Kluwer Law International.

——. 2006. *Zhongguo Falixue Luntan* [Studies on Chinese jurisprudence]. Beijing: Zhongguo Renmin Daxue Chubanshe.

Zhu, Liyu, and Wan Qigang. 2000. Lun Dang de Zhizheng Fangshi Xiang Fazhiguo de Genbenxing Zhuanbian [On the fundamental transition of the Party's mode of governing in the transition to rule of law]. *Zhongguo Renmin Daxue Xuebao* 5:74.

Zhu, Pu. 1938. *Zhang Fakui Jiangjun* [General Zhang Fakui]. Hankou: Qunli Shudian.

Zhu, Shan. 1987. *Jiang Qing Mizhuan: Zhongguo Xiandai shi shang di ye xin jia, qi nü Zi* [A secret biography of Jiang Qing]. Hong Kong: Xingchen Chubanshe.

Zhu, Shoupeng (Qing). 1958. *Quangxuchao Donghualu*. 5 vols. Beijing: Zhonghua Shuju.

Zhu, Suli. 1997. Houxiandai Sichao yu Zhongguo Faxue he Fazhi [Post-modern thought and the jurisprudence and legal system of China]. *Faxue* 3:11.

Zhu, xi. 1990. *Learning to be a sage*. Trans. D. K. Gardner. Berkeley: University of California Press.

———. 1991. Modes of tinking and modes of discourse in the Sung: Some thoughts on the Yu lu ('Recorded conversations') Texts. *Journal of Asian Studies* 50:574–603.

Zhu, Xinli. 1996. Lun Xingzheng Chaoyue Zhiquan [Administrative excess of authority]. *Faxue Yanjiu* 2:112.

Zhu, Yuanzhang. 1965. *Yuzhi Wenji* [Collected works of Emperor Zhu Yuanzhang]. Taibei: Xuesheng Shuju.

———. 1969a. Da Gao [Great warnings]. In *Huang Ming Zhishu*, ed. Zhang Lu et al., 1: 22–153. 6 vols. Taibei: Chengming Chubanshe

———. 1969b. Yuzhi Zishi Tongxun. In *Huang Ming Zhishu*, ed. Zhang Lu et al., 1: 478–485. 6 vols. Taibei: Chengming Chubanshe.

———. 1988. *Yuzhi Dagao* [The imperial grand pronouncements]. In *Ming Dagao Yanjiu* [Studies of Ming Dagao], ed. Yang Yifan, 195–452. Nanjing: Jiangsu Renmin Chubanshe.

——. 1994. Huang Ming Zhaoling. [Imperial edicts of the August Ming]. In *Zhongguo Zhenxi Falü Dianji Jicheng*, ed. Liu Hainian and Yang Yifan, 2nd ed., vol 3, 1–91. Beijing: Kexue Chubanshe.

Zhu, Zongzhen, and Wang Chaoguang. 1996. *Tiejun Mingjiang: Chen Mingshu* [Famous general of an iron army: Chen Mingshu]. Lanzhou: Lanzhou University Press.

Zhu, Zongzhen, and Yang Guanghui. 1983. *Minchu Zhengzheng yu Erci Geming* [The war at the early Republic and the second revolution]. 2 vols. Shanghai: Renmin Chubanshe.

Zhuang, Jifa. 1981. *Qingdai Tiandihui Yuanliukao* [Studies in the origin of the Qing Heaven and Earth Society]. Taipei: Gugong congkan bianji weiyuanhui.

——. 1982. *Qing Gaozong Shiquan Wugong Yanjiu* [A study of the ten great military campaigns of the Qing Gaozong Emperor]. Taipei: National Palace Museum.

——. 1988. Qingdai Min-Yue Diqu de Renkou Liudong yu Mimi Huidang de Fazhan [Population movement in Qing dynasty Fujian and Guangdong and the development of secret societies]. In *Jindai Zhongguo Chuqi Lishi YantaoHui Lunwenji*, 737–773. Nangang: Academia Sinica.

——. 1989. *Development of secret societies in the Ch'ing dynasty and Changes in Ch'ing statutes governing them.* Paper delivered at the 104th annual meeting of the American Historical Association, December 27–30, San Francisco.

——. 1990a. Cong Qingdai Lüli de Xiuding Kan Mimi Huidang de Qiyuan Jiqi Fazhan [The origin and development of secret societies from the perspective of changes in Qing laws]. *Guoli Taiwan Shifan Daxue lishi xuebao* 18:107–168.

——. 1990b. Qingdai Hu-Guang Diqu de Renkou Liudong yu Mimi Huidang de Fazhan [Population movement in Qing Dynasty Hu-Guang and the development of secret societies]. *Danjiang shixue* 2:149–176.

Zhuang-zi, Ji-lie. 1968. *Collected commentaries on Chuang-zi.* Vol. 3. Beijing: Zhu-zi ji-cheng.

Zhuo, Jian'an. 1982. Gu Zhenglun yu Goumindang xianbing [Gu Zhenglun and the Guomindang military police]. *Guiyang wenshi ziliao xuanji* 3:225–254.

Zhu-zi, kao yin. 1958. *Zhu-zi, kao yin.* Beijing: Renming Chubanshe.

Zi, Xuzi. 1988. *Xiang shi ji, Xu Shichang* [Hunan record, Xu Shizhang]. Taipei: Wenhai Chubanshe.

Zou, Rong. 1998. Xingzheng Susong de Yuangao Zige Yanjiu [Study of standing to sue in administrative litigation]. *Faxue* 7:61.

Zou, Weimin. 2000. *Bianqian yu Gaige: Fayuan zhi Xiandaihua Yanjiu* [Change and reform: Research on the modernization of the judiciary]. Beijing: Falu Chubanshe.

Zuo, Lu. 1984. Deng Tuo Shengping, Gongzuo Pianduan: Xinwenshi Shangde Qiju [Fragments of Deng Tuo's life and work: A miracle in the history of journalism]. *Xinwen Jizhe* 11:28–30.

Zuo, Yunpeng. 1983. *Mingmo Nongmin Zhanzheng de Lishi Genyuan* [The historical origins of the late Ming peasant wars]. *Mingshi yanjiu luncong* 2:281–301.

INDEX

Lightning Source UK Ltd.
Milton Keynes UK
07 June 2010

155245UK00001B/79/P

9 781604 976045